Sustainability in the Hospitality Industry

Sustainability is one of the single most important global issues facing the world. A clear understanding of the issues surrounding climate change, global warming, air and water pollution, ozone depletion, deforestation, the loss of biodiversity and global poverty is essential for every future manager in the hospitality industry. Present and future hospitality executives need to know how sustainable management systems can be integrated into their businesses while maintaining and hopefully improving the bottom line.

Sustainability in the Hospitality Industry, second edition, is the only book available introducing students to the economic, environmental and social sustainability issues specifically facing the industry as well as exploring ideas, solutions and strategies of how to manage operations in a sustainable way.

Since the first edition of this book there have been many important developments in this field and this second edition has been updated in the following ways:

- Updated content to reflect recent issues and trends, including hotel energy solutions and green hotel design.
- Two new chapters on sustainable food.
- Updated international case studies throughout to explore key issues and show real-life operational responses to sustainability within the hospitality industry.
- New case studies on growth hotel development markets, Asia and the Middle East.
- New practical exercises throughout to apply your knowledge to real-life sustainability scenarios.

This accessible and comprehensive account of sustainability in the hospitality industry is essential reading for all students and future managers.

Philip Sloan Department of Hospitality Management, International University of Applied Sciences, Bad Honnef, Bonn, Germany.

Willy Legrand Department of Hospitality Management, International University of Applied Sciences, Bad Honnef, Bonn, Germany.

Joseph S. Chen Department of Recreation, Park and Tourism Studies, Indiana University, Bloomington, USA.

'This book is a unique addition to the scholarly literature of tourism and hospitality. Although there is an abundance of books on tourism and sustainability in general, this second edition is the only book available to introduce students and practitioners of hospitality to the essential aspects of sustainability and the challenges that face our industry in today's highly competitive business environment. The book also explores ideas, solutions and strategies to manage operations in a sustainable way. Without doubt, this is one of the most needed and refreshing books we have in the field.'

Muzaffer Uysal, Professor of Tourism and Hospitality
Management, Virginia Tech University, USA

'*Sustainability in the Hospitality Industry*, second edition takes a holistic approach to sustainability which will support the hospitality industry in taking the next steps forward in the integration of sustainability in its strategy and operations. This book contains examples of best practice which engage the reader and help both practitioners and students to better understand the opportunities offered by the application of sustainability principles to the practice of hospitality. It also clearly illustrates the impact of choices made which gives the industry a clear picture of their responsibilities towards solving them. Finally, this book highlights the importance of sustainable consumer behavior. This is something which is often overlooked but here the authors present the advantages of involving clients and staff in the sustainability effort. This makes this book essential reading for all students and practitioners in the hospitality industry.'

Elena Cavagnaro, Professor of Service Studies,
Stenden University of Applied Science, the Netherlands

Sustainability in the Hospitality Industry

Principles of sustainable operations

Second edition

Philip Sloan, Willy Legrand and Joseph S. Chen

Routledge
Taylor & Francis Group

LONDON AND NEW YORK

First edition published 2009 by Elsevier Inc.

Second edition 2013
by Routledge
2 Park Square, Milton Park, Abingdon, Oxon OX14 4RN

Simultaneously published in the USA and Canada
by Routledge
711 Third Avenue, New York, NY 10017

Routledge is an imprint of the Taylor & Francis Group, an informa business

British Library Cataloguing in Publication Data
A catalogue record for this book is available from the British Library

Library of Congress Cataloging in Publication Data
Sustainability in the hospitality industry: principles of sustainable operations/
  Philip Sloan, Willy Legrand, Joseph S. Chen. – 2nd ed.
  p. cm.
  Includes bibliographical references and index.
  1. Hospitality industry – Management. 2. Hospitality industry – Environmental
  aspects. 3. Social responsibility of business. 4. Sustainability. I. Sloan, Philip.
  II. Legrand, Willy. III. Chen, Joseph S.
  TX9111.3.M27S87 2012   338.4'791068–dc23
  2012014140

ISBN: 978-0-415-53123-8 (hbk)
ISBN: 978-0-415-53124-5 (pbk)
ISBN: 978-0-203-11626-5 (ebk)

Typeset in Helvetica Neue
by Florence Production Ltd, Stoodleigh, Devon

Printed and bound in Great Britain by
TJ International Ltd, Padstow, Cornwall

Contents

Illustrations

Figures

Pictures

Tables

Preface

The hospitality industry at large and hotel companies in particular have increased their involvement in matters of sustainability during the past decade. Fuelled by increasing energy costs, public scrutiny and regulatory constraints, large, medium-sized and small hotels are keen to polish up their image while doing something good for the planet.

For the past three decades, the oil and chemical industries have long been in the spotlight due to their visible and often negative environmental image. While not in the front seat of environmental pollution and consumption of non-renewable resources compared to heavy industries, the hospitality industry is often thought to be at the forefront of the service industry in terms of resource usage. While issues surrounding the management of waste produced or water consumed in hotels are important features of any environmental management programme, carbon dioxide (CO_2) emissions have taken the central stage in the mitigation of environmental impacts. The partnership formed to develop Carbon Footprint Standards between the International Tourism Partnership (ITP), the World Travel & Tourism Council (WTTC) and hotel players such as Accor, the InterContinental Hotels Group, MGM Resorts International, Mövenpick Hotels & Resorts, Red Carnation Hotel Collection, Starwood Hotels & Resorts Worldwide, Inc., Premier Inn-Whitbread Group and Wyndham Worldwide is yet one more recent initiative aimed at making carbon measurement possible. It is important to realize that due to a resource-intense utilization of energy, water and consumables in hotel facilities, the environmental footprint of hotels is typically larger than those of buildings of similar size. This is partly explained by the fact that hospitality operations are made up of a diversity of small operations from restaurants and banqueting to housekeeping and spas. Each of those operations accounts for a rather small share of environmental pollution in terms of energy and water consumption, food, waste and other resources but it is *the whole which is greater than the sum of its parts* (Aristotle).

This book is of particular interest for three reasons. First, there is acute pressure on the private sector to clean up after itself. All stakeholders, including investors, employees, customers, environmental and ethical groups as well as the general public, now expect companies to show best performance concerning all dimensions of the 'triple bottom line' of social, environmental and economic management, and companies are increasingly being judged as to their transparency in this system. Although the restaurant sector does not rank as highly among the great polluters such as the metallurgical or chemical industries, the size and rapid growth of the industry make it clear that environmentally sustainable action is necessary. This book reviews best hospitality industry practices regarding water and energy consumption, material and food procurement and analyses trends in environmental protection and social equity.

Second, legal implications are expanding and becoming increasingly important, with stricter emission and pollution controls than ever before. The tourism industry, as a whole, is one of the largest industries in the world. For businesses, the challenge is to be a step ahead of legislation, rather than being forced to implement certain practices afterwards. This book examines how hotels and restaurants implement environmental management systems, and take advantage of possible certifications or eco-labelling schemes enabling businesses to operate more efficiently and hence improve their competitive position considerably.

Third, by incorporating responsible marketing and corporate social responsibility, hospitality businesses can enhance their reputation and attract investment. This book examines the behaviour of the responsible consumer and discusses which marketing practices would be considered sustainable to attract such consumers.

Sustainability in the Hospitality Industry seeks to provide some answers to questions, attempts to resolve challenges and give guidance. Finally, it provides a new intellectual framework designed to stimulate discussion on conducting business which future generations can benefit from.

Organization of the book

1 The rationale for sustainable development: the environment, the people, the economy

The book starts with a review of the current global challenges faced by nations. Chapter 1 looks at the concept and roots of climate change. It develops further by addressing the management of natural resources and the effects on economic development. The chapter closes by clarifying the links between those global issues and the relationship between economics, people and the environment.

2 Sustainable development in the hospitality industry

Chapter 2 introduces the general concept of sustainability and sustainable development. It develops the idea that financially profitable hospitality operations can be combined with the principles of environmental management and societal engagement. The chapter also describes the various actions undertaken over the past two decades in the field of sustainable hospitality management.

3 Energy efficiency

Chapter 3 describes the issues concerning energy consumption in hospitality operations and defines the term carbon footprint, including calculation and offsetting options. The concepts of renewable and non-renewable energy sources are explained, followed by a detailed analysis of the possibilities and application of the different forms of energy used in hotels: solar, wind, geothermal, wave, hydro and biomass. The chapter also discusses the use of energy-efficient technologies in hotels and the process involved in installing an energy management programme as well as the tools available for energy usage self-audits.

4 Waste management

Chapter 4 starts by describing the various forms of waste and explaining the impacts of waste on the environment and communities. It follows with a discussion on waste management strategy, including waste avoidance, waste reduction, waste recycling and waste disposal methods in the hospitality industry.

5 Water conservation

Chapter 5 focuses on the issues surrounding water usage, water quality, water availability and water conservation. Techniques for water conservation and use of technology to manage water are discussed, including solar water heating and rainwater harvesting.

6 Eco-design in hospitality architecture

Chapter 6 starts by explaining the impacts buildings and hotels have on the natural and societal environments. The chapter continues by underlying the principles of eco-design in construction and architecture as well as site selection. It also explains the theory of embodied energy in construction material and discusses the waste created and resources used in the construction of a hospitality operation. Finally, the chapter reviews the leading construction certification systems available.

7 Food security

Chapter 7 starts by analysing the current food crisis and challenges as well as the impacts linked to conventional agriculture and food security. Food production systems and food scares are discussed. The linkages between agricultural inputs and the Western diet are examined. Finally, issues of animal welfare are reviewed.

8 Sustainable food issues and food sourcing

Chapter 8 continues from Chapter 7 by introducing issues in sourcing the most important input of restaurant operations, i.e. food. A brief insight into agriculture to pave the way for a deeper understanding of the effects of sourcing food is given with definitions of the following terms: conventional, integrated, organic and biodynamic farming. The chapter also defines the concept of food miles, sustainable food and a comprehensive analysis of regional food systems is provided.

9 Sustainable food and beverage management

Chapter 9 continues on from Chapter 8 and explores the opportunities and limitations of sustainable food, taking into consideration aspects such as regionality, seasonality, meat and fish dishes, and vegetarian and vegan food. Issues surrounding genetic engineering are discussed and categories of sustainable food are presented. The chapter continues by discussing nutrition in relation to human health.

10 Green marketing and branding

Referring to the discussion in previous chapters, Chapter 10 defines what it takes to establish a sustainable marketing strategy. To do so, the chapter identifies the principles of green marketing for hotels and examines the concept of sustainable development in relation to external communication and green marketing. It examines responsible marketing as part of a company's ethical strategy and discusses the four new Ps of green marketing.

11 Consumer typology and behaviour

Chapter 11 examines the changes in consumer behaviour in relation to sustainable development. The chapter examines the importance for companies in tourism to identify the motives of the responsible tourist. The chapter also discusses the techniques used by hospitality operations to involve consumers in sustainable management practices. The chapter closes on a discussion to understand behavioural variances toward consumption.

12 Corporate social enterprises

Chapter 12 identifies the underlying principles of sustainable business management and discusses the concept of corporate social responsibility as well as the concept of social entrepreneurship. The chapter discusses the relevance of each strategy in the hospitality industry.

13 Hospitality industry environmental management systems

Chapter 13 starts with defining what an environmental management system is. It continues by discussing the ways to implement such a system in hospitality operations and examines the challenges and opportunities associated with environmental management systems. A set of recommendations for the successful implementation of an EMS are discussed.

14 Certification processes and eco-labels

Chapter 14 defines what is meant by 'certification' and evaluates the various certification schemes available to hospitality managers. The chapter continues by discussing the major benefits associated with certification as well as the costs associated with certification. The chapter introduces a set of well-established standards and discusses how hotels communicate performance.

15 Financing, investing, measuring and accounting in sustainable hospitality

Chapter 15 explores the possibilities of accessing the finance investment needed for new green technologies or green refurbishing in hotels. The chapter provides examples and an overview of green financing schemes. The chapter also discusses green accounting, defines the concept of externalities and presents a series of environmental performance indicators and sustainability performance indicators. A sustainability performance framework is presented and online environmental self-auditing tools are discussed.

Epilogue: sustainability education in hospitality

The Epilogue discusses the issues and challenges in providing sustainability in hospitality curricula in universities.

Glossary

At the back of the book there is also a full glossary of terms used. These terms are shown in bold on their first occurrence in the chapter.

Companion
website resources

A companion website accompanies this book at www.routledge.com/cw/sloan, and includes additional resources for both students and lecturers.

Student resources

- A test bank of questions for each chapter for students to test their understanding.
- Links to relevant videos and websites to provide further insight into the industry.

Lecturer resources

- PowerPoint slides of all the tables, line figures and photographs from each chapter.
- Additional case studies to provide further examples of theory in practice within the hospitality industry.

Acknowledgments

We ought first to thank our families and friends for their support, who relentlessly encouraged our endeavour and shared our effort in assisting the book project.

We are thankful to Anna Birk, Micheal Bösch, Nadine El Rahman, Cornelius Kirsche and Gabriel Laeis who have continuously showed support and provided numerous case studies for this book.

We are so grateful to our affiliations, the International University of Applied Sciences Bad Honnef-Bonn and the Department of Recreation, Park and Tourism Studies at Indiana University, which have sponsored our research efforts concerning sustainable hospitality management, while being intellectually in debt to those colleagues leading us to a new scholarly horizon.

We are grateful to the hotels and restaurants which constantly strive to improve business in a sustainable manner that have provided this book with so much valuable material.

Finally, we would pass on our sincere thanks to the all hospitality students around the globe who have over the years provided valuable support in terms of research, ideas and discussion on the theme of sustainability in the hospitality industry.

The rationale for sustainable development

The environment, the people, the economy

CHAPTER OBJECTIVES

The objectives for this chapter are:

- To explain the way the activities of mankind are affecting the planet
- To describe the various forms of environmental degradation
- To analyse the reasons for the over-exploitation of water, minerals and oil
- To describe the effects of over-population
- To analyse the relationship between economics, people and the environment
- To define sustainable economics

Emerging challenges for the planet

Impact on the planet

Humankind consumes what nature has to offer and in return we create waste and deplete the Earth's natural reserves. All our actions have an impact on the Earth's **ecosystem**s that are only able to renew themselves at low levels of consumption. For many thousands of years man's impact on the **environment** was negligible, however, at the dawn of the Industrial Revolution all this changed. We now consume more of the Earth's resources than the planet can regenerate, hence, the planet is in 'ecological overshoot'. Our current consumption levels are simply too high and action needs to be taken soon as the planet's non-renewable resources are quickly being depleted. This depletion is accelerated by the continuous growth of the world population and its changing consumption patterns.

Climate change

Proven by recent incontrovertible scientific evidence, the climate has been changing as a consequence of human activity during the past 150 years. Within the troposphere (the lower part of the atmosphere about 10–15 kilometres deep), there are what is known as **greenhouse gases**. When sunlight reaches the Earth, some of it is converted to heat. Greenhouse gases absorb some of the heat and trap it near the Earth's surface, so that the Earth is warmed up. The most important greenhouse gases are **carbon dioxide**, CFCs (chlorofluorocarbons), nitrogen oxides and methane. This process is commonly known as the **greenhouse effect**. Life, as we know it, exists only because of this natural greenhouse effect which regulates the Earth's temperature. Without these gases, the surface temperature on Earth would be approximately 30°C lower. However, it is now clear there have been increases in the concentration of these gases which have exceeded the amount sequestered in the **biomass**, the oceans and other sinks. This has led to increases in air temperatures around the globe ranging from −0.26°C in 1880 up to 0.63°C in 2011 (National Aeronautics and Space Administration, 2011) known as **global warming**. It is suspected that this phenomenon may be causing increases in storm activity, the melting of ice caps on the poles resulting in flooding in lowlands, and other environmental problems. Scientists expect sea levels to rise between 10 and 90 cm by 2100 and ocean temperatures to increase. This of course is serious in the extreme for all nations but developing nations of the world simply lack resources to respond to this form of environmental **degradation**. For example, in Bangladesh, a 50 cm rise in sea level will place approximately 6 million people at risk from flooding. Carbon dioxide, one of the greenhouse gases, is also essential for internal respiration in the human body. It is the guardian of the pH (the measure of the acidity or basicity) of the blood, which is essential for survival. Apart from being an essential buffer in the human system, carbon dioxide is also known to cause health effects when the concentrations exceed a certain limit.

World leaders met in Kyoto, Japan, in December 1997, to consider a world treaty restricting emissions of greenhouse gases, mainly of carbon dioxide, that cause global warming. Unfortunately, while the **Kyoto Protocol** has worked for a while, America, the world's largest polluter, has never signed up. At the United Nations (UN) climate control talks in December 2011 in Durban, the protocol was dealt a major blow with Canada announcing its decision to pull out. Russia and Japan also oppose any extension of their commitments. The extension of the protocol beyond 2012, when the first round of commitments expires, was agreed on the last day by industrialized countries only after developing countries gave their nod for a new treaty for emissions reduction from 2020 onwards.

Damage to biodiversity

One reason for the catastrophic losses and degradation to the world's **biodiversity** (up to 60 per cent of the world's ecosystems are degraded or used unsustainably, according to the European Commission in 2011) is global climate change. The distribution of species (biogeography) is largely determined by climate, as is the distribution of ecosystems and plant vegetation zones (biomes). Climate change sometimes shifts these distributions but, for a number of reasons, plants and animals cannot always adjust.

Over-hunting has been another significant cause of the extinction of hundreds of species and the endangering of many more, such as buffalo in the nineteenth century and many African large mammals. Most extinction over the past several hundred years is mainly due to over-hunting for food, fashion and profit, in addition to environmental degradation.

One of the best-known models of commercial exploitation is the whaling industry, where whales are slaughtered for oil and meat. This custom has led to many whale species being brought to the brink of extinction. A century ago, humans could not seriously threaten whale populations because of rather primitive technology. At that time, a three-year-long whaling trip would kill fewer than a hundred whales. However, by 1967, about 60,000 were being killed yearly, yielding roughly 1.5 million barrels of oil. Not only the whaling industry but the fishing industry has developed exponentially as well. Larger, faster ships, sonar, better nets and other similar improvements have increased the ability of commercial fishermen to catch more fish and put the survival of species in danger.

Between 1966 and 1970, world herring catches decreased by almost a hundred-fold, from 1.7 million tonnes to 20,000 tonnes. Indeed, marine fisheries have been wiped out because their catches are no longer profitable. The California Sardine Fishery took 750,000 tonnes in the 1936–1937 season, but 21 years later, only 17 tonnes were brought in. The local fishing industry has not, to this day, recovered. In addition, when a specific type of fish becomes rarer, its value and price increase. Consequently, fishermen are given greater incentive to hunt it. It then becomes even more difficult for that species to survive.

However great over-exploitation is, the greatest damage to marine life is the result of general environmental degradation. Most sea aquatic life is concentrated in shallow waters close to land, where marine populations that are already exploited are also most subject to heavy **pollution** (because most pollutants are dumped into the sea near the shore). Moreover, many organisms live in estuaries, the mouths of rivers and streams where fresh and salt waters mix. These areas are threatened because of industrial and human waste in some parts of the world and fertilizers washed off agricultural land that interfere with the delicate natural equilibrium of these environments. Habitat loss and degradation caused by human activity are important causes of **flora** and **fauna** extinctions. As **deforestation** proceeds in tropical forests, more loss of biodiversity can be expected. All species have specific food and habitat needs, the more specific these needs and localized the habitat, the greater the vulnerability of species to loss of habitat through agricultural land

and livestock enlargement and to roads and cities. As the human population passed the seven billion mark in 2011, roughly half of the world's forests and natural habitats have been transformed, degraded or destroyed. Tropical forests are important because they are home to at least 50 per cent, and perhaps more, of the world's biodiversity, and they also act like sponges, releasing vast quantities of moisture into the atmosphere to fall as rain elsewhere and perform the vital task of absorbing carbon dioxide from the atmosphere. The original extent of these forests was 15 million square kilometres (km^2), now there remains about 7.5–8 million km^2. While there is uncertainty regarding the rate of loss, and what it will be in the future, the likelihood is that tropical forests will be reduced to 10–25 per cent of their original extent by late twenty-first century. Habitat fragmentation is a further aspect of habitat loss that often goes unrecognised. Forests, meadows, boglands and other habitats that are divided by human development remain generally small and isolated and can only maintain very small animal populations at best. Any species that requires a large home range, such as the grizzly bear, will not survive if the area is too small.

Over-exploitation of water, minerals and oil resources

Materials removed from the earth are needed to provide humans with food, clothing, and housing in the process of the continual standard of living upgrading that most people expect. Some of the materials needed are renewable resources, such as agricultural and forestry products, while others are non-renewable, such as minerals and oil. The United States Geological Survey has reported in 'Materials Flow and Sustainability' that there is increasing demand for non-renewable resources. Primarily due to the new developing **BRIC** (Brazil, Russia, India and China) economies, world commodity prices maintain their relentless push higher and higher as vital minerals such as ores of copper or aluminium become depleted. High oil prices are here to stay, the European Union's Energy Commissioner Guenther Oettinger warned in 2011. The lower prices of the previous three years had been the result of the financial crisis and recession, but escalating demand is now pushing up prices. The over-use and waste of valuable natural resources are threatening to produce a fresh economic crisis, Janez Potočnik, chief of the European Union's Commission for the Environment, warned in the same year. He said:

> It's very difficult to imagine [lifting Europe out of recession] without growth, and very difficult to imagine growth without competitiveness, and very difficult to be competitive without resource efficiency. Unless consumers and businesses take action to use resources more efficiently (from energy and water to food and waste, and raw materials such as precious metals), then their increasing scarcity, rising prices and today's wasteful methods of using them will drive up costs yet further and reduce Europe's standard of living.

This stark warning highlights the increasing **scarcity** and rising price of some key resources, including energy and water, but also food and raw materials such as metals, ores and minerals.

Some essential minerals can be recycled, such as phosphorus, potassium and nitrogen but the number of people that even the most efficient **recycling** could support may be much less than today's world population. In 1997, Canadian geographer Vaclav Smil calculated that were it not for the industrial fixation of nitrogen, the world's population would probably not have exceeded 4 billion people, 3 billion fewer than are alive today. It's likely that **organic agriculture** can feed many more people than it currently does, but the hard accounting of the nutrients in today's 7 billion human bodies, let alone tomorrow's projected 10 billion, challenges the hope that a climate-neutral agriculture system could feed us all. The bonanza forecast by some economists of cheap bio-fuels is beginning to backfire since land that was previously used for producing food is now used to produce crops to fuel cars. In the United States, which harvested 416 million tonnes of grain in 2009, 119 million tonnes went to ethanol distilleries to produce fuel for cars which is enough to feed 350 million people for a year. The result has been a massive increase in world food prices. The massive United States investment in ethanol distilleries sets the stage for direct competition between cars and people for the world grain harvest. In Europe, where much of the auto fleet runs on diesel fuel, there is growing demand for plant-based diesel oil, principally from rapeseed and palm oil. This demand for oil-bearing crops is not only reducing the land available to produce food crops in Europe, it is also driving the clearing of rainforests in Indonesia and Malaysia for palm oil plantations. On the demand side, the other reasons for the huge food price increases in the early years of the twenty-first century are population growth and the rising affluence of 300 million inhabitants of the BRIC countries. On the supply side: aquifer depletion, the loss of cropland to nonfarm uses, the diversion of irrigation water to cities, the plateauing of crop yields in agriculturally advanced countries, and, due to climate change, crop-withering heat waves, melting mountain glaciers, ice sheets and soil erosion. These climate-related trends seem destined to take a far greater toll in the future. An estimated one-third of the world's cropland is losing topsoil faster than new soil is forming through natural processes – and thus is losing its inherent productivity. Two huge dust bowls are forming: one across north-west China, western Mongolia and central Asia; the other in central Africa. Each of these dwarfs the US dust bowl of the 1930s.

In 2002, the United Nations asked 1500 experts to study the **social** effects of water scarcity in developing countries. One year later teams of executives from the world's largest water, oil and chemical companies tried to forecast the effect of future water scarcity on their own and national economies. Both groups reported back with alarming unanimity and predicted supply, health and economic crises coming sooner rather than later if there is no radical change in the way water is used. Reasons for water shortages can be found in the phenomenal pace at which glaciers are melting. Glaciers that used to gently supply communities in the summer season with a steady water supply are now melting so fast as to cause unseasonal floods and mud slides.

If all the ice in the polar ice caps were to melt, the oceans would rise by an estimated 70 metres. Even present low level melting is affecting coastal life and coral reefs, which are disappearing. Droughts, too, are becoming more frequent and lasting longer, rains are coming more irregularly. But the really big water deficits are caused by over-pumping of the water aquifers and wasteful irrigation techniques. In India, the World Bank numbers indicate that 175 million people are being fed with grain that is produced by over-pumping. In China, over-pumping provides food for some 130 million people. In the United States, the world's other leading grain producer, the irrigated area is shrinking in key agricultural states such as California and Texas. As water becomes scarcer, some countries may have to give up growing certain crops and rearing animals. A one quarter-pound hamburger needs about 11,000 litres of water, a cotton T-shirt 7,000 litres, a kilo of rice 5,000 litres. When the water needed to grow crops has to be pumped hundreds of metres from below, the true cost of food on supermarket shelves becomes clearer. Rather than digging deeper and moving water further, the future will be about recycling water. Waste water is increasingly being collected from kitchens, gardens and bathrooms, treated and reused. The technology is proven, and it is being used everywhere from golf courses in southern Spain to desert farms in Jordan and breweries in Ghana. Singapore, a city right on the equator with seemingly no shortage of fresh water, is using waste water for all its industries and most of its housing. Cities that do not want to ask their citizens to save water are moving rapidly to desalination. California and the Middle East, led by Dubai, are increasingly dependent on the technology. Most coastal cities around the world and even London may soon build a plant as desalination becomes a US$100 billion-a-year industry. In most cases, however, desalination is the most expensive and least sensible option for the time being. Studies suggest that most communities can find additional water, more quickly and for less money, by improving efficiency and management. The downsides of desalination are the enormous amounts of power needed and the vast quantities of salt that are extracted and must be disposed of. In the next decade, however, the cost is expected to fall as the technology improves, and desalination plants will increasingly be linked to waste heat from factories or solar power stations.

Over-population

Few experts question the received demographic wisdom that the Earth will be home to roughly 9 billion people in 2050 and become stable at 10 billion by the end of the century. Demographers also project that life expectancy will keep rising while birth rates drift steadily downward, until the human population stabilizes at nearly 3 billion more people than today's 7 billion residing on this planet. Amazingly, 2 billion people are overweight and paradoxically another 1 billion do not have enough food on the table to eat every evening. It appears difficult to square this projected growth in the population with the ecological limits that we appear to be meeting and perhaps surpassing. There is little scientific dispute that the world is heading toward a warmer and harsher climate, less dependable water and energy supplies, less intact ecosystems with fewer species, more acidic oceans and less naturally productive soils. Some analysts, ranging from scientists David Pimentel of Cornell University to financial advisor and philanthropist Jeremy Grantham, dare to underline the possibility of a darker alternative future, suggesting that humanity long ago overshot a truly **sustainable** world population.

Most scientific commentators on the environment and population do not sign up to such predictions. However, questions should be asked about whether such possibilities are real enough to temper the usual demographic confidence about future population projections.

Climate change, water aquifer depletion and natural resource depletion all provide daunting challenges to the present-day population. The world's net land under cultivation has scarcely expanded since 1960, with millions of acres of farmland gobbled up by urban development while roughly equal amounts of less fertile land have come under the plough. The doubling of humanity has cut the amount of cropland per person in half. Much of this essential asset is declining in quality as constant production saps nutrients that are critical to human health. Fertilizer helps restore fertility (though rarely micronutrients), but at ever-higher prices and through massive inputs of non-renewable resources such as oil, natural gas and key minerals.

It is certainly possible that ingenuity, resilience and effective governance will manage the stresses humanity faces in the decades ahead and will keep life expectancy growing in spite of them. Slashing per-capita energy and resource consumption would certainly help. A sustainable population size will be easier to maintain if societies also assure women the autonomy and contraceptive means they need to avoid unwanted pregnancies. However, it seems foolish to treat projections of 10 billion people at the end of this century with total serenity. More humility about population growth is needed in an uncertain and dangerous century where **conservation**, correct management and political leadership have never appeared so important.

The economy, present and future

The economy, the human population and the Earth's ecosystems are all inextricably linked. What affects one affects another, the change in state of each one of these components affects the states of the other components. The present economic model creates momentum for certain processes it creates and drives growth. However, the economy is constrained by a wider ecosystem **carrying capacity** so the economic model cannot drive growth indefinitely. When growth starts to impact on the ecosystems, i.e. it is nearing the ecosystem carrying capacity, the ecology/economy will start dragging population growth down. This is because the population growth is dependent on the economy/ecology to sustain it and maintain it. Ecological carrying capacities are not simply caused by the finite limits of natural resources. In practice, it is the ability of a species to access its essential resources, which become constricted. To a large extent, cooperation is necessary for things to work and as limits are reached, the social efficiency of the functioning of a species is affected. In the case of mankind, it will be our economic patterns, governments and infrastructures which will need to change. This will be the mechanism by which this growth will be restricted, not resources running out completely.

Our present system of capitalism has been described as 'a financially profitable, non-sustainable aberration in human development' but no-one can deny that it has been prodigiously productive. Nearly everyone alive in Western Europe today has a higher real income than they would have had if capitalism had never existed. The trouble is that among the things that have been destroyed in present-day capitalism is the way of life on which capitalism in the past depended.

Defenders of capitalism argue that it offers everyone the benefits that in Karl Marx's time 150 years ago were enjoyed only by the bourgeoisie, the settled middle class who owned capital and had a reasonable level of security and freedom in their lives. In the nineteenth century, most people had very little. They lived by selling their labour more often than not on a daily basis and when the mill or the farm had less work, they faced hard times. But as capitalism develops, its defenders say, an increasing number of people will be able to benefit from it. Fulfilling careers will no longer be the prerogative of a few. People will no longer struggle from month to month to get by on a meagre wage without security. Protected by a cushion of economies, a house they own and a decent pension, they will be able to plan their lives without fear. With the growth of democracy and the spread of wealth, no-one needs to be shut out from the aspirations for a better life. Everybody can be middle-class.

In fact, in many developed countries over the past 20 or 30 years, the opposite has been happening. Few people have job security, life-long careers are barely memories and the trades and many professions of the past have largely gone.

While previous generations could comfort themselves with significant savings and property ownership, credit has now become so tight and employment so irregular that house purchasing is a distant dream for many. In many parts of Europe and North America, house ownership has become the scourge of negative equity as prices stagnate and the value of bricks and mortar falls. A dwindling minority can count on a pension on which they can comfortably live but many regard their working lives extending into what was until recently considered to be the golden years. The future is insecure, the art of living from day to day is becoming a necessity for many.

For the more fortunate individuals who do have work, disposable incomes are far higher than in the past and the remnants of the post-war welfare state still provide care, infrastructure and medical treatment, albeit often limited. The model of free, comprehensive welfare for all as created by Aneurin Bevan in the UK is no more than a distant memory.

Job scarcity and security are becoming a generational issue, the situation for many younger people is worse. Increasingly, higher education is no longer a birth right, it is a business transaction. Gaining knowledge and skills has become an issue of wealth and financial debt. At a time when savings are diminishing due to low interest rates, being thrifty can make the situation worse. It is the cavalier business person who borrows heavily and is not afraid to declare bankruptcy who survives and goes on to prosper. In a market place where mobility is expected, it is those who are always ready to try something new who have the most promising future. Those who stick dutifully to their old ways risk falling by the wayside.

In 2008, the bubble economy of the Western economies burst and in 2012 global markets are in a state of reconfiguration. The USA and Europe were ready to embrace **globalization** only when it seemed the process would produce their version of capitalism. As the global crisis unfolds, there is unlikely to be any alteration in human behaviour. The reflex of people is to turn to governments for security from the thunderclouds while governments, as always, will be mainly concerned with their own survival. Until now, bank bail-outs have stopped the financial system from disintegrating and policies of monetary expansion attempt to kick-start economies. The growth produced in the bubble economy leading up to the crisis was unsustainable; attempts to re-start it might well be self-defeating. Resource scarcities, upon which much of this temporary prosperity is built, will be become more obvious and more threatening to the planet.

The model of globalization in place over the last generation appears to be undergoing an irreversible collapse. The global free market was only stable when resting on the assumption that it could be self-regulating, but since economies are so closely connected, the whole system has become fragile with different fractions pulling it apart. In the past, destabilization suffered in one economy would not be passed like a virus to the next. In the present integrated system where countries and economies rely on each other, it is likely to break down when one part ceases to function. When the American sub-prime mortgage crisis struck and brought down the whole financial system, shock waves were sent around the globe and shortly after its real economy went into reverse and those of its trading partners.

A new style of sustainable economics is needed. The present freedom of markets is there only for the benefit of human beings, and then, it can be argued, only for a minority and generally not for the environment. In the global free market, societies and individual governments have little control over the economic instruments used by it. The spread of new communication technologies throughout the world does not make Western values universal or the rise of a single economic civilization more likely. On the contrary, it makes a world rich in cultural diversity a distant memory.

Towards sustainable economics

Some environmentalists and economists argue in favour of a sustainable economy which implies including all resources that contribute to sustainable human activity. In the current market economy allocation system, most non-marketed natural and social capital **assets** and services that are critical contributors to human well-being and that of the planet are excluded. In sustainable economics contributions of natural and social capital are included and approximate to real economic efficiency. In a sustainable economy, the use of *renewables* are maximized, such as from wind, water, the sun or another **renewable resource** for power production, rather than burning fossil fuels, of which there are limited supplies.

It means that society would desire a more constant Gross National Product (GNP), with some sectors growing and others declining at an equal and opposite rate. Those sectors of the economy that increased the **sustainability** of the environment, such as **renewable energy** or the production of long-lasting goods, would be encouraged to grow. Where new technologies make growth possible without decreasing sustainability, growth would be stimulated. Likewise, growth would be encouraged in service industries where a high proportion of human capital is involved. Rather than consuming natural resources and depleting biodiversity, the sustainable economy seeks to use what is already taken, leaving natural resources as a backup supply. Biological capital is viewed as being of equal importance to financial capital.

In order to stimulate the sustainable economy, incentive systems would be used to reward those who minimize the toll they exert on the environment, and produce environmentally friendly items for human use. The levels of consumerism that exist today in the Western world are simply not sustainable. The planet does not have enough resources to provide the new BRIC countries with the same levels of consumerism as exist today in the Western world on a long-term, sustainable basis. We all need to make do with less; people should be encouraged to use goods and services that bring comfort and well-being rather than happiness as defined by the number of cars parked in the drive or by the size of one's house. Finally, a sustainable economy would attempt to build a more egalitarian society. While trying to minimize the number of goods people used, the economy would also try to equalize what goods people have.

EXERCISE

SMALL GROUP QUESTION AND GROUP DEBATE

Read the article entitled 'The Economics of the Coming Spaceship Earth' by Kenneth E. Boulding. Then read the article entitled 'Lifeboat Ethics: The Case Against Helping the Poor', by Garrett Hardin. Which analogy, Hardin's lifeboat or Boulding's spaceship, more accurately describes the current condition of human civilization on Planet Earth? Provide some argumentation and be ready to discuss in class.

References

Boulding, K. E. (1966) 'The economics of the coming spaceship Earth', in H. Jarrett (ed.), *Environmental Quality in a Growing Economy*. Baltimore, MD: Johns Hopkins University Press, 3–14. Available at: http://www.eoearth.org/article/The_Economics_of_the_Coming_Spaceship_Earth_%28historical%29).

European Commission (2011). *Our Life Insurance, our Natural Capital: An EU Biodiversity Strategy to 2020*. Available at: http://ec.europa.eu/environment/nature/biodiversity/comm2006/pdf/2020/1_EN_ACT_part1_v7%5B1%5D.pdf.

Hardin, G. (1974) 'Lifeboat ethics: the case against helping the poor', *Psychology Today*. 8: 38–43. Available at: http://www.garretthardinsociety.org/articles/art_lifeboat_ethics_case_against_helping_poor.html).

National Aeronautics and Space Administration (2011) *Global Climate Change: Vital Signs of the Planet*. Available at: http://climate.nasa.gov/news/?FuseAction=ShowNews&NewsID=467.

USGS. (n.d.) *Material Flow and Sustainability*. Available at: http://pubs.usgs.gov/fs/fs-0068-98/fs-0068-98.pdf.

Resources

Earth Policy Institute: http://www.earth-policy.org/.

Gray, J. (2009) *False Dawn: The Delusions of Global Capitalism*. Revised edn, London: Granta Books.

Greenpeace: http://www.greenpeace.org.

GRIST: http://www.grist.org/.

Lovelock, J. (2009) *The Vanishing Face of Gaia: A Final Warning: Enjoy It While You Can*, London: Allen Lane.

Sustainable Economics: http://www.sustainableeconomics.org/.

The Guardian: Guardian Environment Network. Available at: http://www.guardian.co.uk/environment/series/guardian-environment-network.

The Ecologist: http://www.theecologist.org/.

U.S. Department of Energy Efficiency and Renewable Energy (US DOE EERE): http://www.eere.energy.gov/.

World Business Council on Sustainable Development (WBCSD): www.wbcsd.ch.

World Economic Forum (WEF): http://www.weforum.org/en/index.htm.

Yale Environment: http://e360.yale.edu/.

Additional material

Go to www.routledge.com/cw/sloan to find PowerPoint slides of all the figures and tables from the book, additional case studies, a test bank of questions and extra links to useful videos.

2

Sustainable development in the hospitality industry

CHAPTER OBJECTIVES

The objectives for this chapter are:

- To explain the way the activities of mankind are affecting the planet
- To describe the various forms of environmental degradation
- To define sustainable development and explain its history
- To explain the three pillars of sustainability
- To give reasons why the hospitality industry needs to become more sustainable
- To give examples of sustainable practice in the hospitality industry
- To explain the concept of eco-advantage

Emerging challenges for the planet

Human activities have influenced the Earth's **ecosystem** for many thousands of years. Nowadays the negative consequences of human actions can be noticed everywhere. Because it is one of the larger industries in the world, the **hospitality industry** is an important contributor to these problems. This chapter explains why hospitality operations need to manage their **environmental impacts** and exactly what is involved in running a profitable business in line with the principles of **environmental stewardship** and to the benefit of society, i.e. **sustainable** hospitality management.

Problem definition

The boom in tourism and hospitality has given rise to millions of new jobs and increased economic prosperity in countries around the world. As the world's largest service industry, tourism and hospitality contribute an estimated 5 per cent to worldwide **Gross Domestic Product (GDP)** and employ around 234 million people worldwide, corresponding to 8.7 per cent of the total global workforce which implies substantial **impacts** on society and the **environment**. The industry is therefore faced with a range of increasingly pressing challenges.

Although the numbers of international arrivals decreased by 4 per cent in 2009, international arrivals grew by 4.4 per cent in 2011 and the United Nations World Tourism Organization (**UNWTO**) forecasts a continued growth in 2012, reaching the 1 billion international arrivals by the end of the year (UNWTO, PR No. PR12002, 2012). In 2008, tourism and hospitality generated US$946 billion in export earnings in the United States alone. Consequently, there is growing potential for enterprise development and employment creation, which in turn, stimulates further investment and supports the development of local services. The industry also earns substantial foreign exchange and makes a large contribution to the balance of payments.

When describing a phenomenon such as the hospitality industry, it is difficult to define not only its size and activities but also its role in society. The diversity of its products and services, from luxury hotels, to cruise ships, to casinos, to catering firms, even to hot dog stands outside sports stadiums, defies the conventional definition of an industry as being a set of firms all making the same product. Naturally, the provision of hotels falls within the general context of hospitality, an aspect of human activity which has important **social** dimensions as well as meeting the physiological needs of shelter and comfort. From an international perspective the notion of a hotel is understood as a culturally bound phenomenon that represents a certain set of assumptions. Managing a hotel in the twenty-first century is a challenging task. Welcoming and taking care of guests from different backgrounds and offering food and shelter are always constant but the demands made on hoteliers have drastically changed. The modern-day hotelier requires an in-depth knowledge of the traditional fields of operations, finance, marketing, customer relationships, branding, media and communication but also of **stakeholder** relationships, environmental management, ethics and social responsibility. Many hotels now consist of multiple units including restaurants, bars, clubs, entertainment facilities, spas and recreation facilities operating 24/7, 365 days a year, and consequently have a relatively high environmental impact and may cause a strained relationship with people both locally and internationally in the global market place. Indeed, the expansion of the hotel industry is dramatic with dozens of new properties opening weekly. This expansion is in direct response to increases in prosperity and the desire to travel. The result is direct pressure on non-renewable resources both in the 'design and construction phase' and the 'operation and occupation phase' of hotel properties. New sustainable building and management systems are now needed to relieve the unrelenting pressure on the natural environment that is reaching the limits of its **carrying capacity**.

Why should hotels become more sustainable?

Hotels, motels and all the various forms of accommodation comprise the largest sector of the travel and tourism industry and have been shown to have the highest negative influence on the environment, of all commercial buildings. **Pollution**, waste, **greenhouse gases** and environmental hazards do not necessarily spring to mind when considering the hospitality and tourism industries. Environmental **degradation** is more readily associated with industries such as manufacturing, energy production, the steel industry, oil production or the chemical industry. But according to estimates, an average hotel releases between 160 and 200 kilograms (kg) of **carbon dioxide (CO$_2$)** per square metre of room floor area per year, and water consumption per guest per night is between 170 and 440 litres in the average five-star hotel. On average, hotels produce 1 kg of waste per guest per night. The US Environmental Protection Agency calculates during a one-night stay in a hotel room 29.53 kg of CO$_2$ are produced on average in an average hotel. For upscale hotels, emissions are calculated at 33.38 kg CO$_2$ per room day. In 2007, InterContinental Hotels surveyed a representative sample of 26 of their hotels. Extrapolating this data gave an idea of the **carbon footprint** throughout the company's complete hotel portfolio:

- The total estimated carbon footprint is approximately 9 million metric tonnes, roughly equivalent to 4,777 Empire State Buildings.
- Roughly 4.6 million tonnes come from energy usage while 4.4 million tonnes are indirect emissions from consumption of other resources, including materials and waste.
- At 59 kg per night, their average hotel room carbon footprint is roughly equal to the average US home.

According to the report, the carbon footprint of a customer in their best performing hotels is significantly lower than if he had stayed at home. The study also demonstrated that the environmental aspects of hotel activities such as heating, ventilating and air conditioning systems can be managed to lower our carbon footprint. In addition, we discovered we have opportunities to reduce carbon emissions in all our hotels. The US Environmental Protection Agency also calculated that the average person's diet contributes 2920 kilograms of CO$_2$ to the atmosphere each year. By dividing by 365, it is deduced that a person emits, on average, 8 kg CO$_2$ a day from their meals. Emissions for food preparation are not included in this calculation.

To the uninformed onlooker, environmental protection seems much more necessary in industries where the pollution is actually visible. However, while the processes that are necessary in the assembly of service products may be intangible, perishable and consumed as they occur, they often involve the support of a wide spectrum of physical components and reliance on natural resources. Hotels need to reduce their impact on the environment as they count among the greatest polluters and resource consumers within the service industries. Major hotel chains that constitute a large percentage of rooms worldwide have a significant potential to decrease their impact on the environment. Moreover, large hotel brands have the financial capacity to invest in technology. Hotel chains also have the opportunity to introduce environmental policies on a corporate strategic level and therefore reduce environmental impact on a large scale.

Over the past few years, hotel companies have made a determined effort to deal with the impact their business activities have on the environment, particularly by measuring and reducing their carbon and water **footprints**. Both major international hospitality companies and small businesses recognise that there are tangible benefits in doing this, including real efficiency gains and an improved corporate reputation. Another closely linked challenge for companies is how to manage the ethical operation of their business. Ethical issues arise in four main areas: the supply chain, the local community (in the tourism destination), the workplace and the customers. There may be concerns about exploitative labour practices in the supply chain or exploitation of migrant workers in hotels and restaurants. Local people may often rightly perceive that they have little or no share in the economic benefits of tourism while bearing a disproportionate burden from environmental degradation. The development of **tourist** destinations produces demand for generally low-paid hotel operatives and destroys traditional employment opportunities such as fishing and farming, local living prices normally increase and many of the original population are obliged to leave. In 1999, the UNWTO devised and adopted a global **code of ethics** for tourism, designed to minimize the negative effects of tourism activity on destinations and local communities, which was officially recognised by the UN in 2001. In 2011, the UNWTO held the first International Congress on Ethics and Tourism, arguably it was the first opportunity to evaluate whether the industry had moved beyond symbolic statements and agreed on codes of practice leading to concrete actions. Encouragingly, there is evidence that the hotel industry is assuming a proactive, collective approach to human rights and business ethics, incorporating human rights risk mapping, employee training on responsible business and sustainable local benefits. Major hotel companies have taken significant steps in the past decade to integrate policies on human rights into their stated policies on business conduct and ethics.

An example is Marriott International, who re-launched their business ethics awareness programme in 2010, to provide employees with information on how to identify potential ethical and compliance issues and raise them with the organization. Included in this scheme are new training videos for all newly hired workers and quarterly bulletins with tips on problem prevention. For their global operations, the company recently developed human rights and specifically child protection policy for their security officers.

Another company with a proactive ethical policy is the Hong Kong-based hotel group, Shangri-La Hotels and Resorts, that operates globally, although half of its properties are in China. They launched a **code of conduct** for suppliers in 2009 which is externally audited and conducted site visits to their top 150 suppliers to check employee wages and conditions, health and safety, management systems and environmental practices. They also have a group-wide programme linking hotels with a local school or orphanage for five to 10 years, including providing training in hotel skills. The examples of Marriott and Shangri-La highlight **best practice** rather than industry-wide reality, where much more needs to be done. A code of ethics, an employee's charter and human rights policy are no longer enough: companies need to show practical examples of where they have made a difference through the supply chain, local communities, their workplace and to their customers' behaviour. Similar to hotels displaying examples of their environmental stewardship policy, customers regard a firm ethical policy as an attractive selling point. Sustainable core business strategy makes good business sense as it potentially enhances a company's profits, management effectiveness, public image and employee relations. The likely winners in a fast-changing hospitality industry are companies that take a long-term **triple bottom-line** approach.

Travel industry emissions

The hospitality industry is very much part of the travel industry where ethical behaviour and environmental emissions are also on the corporate agendas. However, for the purposes of this book, the authors make no attempt at providing solutions to the impacts resulting from travel to and from destinations but merely offer tentative advice on how to reduce personal environmental impacts while travelling.

Arriving in hotels generally requires the burning of fossil fuels on an impressive scale in one form or another. Since greenhouse gases are mostly invisible, most travellers do not make a direct connection between boarding a plane and villages being flooded in Tanzania. Unfortunately there is a connection through the carbon dioxide emitted from the jet's engine and climate change.

According to Climate Care, a UK **carbon-offsetting** company, cruise ships emit nearly twice as much carbon dioxide as aeroplanes per passenger kilometre. Justin Francis, co-founder of responsibletravel.com, a directory of environmentally friendly holidays that partners with Climate Care, said that, 'Add to that the fact that many passengers fly to the port of departure of the cruise ship before boarding and you have a double carbon whammy.' The organization also claims that carbon dioxide emissions are just a drop in the ocean when it comes to environmental problems on luxury liners. Most ships run on so-called bunker fuel, the cheapest and dirtiest fuel oil, which not only powers the vessel, but also all the amenities on board: restaurants, swimming pools and nightclubs among them. In 2011, Royal Caribbean launched its largest ship yet, the *Oasis of the Seas* with a capacity of 5400 passengers. Its amenities include a microclimate-controlled Central Park, with irrigation and drainage systems, as well as trees that tower more than two and a half decks high. The environmental group Friends of the Earth claim that a one-week voyage of such a large ship is estimated to produce 210,000 gallons of sewage, a million gallons of grey water (runoff from sinks, baths, showers, laundry and galleys), 25,000 gallons of oily bilge water, 11,550 gallons of sewage sludge and more than 130 gallons of hazardous wastes. Marcie Keever, director of the Clean Vessels

Campaign of Friends of the Earth, said, 'These are floating cities that go back and forth through our waters, dumping toxins from their enormous amount of waste.' She added that cruise ships also pollute the coast lines by affecting marine life, beaches and coral reefs, as well as the air (sulphur dioxide and nitrogen oxide emissions from their massive engines). Due to the sheer volume of their passengers, when cruise ships arrive, often several at a time, in small resort towns like Dubrovnik in the Adriatic Sea, their passengers tend to take over the whole landscape. This form of mobile tourist destination has the same effect as clusters of hotels on the local society and the environment. There is, however, some positive environmental news beginning to emerge thanks to increased pressure from the US Environmental Protection Agency, as well as various environmental campaign groups, and stricter regulations are being passed. Cruise ships are slowly converting to burning low-sulphur diesel fuel instead of the cheaper fuels and ships are voluntarily starting to discharge raw sewage, grey water and oily bilge water well away from shores.

Another worrying component of the travel industry is aviation, which accounts for 1.6 per cent of global greenhouse emissions currently, but will soon become the biggest emitter in the developed world if it grows unchecked. The UK government's advisory body, the Committee on Climate Change, warned ministers in 2010 that aviation will account for a quarter of all emissions in the developed world even if it caps 2050 emissions at the growth rate witnessed at the beginning of the century.

The airline industry may be cleaner than the cruise industry on a per passenger/ kilometre basis but it is still nowhere near going green. In 2009, the British Airways chief executive, Willie Walsh, unveiled an agreement between airlines, airports and aircraft companies to cut emissions to 50 per cent below 2005 levels by 2050. This ambitious target was based on small increases in airplane engine efficiency and blending aviation fuel 50:50 with bio-fuel. A study by a team from Purdue University found that the use of drop-in bio-jet fuel (produced from US feedstocks) would not be sufficient to achieve the aviation emissions reduction target of 50 per cent below 2005 levels by 2050. Producing bio-fuels is conditional on two major factors: oil price and land availability. Biomass-based bio-jet fuel only becomes viable when the oil price is high. Oil-producing feedstock (i.e., camelina and algae) can be competitively produced when the oil price is lower but it requires fertile land that could be used to produce food for people.

Carbon offsetting for travel

For those travellers who reduce the distance they travel, going on holiday will most likely involve travelling some distance away from home. Simple methods exist for reducing individual contributions to **global warming**. Trains use far less fossil fuel than other forms of mechanized transport, except of course walking and cycling which are becoming increasingly popular, healthy, low environmental-impact alternatives. Car pooling is also becoming a means to reduce carbon footprints; many cities now centralize destination offers where the thrifty traveller can also reduce travel costs. Addressing the challenge of transitioning to a **renewable energy** economy will require a sustained effort for many years to come. For the time being, all direct reductions of personal carbon emissions are the best solutions. However, for those remaining emissions that are unavoidable, carbon offsetting through credible projects is a relatively easy way to invest in high quality vetted renewable energy, energy efficiency and forestry-related projects around the world.

Organizations like Sustainable Travel International support individuals and businesses to reduce environmental impacts by providing comprehensive carbon management and reduction services.

Defining sustainability and sustainable development: a historical perspective

The Greeks, the Romans and von Carlowitz

The Greek and Roman philosophers already reflected on the diverse and sometimes complex relationships between humans, and in particular human activities, and ecosystems in which those activities take place. Plato (400 BC) examined issues related to the size of population versus the availability of fertile land and natural resources. Aristotle discussed nature's role and purpose. The Roman army commander, natural philosopher and author, Gaius Plinius Secundus, known as Pliny the Elder (first century AD), pointed out the improper use of raw material and the disappearance of forests with the known consequences of **deforestation** such as soil erosion, floods and a decrease in soil fertility in his publication, *Naturalis Historia* (Natural History). But it was not until the turn of the eighteenth century that such philosophical discussions moved into the spheres of agriculture, management and business. In a book published in 1713, entitled *Sylvicultura Oeconomica*, German tax accountant and mining administrator, Hans Carl von Carlowitz laid the grounds of the modern interpretation of **sustainable development** (Grober, 2010). He argued against short-term financial gains in managing primary resources in general and wood in particular. Located in Freiberg, Saxony, von Carlowitz further reasoned that along with the careful harvesting of wood, a plan for reforestation must be devised. Von Carlowitz was an advocate of improved thermal insulation in construction and the use of energy-efficient furnaces and ovens. *Sylvicultura Oeconomica* is considered one of the first scientific publications on forestry. Von Carlowitz coined the word 'sustainability'.

From Freiberg to Rio

The nineteenth-century German sustainable forestry science gained international acclaim. However, the concept of **sustainability** and sustainable development was going to be tested by rapid economic growth in the second half of the twentieth century. This growth was based heavily on the depletion of natural resources.

Sustainable development, a concept that gradually came about over centuries, gained momentum in the 1950s and 1960s. In 1951, the IUCN (the International Union for Conservation of Nature) published the first report on the state of the environment in the world (IUCN, 1951), a pioneering report in its quest for reconciliation between the economy and ecology. In 1966, economist Barbara Mary Ward published *Spaceship Earth* (Ward, 1966) and economist Kenneth Ewart Boulding wrote an essay entitled 'The Economics of the Coming Spaceship Earth' (Boulding, 1966). The basic premise of both publications rests on the realization that Planet Earth is 'a single spaceship, without unlimited reservoirs of anything, either for extraction or for pollution, and in which, therefore, man must find his place in a cyclical ecological system' (ibid.).

The international think tank, the Club of Rome, was founded in the late 1960s and commissioned the report entitled *The Limits to Growth*, which landed on the bookshelves in 1972. The basic thesis was the linkage drawn between rapid population growth and the finite supply of primary resources (Meadows *et al.*, 1972). In the same year, the United Nations organized the Stockholm United Nations Conference on the Human Environment, which investigated the linkages between the environment and development. The United Nations Environment Programme (**UNEP**) was born out of the 1972 Stockholm Conference. However, the modern version of the definition of sustainable development is best summarized in one simple sentence created by the World Commission on Environment and Development in 1983 and published in the final report entitled *Our Common Future*, better known as the Brundtland Report, in 1987 (WCED, 1987). Sustainable development is defined there as: 'development that meets the needs of the present without compromising the ability of future generations to meet their own needs'. Building upon this definition, but changing its focus from humankind's responsibility towards future generations to the current balance of the Earth's ecological systems, is the definition of sustainable development in the 1991 publication *Caring for the Earth: A Strategy for Sustainable Living* by the United Nations Environment Programme (UNEP), the International Union for the Conservation of Nature (IUCN) and the World Wide Fund for Nature (**WWF**): 'improving the quality of human life while living within the carrying capacity of supporting ecosystems'. The addition of economic and socio-cultural aspects to the notion of sustainability came about from the Earth Summit in June 1992, from the United Nations Conference on Environment and Development (**UNCED**) in **Agenda 21**. Furthermore, this conference focused attention on the role of education, more specifically education that encourages values and attitudes of respect for the environment. Under Agenda 21, to engage in sustainable development requires adopting, changing or improving behaviours by following five principles:

1. *The principle of precaution*, i.e. to prevent any risks occurring that are deemed possible.
2. *The principle of responsibility*, i.e. to adopt social and environmental responsibility for all activities and decisions.

3. *The principle of transparency*, i.e. to make all relevant information available to stakeholders.
4. *The principle of social and technological innovation*, i.e. to move forward technological innovation in a way that benefits humankind and the planet.
5. *The principle of responsible citizenship*, i.e. to contribute to local, national and global tasks.

Post-Rio and the current situation

Many conferences followed, on all topics within the field of sustainable development. The subject of climate change was projected to the forefront of sustainable development when it was discussed in 1997 in Kyoto, Japan. An agreement was reached by 38 industrialized countries to reduce their combined greenhouses gas emissions by 5.2 per cent on average by 2012 compared to 1990 levels (United Nations Framework Convention on Climate Change, n.d.). The agreement entered into force in 2005. The same year, author and entrepreneur John Elkington published a book entitled *Cannibals with Forks: The Triple Bottom Line of 21st Century Business* in which he coined the term triple bottom line, or TBL (Elkington, 2005). Elkington argues that measuring success means capturing, analysing and reporting ecological and social performance in addition to the financial performance of an organization.

In 2000, world leaders gathered and adopted the eight **Millennium Development Goals (MDGs)**. The goals to be achieved by 2015 include eradicating extreme poverty, reducing child mortality rates, fighting disease epidemics such as AIDS, and developing a global partnership for development. The World Summit on Sustainable Development (WSSD) or Earth Summit +10 took place in Johannesburg, South Africa, in 2002, ten years after the Rio Summit. The Johannesburg Summit broadened the definition of sustainable development even further, by including the notions of social justice and the fight against poverty. Additionally, to reinforce the focus on sustainability and education following a proposal from the Johannesburg Summit in 2002, the United Nations General Assembly proclaimed the period 2005–2014 to be the 'Decade of education for sustainable development'. Gatherings of environmental specialists, government representatives and non-governmental organizations (**NGOs**) discussing climate change matters corroborate the media and general public interest. In 2009, the United Nations Climate Change Conference was held in Copenhagen, Denmark. The summit was a missed opportunity for world leaders to agree on a framework for the mitigation of climate change beyond 2012, when the **Kyoto Protocol** expires. According to present economic theory, the existing world economy is required to grow ever more in order to meet the escalating needs of an ever increasing global population, where wealth is unevenly distributed. The principles of sustainability will have to be applied increasingly if the planet is to avoid cataclysmic consequences. Countries that are classified as poor need to grow in order to improve the living standards of their populations and scarce resources have then to be distributed between a world population that is set to reach 9 billion by 2050 (according to WTO figures), an increase of another 2 billion compared to the present day. Countries with lower standards of living, where the infrastructure is on the threshold of development have the chance to implement the principles of sustainability from the beginning. Without giving up on growth, they have the possibility to develop in a way that is sustainable for the present generation and will ultimately benefit future generations as well. An agreement was reached to restore the world's depleted fisheries for 2015 and discussion took place on how best to achieve the Millennium Development Goals.

Other definitions of sustainability

World Business Council on Sustainable Development

Sustainable development is, according to the World Business Council on Sustainable Development (**WBCSD**):

> Forms of progress that meet the needs of the present without compromising the ability of future generations to meet their needs. Given the scale of world poverty today, the challenge of meeting present needs is urgent. But we must look ahead and do our utmost to ensure that what we do today for our ever-growing population does not compromise the environmental, social and human needs of our descendants.
>
> (WBCSD, 2006)

United Nations World Tourism Organization

According to the United Nations World Tourism Organization (UNWTO) (2004): 'Sustainability principles refer to the environmental, economic and sociocultural aspects of tourism development, and a suitable balance must be established between these three dimensions to guarantee its long-term sustainability.'

Defining a sustainable hospitality operation

Using the Brundtland Report's definition as a starting point, a sustainable hospitality operation can be defined as: a hospitality operation that manages its resources in such a way that economic, social and environmental benefits are maximized in order to meet the need of the present generation while protecting and enhancing opportunities for future generations. For greater clarity, this statement requires examination of the following questions:

- Which resources used by a hotel impact directly on economic profit, society and the environment?

- How can the principles of sustainability be incorporated into a hospitality management system?
- What does it mean for a hotel to meet the needs of the present generation while protecting and enhancing opportunities for future generations?

Sustainable hospitality operations or 'green hotels' aim to reduce their impact on the environment and society. The American association, Greenhotels, provides a more resource-oriented definition: 'Green Hotels are environmentally sustainable properties whose managers are eager to institute programmes that save water, save energy and reduce solid waste while saving money to help protect our one and only earth.'

Critics of sustainability

Although interest and support for sustainable development are growing continuously, critics of the movement and sceptics still exist. Since numerous definitions of the term 'sustainability' have been created and received media coverage, the concept is often claimed to be difficult to understand. For some, the concept is vague and fuzzy and the limited availability of sustainable models is often criticized as well. Sustainability is not a panacea for all the ills of the world though some consider it a quick-fix solution.

Obstacles to environmental sustainability

Investing in sustainable hospitality operations is often impeded by misconceptions about what the bottom line is. Many managers and owners of hotels only consider the initial investment costs that are indeed higher when compared to unsustainable solutions. However, the sustainable running costs are generally much lower than those properties that have inefficient equipment. The longer-term return of such investments is most often positive purely in financial terms, even without considering the triple bottom line of environment, society and economics.

Another obstacle lies in the internal communication and control within hotel chains. Several hotel corporations already have **environmental management programmes** in place, and some of them are even included in the **Dow Jones Sustainability Index**. But an important factor determining the effectiveness of these programmes is the translation of corporate environmental policies to the individual hotels, i.e. the translation into real actions by hotel workers. Many hotels until now have had problems in articulating in-house or corporate environmental management activities. Most often a manager of a hotel has the freedom to determine the strategies and procedures that seem fit to him. Therefore his attitude towards specific subjects will for the most part determine the hotel's actions with respect to that subject when the corporate framework gives him the freedom to do so. Furthermore, a difference is made between company-owned and managed hotels. Different levels of involvement in franchise agreements exist, all with different levels of imposed procedures. Less demanding franchise formulas give the manager more freedom to design his own strategies with regard to sustainability.

Sustainable development in the tourism and hospitality industry

The hospitality industry set about incorporating the philosophy of sustainability in the early 1990s. With the publishing of **Agenda 21** for the Travel and Tourism Industry, for the first time, individual businesses and the hospitality industry were encouraged to adopt codes of conduct promoting sustainable travel and tourism best practice. Gradually voluntary guidelines and examples of best practices were established in the industry followed by the introduction of **eco-labels** and **certification** procedures. An increasing number of hotels and restaurants are now becoming more sustainable as they embark on a wide range of measures designed to reduce their impact on the environment. Around 80 per cent of European hoteliers are involved in some kind of activity oriented towards the environment, and the areas most concerned are:

* energy-saving measures;
* water-saving measures;
* green purchasing;
* waste minimization practices.

Hospitality management associations are paying increased attention to providing the industry with best practice examples and guidelines. An example is the International Tourism Partnership which has produced a set of sustainable hotel siting, design and construction principles. Another example for the restaurant industry is the American National Restaurant Association, which has inaugurated a set of guidelines that move the restaurant industry towards more environmentally sound practices and sustainable initiatives. The International Hotel & Restaurant Association (**IH&RA**) recently realized the need for more sustainable practices and has developed a set of ecological, business-smart solutions. Some of the practices they promote include **conservation** of energy, water and other natural resources, increasing recycling and encouraging the use of sustainable materials and alternative energy sources. Founded in 1919, the IH&RA is the leading business association for the restaurant industry. It comprises 945,000 restaurants and food outlets employing 13.1 million people in the United States.

The Green Restaurant Association, a US non-profit, consultative and educational organization with the mission 'to create an ecologically sustainable restaurant industry', also conducts research in various environmental areas. They have established several environmental guidelines for restaurants and promote examples of best practice in order to facilitate achieving environmental sustainability. An example is their 'Guide of Endorsed Products', a compendium of environmentally responsible products for the restaurant industry, in which they provide information about organically certified, recycled, chlorine-free and other environmentally preferable product choices. These examples show that in the hospitality industry sustainable awareness is growing but is still in its very early stages.

Figure 2.1 presents a holistic perspective of the theoretical framework for sustainability. Taking the definition of a sustainable hospitality operation, the whole value-chain and **life cycle** of an operation has to be taken into consideration when identifying critical aspects that impact on sustainability. Everything from construction to furnishing; from food and beverage sourcing to production and waste management; to all the various day-to-day operations, everything has to be in harmony with the environment, society, as well as operational profitability.

The environmental dimension

The environmental dimension focuses on an organization's impact on the **flora** and **fauna** that make up the ecosystems in addition to the air we breathe, the water we drink and the land we enjoy. It involves looking at a company's environmental footprint in regard to all its operations, facilities and finished products. Thus, all waste and emission elimination must be examined in detail. Productivity maximization and efficiency of all **assets** and resources must be strived for. The overall objective is to minimize all practices that might adversely affect the enjoyment of the planet's resources by present and future generations. Avoiding short- and long-term environmental damage and maintaining and promoting natural diversity are the main objectives of this dimension.

Hospitality operations can impact on the environment during building construction, during the manufacture and use of fixtures and fittings, during the cultivation of food, as well as when using energy and water or producing waste. This examination of

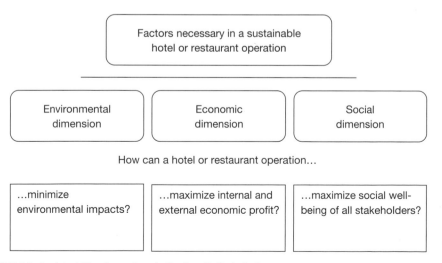

FIGURE 2.1 Sustainability dimensions in the hospitality industry

environmental impacts before and during hospitality operations is known as an environmental life cycle analysis.

The economic dimension

The main aim of all private sector organizations is to make a profit. They have other aims as well, but if their main aim is not fulfilled, they will sooner or later stop operating. Profit maximization, whether stated as the primary objective or not, is essential for all commercial organizations, as without profits they simply go out of business. In recent years it has become obvious that some practices that contribute to environmental sustainability can also provide significant short- and long-term business benefits. Saving costs through installing energy- and water-efficient technologies, using energy-efficient equipment and ensuring efficient and fair staff practices can increase internal profitability. Additional business benefits of improved relationship with stakeholders, improved staff morale and motivation, enhanced public reputation, increased market share can all result from sustainable management systems.

A hospitality company committed to a sustainable business policy supports and participates in the development of the local economy and will aim to generate economic benefits for local people through increased local employment opportunities, business linkages and other income-generating opportunities.

The social dimension

The social dimension deals with the impact an organization has on the society in which it operates. The main consideration of the social dimension is how the hospitality operation can positively contribute to the lives of local people in the present and in the future. A company committed to sustainability therefore has to deal with issues such as: public health, social justice, human rights, labour rights, community issues, equal opportunities, skills and education, workplace safety and working conditions, maintaining and promoting social and cultural diversity, involving communities, consulting stakeholders and the public as well as training staff with regard to sustainable practices.

A hospitality operation needs to be able to assess the social impact of its activities in order to enhance the well-being of individuals and communities. Issues such as fair trade and fair prices with regard to sourcing products and food items require consideration. Local food and beverage sourcing should be considered. Careful attention must be given to food safety issues and human health considerations as far as the food and beverages offered is concerned.

In order to turn the three above-mentioned dimensions into practices, a broad commitment of multiple stakeholders must take place to ensure a common and holistic approach to sustainability (see Figure 2.2). Sustainable hospitality does not translate into one company doing its very best in a given market but rather, as presented in the framework in Figure 2.2, partnerships must be developed, responsibility ensured and practices implemented in collaboration with other businesses linked to tourism: regulators, local government, educational establishments, non-government bodies and citizens' groups. Partnerships must be developed between stakeholders to facilitate conflict resolution, to harmonize plans and to bring about action for environmental improvement. Industry networks within and between the broader service sectors of tourism (including transport, tour operators, hospitality, travel agents and the leisure sectors) are critical, as they will provide for the sharing of experience and expertise and the establishment of mutual beneficial sustainable projects. Realistic **indicators** for environmental improvement and sustainable development need to be established, on which overall progress can be monitored and assessed.

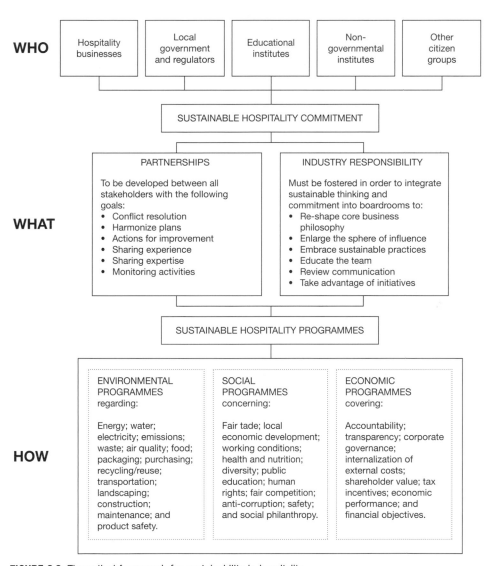

FIGURE 2.2 Theoretical framework for sustainability in hospitality

The hospitality industry must take environmental and societal responsibility and integrate sustainable management into its daily operations and business practices. Taking responsibility requires business leaders and managers to reconsider seven traditional principles including:

- the company's positioning within a market;
- the image perceived by consumers, suppliers and other stakeholders;
- the legitimacy of the environmental positioning of the company;
- the acceptability of sustainable products and services for its customers;
- the suitability of its suppliers to engage in a sustainable supply chain;
- the readiness of intermediaries to support sustainable initiatives;
- the consumer expectations and perceptions of benefits that sustainable products and services will offer.

The savings in costs and revenues earned through sustainable management systems should be injected back into continued environmental improvement. Additional environmental training and information dissemination are especially important for small and medium-sized enterprises (**SMEs**). Finally, the complete communication strategy must be revised to reflect the sustainable initiatives and programmes undertaken by the business. Initiatives may range from voluntary self-regulation schemes such as environmental certification schemes and eco-labels, to tax rebates on environmental investments and low-interest financing schemes for clean and resource-efficient technology.

Following the development of partnerships coupled with industry responsibility, sustainable hospitality programmes can be established encompassing the three pillars of environmental, social and economic programmes. Each programme should cover a wide range of initiatives to be undertaken by hotel managers and owners, from concrete planning calculations and reductions of emissions created by a hotel to tactics in getting the most from and giving the most to local communities while creating a business system whereby the external environmental costs of doing business are accounted for internally within the business model. Leading hospitality companies understand that sustainable business models have far-reaching implications and are not merely incremental improvements in today's business operations.

Sustainable competitive advantage in the hospitality industry

A strong motivation for hospitality companies embarking on sustainable business initiatives is the competitive advantage that can be achieved. Although competitive advantage is seen to be necessary, it must be stated that in fast-changing macro-economic environment conditions, competitive advantages do not last very long. Furthermore, gaining sustainable competitive advantage in the hospitality industry can be difficult due to the hyper-competition that exists. As in all hyper-competitive industries, rivalry is abnormally high and competition is fierce. In this situation, companies observe very closely the moves of competitors and industry leaders and immediately copy their successful strategies as soon as they are introduced.

Competitive advantage cannot be gained by only one single improvement, it requires a company to constantly question its strategic position. Thus, competitive advantage through sustainability can only be achieved by constant screening of competitors and constant innovation. It must be emphasized that in this respect technology plays a vital role in increasing competitiveness for a hotel company.

Competitive advantage and technology

In the past few decades, the number of technological patents has vastly increased and technology has become a dynamic energizer of many businesses. Better technology often leads to greater efficiency and often to shorter product life cycles. Businesses are forced to carefully assess which technologies to put into practice. In addition, new technologies usually require large capital investment and commit companies to using the new technology for long periods. In this process, hotel customers have become more knowledgeable regarding technology and their needs have changed accordingly. Hotel guests request the same standard of technology in their hotel room as they have at home.

Technological innovation is one of the most powerful sources of competitive advantage; and applying superior technology has helped many firms to achieve a better competitive position within the hospitality industry.

CASE STUDY 2.1 Inkaterra Authentic Nature Travel: beyond hospitality: pioneering ecotourism in Peru

For over 37 years, Inkaterra has been an active player in developing and promoting **sustainable tourism** in Peru. Each year Inkaterra hosts more than 65,000 travellers providing authentic nature experiences in Peru. The Inkaterra Machu Picchu Pueblo Hotel in the heart of the Andean cloud forest, and Inkaterra Reserva Amazonica Rainforest Lodge, on the banks of the Madre de Dios River in the Amazonian forest and Inkaterra La Casona in Cusco are examples of Inkaterra's work in rescuing, presenting and showcasing Peru's unique culture and nature.

Inkaterra's mission is:

Excellence in Ecotourism and Conservation, re-evaluating the real cultural, social and natural values, creating authentic experiences.

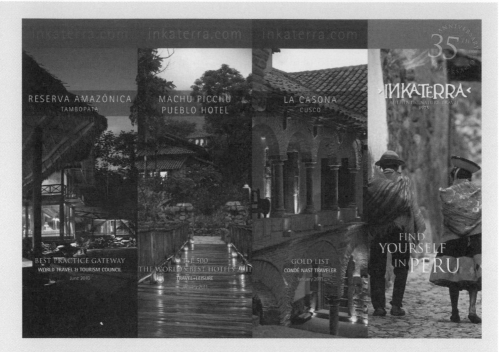

PICTURE 2.1 Inkaterra Reserva Amazónica, Pueblo Hotel and La Casona

Inkaterra's extensive *Sustainability Policy* is based on 14 points:

1. Define and respect authentic cultural, social and environmental values.
2. Create professional development opportunities and encourage the recruitment and training of local staff.
3. Develop an ideal work environment providing better living conditions than those covered by labour law.
4. Develop activities in accordance with current legislation, such as corporate, tax, labour and the concepts of sustainable development.
5. Provide experience in the formulation of standards and creation of protected areas.
6. Develop contingency plans for natural, social or financial disasters.
7. Continuously update analysed financial statements in order to facilitate the decision-making process and the decentralization of administrative actions. Raise awareness within partners, travellers and locals on the conservation of the environment, with activities and materials.
8. Encourage the development of local communities, taking into consideration their environment and culture.
9. Use environmentally friendly products and maintain good communication with suppliers.

10. Use energy and water efficiently, and provide adequate waste treatment.
11. Develop continuous improvement in our management and process controls by minimizing negative impacts.
12. Identify the positive and negative effects generated by human action.
13. Offset the greenhouse gas emissions generated by the organization's operations, in order to be carbon neutral.
14. Be a replicable business model of low initial cost and high positive impact on local populations.

Inkaterra's Sustainability Policy is turned into seven themes for a responsible approach to travel.

I Built-in sustainability

Inkaterra Asociación (ITA) invests over USD$300,000 annually in the preservation of ecological reserves, the protection of animal species and the management of natural reserves. Additionally, all staff at Inkaterra undergo in-depth training on social and environmental issues. Staff take part in activities linked to the celebration of environmental days such as Earth Day, Water Day, Responsible Tourism Day and Environmental Day.

PICTURE 2.2 Big Birding Day

PICTURE 2.3 Cleaning of river banks during Environmental Day

II Long-term projects

Inkaterra has established research and conservation programmes. Those include programmes on butterflies, birds, hummingbirds, orchids, amphibians, ants and spectacled bear rescue project. The conservation programmes includes the study of ecosystems, an inventory of flora and fauna, a behavioural analysis of living things and their inter-relationships, the conservation of endangered species, sociological studies as well as **environmental education** and community training programmes.

III Local impact

Since 1975, Inkaterra has trained over 2000 local people and provided community workshops in Tambopata, Madama and La Tormenta communities. Inkaterra ensures the involvement of local institutions (municipalities, schools, guide associations, community boards, NGOs, etc.) and gives priority to local suppliers. Knowledge is shared and transferred across cultures via interpreters. Inkaterra strives to hire locally (an average 80 per cent of employees working for Inkaterra are locals) and respects local and national employment benefit laws.

PICTURE 2.4 *(left)* Planning with local institutions

PICTURE 2.5 *(right)* Job creation for local people

IV Positive footprint

Inkaterra has been carbon neutral since 1975. Over 17,000 hectares of protected forest contributes to CO_2 offsetting operations each year. Energy, fuel and water **conservation** as well as the **recycling** of paper, plastic, glass and organic residue are examples of activities undertaken at Inkaterra. Using local materials and local contractors is a priority.

PICTURE 2.6 Monitoring wildlife with volunteer programmes

V Sense of place

In order to offer an authentic experience, the respect for local culture and character and the use of design inspired by local traditions ensure that properties adapt to local geography, minimizing and diminishing the visual impact.

PICTURE 2.7 Design inspired by local traditions

VI Engaging experience

Inkaterra is about transformative experiences. The traveller receives the message of conservation and sustainability throughout all Inkaterra products.

VII Profitability

Inkaterra strives for economic stability by generating income from hotel and travel experiences, the Canopy and Anaconda Walk, the Spectacled Bear donation and the Native Farm Machu Picchu.

The business philosophy is best described using Inkaterra's slogan: 'We offer more than accommodations, we define sustainable tourism.'

Source: Inkaterra, http://www.inkaterra.com/.

CASE STUDY 2.2 Farnek Avireal encourages hoteliers to optimize sustainability goals with industry-specific, web-based technology

About Farnek Avireal

Established in 1980 in the United Arab Emirates (UAE), Farnek Avireal is a joint venture between Khalifa Juma Al Nabooda Group and the Zurich-based international facilities management company Avireal AG Switzerland. Farnek Avireal is a leader in sustainability and is a member of the US Green Building Council, has associations with international organizations such as **Green Globe** and myclimate and has already been awarded the prestigious Emirates Energy Award. Farnek Avireal manages 1000 properties and operates the maintenance contract for the world's tallest building, the Burj Khalifa.

The Farnek Avireal Hotel Optimizer programme has been created to help the region's hoteliers effectively manage and reduce both the costs and consumption of energy, water and waste disposal via easy-to-use web-based **benchmarking** software.

According to a recent study conducted by the Farnek Avireal, five-star city hotels in Dubai are using up to 225 per cent more energy than their European counterparts. 'With energy saving directly related to cost saving, the findings have highlighted significant savings for hotels in Dubai and throughout the region, thereby potentially boosting bottom line performance,' said Markus Oberlin, General Manager, Farnek Avireal.

The study, which benchmarked Dubai hotel average consumption against comparable European properties, revealed that hotels in the Emirates use up to 1,250 litres of water per guest compared to 350 litres in Germany, with power usage of 275–325 kilowatt-hour (kWh) per square metre versus 100 kWh in German hotels.

Oberlin remarked:

> As a market leader in sustainability, we have been helping hotels and resorts to reduce their carbon footprint through our exclusive association with Green Globe, the international sustainability certification programme for the tourism and hospitality industry, and the Hotel Optimizer software is a complementary product that enables our environmentally-focused clients to make significant cost savings of between 15 to 20% across key areas of their operation.

He added: 'Using our advanced technology, customers can calculate their carbon dioxide (CO_2) emissions including the real cost of wasteful energy and water consumption, as well as non-recyclable waste production.'

The Hotel Optimizer functionality enables hotels to easily identify cost-saving opportunities and set realistic annual targets at the click of a button, as well as download unbiased overviews of operational water and energy costs.

Farnek Avireal will also launch the next generation edition of Hotel Optimizer software with programme upgrades including detailed analytics and cost-saving indications, a month-on-month comparison chart spanning four years that allows users to track progress, and the ability to add property-specific commentary. 'We have also refined the actual graphic display to enhance functionality and make it even more user-friendly,' said Oberlin.

Source: Farnek Avireal, http://www.farnek.com/home.php.

EXERCISES

1   GROUP DISCUSSION, GROUP PROJECT OR WRITTEN ASSIGNMENT

- Outline the major environment threats and social challenges facing the world today.
- How are these issues impacting your country or region?
- Critically examine how the resulting environment and social changes are affecting the tourism and hospitality industry in your country or region.

2   GROUP DISCUSSION OR GROUP PROJECT

Mitigating environmental challenges

- What are the major environmental threats facing your country or region?
- What control measures are in place to combat these threats?
- Do you feel that these control measures are resulting in environment improvement?
- Give a 10–15-minute presentation of your findings.

3   GROUP PROJECT

Environmental and social issues in media

- Review the environment-related issues that have caught the attention of your local and national media over the past month.
- How have these issues affected tourism in your city or region?
- Give a 10–15-minute presentation of your findings.

4   GROUP PROJECT OR WRITTEN ASSIGNMENT

Hospitality and sustainability challenges

- What is the biggest environmental and societal issue facing the hospitality industry in your country?
- How does it affect the tourism and hospitality business?

- To what extent does tourism and/or hospitality contribute towards this issue?
- Develop a feature article for a local newspaper responding to these questions.

5   GROUP PROJECT

- Develop an outline for a television or radio programme that will raise public awareness of environmental issues and related control actions in your country.

6   WRITTEN (AND RESEARCH) ASSIGNMENT

- Select a case study on tourism and hospitality. Identify how tourism and hospitality contribute towards climate change, depletion of the ozone layer, biodiversity loss, land degradation, acid deposition and air pollution.

Acknowledgments

The exercises proposed in this chapter were originally set by the International Association of Hotel Schools (EUHOFA), the International Hotel & Restaurant Association (IH&RA) and the United Nations Environment Programme (UNEP) in a document entitled *Sowing the Seeds of Change: An Environmental Teaching Pack for the Hospitality Industry* published in 2001 and updated in 2008. Thank you to EUHOFA (http://www.euhofa.org/), IH&RA (http://www.ih-ra.com/), UNEP (http://www.unep.org) and François-Tourisme-Consultants (http://www.francoistourisme consultants.com).

References

Boulding, K.E. (1966) 'The economics of the coming spaceship Earth', in H. Jarrett (ed.) *Environmental Quality in a Growing Economy*. Baltimore, MD: Johns Hopkins University Press, 3–14. Available at: http://www.eoearth.org/article/The_Economics_of_the_Coming_Spaceship_Earth_%28historical%29.

Elkington, J. (2005) *Cannibals with Forks: The Triple Bottom Line of 21st Century Business*, Oxford: Capstone Publishing.

Grober, U. (2010) *Die Entdeckung der Nachhaltigkeit*, Munich: Antje Kunstmann.

IUCN (International Union for Conservation of Nature) (1951; 2011) *First Report on the Condition of the Environment*, Gland: IUCN. Available at: http://www.iucn.org/.

IUCN, UNEP and WWF (1991) *Caring for the Earth: A Strategy for Sustainable Living*, Bern: Union Internationale pour la Conservation de la Nature et de ses Ressources.

Meadows, D.H., Meadows, D.L., Randers, J. and Behrens, W. (1972) *The Limits to Growth*, New York: Signet Books.

Nemeth, E. and Neurath, P. (1994) *Otto Neurath oder Die Einheit von Wissenschaft und Gesellschaft*, Wien: Böhlau.

United Nations (2012) *Millennium Development Goals*. Available at: http://www.un.org/millenniumgoals.

United Nations Framework Convention on Climate Change (n.d.) *Uniting on Climate: A Guide to the Climate Change Convention and the Kyoto Protocol*. Available at: http://unfcc.int/resource/docs/publications/unitingonclimate_eng.pdf.

United Nations World Tourism Organization (UNWTO) (2004) *Sustainable Development of Tourism: Definition*. Available at: http://sdt.unwto.org/en/content/about-us-5.

UNWTO (2012) Press Release No. PR12002. Available at: http://www.unwto.org/facts/menu.html.

Ward, B. W. (1966) *Spaceship Earth*, New York: Columbia University Press.

World Business Council on Sustainable Development (WBCSD): http://www.wbcsd.ch.

World Commission on Environment and Development (WCED) (1987) *Our Common Future*. Available at: http://www.un-documents.net/wced-ocf.htm.

Resources

American Hotel and Lodging Association (AHLA): http://www.ahla.com.

Conservation International (CI): http://www.conservation.org/Pages/default.aspx.

Convention on Biological Diversity (CBD): *Text of the CBD*. Available at: http://www.cbd.int/convention/text/.

Greenhotels: http://www.greenhotels.com.

Greenpeace: http://www.greenpeace.org.

International Hotel & Restaurant Association (IH&RA): http://www.ih-ra.com.

National Restaurant Association (NRA): http://www.restaurant.org.

United Nations (UN): *Millennium Development Goals*. Available at: http://www.un.org/millenniumgoals/.

United Nations Environment Programme (UNEP) *GEO Yearbook Series*. Available at: http://www.unep.org/yearbook/2012/uyb_series.asp.

United Nations Environment Programme (UNEP) *Making Tourism More Sustainable: A Guide for Policy Makers*. Available at: http://www.unep.fr/scp/publications/details.asp?id=DTI/0592/PA.

United Nations Environment Programme (UNEP) *Sowing the Seeds of Change: An Environmental and Sustainability Tourism Teaching Pack for the Hospitality Industry*. Available at: http://www.unep.fr/sowingtheseeds/.

United Nations World Tourism Organization (UNWTO): http://www.unwto.org/facts/menu.html.

World Business Council on Sustainable Development (WBCSD): http://www.wbcsd.ch.

World Commission on Environment and Development (WCED) (1987) *Our Common Future*. Available at: http://www.un-documents.net/wced-ocf.htm.

World Economic Forum (WEF): http://www.weforum.org/en/index.htm.

World Wildlife Fund (WWF): *Climate Change*. Available at: http://wwf.panda.org/about_our_earth/aboutcc/.

World Wildlife Fund (WWF): http://www.worldwildlife.org/who/index.html.

Additional material

Go to www.routledge.com/cw/sloan to find PowerPoint slides of all the figures and tables from the book, additional case studies, a test bank of questions and extra links to useful videos.

Energy efficiency

CHAPTER OBJECTIVES

The objectives for this chapter are:

- To describe the issues concerning energy consumption in a hospitality operation and define the term carbon footprint
- To differentiate between renewable and non-renewable energy sources
- To describe solar, wind, geothermal, wave, hydro and biomass energy
- To explain carbon offsetting and carbon neutrality
- To describe the process involved in an energy management programme
- To describe examples of energy-efficient technology

Energy use in the hospitality industry

Hotels are the largest consumers of energy not only in building construction but also as establishments with complex installations, which provide guests with high levels of multi-faceted comfort and exclusive amenities, treatment and facilities. Many of the services provided to hotel guests are highly resource-intensive whether it concerns energy, water or raw materials. A significant amount of the energy used is wasted, leaving ample room for intelligent measures of energy efficiency and **conservation**. Since the installation of techniques that can save energy, water and raw materials in hotels can achieve environmental progress and offer competitive advantages to hotels in outperforming their counterparts, many new energy-saving facilities have been introduced by the hotel sector in the past few years following technological advances.

On a worldwide basis, the energy used in hotels is predominantly fossil fuel-based, often produced by nuclear reactors. A truly **sustainable** hotel must not only consider ways to use energy wisely but should also consider the possibilities of enhancing the use of energy from renewable sources. Renewable and non-renewable energy alternatives are typically not compared with each other from the perspective of their entire **life cycle** impact and cost. With few exceptions, insufficient or no value is attached to the knock-on effects of energy production and use on the **environment**, **biodiversity**, human health and the overall quality of life, all of which would substantially benefit from the enhanced use of **renewable energy** resources and energy-efficient technology.

The **carbon footprint** is a measure of the **impact** the activities of individuals or businesses have on the environment and in particular on climate change. It relates to the amount of **greenhouse gases** produced in our day-to-day lives through burning fossil fuels for electricity, heating and transportation, etc. The carbon footprint is a calculation of all the greenhouse gases we individually produce and is measured in tonnes or kilogrammes of **carbon dioxide (CO_2)**. In some cases it can be reduced or neutralized by a variety of measures. The first being to reduce dependence on non-renewable energy sources in favour of renewable energy alternatives.

Non-renewable energy sources

Some 85 per cent of the energy used in the world today is produced using non-renewable energy sources. This percentage is forecast to remain the same till 2030 unless something changes drastically, such as the widespread enactment of legislation, breakthroughs in energy technology or the development of abundant, inexpensive new energy sources. Non-renewable fuels are also known as fossil fuels because they are the fossilized remains of plants and animals which died up to 300 million years ago and became buried beneath the surface of the earth and the ocean floors. Time, pressure and heat transformed this material into hydrocarbons which we burn to extract energy.

The public debate about energy sources often pits **environmental impacts** against low price; clearly, sustainable solutions lie in resolving both sides of the argument. However, discussions over price and planetary **impacts** often miss some important facts. For example, the price paid by the consumer for electricity from nuclear energy excludes two large economic factors that are relevant to power generation: **subsidies** and **externalities**.

Subsidies are direct financial incentives given to power generators, often in the form of tax breaks. In some countries, such as France, where electricity is cheaper than in most other European countries, it is because the state has long subsidised the development of nuclear power. As in many other countries, in France the regulated tariff does not include the cost of dismantling old nuclear power stations, their replacement, **waste management**, accident risk and various operating costs. The cost of decommissioning old nuclear plants in the UK is estimated to be at least €100 billion. It could reasonably be expected that anyone wishing to build new nuclear power stations should have to put that sort of sum into an upfront clean-up fund. Unfortunately, of course, as nobody seems willing to do so, nuclear power is uninsurable. Since the 1980s, nuclear power programmes have undergone considerable cost increases. In an article published in the scientific journal *Energy Policy*, the investment cost in French nuclear power plants has multiplied by 3.4 in 25 years. Nuclear power has always been an expensive white elephant, in the UK, taxpayers subsidise nuclear power to the tune of £1 billion a year. Only two nuclear power stations are under construction in Western Europe: one in France and one in Finland. The Finnish reactor is supposed to be the first of a new generation of safe and affordable units and it is being subsidised by the French nuclear industry as a loss leader in the hope that it will spark a new nuclear building boom. The project has been plagued with cost overruns and delays and is under investigation by the Finnish nuclear safety regulator. Considering the astronomical price paid in subsidies by taxpayers, the inherent dangers of nuclear radiation as witnessed in nuclear disasters like Long Mile Island, Chernobyl, Fukushima and the indefinite stockpiling of highly dangerous nuclear waste it is not difficult to understand why building new nuclear plants is a such a controversial subject.

It is not only nuclear power that receives large doses of government funding. A 2009 independent study by the Environmental Law Institute looked in detail at subsidies to both renewable and non-renewable energy sources in the USA. Renewable subsidies totalled US$29 billion over the study period (2002–2008), with corn ethanol claiming about half of that amount. Non-renewable subsidies over this time period totalled US$72 billion, most of which was consumed by transportation fuels. The study also noted that most of the renewable subsidies were only temporary or had provisions to end, whereas the non-renewable subsidies were permanent provisions in the US tax code. The total costs of non-renewables like coal may be high, but the total costs of nuclear power are, in any meaningful sense, incalculable. Investors face cost overruns that could burn through even the deepest pockets. The true cost of waste disposal is still not known. The cost of decommissioning, even decades away, is also unknown in some cases. And the cost of catastrophic failure is more than any private company is willing to face. How can any investor calculate the return on investment with such large uncertainties?

Externalities or external environmental costs, are benefits to society that are not included in the market price of an item but have to be paid for at some point, thus, forming the basis for the idea of true cost. **Pollution** of the air, of the groundwater or landscape is the most commonly cited negative externality because the buyer or the seller of a polluting consumable does not directly bear the cost of clean-up.

One good example is gas and oil extracted from shale gas and tar sands in Canada. Energy-intensive and messy to extract, the fossil fuel industry sees them as a buffer during the dying days of conventional cheap oil. Both the mining and the processing of tar sands cause significant environmental impacts, including huge emissions of **global warming** gases, destruction of wildlife habitat and impacts to air and water quality. In addition to producing greenhouse gas-emitting fossil fuels, tar sands development is significantly more energy-intensive than conventional oil and gas development. World Energy Outlook suggests that alongside conventional sources of gas, unconventional sources like shale gas could supply the world's gas needs for 250 years at current levels of consumption. At present, the majority of shale gas output is in the US, but the announcement that there may be large reserves in the UK suggests that shale gas could become a very significant part of energy supplies here, too.

The rapid rise of shale gas has been possible thanks to recent developments in hydraulic fracturing, better known as fracking: this is basically drilling horizontally into rock formations deep underground using charges to blow cracks in the rock, then using fluid (over 99 per cent of which is water and sand) to keep the cracks open to allow gas to escape. Burning gas produces fewer greenhouse gas emissions than coal or oil because the ratio of hydrogen to carbon in methane is higher. It is not a low-carbon energy source, like renewables or nuclear power, but it is certainly lower in carbon. However, research by Cornell University, published in 2011, suggested that shale gas was as bad, if not worse, than coal. There is also significant evidence of health impacts in rural communities where fracking is taking place, mostly the US Midwest and Pennsylvania. There are reports of contaminated wells, highly polluted air, patterns of similar human illnesses and sick or dying farm animals in communities where shale gas drilling and fracking are taking place. In addition, evidence is mounting of risk of contamination of drinking water sources for urban areas downstream from fracking sites. These risks, especially to water, but also to air, soil, health and rural environments, have made fracking a hot issue in the USA, Canada, South Africa and Europe.

When subsidies and externalities are considered, non-renewable energy, especially coal, is significantly more expensive than most renewable options. Coal provides around half the electricity used in the USA, and has the highest total subsidy cost to society. Researchers from Harvard recently published a study entitled 'Full cost accounting for the life cycle of coal' (Epstein *et al.*, 2011), it calculates the full health and environmental costs of coal power in the USA to be from US$175 billion to US$523 billion annually. The costs in China, where health and environmental protections are low, may well be much higher. Reducing the use of coal is perhaps the single most important thing we can do to reduce air pollution and protect our climate.

Renewable energy usage

There are only two types of energy: renewable which is unlimited, and non-renewable which, by definition, will eventually run out. Worldwide energy consumption for the period from 1995 through 2005 witnessed an average annual growth of 2.4 per cent. World energy production grew from 34.5 trillion kilowatt-hours (kWh) in 1995 to 43.6 trillion kWh in 2005. Oil and oil derivates remained the most important energy sources in 2005, accounting for 36.8 per cent of the total amount of the primary energy sources, although this represents a somewhat lower amount than in 1995 (39 per cent). During the same period, renewable energy sources in the form of geothermal, solar and wind energies, as well as biomass, grew to 370 billion kWh in 2005 but only represented 0.93 per cent of the total world energy production. In 1995 it accounted for 0.6 per cent (International Energy Agency, 2005).

In 2010, world energy consumption grew by over 5 per cent after the slight decrease of 2009. Consumption in the Organization for Economic Co-operation and Development (the OECD is an international economic organization of 34 countries) countries grew by 3.5 per cent, the strongest growth rate since 1984, although the level of OECD consumption remains roughly in line with that seen 10 years ago. Non-OECD consumption grew by 7.5 per cent and was 63 per cent above the 2000 level. Consumption growth accelerated in 2010 for all regions, and growth was above average in all regions. This strong increase is the result of two converging trends. First, industrialized countries experienced sharp decreases in energy demand in 2009, following the global financial crisis but recovered firmly in 2010. Second, China and India, which showed no signs of slowing down in 2009, continued their intense demand for all forms of energy. Chinese energy consumption grew by 11.2 per cent, and China has surpassed the USA as the world's largest energy consumer. Oil remains the world's leading fuel, at 33.6 per cent of global energy consumption, but oil continued to lose its market share for the 11th consecutive year. As the data from the International Energy Agency show, China has gone from using 1107 million tonnes of oil equivalent (Mtoe) in 2000, to 2131 Mtoe in 2008 and is estimated to have consumed 2265 Mtoe in 2009. Meanwhile, US energy consumption was only marginally higher in 2008 (at 2281 Mtoe) than it was in 2000 (2270 Mtoe), and is still gradually falling (International Energy Agency, 2010).

In 2011, global investment in renewable, clean energies reached a new high of US$260 billion despite the financial crisis. This figure includes investment in renewables such as bio-fuels and smart technologies. It does not include natural gas, nuclear energy or clean coal. Bloomberg New Energy Finance (BNEF), which tracks renewable energy investment, reported a 5 per cent increase over 2010, made possible by large amounts of investment going to the solar industry which alone saw a 36 per cent rise over the previous year, totalling US$136.6 billion. For the first time since 2008, the USA invested more than China in clean energy: US$56 billion compared to US$47.4 billion, with 29 US states requiring utilities to generate a share of their electricity form wind, solar, geothermal and biomass. However, there were also big losers in the clean energy world in 2010. Investment in wind power fell 17 per cent to US$74.9 billion. Meanwhile, manufacturers of wind turbines and solar panels are being squeezed by a drop in the price of raw materials and oversupply.

Although renewable power development is well established in developed economies, there is also strong interest in developing countries, with emerging economies such as India and Brazil needing more power. India's transformation into a clean technology powerhouse surged forward in 2011 when it racked up investments of US$10.3 billion in the sector, a growth rate of 52 per cent year on year that dwarfed the rest of the world's significant economies. Solar investments led the growth with a seven-fold increase in funding, from US$0.6 billion in 2010 to US$4.2 billion in 2011, just below the US$4.6 billion invested in wind power during that year, according to figures released by analysts BNEF. A record 2827 megawatt (MW) of wind energy capacity was added in 2011, which kept India third behind China and the USA in terms of new installations.

Also, according to BNEF, on a business-as-usual basis, US$1.7 trillion will be invested globally in clean renewables by 2020; this would still be US$546 billion less than is needed to prevent dangerous climate change.

Renewable energy forms

The mainstream forms of renewable energies include wood or other biomass, wind energy, solar energy and hydropower. Non-renewable energy includes fossil fuels, coal, geothermal energy and nuclear fission. Some proponents of nuclear power, which is a low carbon power generation source, argue that it should be classified as a renewable energy. However, conventional nuclear power uses uranium as its source of fuel. Uranium is a non-renewable resource which would eventually be exhausted when used at present rates to produce electricity.

Solar energy

Solar energy can be used in different ways in buildings to provide electricity, mechanical power, heat and lighting. Since the beginning of mankind, dwellings have been positioned to attract the maximum of the sun's heating potential in cold climates and, conversely, to reduce the sun's heat in hot climates. **Passive solar design** for heating and cooling can save substantial electricity bills, thus, the design of a building is very important for tapping passive solar energy:

- *Passive solar heating*: Well-positioned and well insulated windows with double or triple glazing can also result in net gains of heat. Once the heat is inside the building, various techniques can be adopted to keep and spread it. Sophisticated insulating methods can ensure buildings trap and keep virtually enough natural sunlight to keep their inhabitants warm with very little additional space heating. Negative energy buildings in fact do not require any supply of non-renewable energy. By the deployment of **photovoltaic cells** and wind turbines they often produce more electricity than they need.
- *Passive cooling*: Here buildings are designed to keep the solar and air heat away by correct siting that maximizes the effect of cooling breezes and good ventilation. Shading devices reduce solar radiation. One of the best forms is deciduous trees that prevent radiated heat penetrating buildings in the summer but allow the sun's warmth into the building during the winter when the leaves have fallen. External heat gain can also be minimized by good insulation, reduced window size and by the use of reflective materials in the walls and roof.
- *Natural daylight*: A commercial building can reduce its electricity bill by using the overall light of the surrounding sky and not just daylight. Traditional day

lighting techniques include roof light wells, tall windows and courtyards. Modern alternatives include light monitors, light reflectors or optical fibres used to transport light.

Passive solar design makes the most of natural sunlight and airflow. Buildings with a passive architectural design take into account the daily cycle of the sun shape, the need for artificial light. Cooling and heating can be reduced considerably while creating a comfortable indoor atmosphere. Designing buildings to maximize the use of natural lighting can reduce energy consumption by 40 to 60 per cent compared to conventional buildings. Passive solar energy utilizes building constituents such as walls, floors, roofs, windows, exterior building elements and landscaping to control heat generated by sun. Solar heating designs try to trap and store thermal energy from sunlight directly. Passive cooling minimizes the effects of solar radiation through shading or generating air flows with convection ventilation.

Active solar design for energy both produces electricity and heats water for domestic and industrial use. Solar water heating is a sustainable source for hot water supply. Usually the collector panels are installed on the roof in order to optimise exposure to sunlight. Solar energy is not constant, however, as overcast skies, shortened days in winter and long nights restrict the production of solar energy.

Photovoltaic (solar) cell systems

Photovoltaic solar panels contain solar cells that convert daylight into electricity and can be placed on roofs or can be integrated into the roof or side of the building as sunscreens that can reduce the need for air-conditioning. When sunlight is absorbed by these materials, the solar energy knocks electrons loose from their atoms, allowing the electrons to flow through the material to produce electricity. This process of converting light (photons) to electricity (voltage) is called the photovoltaic (PV) effect. Solar cells are typically combined into groups that mass together about 40 cells; a number of these groups are mounted in photovoltaic arrays that can measure up to several metres across. These flat photovoltaic arrays are mounted at a fixed angle, usually 30 degrees facing south. Several connected photovoltaic arrays can provide enough power for a household and are gaining increasing prominence on the roofs of buildings and often hotels. The electricity produced can either be used directly in the building or in many cases sold to the local utilities company.

Solar furnaces

Solar furnaces have been around for centuries. In the third century BC, Archimedes allegedly used a mirror to burn up the entire Roman fleet during the siege of Syracuse. The technology uses the rays of the sun to produce incredibly high temperatures. In developing countries, solar ovens employ the heat of the sun for everyday cooking. At Odeillo in France, a solar furnace reaches temperatures up to

3,000 degrees Celsius. This kind of heat can then be used to create electricity, melt steel or produce hydrogen fuel. The thermo-electric solar plant at Sanlucar La Mayor, near the city of Seville in Spain, has an 11 megawatt (MW) capacity, slightly more than its 10-megawatts counterpart at Pocking in Germany, which to date is Europe's largest solar energy producer. Spain plans to build eight reactors with an overall capacity of 302 MW in the next few years. When all eight are running, there will be enough electricity produced to supply 180,000 homes, the equivalent of a city such as Seville itself.

Wind power

Wind power is nothing new. Sailing boats have been around for thousands of years and windmills for grinding corn since the Middle Ages in Europe. The Babylonians and Chinese were using wind power to pump water to irrigate crops 4000 years ago. Wind turbines capture the kinetic energy of wind and convert it into electricity. Wind farms are constructed normally where wind funnels through mountains or hills. Wind power is environmentally safe; however, it can be intermittent. Significant power generation requires a good deal of windmills on one farm, thus affecting the scenic landscape. This issue has been partly offset by building wind farms out at sea. The world's biggest offshore wind farm was opened in 2012 at a cost of €1.2 billion off the coast of Cumbria in the north-west of England, more than 100 turbines are generating enough power for 320,000 homes. The 'London Array' wind farm is scheduled to bring its 630 turbines onstream by the end of 2012.

Hydro and wave power

Hydro power is electrical energy that is generated by using the flow of water through a turbine with a generator, usually derived from rivers or man-made installations. Like the wind, running water has been an energy source for thousands of years, mainly to grind corn. The first large-scale hydro-electric generator was built in 1882 on the Fox River, in the USA, the hydro-electricity produced was enough to power two paper mills and a house. Nowadays hydro-electric power stations provide around 20 per cent of the world's electricity. For the adventurous restaurateur or hotelier sited near a fast-flowing river, a small hydro power system could be the solution to self-sufficiency in power. For hotel properties located on a coastline, wave power may be a future source of energy.

Ocean waves are created by the wind as it blows across the sea. While wind turbines out at sea can generate electricity, so can the waves. Harnessing this energy and converting it into electricity in large amounts is not easy but examples of wave power stations and tidal power stations (such as at La Rance, Brittany) harnessing the power of the tides, are to be found. There are several methods of obtaining energy from waves. The most common works like a swimming pool wave machine in reverse. At a swimming pool, air is blown in and out of a chamber beside the pool, which makes the water outside bob up and down, causing waves. At a wave power station, the waves arriving cause the water in the chamber to rise and fall, which means that air is forced in and out of the hole in the top of the chamber. Inside this chamber is a turbine which is turned by the air rushing in and out and produces the electricity. The world's first and still one of the most productive wave power stations was built off the coast of Scotland in 2000. The Islay island wave power generator was designed and built by Wavegen and researchers from Queens University in Belfast. Known as Limpet 500 (Land Installed Marine Powered Energy Transformer), it feeds 500 kilowatts of electricity into the island's power grid.

Geothermal power and heat pumps

Geothermal power is energy that is gained by heat stored beneath the surface of the earth. The heat from the Earth's own molten core can be converted into electricity. This core consists primarily of extremely high temperature liquid rock known as magma. Geothermal heat circulates within the rock or is transferred to underground reservoirs of water, which also circulate under the Earth's crust.

Geothermal resources have been harnessed as an energy source since the dawn of civilization, when natural hot springs were first used for cooking and bathing. Pumps bringing heat from beneath our feet can be used to directly heat hotels and other buildings or used as a source of power that drives steam turbines to produce electricity. In some places this heat source is close to the surface and can provide a cheap and efficient source of energy. However, in most surface areas, bore holes would have to be made to uneconomical depths to bring up the energy. Capital costs for the construction of geothermal power plants are much higher than for large coal-fired plants or new natural gas turbine technologies. But geothermal plants have reasonable operation and maintenance costs and no fuel costs. Though more expensive than wind power in most cases, new geothermal electricity generation facilities are increasingly competitive with fossil options.

Geothermal technologies are used extensively in Iceland and in northern California where steam technology is used in the world's largest geothermal power plant at The Geysers. In this case, highly pressurized geothermal vapour is used directly to drive a turbine.

Heat pump systems

Especially useful for private dwellings and buildings such as hotels are heat pumps. In climates with moderate heating and cooling needs, heat pumps offer an energy-efficient alternative to gas and solid fuel-powered central heating boilers and air-conditioning. Geothermal heat pumps transfer heat between the inside and the outside of the building from the ground or a nearby water source. Although they cost more to install than conventional heating systems, geothermal heat pumps have low operating costs because they take advantage of relatively constant ground or water temperatures.

A simpler technology that makes use of varying air temperatures inside and outside buildings are heat pumps that work in a similar way to refrigerators. Heat pumps use electricity to transfer thermal energy from a heat source to a heat sink. In the winter heat pumps draw heat from the ground into the conditioned space and vice versa in the summer. Since they move heat rather than generate heat, heat pumps can provide up to four times the amount of energy as they consume.

Biomass

Wood was once the main fuel of mankind, burnt to heat and cook food over the centuries but in the past century until the oil crisis in the 1970s it was in a headlong decline in developed countries. Even now in other parts of the world, more than a billion people still lack access to electricity, and 3 billion still rely on dung, wood and other **biomass** fuels for cooking and heating. Biomass plants release carbon dioxide (CO_2), the primary greenhouse gas. However, during the growing cycle, processing and burning biomass recycles CO_2 from the atmosphere. If this cycle is sustained, there is little or no net gain in atmospheric CO_2. As fossil fuel use rose in price, interest in wood heating resurfaced as a renewable energy alternative. Recently pellet fuel appliances are increasingly being installed in commercial buildings and hotels. This new generation of wood- and pellet-burning appliances are clean burning and efficient. They burn small pellets that look like rabbit feed and measure a couple of centimetres long. Pellets are made from compacted sawdust or wood. Other solid wastes can be burned to provide heat or used to make steam for a power station. One example is 'bagasse', the left-over cellulose material from sugar cane after harvest. Because biomass technologies use combustion processes to produce electricity, they can generate electricity at any time, unlike wind and most solar technologies, which only produce when the wind is blowing or the sun is shining. Biomass power plants currently represent 11,000 MW in the USA, the second largest amount of renewable energy in the country.

Bioconversion uses plant and animal wastes to produce bio-fuels such as methanol, natural gas and oil. These renewable energies can be produced from food waste in hotels, supermarkets, farms and council refuge collection. For this process, anaerobic digesters are widely used in some countries like Germany to extract biogas, a combination of methane, carbon dioxide and traces of other contaminant gases. This biogas can be used directly as cooking fuel or in combined heat and power gas engines or upgraded to natural gas quality. The nutrient-rich digestate also produced can be used as fertilizer.

In Europe, biomass energy production has become one of the standard technologies in the treatment of organic waste, where countries like Germany, Denmark and Austria are leading the way. For hotels with a large number of vehicles, the bio-fuel ethanol can be a viable alternative to petrol. Brazil has declared energy independence by producing large quantities of another biogas ethanol from sugar cane and maize. An unpleasant side effect of the production is the price of maize which has more than doubled in the period 2009–2012. Since it is the main feed used in beef production and for milking cows, using ethanol to power vehicles is pushing up the price of beef and milk. In the USA over a third of all corn production goes to the ethanol distilleries to produce biogas to run cars. Even with so many promising alternative renewable energy sources, hoteliers should not forget that conservation is the key to efficient energy use, no matter what the source of the energy may be.

Buying green electricity

As already explained, green energy means energy that has been produced in a more sustainable way. Public utility companies are in some cases beginning to use renewable technologies, such as wind, biomass, geothermal, hydro or solar power for electricity generation. This energy is then sold to private users or businesses. A hospitality operation wishing to purchase green energy should refer to labels such as the European Green Electricity Network (EUGENE) label, to ensure that the purchased energy really is green. This independent European **eco-label** guarantees the electricity comes from the following sustainable energy sources:

- solar, wind or geothermal;
- green biomass (agricultural and forestry wastes, other organic wastes, sewage gas);
- green hydropower (the plant has to meet basic ecological criteria at local scale, so that the river system's principal ecological functions are preserved. New or expanded power plants can only be labelled as green if the hydropower facility leads to a substantial improvement of the local and regional ecological quality, in excess of legal compliance);
- highly efficient natural gas-based co-generation (up to a maximum share of 50 per cent and only in certain countries).

Imports of green electricity are allowed only if the imported electricity is generated from eligible sources and meets the standards defined in both the exporting and importing country.

Carbon offsetting

Reducing carbon footprints by purchasing **carbon offsets** is becoming a popular idea throughout the world and increasingly in the tourism industry. However, the system of carbon offsetting is controversial, while some people feel it is a great solution, others believe that carbon offsets lull people into a false sense of well-being about their ecological **impact** on the Earth. Carbon offset programmes essentially allow companies or individuals to 'make up' for the carbon dioxide created by their actions – from creating products or services, driving a car, to the energy needed to sustain a hotel room. Many carbon emissions for the **hospitality industry** simply cannot be avoided. Guests must fly, drive or take the train to the hotel. The hotel creates carbon emissions, although sometimes small, at all stages of the guest stay, including the room where he or she sleeps, the meals eaten, the facilities used and the preparation necessary for the entertainment enjoyed. Even the best consumption reduction programmes cannot completely eliminate carbon emissions. To make up for these emissions, hospitality executives and guests can participate in carbon offsetting programmes to 'buy' their way out. Carbon offsetting organizations make an estimation of the carbon dioxide created during the hospitality guest stay and attach a price to it. This can be on a departmental basis or an average guest stay basis, a degree of guesswork is inevitable in this process since tools that make a precise assessment of carbon emissions are still in development. The funds collected from the carbon offset customers are directed to programmes that generate clean energy such as solar arrays and wind farms, which can, in turn, be used to power hospitality operations.

Carbon offset programmes are now numerous and they have different methodologies for measuring and verifying carbon emissions; questions include how much should be charged, or even how many kilogrammes should constitute a legitimate offset. Some projects donate a larger percentage of revenues to actual offsetting projects, while others keep more for their business overheads.

Hospitality executives and guests interested in these programmes need to do the following:

- Understand how the programme chosen calculates carbon emissions and how they calculate the offsets.
- Consider the **certification** for the offsetting programme. No universal standard for certifying carbon calculators or carbon offsetting programmes exists but the non-profit-making organization Clean Air/Cool Planet has produced an annual consumers guide.

Steps to achieving carbon neutrality

According to Clean Air/Cool Planet, there are six steps to achieving **carbon neutrality**:

1. Assess carbon footprint.
2. Deduct emissions-free electricity purchases.
3. Implement emissions reduction measures.
4. Compute remaining carbon emissions.
5. Purchase offsets.
6. Communicate carbon neutrality.

The first of the six steps towards achieving carbon neutrality is to measure the carbon footprint of the hospitality operation, as without this data it is impossible to start offsetting or reducing. Step two is to ensure the request for proposal contains a green element. For example, if the property is purchasing electricity from a wind farm that is already carbon neutral, this is deducted from the carbon footprint assessment of the property. Step three establishes the total carbon footprint and in step four negotiations and contracts are made with the carbon offsetting organization. Step five is purchasing the offsets. Step six consists of measuring the effectiveness of the carbon offsetting policy and communicating the results to all **stakeholders**.

Carbon dioxide by the numbers

One tonne of carbon dioxide is emitted when you do the following:

- Travel 2000 miles on a plane.
- Drive 1350 miles in a large sport utility vehicle.
- Drive 1900 miles in a medium-sized car.
- Drive 6000 miles in a hybrid gasoline-electric car.
- Run the average American household for 60 days.
- Graze one dairy cow for eight months.

According to Clean Air/Cool Planet, to offset 1000 tonnes of carbon dioxide you could do the following:

- Move 145 drivers from large SUVs to hybrid cars for one year.
- Run one 600 kW wind turbine for an average year.
- Replace 500 100-watt light bulbs with 18-watt compact fluorescent lights.
- Replace 2000 refrigerators with the highest-efficiency model.
- Install 125 home solar panels.
- Plant an acre of Douglas fir trees.

From the hospitality business perspective, participating in carbon offsetting schemes makes sense because a growing number of consumers are impressed by companies that demonstrate **environmental stewardship**. This form of eco-advantage is not negligible in a rapidly changing economy. Since many carbon offsetting projects are located in developing countries, this action raises the ethical profile of the hospitality company. Lastly, no one yet has all the solutions to solving all the issues of environmental **degradation**. Although carbon offsetting may not be the perfect solution, it does allow individuals and companies to be at the cutting edge of experimental and innovative approaches to solving these issues.

The use of energy in hotels

There are substantial differences in energy use between different types of hotels depending on hotel size, class/category, number of rooms, customer profile (business/vacation), location (rural/urban, climate zone), in addition to the types of services/activities and amenities offered to guests.

A hotel can be seen as the architectural combination of three distinct zones, all serving distinctly different purposes:

- *the guest room area* (bedrooms, bathrooms/showers, toilets), individual spaces, often with extensive glazing, asynchronous utilization and varying energy loads;
- *the public area* (reception hall, lobby, bars, restaurants, meeting rooms, swimming pool, gym, sauna, etc.), spaces with a high rate of heat exchange with the outdoor environment (thermal losses) and high internal loads (occupants, appliances, equipment, lighting);
- *the service area* (kitchens, offices, store rooms, laundry, staff facilities, machine rooms and other technical areas), energy-intensive requiring advanced air handling (ventilation, cooling, heating).

Typically, about half the electrical energy is used for space conditioning purposes. According to the US Environmental Protection Agency, some 47,000 hotels spend US$2196 per available room each year on energy which represents about 6 per cent of all operating costs.

Depending on the category of the hotel, lighting may account for up to 20 per cent or even more. The demand for domestic hot water varies appreciably within hotel categories ranging from 90 to 150 litres or sometimes more. Supplying domestic hot water accounts for up to 15 per cent of the total energy demand. For a medium category hotel with an average annual occupancy of 70 per cent, this is the equivalent to 1500–2300 kWh/room. Catering and other facilities also account for an important share of overall energy use. By comparison, operating elevators, pumps and other auxiliary equipment accounts for only a small percentage of total energy expenditure. Through a carefully managed strategic **energy management** approach to energy efficiency, a 10 per cent reduction in energy consumption would have the same financial effect as increasing the average daily room rate (ADR) by US$0.62 in limited-service hotels and by US$1.35 in full-service hotels (Energy Star, 2009).

There is a widespread misconception in the hospitality industry that substantial reductions in energy used can only be achieved by installing advanced, high-maintenance and prohibitively expensive technologies. While this may be true in some contexts, in the majority of cases, major energy savings can be achieved by adopting a common-sense approach, requiring neither advanced expertise nor excessive investments. When embarking on an energy management programme, the first step is to establish exactly how much energy is being used and in which way. This is achieved through an energy audit.

Energy audit

An energy audit is the systematic review of each fuel- and energy-consuming system in the establishment. It commences with the collection and analysis of all information that may affect energy consumption, and inspects the condition and performance of existing systems, installations, existing management techniques and utility bills. The findings are then compared to the energy performance published standards (**benchmarks**) in other similar establishments and proposals are made. An energy audit is not an excuse for cutting energy consumption, rather better managing the usage to maintain and or improve hotel guest and worker comfort. An annual energy audit is much like an annual accountant's review, stating the past and current energy balance.

Energy consumption goal setting

Once a clear picture of energy consumption has been created, goals for improvement can be made. Measurability is an important key to the success of an energy management programme and helps the establishment to identify progress and setbacks at operational level. A clear energy programme that embodies attainable goals demonstrates commitment to reducing environmental impacts and has a motivational effect on staff and guests.

The energy management team should create departmental targets and establish a tracking system to monitor progress. This system should also embrace timelines for actions, including regular meetings with personnel to discuss completion dates, milestones and expected outcomes.

Defining and implementing an action plan

Determine which members of staff should be involved and what their responsibilities will be. To ensure the success of an energy management programme, the support of all personnel is required with leadership coming from the top. Specifically, some departments will have certain responsibilities; Finance = capital investment and budget planning; Human Resources = training and performance standards; Supply management = procurement procedures, energy, equipment and material purchasing. For each part of the action plan, estimate the cost for each item in terms of both human resources and capital/expense outlay. Develop the business case for justifying and gaining funding approval for action plan projects and resources needed.

Staff warrants recognition when results are reached and accomplishments should be highlighted. Tracking sheets, scorecards, bonuses and prizes can be motivational. Good communication stimulates interest among stakeholders and commitment from staff. All information on energy use, environmental impacts and energy-saving options should be published for the general audience of the establishment's web site and in the local news media.

Energy-efficiency technology

Heating, ventilation and air-conditioning (HVAC)

Depending on the hotel's geographic location, HVAC can account for up to 50 per cent of a hotel's total utility costs: electricity, water, gas and fuels. The latest generation of air conditioners consumes up to 30 per cent less energy than those manufactured 20 years ago. Modern chiller units not only save energy but are even able to recover the heat they produce during operation. The heat, which is normally expelled to the atmosphere, can now be used to pre-heat water for laundry or swimming pools, thus creating savings.

Not only has air-conditioning technology been improving over the past decades, but also heating systems have become more efficient, requiring less maintenance. Air-conditioning units, called heat pumps, can now supply hotels with hot air as well as cold air. Geothermal heat pumps are similar to ordinary heat pumps, but use the ground instead of outside air to provide heating, air-conditioning and, in most cases, hot water. Because they use the Earth's natural heat, they are among the most efficient and comfortable heating and cooling technologies currently available.

Probably the most cost-efficient system of heating is a gas-fired condensation boiler. They are capable of converting 88 per cent of the fuel used into heat, whereas older models only achieve 80 per cent. Those recent boilers contain a second heat exchanger to use the heat that would usually escape through the chimney. Hotels seeking a very effective and comprehensive energy solution might choose to invest in the new combined heat and power systems which work like mini-power stations converting gas into electricity, heat and hot water. These systems are advantageous because their combustion efficiency is only about 10 to 20 per cent less efficient than fuel-burning public power stations and they also produce less carbon dioxide and sulphur because they run on gas.

CASE STUDY 3.1 Romantik Hotel Muottas Muragl: plus-energy concept

On 18 December 2010, the first plus-energy hotel in the Alps was opened on Muottas Muragl, overlooking Samedan. Situated on Switzerland's sun-blessed mountain terrace, the hotel is based on a ground-breaking energy concept: taken over the entire year, the mountain and the photovoltaic system together produce more energy per annum than the Romantik Hotel Muottas Muragl needs to run itself.

In spite of increasing the heated floor space by 50 per cent, two-thirds less energy is required. The energy consumption of the hotel building is fully covered by solar energy, thus doing away with CO_2 emissions totalling 144 tonnes per

PICTURE 3.1 Romantik Hotel Muottas Muragl overlooking Samedan, Switzerland
Source: Christof Sonderegger.

annum. Solar panels (flat-plate and pipe solar collectors, Pictures 3.2 and 3.3) generate solar power for heating both space and water.

Additionally, excess solar energy is stored in the thermal loop field in the ground and drawn on when required by means of a heat pump. The energy supply is based on the use of five energy levels, storing energy, using energy and plus energy building as explained as follows. In total, the renovation period of the Romantik Hotel Muottas Muragl took 10 months and construction costs amounted to CHF20 million.

PICTURE 3.2 Flat-plate solar collectors
Source: kmu-fotografie.ch.

PICTURE 3.3 Pipe solar collectors
Source: kmu-fotografie.ch.

Storing energy

Natural sunlight shining on the window surfaces is captured and stored in the building structure. Solar energy is channelled via the flat-plate and pipe solar collectors and directly used to heat room space and water. Excess solar energy is stored in the thermal-loop field. Waste heat from the cooling units and the train traction is used for space heating, preheating the water and thermal-loop regeneration. Electricity generated by the photovoltaic panels is directly channelled into the system; excess energy is stored in the power grid.

PICTURE 3.4 Central thermal-loop and pumping station Source: kmu-fotografie.ch.

Using energy

Geothermal heat is collected and topped up to a usable level by means of a heat pump. Waste heat from the cooling units and the train traction is used to increase the heat-pump flow temperature. Low-temperature gain (diffuse radiation) from the solar panels is used to increase the heat-pump flow temperature. Electricity stored in the power grid is used (heat pump, operational and household power).

Plus-energy building

The first low-energy buildings made their debut in the 1980s in the wake of the 1973 oil crisis. Ten years later, **zero-energy buildings** appeared on the scene. Nowadays, the focus is on plus-energy buildings. These are concepts that generate more renewable energy for heating, hot water production and air replenishment than they actually need themselves. Plus-energy is not to be confused with the notion of self-sufficiency; for safety reasons, the hotel is also connected to the local power grid. This project is particularly laudable because it demonstrates that a plus-energy concept is possible even in such a high-alpine location. As a result, Muottas Muragl provides an excellent example of sustainable energy.

The Romantik Hotel Muottas Muragl has won not only the Swiss Solar Award 2011 in the Building Renovation category, but also the PlusEnergieBau(r) (PEB) Solar Award 2011, the only prize in the world for plus-energy buildings. Since

2000, the specialist magazine *htr hotelrevue* has also been acknowledging particularly outstanding projects and people in the Swiss tourism industry with its 'MILESTONE' award.

In 2011, the Romantik Hotel Muottas Muragl, together with the **tourist** destination, Engadin Scuol Samnaun, were named winners in the Environmental Award category. For years, Bergbahnen ENGADIN St. Moritz AG has been implementing various measures to embrace the careful and sustainable use of the surrounding nature – in effect, the 'employer' of a mountain railway such as this.

PICTURE 3.5 A designed room with a view
Source: Daniel Gerber.

PICTURE 3.6 Sustainable use of local resources in room design
Source: Daniel Gerber.

For the hotel, winning these awards reaffirms the company's long-standing efforts regarding sustainable use of energy.

Source: Romantik Hotel Muottas Muragl, http://www.muottasmuragl.ch/en/.

Intelligent room functions

Thanks to the application of new technologies which enable the rational use of energy, hospitality companies can reduce power consumption per night. Using so-called intelligent hotel room systems, electricity can be saved by adjusting air-conditioning, heating and lighting systems according to the guest's presence in a room. Some hotels have sought benefits in this area by interconnecting the hotel's energy management system with its property management system to ensure consumption reduction when a room is unoccupied. The linking of energy use and room occupancy presents a natural synergy for conservation. At the time of checkout, all non-critical equipment in a guestroom can be automatically controlled or turned off. Items such as alarm clocks and refrigerators are not affected, while thermostatic controls, television sets, select room lighting and related components might well be subject to a power-down condition.

According to Energy Star, additional energy saving initiatives for HVAC include:

- Limit thermostat control in guest rooms and public areas.
- Use outdoor air for cooling where possible.
- Ensure heating and cooling cannot be provided simultaneously.
- Regular maintenance to optimize efficiency.
- Install curtains to control solar heat gain.
- Shade sun-oriented windows with awnings.
- Insulate hot/chilled water tanks, pipes and air ducts.
- Insulate the entire building correctly.
- Zone guest occupancy and turn off heating/cooling on unoccupied floors.

Daylight and electric light

One way to greatly enhance the **thermal mass** performance of windows is to install Low-E glass, i.e. glass that is manufactured with a microscopically thin and transparent layer of metal or metal oxide that reflects infrared 'heat' energy back into the building.

Electric lighting is another element of the hotel guest experience that is affected in many different ways. However, with lighting costs accounting for an estimated 20 or more per cent of total energy usage, energy-efficient lighting can help reduce energy consumption costs. Energy-efficient lighting has sometimes been characterized by low quality lighting, with poor colour rendition. Recent lighting technology is radically changing all this. Compact fluorescent lights (CFLs) use about 75 per cent less energy than standard incandescent bulbs and last up to 10 times longer. CFLs provide the greatest savings in fixtures that are on for a substantial amount of time each day. For this reason, they are typically used in guestrooms and corridors as well as in the back of the house. Due to major improvements over the last few years in their colour-rendering abilities, CFLs are now a viable alternative to incandescent lamps.

Where colour options or different effects are desired, light-emitting diode (LED) lighting is now a good choice. LED bulbs can provide bright lighting as well as increasingly better colour rendition with less energy use. Typical uses include cove lighting in corridors, display lighting and increasingly different alternatives as the technology continues to expand rapidly. LEDs last from 100,000 hours to 1,000,000 hours compared to a 30,000 maximum life span of fluorescent bulbs, plus they do not contain the harmful mercury found in fluorescent bulbs.

Additional energy-saving initiatives for lighting include:

- Adjust lighting levels to demand and types of fixtures.
- Use time and motion sensors to turn off lights where appropriate.
- Use dimmer controls in dining and public areas.
- Clean bulbs and reflecting surfaces regularly for maximum efficiency.

CASE STUDY 3.2 The Derag Livinghotel Campo dei Fiori in Munich, Germany: a zero-energy building

Derag Livinghotels' first zero-energy building has enjoyed huge public interest from the very start of its construction phase. The reason for the interest lies in the innovative energy concept of the Derag Livinghotel Campo dei Fiori, which is geared towards a zero-energy balance through the optimal interplay of various initiatives. Following the opening in September 2011, the Campo dei Fiori was awarded the GreenBuilding certification by the European Commission.

PICTURE 3.7
Front view of Derag Livinghotel Campo Dei Fiori, Munich, Germany

The European Commission GreenBuilding certificate is anchored in the ecological, the economic as well as the **social** and functional quality of a building. Natural resources should be preserved, the life cycle costs lowered, ecological and social values maintained and a convenient working environment established.

The entire building aims to cover the required energy for heating, cooling, water heating and lighting by using self-generated, sustainable energy. This innovative technique not only brings **sustainability** closer to guests of the hotel, it also increases the level of comfort, e.g. due to steam wellness-showers.

With an overall investment of €4.3 million, the costs for the zero-energy-building are approximately 20 per cent higher than for a conventional building. However, the additional investment will be recovered through considerable savings in energy costs. 'This project proves that ecological and economic aspects of energy efficient buildings in the hospitality sector can be combined,' explains Prof. Dr. Max Michael Schlereth, board member of the family business Derag Group.

The high level of energy efficiency of the building is being realized by an integrated concept supported by a long list of interconnected measures. The renewable energy is mainly produced by solar heating and photovoltaic systems, but also by making use of waste heat coming from individual air-conditioners and grey water **recycling** facilities as well as cooling and freezing facilities. Additionally, the hotel has buffer storages to stock as large an amount of energy as possible. For energy efficiency, the high thermal insulated glass building envelope with triple glazing builds a key feature of the energy-efficient architecture.

Heating and cooling are performed by using warm and cold water circulation within the floors and ceilings. The climate surface reacts in an innovative system, which is very similar to ordinary air-conditioning systems, and offers even more comfort as the effect of feeling the heat instantly occurs.

The heating of the drinking water is done separately for each hotel room, which saves further energy. Water, as a valuable resource, runs in separate systems. For example, shower water first runs through a water treatment plant where it is cleaned and afterwards used for toilet flushing, before it is declared waste water.

The hotel offers 43 state-of-the-art rooms and apartments with a size between 22 and 43 square metres. All apartments contain a complete set of a kitchenette with a minibar, induction cooker, microwave, coffee machine or water boiler, flatware, a living and working area, free Wi-Fi access, as well as flat screen televisions. One highlight is the innovative oil-vital bed in each room that combines aspects of air-water beds as well as regular mattresses. Within seconds, the core of the bed can be adjusted individually to change its hardness.

PICTURE 3.8 Executive double room with oil-vital bed

A high quality, washable climate sheet with silver threads against mites and bacteria is used. Highest showering comfort is guaranteed by a steam-wellness-shower with low energy consumption. Additionally, each room is equipped with a steam cleaning system in order to achieve the highest level of cleanliness, thus removing the use of aggressive detergents.

Based on the success of the Campo dei Fiori, Derag Livinghotels has decided to switch to green energy for all of its German properties from 2012 onwards.

Source: Derag Livinghotels, http://www.deraghotels.com/.

CASE STUDY 3.3 Soneva Resorts: decarbonizing your business

Soneva recognises that climate change is a serious concern for both its business existence and the planet as a whole. A central part of climate change is that too much carbon emissions are emitted globally. Soneva feels immediate and bold actions are needed to make a difference. For this reason, it has set a vision for the company to be decarbonizing by 2020.

Soneva aims to remove its net carbon emissions from its overall operations by 2020, that is, to decarbonize. Energy efficiency will be achieved by creating an oversupply of clean energy (i.e. generating 'excess energy' from renewable resources) at the source and offsetting unavoidable emissions (e.g. through clean technology or planting trees that absorb CO_2 and produce O_2).

Through operational and energy efficiency, the resorts and spas will improve their ecological **footprint**. An over-supply of clean energy in addition to carbon offsetting unavoidable emissions will decarbonize the Soneva's operations. The scope of these efforts makes up our full ecological and carbon footprint, including guest transportation, supply chain, energy, water, waste and biodiversity.

We are confident that our high standard and innovative practice, combined with our biophilic approach, may even mean some of our resorts become a carbon sink. This vision is one of the company's most pressing and immediate priorities, and the reasons for it could not be more important to us.

Carbon calculator

What you cannot measure, you cannot manage. This applies very much to responsible business practices. For this reason, Soneva has developed a carbon calculator based on the greenhouse gas protocol to monitor its carbon footprint, covering not only energy emissions but also air travel, ground travel, freight, food, paper, waste and water.

The carbon calculator gives Soneva an in-depth overview of emissions and covers far more than most companies consider. For example, of the 59,335 tonnes of carbon emission emitted in July 2010–June 2011 by the three Soneva resorts, only 16 per cent or 9244 of the emissions are from energy used at the resort level.

Emissions from energy consumption, also referred to as Scope 1 and 2 emissions in the Greenhouse Gas Protocol, are the common measure that most companies consider when measuring their carbon footprint. The reason for this is that these are the ones that can be directly influenced and improved by the company. Soneva feels one has to consider beyond this and therefore include Scope 3 emissions such as air travel, ground travel, freight, food, paper, waste and water. Some 76 per cent of the Soneva resorts' emissions are derived from guest air travel, emissions that cannot be controlled by the company.

Soneva's focus is on energy management through improving energy efficiency and increasing the use of clean energy. To mitigate these emissions such as air travel and freight, a Carbon Sense Fund has been established.

Renewable alternatives

The best way to improve your carbon footprint is to be more efficient with the energy you use. Soneva recognises this, and incorporates that philosophy in all of its new and innovative designs. Energy management can take many forms, and requires many different approaches to fully address those issues. However, we feel that we have to work on switching to renewable energy and have been bold in our approach to experimenting and pioneering new technologies and systems in our attempt to make our practices as low carbon as possible. We experimented with a Deep Sea Water cooling project that unfortunately failed and cost us time and money. However, the willingness to take pioneering risks is achieving our goal. We have successfully implemented solar technologies such as a 70 KW solar PV system at Soneva Fushi in 2009 (Picture 3.9) and will continue to invest in clean energy.

One of the main challenges we face at Soneva Fushi in the Maldives is energy storage, as we are off the grid. However, with prices coming down, we expect to significantly increase the solar PV capacity in 2012 and invest in other clean energy sources as this is core to our decarbonizing goals. The biggest challenge is the last 20–30 per cent, especially as many of our resorts are on a desert island and not connected to the grid. With **eco-technology** improving at an impressive rate, the goal is achievable and future investment, either in bio-fuel or battery storage, is needed to take care of the demand at night.

The need for mitigation

By investing in clean energy and improving our practice, we can make decarbonizing a reality, but some of the carbon emissions we incur cannot be avoided. Because of the necessity of air travel to transport our guests, hosts and supplies, we have integrated a Carbon Sense Fund that enables carbon mitigation projects.

PICTURE 3.9
Solar panels at
Soneva Fushi

An acknowledgment must be made of the reality of those carbon emissions the industry cannot avoid, but can mitigate. The source of these emissions could be related to a locality, or a practice which the industry is reliant upon – such as air travel. Soneva does recognise these issues, and works pro-actively to incorporate them into its decarbonizing goals. It is important to be clear about the reality of these issues, and to sincerely put in place any change of practice, or available new technology which could further mitigate these unavoidable emissions. Furthermore, one has to take into consideration the positive impacts tourism have, which, if done responsibly, far outweighs the negative carbon emissions from air travel.

The Carbon Sense Fund

As Soneva considers carbon scope beyond our operation, energy used at resorts only counts for 16 per cent of the resorts' emissions. For this reason, a Carbon Sense Fund has been established to mitigate emissions that cannot be controlled, such as guest flights. A 2 per cent levy on room rates is charged. This capital is then invested in our carbon mitigation projects not directly located on Soneva resorts through the Soneva SLOW LIFE Trust. The fund gives us the ability to mitigate the carbon emissions we cannot control, such as those incurred through air travel. Through the Soneva SLOW LIFE Trust we are trying to find the most effective ways of balancing our unavoidable carbon emissions, focusing on clean energy, biodiversity and social impact.

The Darfur Stoves Project

The Soneva SLOW LIFE Trust will provide US$660,000 of development funding to the Darfur Stoves Project, an **NGO** that is providing energy-efficient cooking stoves to women in Darfur, Sudan.
The Darfur Stoves Project aims to do the following:

1. Distribute more than 150,000 energy-efficient cooking stoves over seven years to residents of the internally displaced person (IDP) camps in the area.
2. Dramatically reduce the amount of time women must spend collecting firewood in unprotected areas – an activity that can take up to 25 hours per week.
3. Reduce the carbon emissions resulting from cooking fires by an estimated 300,000 tonnes over a seven-year period.
4. Reduce pressure on the local biosphere and **deforestation** in surrounding areas by reducing demand for wood-fuel.
5. Reduce indoor air pollution from cooking fires which is a major cause of premature death among women and children in rural Africa.

Forest Restoration Project, Thailand

2011 is the international year of the forest, and Soneva SLOW LIFE Trust is working with the PATT Foundation to make this year really live up to its name.

The aim is to establish a large forest **restoration** project linked to existing forest areas. Some 200,000 trees covering 200 acres, with first site in Sri Lanna National Park, Northern Thailand, will be planted annually. Not only will this mitigate 160,000 tonnes of carbon per year, but it will create wildlife corridors, prevent erosion, restore biodiversity and generate local jobs.

Between 20–30 different species of tree will be planted. This is following the Framework Species Method of Forest Restoration, which indicates that birds and mammals, attracted to the plots, bring with them the seeds of many other forest trees and thus help to re-establish a species-rich forest tree community of up to 90 species, similar to that of the original forest. Rather than just a mono-type plantation, the result is a rich biodiverse forest. The new planted forest will provide a sanctuary for rescued and endangered animals, and its management will be carried out by local people to provide income and support for their communities.

Soneva SLOW LIFE Trust recognises the need to involve and include the local communities on whose shoulders the long-term success of the project rests. The ongoing management of the forest, which follows the principle of natural seed distribution, will require the input of local people. Some 20–30 species of indigenous tree will be planted, whose seeds will be collected, grown and replanted by locals. Over time and with support, native bird species will begin to distribute seeds naturally, which could mean an ecosystem supporting up to 90 species of trees and a vast rich ecology. The protection and continuation of this project are intertwined with the local people who will support it.

Wind Turbine Project

Soneva SLOW-LIFE's first carbon mitigating project was a Wind Turbine Project that was established to provide clean energy in Tamil Nadu, India. A 1.5 megawatt (MW) Suzlon wind turbine was built. Not only will this mitigate 70,000 tonnes of carbon over a 20-year period through the production of 80,000 MW clean electricity, but it will also encourage other wind turbines to be built and support local communities and create additional 30,000 tonnes of carbon reductions. A portion of the revenue generated from the electricity sale to the grid is invested in other wind turbines. In addition, a portion of the revenue will be donated to local community projects to support climate change adaptation and projects that help to break the poverty cycle. The Wind Turbine Project is run by The Converging World, a registered UK charity. In the local community projects, they cooperate with SCAD, a registered Indian NGO.

About Soneva – intelligent luxury

Soneva is committed to offering luxury of the highest standard in an environment that nurtures the indigenous feel in design, architecture and service. The simple sophistication of a Soneva resort is enhanced by continually embracing innovations that result in the creation of a unique experience for guests. Traditional conventions are re-evaluated so that the concept of the place should reward all the human senses. Cuisine is a fusion of international influences and the reality of the location, together with the freshest ingredients from the resort's own organic gardens.

A Soneva resort has a limited amount of accommodation, allowing exceptional and inspired service. Furnishings and finishes are crafted from renewable and sustainable sources, while generous personal space and the fusion of nature with guest experiences create destinations unto themselves, and further expound the Soneva theme – intelligent luxury.

Source: Soneva Resorts, http://www.soneva.com/.

EXERCISES

1 **GROUP DISCUSSION, GROUP PROJECT OR WRITTEN ASSIGNMENT**
Private electricity demand versus hotel electricity demand
 • Based on your typical day, estimate when electricity demand is greatest, and when it is least.
 • Does the electricity demand in hotels follow a similar pattern?

2 **GROUP DISCUSSION**
Renewable energy versus fossil fuel
 • Do you think renewable energy resources could replace all use of fossil fuels by 2020?
 • Explain your answer.

3 **GROUP PROJECT**
Carbon offsetting
 • When you drive or fly, you can offset your greenhouse gas emissions by purchasing 'carbon offsets' also known as green offsets, greentags or renewable energy certificates. The money you pay goes to develop alternative energy projects (typically wind or solar) or is invested in tree-planting projects. Some environmentalists consider carbon offsets counterproductive, feel-good environmentalism. Research the issue and discuss why this is so and whether you agree.

4 **GROUP PROJECT OR WRITTEN ASSIGNMENT**
Hospitality emissions and carbon offsetting
The tourism industry at large (which include transport, accommodation and gastronomy as examples) is estimated to be responsible for 5 per cent of the world's carbon dioxide (CO_2) gas emissions. The hotel sector represents 20 per cent of the tourism industry's emissions – in other words, 1 per cent of all CO_2 gas emissions.
 • Should hotels have a clear understanding of their individual property CO_2 emissions?
 • How should a hotel mitigate its CO_2 emissions?
 • Is the business of buying carbon offsets an easy way out for the hospitality industry?

5 WRITTEN (AND RESEARCH) ASSIGNMENT

The use of energy in hotels greatly impacts upon the environment but is invisible to hotel guests, who have a seemingly unlimited supply of energy available, e.g. to switch the lights on or turn the TV on. Energy is used everywhere in hotels, for HVAC, in the guest rooms, the kitchens, for the laundry, the pool, the lifts and escalators and so on.

- What alternative sources of energy to the traditional fossil fuels are available to hoteliers with possibly less impact on the environment?
- What should a hotel implement as an example of a solution to reduce the overall energy consumption and how much would be the capital investment (if any) to implement this?

References

Bloomberg New Energy Finance (BNEF) (2012) *Press & Publications*. Available at: http://www.bnef.com/bnef/press-publications/.

Energy Star (2009) *Hotels: An Overview of Energy Use and Energy Efficiency Opportunities*. Available at: http://www.energystar.gov/ia/business/challenge/learn_more/Hotel.pdf.

Epstein, P.R., Buonocore, J.J., Eckerle, K., Hendryx, M., Stout III, B.M., Heinberg, R., Clapp, R.W., May, B., Reinhart, N.L., Ahern, M.M., Doschi, S.K. and Glustsom, L. (2011) 'Full cost accounting for the life cycle of coal', *Annals of the New York Academy of Sciences*, 1219: 73–98.

International Energy Agency (2005) *Publications & Paper*. Available at: http://www.iea.org/publications/free_all.asp.

International Energy Agency (2010) *Publications & Paper*. Available at: http://www.iea.org/publications/free_all.asp.

Resources

Clean Air/Cool Planet: http://www.cleanair-coolplanet.org/.

Energy Star: http://www.energystar.gov/.

European Green Electricity Network: http:// www.naturemade.ch.

Green Energy Standard EUGENE. http://www.eugenestandard.org/.

International Energy Agency: http://www.iea.org/.

U.S. Energy Information Administration (EIA): *International Energy Outlook*. Available at: http://www.eia.gov/forecasts/ieo/index.cfm.

US Environmental Protection Agency: http:// www.epa.gov.

Additional material

Go to www.routledge.com/cw/sloan to find PowerPoint slides of all the figures and tables from the book, additional case studies, a test bank of questions and extra links to useful videos.

Waste management

CHAPTER OBJECTIVES

The objectives for this chapter are:

*   To explain the impacts of waste on the environment
*   To describe the various forms of waste
*   To explain how waste can be reduced
*   To explain how product design can reduce waste
*   To explain a strategic approach to reusing waste
*   To give examples of ways to recycle waste

Waste and the environment

Forty years ago in *The Ecologist* magazine journalist Robert Allen wrote a simple and practical guide of do's and don'ts in order to cut down on waste. The journalist advised **recycling**, keeping a compost heap, not buying disposable goods, not littering and also addressed issues of leaving heaters, lights and taps switched on unnecessarily, a seemingly familiar list of recommendations that any environmentally conscious citizen could recite today.

Over the past four decades there have been improvements in waste production. Every business, including all those in the **hospitality industry**, has seen the economic benefit of recycling. Individuals are no longer laughed at when separating kitchen waste and reusing supermarket carrier bags. Economic reality means that more people have thermostats fitted to radiators and take the train more than they used to due to escalating energy prices. Some hotels boast their policies of cutting back on laundering towels and sheets, which, although meritorious, somehow misses the point when in the same room air-conditioning units pump out cool air when simpler eco-design could provide the same temperature with no environmental impacts.

The media in general have done an excellent job of making the general public more aware today of environmental issues regarding domestic waste and excessive energy usage. It seems that *The Ecologist* did a good job in bringing the many aspects of wastefulness to the attention of the general public. Everything, from insulation in our houses to green rubbish bins and bottle banks, shows the advice has indeed been heeded and woven into the fabric of today's society.

Yet waste issues remain and landfill capacities are continuing to be stretched. In the 1970s, environmentalists were seen as a marginal section of society, *The Ecologist* in responding to their letters complaining that 'something must be done about the waste epidemic' was echoing the feelings of a small minority. Interestingly, the message today is still just as relevant now as it was then, possibly more so in light of the ever-growing recognition of **global warming**. Even though waste is on the front page of every newspaper and magazine, the question must be asked, why is the same advice still being repeated to the general public 40 years on? Have we not yet mastered the undertaking of these simple actions by now? Although it seems the modern-day general public is indeed more environmentally aware and has greater possibilities to be green if it chooses, the evidence shows that their attitudes towards environmentalism and their willingness to act remain ambivalent and tentative at best. The majority of people in developed economies continue with their insatiable appetites for consumerism to create vast swathes of waste and fritter away precious energy resources.

Society cannot turn the clock back, making do with only what you need might have been acceptable to our grandmothers but human nature, coupled with the effect of decades of capitalism, means that consumerism is here to stay for a long time yet. Government-enforced recycling, taxation and a minority who reduce voluntarily the amount they use can only do so much. Encouraging more **sustainable** forms of consumerism is more necessary than ever before. Since the big producers and retailers, like Mars, Walmart, Tesco or in the restaurant and hotel industry, McDonald's, Pizza Hut, InterContinental and Accor, all tend to be multinationals, thus they are relatively unaffected by the laws of individual countries. Through greater awareness and personal motivation consumers could be encouraged to switch their allegiance to products and services with less packaging and sustainable production practices and sourcing. Economics apart, it is only through leadership and education that the tide of waste that society is now faced with can be reversed. Fortunately many businesses who practise and publicize their **waste management** and green credentials are seen to turn their strategies into profit, and in the hospitality industry too, examples do exist.

In rich and poor countries alike, the authorities are increasingly inclined to entrust waste management to the private sector. Waste firms see rich pickings all over the planet as municipalities realize they cannot cope with ever stricter waste regulations. According to Veolia Environnement, a global player in waste management, the more complicated the treatment, the higher the margin. Prices for tipping rubbish have tripled in the past 20 years in the USA, commercial refuse tipping charges are now around US$38 a tonne. The European Union is probably the most zealous regulator: it has separate legally binding directives on waste policy in general, hazardous waste,

CASE STUDY 4.1 The growth of waste

According to OECD forecasts, municipal waste in rich countries will grow by only an average of 1.3 per cent a year up to 2030, or about 38 per cent in total. The real growth in waste is expected in the emerging economies, India's city-dwellers will be generating 130 per cent more rubbish and in China over 200 per cent more during the same period. That increase will come partly from a growing amount of waste generated per person but mainly from a rising urban population. Overall, worldwide waste is expected to double by 2030 (OECD, 2010).

the transportation of waste, **pollution** control, landfills, incinerators and a host of specific sorts of waste, from cars to packaging to electronic goods. Due to this array of legislation, tipping fees are much higher than America's: €74 a tonne in France, for example, and €50 in Italy (Veolia Environnement, 2010).

In many countries, power from landfill gas or waste-to-energy plants (like the one at Spittelau, outside Vienna) attracts **subsidies** of one kind or another because it reduces emissions. In the developing economies these plants can earn UN-backed **carbon credits**. This represents foreign earnings since the credits can be sold to foreign governments or firms that must reduce their emissions under the **Kyoto Protocol**. The city of Mumbai in India, for example, plans to sell such credits when its landfill-gas project at Gorai is completed. Many firms in the waste business regard public concern about climate change as a spur to waste-to-energy projects. Incineration on a global scale could save up to a gigatonne of emissions if widely adopted. That is about one-seventh of the current global total. Already, more power is generated in the 700-plus waste-to-energy plants dotted around the world than in all the world's wind turbines and solar panels put together. In progressively-minded American states waste-to-energy plants could supply as much as 4 per cent of the country's electricity. Incineration is popular in many European countries, Japan and Singapore burn more than 50 per cent of their municipal waste but China currently only burns about 2 per cent of its rubbish. At an investment cost of US$6.3 billion, it has set itself a target of 30 per cent by 2030 (Covanta Energy, 2012).

Top of the league is the United Kingdom for currently offering the biggest incentives to waste firms in an effort to meet targets set by European directives. The UK government heavily taxes landfill sites, as a result, municipalities and businesses are desperate to find other ways of disposing of their rubbish.

Environmental impacts of waste

Serious **environmental impacts** can be caused by the disposal of waste. Burying rubbish in landfill sites which are massive holes dug into the ground can be a dirty and wasteful business. Some waste takes several centuries to rot down and in the process it may smell or generate methane gas, which is explosive and contributes to the **greenhouse effect**. Leaching of contaminated water and toxic substances into the **environment** can be another problem. Surface water, aquifers, soil and air can be polluted which causes more problems for humans, other species and **ecosystems**. Inadequate management of landfill sites may attract vermin or cause litter.

Incinerating waste also causes problems, because plastics tend to produce toxic substances, such as dioxins, when they are burnt. Gases from incineration may cause air pollution and contribute to acid rain, while the ash from incinerators may contain heavy metals and other toxins. Exposure to hazardous wastes, particularly when they are burned, can cause various other diseases, including cancers.

Hence, proper waste management is of the utmost importance and has become a controversial topic in terms of human justice. Many of the burdens associated by landfills are more often borne by the poor, who are forced to live sometimes near badly managed rubbish tips. There is now also a growing market in the international movement of waste which in itself creates more waste of energy. Although most waste that flows between countries goes between developed nations, a significant amount of waste is moved from developed to developing nations.

Sending the European consumers' rubbish to China in container ships has made headline news in recent years and promoted a knee-jerk reaction of condemnation from ecologists. Research has shown that sending plastic bottles and paper for recycling in China actually saves carbon emissions. Shipping these materials more than 10,000 miles produces less CO_2 than sending them to landfill in Europe and using brand new materials. According to the UK government-funded association, Waste & Resources Action Programme (WRAP), in 83 per cent of circumstances recycling paper, card, glass, plastics and metals is preferable to any other option for dealing with them. Recycling these items is estimated to save more than 18 million tonnes of **greenhouse gas** emissions per year in the UK alone.

Any item thrown away, whether it be a used plastic bags or a packet of sausages past its sell-by date, is a waste of resources and, when not disposed of correctly, can lead to grave environmental consequences. The raw materials and energy used in making the items are lost forever. Reducing waste means less environmental impact, less use of resources and less consumption of energy and water, and saves money.

Waste in the hospitality industry

The hospitality industry can become an important actor in the minimization of waste that is currently hauled off and disposed of at landfill sites. The industry can be active in the creation of recycling centres and programmes, using environmentally friendly cleaning supplies and techniques and sourcing locally produced goods and services that reduce transportation expenses.

CASE STUDY 4.2 Hospitality waste report outlines opportunity to save millions

Improved waste management in the hospitality industry not only helps the environment by reducing resource requirements, it often enhances the attractiveness of destinations as well. Money can be saved in the operations, and the green image is good for business as well.

Over 3.4 million tonnes of waste is disposed of by the UK hospitality industry each year. Hotels, pubs, restaurants and quick service restaurants typically produce food, glass, paper and cardboard waste. Of this, 1.6 million tonnes (48 per cent) is recycled, reused or composted, while almost 1.5 million tonnes (43 per cent) is thrown away, mainly to landfill.

Shockingly, 600,000 tonnes was food waste going to landfill, two-thirds of which (400,000 tonnes) could have been eaten.

Improvements in recycling have been made by the industry in recent years but still 70 per cent of the mixed waste going to landfill could be recycled using existing markets. The UK hospitality sector could save up to £724 million a year by tackling food waste alone.

Nearly a million tonnes of CO_2 equivalent emissions could be saved each year if the recyclable waste disposed of by the hospitality industry was actually recycled. This is about the quantity of CO_2 that 300,000 cars make in a whole year. Of course, this amount of emissions could be saved altogether if the avoidable food waste could be prevented.

Richard Swannell, Director of Design & Waste Prevention, at WRAP, believes the findings suggest there is a real opportunity to reduce waste and costs further across the hospitality sector:

> It is clear from our findings that much work has been done by the hospitality sector to reduce waste to landfill in favour of increased recycling, and more could be done. Businesses are keen to recycle, or recycle more, but often come across barriers, such as a lack of space.
>
> Working together, there is a real opportunity to reduce waste and recycle more, delivering reductions in CO_2 emissions, as well as generating cost savings.

The breakdown of key mixed waste materials in mixed waste sent for disposal that could be recycled is as shown in Table 4.1.

TABLE 4.1 Material tonnes of waste and percentage share

Material	Tonnes	(%)
Food	600,000	40
Glass	213,000	14
Paper	196,000	13
Card	134,000	9

Source: Working Together for a World Without Waste, July 2011.

Source: http://www.wrap.org.uk/media_centre/press_releases/hospitality_waste.htm.

As in other businesses, the top priority in the hotel industry is maintaining high guest satisfaction. Thus, there is great concern that any environmental improvements or **conservation** methods implemented will not negatively affect customer comfort and satisfaction. Most people are familiar with the traditional definition of waste management, which basically concentrates on the removal of rubbish from a private dwelling or business premises. In the hospitality industry, the scope of this definition continues to evolve as operators begin to embrace the three 'R's of reuse, recycle and reduce. Probably the newest component in this equation is the strategy to reduce, in other words, reducing the amount of waste operations produce in the first place.

The European Union produces 1.3 billion tonnes of waste each year. In other words, 3.5 tonnes of refuse and liquid or solid waste per European citizen, nearly a third of this is food waste for which the food service industry has a responsibility. Another 40–45 million tonnes of this huge mountain of waste is classed as hazardous, or particularly dangerous. Among other things it can be:

- persistent or non bio-degradable which remains dangerous for a long time, e.g. plastic bottles and tin cans;
- bio-accumulative, which accumulates as it makes its way up the food chain, e.g. some chemical pesticides and herbicides;
- eco-toxic, which causes damage to the environment, e.g. improperly treated used engine oil;
- carcinogenic, which causes cancer, e.g. asbestos.

Every kilo of waste generated in a hospitality operation equates to inefficiently used resources, in addition, the disposal of waste has to be paid for, usually directly in the form of a tipping fee. In some cases the establishment has to pay a haulage fee to have the waste transferred to a municipal landfill site, a transfer station or a recycling centre.

Although there are costs involved in recycling processes, every cardboard box or plastic bottle recycled saves the amount of energy that would have otherwise been used to make it from virgin material. Waste disposal is not an efficient or clean business. Even though standards are improving, waste management facilities are still significant polluters. Aside from the problem of illegal dumping, badly managed landfill sites are a source of pollution; non-biodegradable rubbish for future generations release the greenhouse gas methane into our atmosphere and damage the landscape. Incinerated rubbish can contribute to air pollution if incorrectly handled, likewise recycling and **composting** vegetable material can also pollute if badly run.

Waste is classified as biodegradable (vegetable and animal matter) and non-biodegradable (inorganic matter: plastics, glass, metal). In addition, hotels produce so-called biological wastes (human sewage) and ashes if an incinerator is used in the establishment. Hazardous wastes that are normally associated with heavy industry and also manufacturing industries are also present in hotels and restaurants.

They include the solvents used in paint and floor finishes, the chemicals used in some cleaning products and batteries that contain heavy metals such as mercury. Every effort must be made to either avoid using such products or, if they are indispensable, they should be disposed of correctly.

Food waste

In the hospitality industry, food and beverage operations account for a substantial amount of waste. This waste can be defined as:

*   *Pre- and post-consumer food waste, packaging and operating supplies*. Pre-consumer waste is defined as being all the trimmings, spoiled food and other products from kitchens that end up in the garbage before the finished menu item makes it to the consumer.
*   *Post-consumer waste*, naturally, is any rubbish left once the customer has consumed the meal.
*   *Packaging waste*, especially in the form of plastic that cannot biodegrade naturally, as anything used to hold food coming into the kitchen and going out. Operating supplies encompass every other piece of material used that becomes waste in a food service operation, such as cooking oil and light bulbs.

In both rich and poor countries, a staggering 30–50 per cent of all food produced is never eaten and just rots away. According to the Food and Agriculture Organization (FAO), in developing countries, bad roads and electricity networks mean that much harvested food is wasted because it cannot be stored or transported. In poor countries, most food is wasted on or near the farm. Rats, mice and locusts eat the crops in the field or in storage. Milk and vegetables spoil in transit. These might be considered losses rather than waste but improvements to infrastructure outputs could massively improve the output. Unlike in rich countries, much of the waste in poor ones is due to a lack of investment, not behaviour.

Rich countries waste about the same amount of food as poor ones, around half of what is produced, but in quite different ways. Studies in the USA and the UK find that a quarter of food from shops goes straight into the rubbish bin or is thrown away by shops and restaurants. Top of the list come salad items, about half of which are chucked away. A third of all bread, a quarter of fruit and a fifth of vegetables – all are thrown out uneaten. Households in Great Britain could save 70 Euros a month or 15 billion Euros a year across the UK, by taking steps to tackle the growing problem of food waste. Yet nearly half (46 per cent) admit that they do not know the correct way to store food safely. More than two-thirds (67 per cent) of consumers claim they do not always plan their shopping trips by making a list or meal planning, but spontaneously decide what to buy in the store (WRAP, 2011).

Roughly speaking, the equivalent of 100 kg of food is thrown away every year by every inhabitant of the planet, this adds up to up to 100 million tonnes of food per annum. Included in this amount is one-third of the entire world's supply of meat.

If Western waste could be halved and the food distributed to those who need it, the problem of feeding 9 billion people would vanish. The British consumer organization WRAP found two main reasons for people throwing food out: either too much is cooked or prepared, or food is left to go off, completely untouched or opened but not finished. But supermarkets have also come under fire from environmental groups for throwing away large quantities of food that is still safe to eat. Food wastage in the West results from personal habits and law and partly a reflection of prices: food is cheap enough for consumers not to worry about chucking it out, and prices seem unlikely to rise by enough to change that attitude, at least in the near future (WRAP, 2011).

The millions of tonnes of uneaten food that are thrown into the bin each year equate to a mountain of hidden costs of such waste. On average, twice as much water per year is thrown away in the form of uneaten food as we use for washing and drinking. This situation is aggravated even further when one considers the origin of food. An increasing amount comes from countries where water is scarce; meaning the food we discard has a huge hidden impact on the depletion of valuable water resources across the world in countries that are already experiencing water stress. As more countries suffer from water **scarcity**, these exports can further deplete natural resources and make prices higher for water to poorer consumers. Food waste carries another environmental cost: it accounts for about 3 per cent of annual greenhouse gas emissions (World Wildlife Fund, 2012).

In a western country like the UK, restaurants lose over 800 million Euros per year by throwing away 400,000 tonnes of food, this equates to the amount of food waste one could pack into two medium-sized houses for every single restaurant in the country. Over half of restaurant waste is generated during preparation, but diners with eyes far bigger than their stomachs are responsible for a lot of restaurant waste too. Most of this waste is organic and could be recycled but usually ends up being burnt in municipal incinerators or landfill (Unilever, 2012). Older generations of restaurant owners will remember the famous 'pig bin'. Just about everything left over would go in it, vegetable peelings, bones and meat scraps and uneaten food on plates. EU regulations put an end to this form of recycling, it was deemed to be unsanitary. Since the 1980s restaurateurs have needed imagination to find economic and sanitary ways to recycle waste. Of course, reductions in the kitchen and the dining room are the first step.

In addition to the environmental impacts of waste, restaurants are faced with ever tightening profit margins. Today's food service managers are constantly looking for ways to trim their costs. To do this they continually look for ways to improve productivity and to minimize waste or conversely, increase yield. Cooking to order, rather than bulk food cooking can reduce waste even though labour costs may increase. Often in canteens food that is cooked in bulk and held for a period of time, such as soups, hot entrées, pastas and other foods are thrown away if not consumed. Tracking food waste can work as a useful deterrent. When culinary staff are trained to weigh food trimmings and other pre-consumer waste at the different food preparation stations in the kitchen using special scales as part of a waste management system, the food service manager is able to pinpoint where most of the food waste is coming from. This attention to detail makes the staff more mindful of their cuts during food preparation and reduces excess trimmings going into the dustbin. Management can also introduce incentives for those staff members who produce the least waste.

Many food service managers are horrified at the amount of food left on plates. American and European cities have wrestled with excess food waste for more than a decade but in Hong Kong where shrinking landfill space is a growing concern; the city elders are pushing the inhabitants to adopt a new consumption ethic. In the past five years the amount of food wasted by Hong Kong's restaurants, hotels and food manufacturers has more than doubled, according to the Environmental Protection Department (EPD). In an attempt to change wasteful dining habits one of Hong Kong's 'hot pot' restaurants that offer 'all you can eat' for a fixed price are charging HK$5 (US 64 cents) per ounce for leftovers. In another sushi restaurant, the owner charges HK$10 (US$1.28) per leftover sushi. Restaurateurs are often loathe to reduce portion size in the fear of losing customers, however, by offering 'come back for seconds' options some restaurants are managing to reduce the overall amount of food waste.

CASE STUDY 4.3 Unilever: wise up on waste toolkit

Unilever Food Solutions has developed a waste toolkit for catering venues and restaurants to help food service operators control their costs better. The toolkit gives accurate costs of food waste and gives guidance on how restaurants can carry out waste audits and create menu dishes that use frequently wasted ingredients. Other tips in the toolkit include examining portion sizes based on consumption patterns, accurate measuring of ingredients, using off-cuts to create starter dishes and using vegetable trimmings to make soups. Unilever drew up the toolkit in response to its latest World Menu Report, which highlights the growing problem of food waste when consumers dine out. Some 81 per cent of Australian consumers consider it important for food service operators to dispose of food waste in an environmentally friendly way. In their survey, Unilever found that half would pay more when dining out for a restaurant that was implementing sustainable practices. 'Many only think about disposal expenses when considering food waste, however, we know for a fact that there are a number of other costs to consider when estimating the overheads of waste.'

Source: Unilever Food Solutions, http://www.unileverfoodsolutions.co.uk/our-services/your-kitchen/wiseuponfoodwaste/tools.

Anaerobic digestion is an increasingly viable option for a solution to food waste. This process produces and captures methane gas which would normally end up in the atmosphere. Methane is 21 times more insidious as a greenhouse gas than CO_2 but can be used to generate 'local' electricity and hot water in Combined Heat & Power (CHP) engines. Furthermore, the 'digestate' end product after the methane has been extracted, is a fertilizer which is better than chemical fertilizers since it binds more easily with the soil, improving soil quality. Also, it is not subject to the same run-off into rivers and aquifers that occurs with synthetic nitrate and phosphate chemical fertilizers. Animal manures can be used in anaerobic digestion as well, providing a good method to reduce smells issues around farms and local sewage works. Hotels and restaurants will always produce some food scraps and finding ways to feed animals with it and then digesting what remains through anaerobic digestion plants would ensure a 'sustainable' loop because the 'fertilizer' can be used to grow more food.

CASE STUDY 4.4 Glasgow hotel begins anaerobic digestion project

The William Tracey Group has partnered with luxury five-star hotel, Radisson Blu Glasgow, to deliver the hotel's next major step in achieving zero waste – recycling food waste into electricity!

The new project, which will see all food waste from the Radisson Blu being recycled and converted to **renewable energy**, is the latest in a number of environmental initiatives implemented at the Radisson Blu as part of their ambition to be Glasgow's leading eco-friendly hotel.

The William Tracey Group, which runs recycling and waste operations around the city and across Scotland, is now offering customers the chance to recycle food waste through the process of anaerobic digestion which treats this waste in a biogas process to produce renewable energy and organic fertilizer – a much cleaner, cheaper and environmentally friendly alternative to landfill.

The initiatives which are driven by the hotel General Manager, Graeme Gibson, are not always easy to implement but despite the challenges they face daily, the benefits they have experienced make it worthwhile:

Graeme Gibson comments:

> The hotel team is very excited about our latest figures in terms of recycling scores. We are proud to say that every employee understands and supports the responsible business initiative, from recycling of cardboard and paper, to food waste management, water management and carbon efficiency. Our partnership with the William Tracey Group has driven forward the improvements in our recycling programme. The support and constant feedback from their team are crucial to our business and they are flexible in terms of catering for our needs and challenges.

In addition to our new recycling plan, reporting carried out for the first quarter of 2010 has shown savings of 32.3 per cent in water costs, 6 per cent in electricity and 35.5 per cent in gas and we are dedicated to using local suppliers such as Matthew Algie who supply the hotel with high quality coffee and are also customers of the William Tracey Group, committed to environmental improvement.

Source: William Tracey Recycling & Resource Management Group, http://www.william traceygroup.com/who_we_are/latest_news/glasgow_hotel_begin_food_recycling_.

Reusable food

Many hundreds of programmes throughout the EU and the USA accept food – packaged, fresh, frozen or baked – that restaurants and hotels can no longer use. Donor programmes deliver food to soup kitchens, homeless shelters, senior citizens' programmes, day-care centres and food pantries. If possible, collect unusable food scraps and arrange to have them picked up by local pig farmers for use as animal feed. First, check with the local health department or cooperative extension office, as some countries and municipalities do not allow the feeding of food scraps to animals. Used deep fryer oil is now used successfully by motorists who have modified their car engines to run on this cheap fuel.

Composting

Compost is organic matter that has been decomposed and recycled as a fertilizer and soil amendment that improves the condition of the soil. There are examples of restaurants that transform kitchen and garden waste into useful compost and use this valuable substance to improve their flower beds and herb gardens. Compostable items, i.e. food that cannot be donated, come in many forms, non-fatty waste including spoiled fruits and vegetables, stale bakery items, kitchen preparation trimmings and leftover plate scrapings. Meat and fish leftovers will break down into compost but attract undesirable vermin in the process and are therefore best avoided. The decomposition process is aided by shredding the plant matter, adding water and ensuring proper aeration by regularly turning the mixture. Worms and fungi and aerobic bacteria further break up the material.

Another form of composting is *vermiculture*. A series of bins are used in this process and the active partner in the enterprise is *Eisenia foetida* or the red wriggler worm which is smaller than worms normally found in the garden and will work 24 hours per day, 7 days a week, to transform kitchen waste into rich black loam (humus). An added advantage of vermiculture composting is that unlike rubbish dumps where organic matter produces the greenhouse gas methane, using worms for composting prevents this by turning waste into stabilized organic matter.

CASE STUDY 4.5 Vermiculture to reduce hotel waste

The Mount Nelson Hotel is a luxury hotel in Cape Town. The hotel is an urban sanctuary, situated within a sprawling lush garden estate in the heart of the city's vibrant cultural centre and close to the waterfront and beaches.

The Mount Nelson Hotel recognises the pivotal role such an operation plays in a community. Therefore the hotel is dedicated to working towards the conservation of South Africa's natural resources and in educating the staff to make a difference in the lives of others. The Mount Nelson Hotel has many onsite eco-initiatives including the establishment of an on-site 'worm farm' (or vermiculture centre) to process leftover food and other organic matter into compost, which is used to fertilize the hotel's gardens.

Vermicompost is the heterogenous mixture of decomposing vegetable or food waste. Vermicompost can be mixed directly into the soil as fertilizer. The benefits of vermiculture are many:

- *Soil*: vermicompst enriches the soil with micro-organisms.
- *Plant growth*: It improves root growth and structure.
- *Economic*: It reduces waste flow to landfills. It also requires a low capital investment and uses relatively simple technologies.
- *Environmental*: It recycles waste onsite.

Source: Mount Nelson Hotel, http://www.mountnelson.co.za/web/ocap/in_house_conservation.jsp.

Another, new and worrying waste is the category known as E-waste (electronic waste) coming from computers, mobile phones, fax machines, copiers, etc. Although fairly harmless while in use, these devices contain an assortment of heavy metals such as lead, mercury and arsenic that are difficult to separate. Since recycling is difficult and expensive in terms of time, this waste is often sorted by people in developing countries working in unsafe conditions who sacrifice their health to do it. The remainder ends up in municipal landfill and accounts for an estimated 40 per cent of heavy metals found in municipal landfill sites.

Manufacturers are coming under mounting pressure from legislators and consumers alike to minimize their impact on the environment, leading to the design for the environment concept. This embodies all manner of issues, such as reduced energy usage, transportation, packaging, recycling and waste reduction and disposal. Emerging from the design for the environment concept manufacturers are now trying to embody the principles of design for disassembly (DFD). The aims of DFD are to design a product that can be readily dismantled at the end of its life and thus optimize the reuse, re-manufacturing or recycling of materials, components and sub-assemblies.

Eco-procurement minimizing waste

Eco-procurement means choosing products and services that have the lowest negative impact on the environment while minimizing waste. In order to meet eco-procurement standards, all products and services must undergo a thorough environmental impact analysis – from cradle to grave. This means being able to trace the origin of all raw materials, the **impacts**, if any, during the manufacturing process, the toxins present, packaging, transportation methods, storage and the effect on the environment when using a product. Finally, eco-procurement or eco-purchasing considers not only the traditional specifications of quality, price, delivery, availability, convenience, etc. but also considers the disposal of the item and its packaging after use.

Eco-procurement incorporates the principles of design for disassembly, by which the method for disposing of the product or components of the product by recycling is planned in advance. An example would be looking for alternatives to disposable plastic cutlery and plastic plates; clearly, plastic has no part to play in **sustainable food** service. As a midway between plastic utensils and styrofoam take-away containers a new generation of compostable packaging is entering the market place. World-centric products made from 'agrifibers' (such as sugarcane pulp) and 'bioplastics' (made from various plant starches) are being used in place of the usual paper and styrofoam packaging. Some of these products can be used in the dishwasher and are microwave safe, all are biodegradable.

Principles of eco-procurement foodservices are:

- In preference to using imported foodstuffs or those from far away, local food products should be selected from the region or country in which they are to be offered when the products meet the quality, quantity and price constraints of the operation. Seasonality of products should be respected where applicable.
- Avoid purchasing foods in the knowledge that they have been produced at home or abroad using processes known to damage human health and/or the environment.
- Support producers using organic or responsibly farmed products.
- Endeavour to reduce chemical additives, salt and sugar in foods.
- Information on food provenance and the **sustainability** of food offerings should be made available to consumers so that they can make well-informed choices.
- Ensure food products are processed using facilities that are resource-efficient (i.e. have a commitment to reducing energy consumption, minimizing waste and reducing water consumption).
- Encourage centralized purchasing systems to meet the needs of smaller local and/or regional suppliers.
- Support transportation systems to facilitate fuel-/energy-efficient sourcing and distribution of food from the point of production/processing to the point of consumption.

- Ensure animal food products are sourced from livestock production systems that comply with national regulatory standards and the international standards developed by the World Organisation for Animal Health.

In addition, inventory levels on perishables should be adjusted to minimize waste due to spoilage or dehydration. If coded dairy products or dried-up lettuce are constantly being thrown out in an establishment, it might be because inventory stocking is much too high and/or it is not being rotated properly. Usage levels should be checked to see if it is necessary to adjust either the quantity or frequency of orders. Develop and use hourly or daily production charts to minimize over-preparing and unnecessary waste. Whenever possible, prepare just the minimum.

Waste reduction tactics in hospitality operations

Management should work with suppliers to procure products that promote waste prevention. Some suppliers may be able to change products and packaging to reduce the waste the hotel manages. For example, ask food service vendors if they can deliver items in reusable shipping containers. Consider buying or leasing used or remanufactured furniture, fixtures and equipment. Typical remanufacturing operations performed by suppliers are replacement of worn parts, refinishing of metal or wooden surfaces, repairing of scratches, dents and holes, and reupholstering of cushions. Extending the life of furniture, fixtures and equipment through remanufacturing reduces the rate at which they are discarded. Purchasing in bulk, using recycled products and buying from suppliers that have a proper environmental policy in place, are all measures that help to reduce the amount of waste generated. Moreover, buying products with a longer lifetime will also lead to decreased waste. Creating less waste or eliminating waste before it is created means creating less pollution and saving natural resources. This can be done by working together with suppliers and encouraging them to reduce their packaging, reuse packaging or change to reusable packaging where possible. Purchasing some items in bulk may be another option for reduction. Cleaning materials, for example, can be purchased in concentrated form and mixed in the hotel. Many hotels now supply guests with liquid soaps and shampoos in refillable ceramic containers in the bathrooms. Outsourcing can sometimes help hotels to reduce waste and cut costs. Services such as dry cleaning that require an important **capital expenditure** and that, if badly managed, produce hazardous waste should be considered carefully. Alternatives, such as using a local company could be more cost effective and result in less pollution.

Reduce: a strategic approach

We have all been in hotels where we are asked whether we would like to have our towels and sheets replaced daily, or whether we wish to 'help the environment' by reusing them. In many ways this typifies the early approach to hotels wishing to green their credentials. Although many other ways have now been developed to 'help the environment', reducing laundry is still a worthy task. Besides saving water and energy, reduced laundering will also cut down on the use of detergent and bleach. According to the US National Association of Institutional Linen Management, hotel laundry costs range from US$3 to US$4 per day per room. It is estimated that hotels can save up to US$1.50 per day per room by reminding guests they have the option of choosing not to get freshly laundered sheets and towels each day of their stay.

CASE STUDY 4.6 Straw Wars: London restaurants opt for drinking straws ban

The idea is simple – either get rid of straws completely or provide a straw only when requested by a customer. If they want one, all they have to do is ask. It's that easy.

London restaurants, bars and cafés have joined the 'Straw Wars' campaign which aims at cutting down on the use of plastic drinking straws by customers. Why? Because billions of straws are discarded every year, filtering into landfill and littering the oceans. This is extremely detrimental to the environment, as plastics cannot biodegrade, they last indefinitely – breaking down into smaller pieces, feeding into the food chain and potentially ending up on our dinner plates. More worryingly, plastics are becoming a major source of marine pollution. Organizers of the Straw Wars campaign claim that in the United Kingdom alone, an average of 3.5 million McDonald's drinks are sold with plastic straws every day.

It is thought that around 60–80 per cent of marine debris is made up of plastic waste. Scientists estimate that every year at least 1 million seabirds, 100,000 marine mammals and sea turtles die when they entangle themselves in or ingest plastic pollution.

Source: Straw Wars, http://strawwars.org/.

Reuse: a strategic approach

Another strategy is to reuse as much as possible of the waste generated. This means finding ways to use the waste from one process as the raw material for another one. Reusing material is a better choice than recycling, incineration or landfill. Reusing differs from recycling in that recycling breaks down an item into its basic parts and makes a new product out of it but reusing an item keeps the material in its original form and uses the item over and over again for the same or different purposes. There are many examples of reuse in the hospitality industry; here are just a few that are applicable to both restaurants and hotels regardless of their type and size:

1. *Reusing textiles*: convert damaged textiles, such as uniforms and linens, into useful items. For example, torn bed sheets, towels and banquet linens into reusable guest-room laundry bags, baby bibs, crib bumper pads, aprons, cleaning rags and bar covers either by the establishment itself or by a charity organization. Another possibility: repair torn bed linen and reuse it on smaller cots or cribs. Replace single-use items with reusable items such as napkins, tablecloths and hand towels. When they are worn, turn them into cleaning rags. Dye stained towels a darker colour for reuse at the pool or beach, or as cleaning cloths. Extend the useful life of curtains by rotating them to expose different portions to sunlight.

2. *Reusing containers*: this means that less material is needed to manufacture containers, and there will be less material requiring recycling and disposal. Reuse of packaging can also save money for companies that either ship or receive products by reducing the cost of packaging, disposal and product damage due to shipping and handling. In addition, companies report that they have generated additional long-term cost savings by implementing reusable container systems, including reduced freight, labour, and handling and storage costs.

3. *Reuse bottles and glasses*: hotel and restaurant operators can choose from a wide variety of options when they purchase and dispense beverages. For example, beer can be packaged in kegs, cans or bottles. Bottles are either intended to be reusable or to be used just once, after which they are disposed of or recycled. In some countries like Germany, using reusable bottles is a way of life, in other countries, throwaway plastic bottles and glasses are the norm. A bottle that is filled 20 times eliminates the need for making 19 more bottles, avoiding not only the need to dispose of those 19 containers but avoiding also the environmental effects of material extraction, processing, manufacturing, distribution and recycling.

Recycle: a strategic approach

A recycled product describes a product that is made entirely or partly from secondary material recovered from consumer waste. Some products are reduced to their raw state and re-manufactured into something resembling their original state. In the case of recycled paper, the newspapers gathered from guest bedrooms and the used notepaper coming from the hotel copy shop are reduced back to their raw state of paper pulp which is then used to produce more paper. Unfortunately, many products recycled in this manner come back as lesser quality products. Paper comes back as packaging material or paper towels. This process is known as *downcycling*, and plastic is another such product. When the used plastic is melted down, it loses strength because its long polymer chains of molecules are sheared. This recycled plastic can be made into building bricks or blocks, commonly used successfully in developing countries but if made into plastic bags the result is more flimsy than the original product. For some products, downcycling is not a problem such as metals and food waste. Aluminium can be used over and over again without any loss of its original qualities. Like all metals, there is a considerable cost saving from recycling aluminium and no additional damage.

Recycling has other advantages. It conserves natural resources, saves energy and reduces greenhouse gases and pollution that result when scrap materials are substituted for primary raw materials. If recycled materials can be used, ore does not have to be mined, not as many trees are cut and not as much oil has to be drilled. Extracting metals from ore, in particular, is extremely energy-intensive, especially aluminium extraction. Using recycled aluminium can reduce energy consumption by as much as 95 per cent. Savings for other materials are lower but still substantial: about 70 per cent for plastics, 60 per cent for steel, 40 per cent for paper and 30 per cent for glass. Recycling also reduces emissions of pollutants that can cause smog, acid rain and the contamination of waterways.

Unfortunately, there is a threat to recycling in the form of declining commodity prices, and in our market economy the two are undeniably linked. It seems unfair that environmental protection is linked to market prices. However, since 2009, prices have generally shot up, even though, in the present economic climate, markets are still fragile. Some recyclables – such as glass – have hardly been touched by the price reductions and the demand for glass remains strong. Using recycled glass saves 25 per cent of the energy it would do to make a product from new materials, and aluminium saves 95 per cent of the energy. Very few people now disagree with the idea of recycling and are happy to participate in these programmes. Most people accept that we live in a world of finite resources and that communities across the planet need to work hard not to exhaust the resources that society has yet to plunder.

The departmental organization of hospitality operations is challenging when establishing a recycling programme. The company must provide organizational resources, the most important being enthusiasm. Giving the responsibility of leading the programme to the right person or people is the main key to success. The following guidelines will help any hospitality company that has decided to put into place a recycling programme:

- *Decide on leadership*, who will be the Recycling Programme Manager, who will be in his or her team? This person might already have a position in managing operations; essentially the person must be an organizer and an enthusiastic communicator who can win support throughout the business.
- *Analyse waste streams*, do a waste audit. The act of counting and measuring, although tedious, focuses attention. Many hospitality professionals have stories of checking waste bins and pulling out perfectly useable utensils and crockery that have been dropped in by mistake. Decide how waste is to be separated and set up disposal systems with local municipalities or recycling companies, not only for raw materials like paper, glass, aluminium, etc. but also for fixtures and fittings. Charity organizations are only too happy to take household items.

- *Establish an accounting system* that reflects monthly waste management costs. A monthly report is needed for tracking waste disposal and recycling information. Create recycling goals for departments and waste material reduction. Organize projects and activities that involve the personnel and that incidentally bring positive publicity to the establishment.
- Build ownership by involving employees at all stages of the programme. Post the goals on bulletin boards so all employees are informed.
- *Close the loop*, that is to say, buy recycled products. Recycling programmes need evaluation periodically and refinement if goals are not being reached. Most recycling programmes need stimulation from caring members of staff.

CASE STUDY 4.7 Soneva Resorts: waste to wealth

Following the principles or reduce, reuse and recycle is the best way of eliminating waste, and doing so is an important part of ethical credibility. Humans are very good at wasting energy, resources and food, and excessive **lifestyles** have a massive negative impact on the environment. With careful management, waste can be seen as a resource rather than a waste. With that view in mind, Soneva uses the concept of Waste to Wealth to work towards a zero waste goal.

Waste management strategies

The best way to manage waste is to avoid creating it in the first place. By stopping all imports of plastic bottled water, and replacing it with our in-house brand provided in glass bottles we improved waste and our carbon footprint. Another example is the room amenities, such as shampoo, conditioner, soap and body lotion. Instead of using individual small plastic containers, we use ceramic dispensers that can be refilled. Not only does that eliminate plastic waste, it also looks more aesthetically pleasing.

No to plastic

Most plastic is made from oil, and despite common opinion, it is very hard to recycle en masse. Most recycled plastic is actually burned, putting further toxic chemicals into the air. Plastic is one of the most common man-made materials on Earth, and because it is non-biodegradable, it will be around for a long time yet. The use of plastic on Soneva resorts is negligible, we have reusable glass bottles for our on-site water, ceramic containers for room amenities and use oxo-biodegradable alternatives in the few areas where we use refuse bags and similar products. Reduce plastic, and you seriously reduce the waste you produce.

Reuse and recycle

Finding new uses for old things is a lesson in innovation. You can see examples of this philosophy in all Soneva resorts, but more probably than not you will be unaware of most of our recycling projects. Paper and cardboard are familiar candidates for recycling but finding new interesting ways to use other disposables offers more of a challenge. Glass often finds its way into concrete as aggregate, wood can become biochar for our gardens or charcoal for cooking, food waste can become food for our vegetables and plants. With an ethical outlook, the waste to wealth mentality is common sense.

Waste to wealth Eco Centro

The Eco Centro project on Soneva Fushi is an example of just how comprehensive and effective waste management can be. Designed on permacultural principles, the site has developed into a complex waste recycling centre using a variety of old and new technologies to maximize site efficiency.

Waste separation and composting are the initial steps in the process, but pyrolysis of waste wood into charcoal and the conversion of degrading plant matter into biogas for power generation and cooking are also important parts of the waste to wealth approach. Despite these efforts, more could still be done. Soneva Fushi is already decarbonizing its waste handling. From July 2010–June 2011 Soneva Fushi had a negative 17 tonnes CO_2 from its waste handling.

Bio charcoal and biochar

Making charcoal is a common practice seen in most cultures around the world. Charcoal has many uses including heating, cooking, soil improvement and even art. As such, the production of bio charcoal is important to many communities and each has its own techniques. Pyrolysis is the name given to the process, and requires that the burning wood be in an atmosphere of zero oxygen. This can be difficult to do and at Soneva Fushi's Eco Centro purpose-built Adams Retort ovens are used to maximize productivity.

The ancient Mayans found that the particulate bi-product of charcoal production, known as biochar, had surprising qualities when mixed with soil. The porous and absorbent nature of charcoal, increased many times in a particulate form, can lock and hold both moisture and valuable nutrients. This was great for the Mayans whose rainforest soil was infertile and low yielding. The soil at our Soneva Fushi resort is similarly poor, but using a combination of biochar and compost has meant we can and do grow a great variety of crops.

Permaculture

A contraction of the words 'permanent' and 'agriculture', the term permaculture denotes a design system which emphasizes sustainability and the use of natural resources. It is commonly used in management plans for sustainable human settlements and has important applications for food production. It is a truly organic approach, working with ecology and wildlife to create a harmonic relationship between man and nature.

Compost

Waste is on average 50 per cent organic, and failure to separate this waste often leads to less recycling of other materials as they get contaminated. Furthermore, if sent to an incinerator, the efficiency of the burning process is considerably hampered. Since producing food on site is a really good way of reducing our imports and makes our food as fresh as possible, any way of improving our soil is very useful.

PICTURE 4.1 Composting at Soneva Fushi

Composting is a great way to make use of organic waste and create fertile soil. At Soneva Fushi a mixture of shredded kitchen and garden waste produces high quality compost for our herb and vegetable gardens.

Worm composting

Soneva Kiri has a special workforce of African Night Crawlers involved in its onsite composting. The earthworms are raised in boxes containing animal manures, coconut fibre and sandy loam topsoil and fed with food leftovers from the host restaurant. The earthworms then excrete highly fertile vermicompost rich in minerals and nutrients and high quality plant food for our herb and vegetable gardens.

Herb and vegetable gardens

With soil improvements both from composting soil and biochar production Soneva Fushi has developed an extensive network of herb and vegetable gardens supplying the kitchen with fresh produce. This system is built on permaculture and organic principles. A horticulturist has been hired to support the perma-culturist; 100 per cent of herb needs and about 30 per cent of salads are supplied from the garden, reducing carbon emissions from imports.

We have even built a mushroom hut where we produce a wide variety of mushrooms. For the chef it is great to be able to work with fresh ingredients and one of our regular guest comments is how good the rocket salad tastes. This is of course attributed to the fact that it comes straight from the soil and has not been transported for several days. One of our restaurants – Fresh in the Garden – is even built over one of the herb and vegetable gardens.

PICTURE 4.2
Organic garden,
Soneva Fushi

Glass

The low cost of glass can make **recycling** it uneconomic; often the cost of transport is far more than the glass is worth. For this reason Soneva Fushi had to find new ways of reusing our glass waste. Crushing glass creates a useful form of aggregate which can be mixed with concrete and used to make table tops. Not only are we able to reuse our glass waste, but also this reduces the need for imported cement. And the result is nice-looking table tops.

Driftwood

For many people, driftwood is seen as waste and a hassle in the ocean and on beaches. Soneva Resorts see it as beautiful art and use it to a large extent as both decoration and furniture in the resorts. Soneva Kiri is a great example where driftwood is literally picked up from the ocean and transformed into stunning decoration.

Power cable reels

Power cable reels are often left as waste after the cables has been used. Soneva Resorts make use of this as they function as great tables. Particularly on remote islands like Soneva Fushi, it is useful as it eliminates the need to get rid of the power cable reels as well as bringing in new tables.

Source: Soneva Resorts, http://www.soneva.com/.

EXERCISES

1   GROUP DISCUSSION, GROUP PROJECT OR WRITTEN ASSIGNMENT

Simple waste management checklist

- Create an activity checklist which could be used at a hotel based on the waste management hierarchy.

    Minimum requirements:

    - two activities to avoid waste

    - five activities to reduce waste

    - three activities to reuse waste

    - four activities to recycle waste

2   GROUP DISCUSSION OR GROUP PROJECT

Mitigating waste impact

- In hospitality facilities, solid wastes are significantly generated in the construction phase. When operating the hotel, food waste and well as paper and cardboard waste account for most of the solid waste.

- How should a hotel manage its waste stream and implement a proper waste management strategy?

3   GROUP DISCUSSION OR WRITTEN ASSIGNMENT

Zero waste

- What is the concept of zero waste?

- Can this be implemented in some ways into the hospitality industry?

- Why or why not?

4   GROUP RESEARCH AND DISCUSSION

A question of waste

- Provide answers and critically discuss the following questions:

    - Why is waste a problem for the environment?

    - Discuss the concept of design for disassembly.

    - What is eco-procurement and what can be done to reduce waste?

    - Discuss ways of re-using items that would normally be considered as waste in a hotel.

    - Discuss ways to recycle waste.

    - Do you think composting is a possible alternative for disposing of vegetable waste in a restaurant?

References

Covanta Energy (2012) *Covanta News Issue 12*. Available at: http://www.covantaenergy. co.uk/.

OECD (2010) *OECD Environmental Outlook to 2030*. Available at: http://www.oecd.org/ document/2010,3746,en_2649_37465_39676628_1_1_1_37465,00.html.

Unilever (2012) *Wise up on Waste Toolkit*. Available at: http://www.unileverfoodsolutions. co.uk/our-services/your-kitchen/wiseuponfoodwaste/tools.

Veoila Environnement Our Publications (2010): http://www.veoila.com/en/medias/ publications/.

World Wildlife Fund (WWF) (2012): http://www.panda.org.

WRAP (Waste & Resources Action Programme) (2011) *LCA of Management Options for Mixed Waste Plastics*. Available at: http://www.wrap.org.uk/downloads/LCA_of_ Management_Options_for_Mixed_Waste_Plastics.54c64a6f.5497.pdf.

Resources

Association for Linen Management: http://www.almnet.org/.

Environment Green: http://www.environment-green.com.

Hong Kong Environmental Protection Department: http://www.epd.gov.hk/epd/eindex.html.

How to compost: http://www.howtocompost.org.

Stern Review: http://www.sternreview.org.uk.

US National Association of Institutional Linen Management: http://www.osha.gov/dcsp/ alliances/nailm/nailm.

Waste & Resources Action Programme (WRAP) *LCA of Management Options for Mixed Waste Plastics*. Available at: http://www.wrap.org.uk/downloads/LCA_of_Management_ Options_for_Mixed_Waste_Plastics.54c64a6f.5497.pdf.

World Wildlife Fund (WWF): http://www.panda.org.

Additional material

Go to www.routledge.com/cw/sloan to find PowerPoint slides of all the figures and tables from the book, additional case studies, a test bank of questions and extra links to useful videos.

CHAPTER

5

Water conservation

CHAPTER OBJECTIVES

The objectives for this chapter are:

- To explain the issues of water conservation
- To describe the need to consider water availability in the hospitality development process
- To explain water conservation techniques in hotels
- To describe some examples of modern water-saving technology
- To give examples of pioneering ways to cut down on water use

COMPANION @ WEBSITE

Water conservation: problem definition

Much is said about the need for the global community to reduce its **carbon footprint** but mankind needs to address another ecological imbalance, its 'water footprint'. One third of the world's population must contend with severe water shortage and twice that number has no sanitation. With a rise in global temperatures of 4°C expected this century there will be 3 billion people facing severe water shortages by 2100 (UNEP, 2009). The combination of **scarcity** and bad management of water affects food supplies, health, education, nature and economic development. It means women spend long periods collecting it, families spend up to half their daily income on it, farmers lose their land, and infants die of dehydration.

Most of Africa, the Middle East, South Asia, the western United States, South America, China and nearly all of Australia are already in trouble. In the burgeoning slums of the developing world, water and sanitation problems are now acute. Up to 3 million people die each year of easily preventable water-borne diseases while global consumption of fresh water doubles every 20 years and new sources are becoming scarcer and more expensive to develop and treat. Many Western countries are struggling against depleting aquifers and increasing water needs for which modern **lifestyles** are partly to blame. It is not only the increasing world population that is stimulating demand but also our cravings for garden pools, consumer products and a richer diet of more meat, fish and milk. **Tourist** regions like Mallorca and Almeria in Spain, Baja California, Cyprus, Singapore, Antigua and Barbados all have acute shortages. Although, in global terms, water is a precious and diminishing commodity, many industrial users regard it as just another expense and see little incentive to conserve it because its price is negligible even though it is in constant escalation.

Land is not the issue in the prevention of agricultural expansion but lack of water. Globally, water seems to be abundant but often not situated within reach of those who need it. A quarter of the world gets its supplies from deep aquifers, or groundwater. Alarmingly, many are being emptied 10 times faster than they are being naturally recharged. Water tables in parts of China are dropping almost 1.5 metres a year and 400 of its 600 northern cities face severe shortages. The over-pumping of groundwater leads to other problems. Removing large amounts of water can magnify the concentration of pollutants in the water that remains, and in many cases polluted surface water or salty sea water pours into the aquifer to replace the groundwater, making it impossible to farm except with salt-tolerant genetically modified crops. Potentially hazardous to human health, pesticides, nitrates, petrochemicals, fluorides, heavy metals and mining wastes pollute major aquifers in the industrialized world and water drawn from them needs expensive treatment before it can be used. In the Mediterranean basin, over-exploitation of local surface water sources and aquifers, to meet the needs of tourism expansion is lowering groundwater tables. Saline intrusion, i.e. seawater contamination, can result in coastal areas where water tables fall below sea level. This leads to the destruction of **fauna** and **flora** habitats, resulting in a less attractive ecology for visiting tourists and the local population.

Deep aquifers are a vital link in the hydrological cycle because they release water slowly into rivers, lakes and wetlands in the dry seasons and soak up water to prevent flooding in times of heavy rain. The only reason that many of the world's great rivers such as the Niger and the Nile flow all year round is because of groundwater release. Take too much and the result is dried-up wetlands and riverbeds.

Major rivers such as the Ganges, the Yellow River, the Colorado and the Nile are now so dammed, diverted for farm irrigation or industrial use that little is left to go out to sea. This can have serious knock-on consequences. Huge areas of Baja California in Mexico where the Colorado used to flow before the Hoover Dam was built are now nearly devoid of agriculture. The Indus feeds extensive mangrove forests but irrigation schemes in its delta are drying up and killing the mangroves and consequently destroying major fish breeding grounds which local people have relied upon for generations.

In 2012, the University of Twente in the Netherlands published research on global levels of water consumption. The average water usage per person is merely 127 litres per day. Not very much compared to citizens of the USA, who, per person, use 295 litres. In Dubai, this number even goes up to an astonishing 500 litres.

In 2011, another study by the University of Twente looked at so-called virtual water usage, i.e. water that is used to produce all the everyday articles we use. Every product and service purchased, be it apples, leather shoes, a steak, a television or a weekend including travel and hotel in Venice, involves water. The total global water footprint in 2005 was 9.087 trillion cubic metres. This is about 190 times as much as the content of Lake Constance in southern Germany.

Agriculture is responsible for 92 per cent of the global water footprint and industrial production accounts for 4.4 per cent. China, India and the USA alone are responsible for 38 per cent. Since much of the agricultural and industrial production is traded globally, exporting countries also indirectly export large amounts of water. Whether it be tomatoes, beef or motor cars, water, used to produce a product or service, leaves one country or region to be consumed in another.

The water footprint can be demonstrated by the water consumed to make a cup of coffee: farmers need water to grow the beans. The workers on the plantation have to cook and wash, the coffee needs to be cleaned. Water is needed for refining, transportation and, of course, when making the final drink. Twente University came to the conclusion that 200 litres of water, which is more than the amount that fits into a full bathtub, are needed to produce one cup of coffee. Steak is another good example. A cow lives around three years before it is slaughtered and of course it would not survive without drinking water. Additionally it is fed corn, which is grown using intensive farming methods which are produced with water. Not forgetting the stables that need to be cleaned, no less than 15,500 litres of virtual water is required. In this calculation by the World Wildlife Fund (**WWF**), the water that is sometimes contaminated in the intensive farming process is not even calculated. According to the US Environmental Protection Agency, it takes nearly 4 litres of water to process a hamburger and 39,090 gallons of water to manufacture the average new car. As countries like China and India move away from agrarian economies where meat eating was exceptional rather than the norm, great strain is being put on diminishing water resources. The water required for a meat-eating diet is twice as much as is needed for a 2,000-litre-a-day vegetarian diet.

Managing water resources better is now essential to protect human life and allow society to prosper. **Sustainable development** requires not only engineering solutions but also a change of mindset towards **sustainability** like conserving, re-using and managing water better. It means thinking about river catchment areas as a whole. Huge, wasteful irrigation projects plus evaporation and pipe leakage must be addressed. Stopping pollution before it reaches water sources and completely rethinking industrial processes not only in production industries but also in service industries is necessary.

CASE STUDY 5.1 Bali's hospitality industry threatened by looming water crisis

Bali is world famous for its white sand beaches, turquoise seas and picture-perfect paddy fields, and attracts around 2.5 million foreign tourists yearly to its 1250-plus hotels. Tourism directly supports 55 per cent of the population and 30 per cent of the Gross National Product. It is ironic that in such a lush tropical island with a wet season spanning six months of the year, water scarcity is an issue. Tourism is a major contributor to this impending crisis and, most specifically, the island's hotel industry.

The water crisis in Bali is primarily due to a lack of infrastructure. Aquifers are depleted as more and more hotels are built. Instead of trapping the rainwater in reservoirs, it runs often directly into the sea since forests have been cleared for urbanization and the rain is free to run away off the concrete and tarmac that now covers large urban areas. Much waste water leaches back into waterways, paddy fields and onto beaches, threatening the health of local people and tourists. Over 50 per cent of infant deaths are caused by diseases related to poor sanitation, water and **environment** according to Bali's Ministry of Health. The problem is compounded by inadequate tap water treatment which can harbour bugs.

Access to safe, clean water is a fundamental human right. Water underpins the rights of all people to live in dignity and protect **food security**. However, in Bali, the wealth and power of the tourism business mean that huge amounts of water are diverted away from fertile rice paddies towards hospitality operations. Local villagers reported to Tourism Concern that lack of water is dominating their lives. Water also has a great religious significance in Bali; paddy fields have traditionally been built around water temples. Thus, the conversion of paddy fields to concrete also symbolizes the erosion of an important aspect of Bali's traditional **social** and cultural fabric.

Thankfully, alarm bells are starting to sound in Bali. The government has announced the opening of a water purification centre and sewage network. Bali's Environmental Agency has threatened to revoke the operating licences of hotels and restaurants that fail to properly dispose of their waste and sewage.

Tourism Concern, under their Water Equity in Tourism programme (WET), is helping set up **water management** projects in other water-deprived tourist destinations. However, protecting water resources and ensuring that the water rights of local communities are respected is also the responsibility of the international tourism industry and individual hotels.

Source: Tourism Concern, September 2011, http://www.tourismconcern.org.uk/news.

Water consumption in the hospitality industry

Precise amounts for water consumption in hotel operations are difficult to come by. Direct water use varies between 100 and 2,000 litres per guest night, with a tendency for larger, resort-style hotels to use significantly more water than guest and pension-like establishments. Golf courses, irrigated gardens, swimming pools, spas, wellness facilities and guest rooms are the greatest users of water. In 2003, **UNEP** estimated that in the USA, all tourism and recreation sites put together, including hotels, consumed 946 million cubic metres of water per year, of which 60 per cent is linked to lodging and another 13 per cent to food service. Total yearly water consumption by tourism across Europe is estimated to be 843 million cubic metres, with each tourist consuming 300 litres of fresh water per day on average. 'Luxury' hotel guests are estimated to consume up to a staggering 880 litres per day. On a per capita basis, hotel guests and tourist activities demand more water than local residents. By comparison, average per capita residential consumption in Europe is estimated at 241 litres per day. Five-star hotels in Dubai use 225 per cent more energy than their counterparts in Europe and use between 650 and 1230 litres of water per guest per day. However, many hoteliers are aware of the consumption issues and have started to actively implement various environmental tactics, including **certification**, to reduce the overall usage of resources.

The **hospitality industry** and tourism in general present a number of challenges for the management of water supplies. In tourist destinations and regions there is often a geographical dimension to water supply. The most popular tourist destinations are located in regions with warmer climates and low rainfall, especially during the peak tourist season. Mediterranean climates are the most badly affected in this respect. Moreover, such countries often have a natural predisposition to drought. The annual influx of tourists increases the demand for water well beyond the normal requirements of residents and the possibilities of local water sources. Thus, water supply and demand are usually mismatched seasonally and often dislocated geographically from one another.

While water use by tourism, on a global basis, is far less important than agriculture, industry or urban domestic use, in some countries and regions, hospitality operations can be the main user in water consumption. The industry can also directly affect water quality, for instance, through the discharge of untreated sewage. For example, in the Mediterranean, only 30 per cent of municipal wastewater from coastal towns receives any treatment before discharge. Other coastal tourist destinations around the world are suspected of not faring any better.

Creative, but not entirely sustainable, solutions to solving water shortages in tourist areas have been to ship water in from far away and to produce drinking water from seawater, i.e. desalination. Many Mediterranean islands have to be supplied from the mainland due to water scarcity. Water tankers supply many of the Greek islands on a daily basis and at one time the Spanish island of Majorca was supplied by water coming from the Ebro Valley in Catalonia, in north-eastern Spain. The scheme was abandoned after a few years, due partly to the expense but also because of opposition from the population in north-eastern Spain. The local population in the Ebro Basin protested at the extraction of 'their' water supplies and the environmental damage caused to the wetlands of the Ebro delta.

Compared to fresh water from rivers and groundwater, desalination requires large amounts of energy, usually in the form of fossil fuels, as well as specialized expensive infrastructure. In Dubai, as in other Middle Eastern countries, desalination is used to provide most of the region's needs in water. In fact, the rapid development of the United Arab Emirates has been made possible due to the desalination plants powered by cheap fossil fuel. During the process large quantities of brine are produced that are normally pumped back in the sea. Critics point out the high costs of desalination technologies in terms of the energy required and the marine **pollution** when the brine is pumped back into the oceans at high temperatures.

CASE STUDY 5.2 Greywater recycling and reuse in a hotel building: the Dead Sea, Jordan

In February 2012, a drought was officially declared by the UK government in the south-west of England, however, some countries like Jordan have been fighting against water shortages for decades. Until 2009, during the peak season, the four-star Dead Sea Spa Hotel used to hire a private water supplier to fill the hotel's water tank up to ten times every day. Both financially and environmentally this is a heavy burden. Approximately 80 per cent of the wastewater generated daily by each hotel room at a wellness facility like the Dead Sea Spa Hotel takes the form of greywater. This water comes from baths, showers and wash basins, and can be treated and reused.

Increased business during the last few years meant it was more critical for the hotel owner, Ramzi Nazzal, to try new ways of managing water at the resort. The Dead Sea Spa Hotel became a pilot operation and the first company in the Arab world to install a modern greywater **recycling** plant that allows greywater to be reused within a single building. Using Pontos GmbH's AquaCycle system, greywater from the Dead Sea Spa Hotel is now being turned into high quality industrial service water that meets the hygiene requirements of the EU Bathing Water Directive. Saving 17 per cent of total water consumption in the hotel required an investment in the greywater system of US$80,000. The water is treated without chemical additives in an entirely mechanical-biological process and is subsequently used to flush toilets in 170 guest bedrooms.

With support from the Jordanian water authorities and technical assistance from Deutsche Gesellschaft für Technische Zusammenarbeit (GTZ) GmbH on behalf of the German Federal Ministry for Economic Cooperation and Development (BMZ), a public–private partnership was formed to manage the project. In the first stage Pontos evaluated the biodegradability of the greywater and fine-tuned their equipment to take account of the local high temperatures, local cleaning products and cosmetics used in the spa.

In the next phase, the hotel's technical staff and a group of local plumbers received training to ensure optimum efficiency of the system. Newly installed water balances in both buildings enable exact water inventories to be drawn up, thus determining the saving potential. The Jordanian authorities are now using this information as the basis for drawing up guidelines on greywater management. Following this success, GTZ and Pontos are working to develop other similar greywater recycling plants in the Aqaba region in Jordan in the coming years.

Source: Public Private Partnerships (PPP) Measure, 'Greywater recycling in hotels in Jodan', January 2010. Additional information on the programme is available at: www. develoPPP.de.

Water conservation in hotels

Water **conservation** is perhaps not the first issue that crosses a hospitality manager's mind when making out the management agenda. Issues such as revenue management, marketing and personnel are prioritized. However, from the perspective of the guest, the use of water is an integral part of his or her experience. Water restrictions would result in unhappy guest stays and so maintaining adequate water comfort must be central to all water management strategies. Purchasing water and the disposal of dirty water are becoming increasingly expensive activities. Issues of water scarcity push up prices and as profit margins in the hospitality industry are relatively small, the astute manager's attention is becoming focused on this subject.

The important message for managers, owners and the public is that water efficiency and management programmes in rooms and facilities, together with investments in water-saving technology, all reduce costs and help save a diminishing resource. Alternative hotel garden landscaping, as well as the use of greywater, can make considerable reductions in the grounds outside hotel properties possible. Irrigation of gardens can be optimized by measuring soil moisture content and watering after sunset. Golf courses, hotels with spas and health centres can engage in a range of water-saving initiatives, while new hotel constructions can seek to avoid pool landscapes and other water-intensive uses.

Any water use reduction programme must have the full support of the staff. Some hotels have estimated that only a small percentage of water used is actually consumed by the guest, the remainder is used by the chambermaids during cleaning. Water is a crucial resource for the hospitality industry, as depicted in Figure 5.1.

As with energy and waste, the approach towards decreasing water consumption is to regularly train staff on how they can contribute with simple measures towards decreased water consumption. In contrast, Webster (2000) warns that water policies should not have a negative effect on a hotel's hygiene and cleanliness.

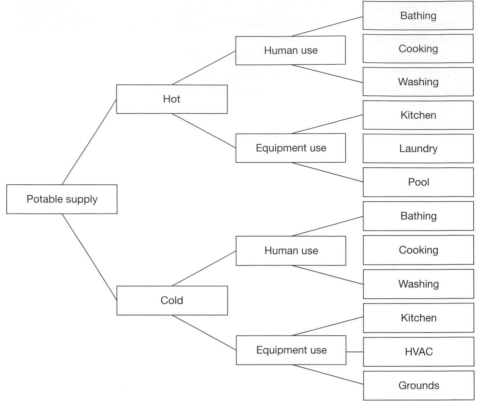

FIGURE 5.1 Building water systems and uses

The attention of all staff needs to be focused on water consumption, repairing small leaks produces immediate gains, hundreds of litres of water can be lost each week in a toilet cistern that is not functioning properly. While the bulk of water consumption in a hotel takes place in the guestrooms (guest showers, sinks and toilets), the kitchen operations, the laundry and the public areas in hotels can represent close to half the water consumption. General awareness, correct staff training and water metering on each floor give employees a clear indication of how much they are using in relation to other colleagues and allow the hotel to set up clear **benchmarking** systems. Water conservation in hospitality operations is achieved as in the management of waste: reduce, reuse and recycle. Water management systems should not affect guest satisfaction.

Water use reduction in hospitality operations

Water use in a hotel is comparable to household consumption, but on a much larger scale. Hospitality operations by definition resemble well-run homes from laundry facilities to kitchens, guestroom toilets and shower heads to irrigation for the gardens. It is estimated that up to 50 per cent of the water that families use could be saved by implementing simple conservation methods, in many cases, the same can be said for hotels.

According to Fairmont Hotels Green Partnership Programme: A Practical Guide to Greening Your Hotel, extraordinary amounts of water use can be conserved by maintaining taps, valves and pipes, maintaining and upgrading toilets, **retrofitting** shower heads with low flow, reusing greywater and involving guests in the conservation process.

Many water-saving technologies installed by hotels and other businesses have short payback times, making them economically attractive. Investments in water-saving systems, greywater reuse and rainwater collection and management systems can help reduce water consumption by 1045 m^3 per year, or a 27 per cent lower volume per guest per night according to the Rainforest Alliance (2010). In research they carried out in 14 hospitality businesses in Latin America (Belize, Costa Rica, Ecuador, Guatemala and Nicaragua), the Rainforest Alliance found the water bill was reduced in 31 per cent of companies, with average annual savings of US$2718, a particularly large number given the very low price of water charged in those countries. Required investment ranged from 1–3 per cent of annual operations costs (US$2,884–US$10,000). Average annual savings were US$2718, for a payback period of 1.1 years (Rainforest Alliance, 2010).

The first step in water management is an efficiently designed and maintained plumbing system. A gravity-fed cold and hot water system delivering low pressure water uses less water than a mains pressure hot water system. Reducing the water pressure from 100 pounds per square inch (psi) to 50 psi can reduce water use by approximately one-third. Such a system might be practicable in lodges and guest houses situated in rural areas but in large hotels guests are used to high pressure showers.

A small leak from a cold water tap, say, a small coffee cup per minute may seem insignificant but over a whole day, nearly a cubic metre of water would be wasted, costing several Euros per day including sewer charges. If this was a hot water tap, the cost would be doubled, based on the energy required to heat the water. Repairing a leaky tap is as simple as replacing a washer. Regular maintenance always pays.

Sinks and showers

Conventional twist taps use around 4 litres per hand wash; water-efficient fixtures can reduce this to 2 litres or less. Flow-controllers or low-flow fixtures can be installed in plumbing where water pressure is less important as in food preparation areas and public toilets. This technology can also be used in showerheads and for baths if the management wishes. Further reductions can be achieved by implementing tap aerators. These spray devices create fine water jets that incorporate air and reduce water flow to 5 litres per minute. Showers in public areas like spas and pools should be equipped with push buttons that limit the water flow to a certain duration. A novel way of encouraging guests to stay in the shower for less time is to place an egg timer in the shower with signage inviting guests to monitor their time spent. The latest generation of sink taps are equipped with infra-red sensors that automatically turn off when a person walks away or when the allotted quantity per wash has been delivered. Again, this system is fine for public areas but can be inconvenient in guest rooms where a hand has to be waved in front of the light to keep it flowing.

Toilets and urinals

Another water-intense facility in hotel bedrooms is toilets and urinals. Conventional flush toilets are responsible for up to 40 per cent of domestic water use. Putting a displacement device or a tank restrictor in the cistern will reduce the cistern capacity but a more efficient solution is to fit a low-flush toilet that uses less than 4 litres of water per flush, cutting water use in half. There are many different models including: dual flush toilets, with a lower flush option for fluids and a standard flush level for solids; gravity toilets, that depend on gravity alone; and pressure-assisted toilets that combine gravity with compressed air.

The Willard Intercontinental in Washington, DC, in the USA, has implemented water-free urinals, resulting in savings of nearly 400,000 litres of water a year since 2005. Environmentally friendly solutions are also used in the laundry which results in saving tonnes of chemicals from entering the water system.

Dry composting toilets

Dry **composting** toilets and urinals are the most water-efficient toilets on the market, using no water at all. They use biological processes to deal with the disposal and processing of human excrement into organic compost material. Waste is transported to a composting chamber below the toilet by gravity; vacuum-flush systems can flush horizontally or upward. There are also commercial systems that use a small amount of water, 'micro-flush', usually about 0.5 litres per use. All work on the same principle: waste material in the toilet is composted in a separate chamber with no interruption of the process, no unpleasant smell and minimal exposure to unprocessed material. Compost toilet systems are beginning to compete with and replace conventional toilets in public facilities. One example is in the University of British Columbia, Canada, in the C.K. Choi Building which contains five compost chambers with 12 toilets for 300 full-time employees. Additionally, they produce nutrient-rich compost for use in the establishment's garden.

Modern water flush urinals are equipped with passive infrared sensors that ensure an economical amount of water is used to flush the urinal after each use. Even better are urinals that do not need to be flushed at all, they are coated with nano-particles creating a hygienic film. A cartridge placed at the bottom of the urinal acts as a funnel directing flow through the liquid sealant, preventing any odours from escaping. This cartridge collects sediment and allows the remaining waste to pass freely down the drain.

Laundry

Hotels that operate laundries on the premises have several options to reduce water consumption. The first is to use front loading machines that consume less water and less detergent than top loading models. Front loaders also have improved spinning performance and extract more water, thus, reducing drying times. A further way to reduce laundry is guest participation in towel and linen programmes where guests have the option to use the same sheets and towels for more than one day. Most guests appreciate these initiatives although in five-star luxury hotels some managers report guest resistance and reluctance to apply reuse programmes.

The Fairmont Royal York in Toronto saves 476,000 litres of water per day by having an installed water softener that reduces water use for laundry. The Otani Hotel in Tokyo, Japan, constructed a water recycling plant, producing 1,000 cubic metres of recycled water daily from kitchen sewage to be used in gardens or staff lavatories.

Swimming pools and spas

Warmer water evaporates more quickly than cooler water, which keeps the pool cooler with slow evaporation. However, this measure could seriously affect guest comfort and satisfaction and should be instituted with care. Pool covers will also reduce evaporation and have the added advantage of reducing heat loss in cooler climates.

Natural swimming pools

Natural swimming pools work on the same principles as ponds and lakes to produce clear and clean water. Natural swimming pools are purposely built to use nature's purifying properties of plants and micro-organisms to produce perfectly healthy swimming water. The basic difference between a natural pool and a conventional swimming pool is that the latter uses chemicals such as chlorine to kill bacteria. Plants and natural organisms are used in natural swimming pools to completely eliminate impurities and bacteria and the need for chemicals and constant cleaning. Natural swimming pools have the added advantage of being a water feature in the grounds of a hotel.

Gardens and water features

Water conservation is important in good garden maintenance. In an attempt to create a prestigious and luxuriant landscape around the property some owners unfortunately use plant varieties that require constant artificial watering. The first rule must be to plant indigenous plant species where possible that are best adapted to the local climate and soil conditions. Such varieties will also save on fertilizers and pesticides. Grass is an example that in many areas requires much attention and is highly water- and fertilizer-intensive. Many properties over-water simply because employees do not understand what the plants require. Watering should also take place either early in the morning or late in the day to reduce the possibility of evaporation in hot weather. Properties investing in fountains and water features should turn off appliances at night and consider the use of greywater.

Waste water recycling

Greywater and blackwater are the two kinds of waste water produced in all buildings and hospitality operations. Greywater comes from baths, sinks, showers and kitchens and can be recycled and reused for watering the garden or flushing toilets. Blackwater comes from toilets, and contains harmful pathogens. It must be properly treated before being discharged into the environment. Reusing greywater for flushing toilets can save up to 50 per cent of domestic water use, but requires some form of treatment such as filtering and disinfectant to remove bacteria and other biological material. If used directly for watering the garden, greywater can be left untreated, but only biodegradable non-toxic household cleaning and toiletry products should be used in the water system. Great care must be taken if using water coming from restaurant kitchens as fats and other additives might be present, resulting in the need for a more sophisticated treatment. Both blackwater and greywater can be effectively recycled on-site using constructed wetlands or reed bed systems.

Rainwater collection systems

Rainwater can be collected from roofs, from driveways and other paved areas, and then, after being filtered, it can be channelled into a cistern or rainwater tank for storage. This water is then used in the garden, or for toilet flushing. Collected rainwater can be used in evaporative cooling equipment for air-conditioning (likewise seawater) or for fire protection systems. Installing point-of-use water heaters ensures that cold water is not wasted while waiting for hot water to come through the taps. Well-lagged and properly positioned pipes will also help keep water hot. Along with plumbing design, water conservation is achieved through the specification and installation of water-efficient appliances and fittings.

CASE STUDY 5.3 Soneva Resorts: clean water for all

One of the key focus areas of the Soneva Resorts is **water management.** Water is seen as an abundant resource, but unfortunately only 2 per cent of all water resources are fresh water and only 1 per cent is available for human consumption.

Soneva resorts are often situated in remote areas where water access is scarce. For this reason, the resorts try to source water sustainably, preferably through rainwater catchment if possible, but in certain instances desalination plants are necessary.

Soneva Resorts also have a zero discharge policy. The resorts have wastewater treatment plants where the treated wastewater is reused, preferably for garden irrigation. The wastewater treatment plants vary depending on location from aerobic gravel filtration plants, anaerobic STP plants and wetland.

Wellness Water Initiative

The Wellness Water Initiative started in 2008 when the properties banned imported water. Instead the resort serves its own produced drinking water – still or sparkling or local water. This groundbreaking initiative was in recognition of the considerable and unnecessary carbon emissions resulting from the shipping of drinking water great distances – often by air - and supports Soneva's move towards a greater use of local and seasonal produce to reduce carbon footprints while adding value to community partnerships.

The drinking water is produced to the highest international drinking water EPA standards, being processed on-site at each one of the resorts. Following stringent filtration, the initial step is carbon and resin filtration followed by reverse osmosis and further ultra-violet purification. The water is then remineralized to make it into a high quality mineral water. Aeration is added to the sparkling style. Bottling is in glass only, sealed with an airtight ceramic stopper clipped in place with a metal clasp. Although use of glass may be the costlier alternative, its use avoids the potential for cross-over contamination recently identified with some plastic bottles.

To further enhance health benefits, the water is poured over VitaJuwel rods and served as Wellness Water. The VitaJuwel rods are gemstones in a crystal rod that improves the molecular structure of the water. It can be noticed in the improved texture of the water with the result that more of the water you drink is absorbed in the body.

PICTURE 5.1 Zero discharge policy at Soneva allows for fabulous snorkelling

PICTURE 5.2 Soneva drinking water at Soneva Fushi

Clean water projects

Sonevas Resorts felt that it was not enough just to stop imports of water and wanted to help tackle water-related issues. The pressing issues are:

* United Nations Millennium Development Goal's number 7 target is to halve, by 2015, the proportion of the population without sustainable access to safe drinking water and basic sanitation.
* 1 billion people globally do not have access to safe drinking water.
* 2.5 billion lack access to basic sanitation services.
* 4 children die of water-related disease every minute.

Source: World Health Organization and the United Nations.

The paradox is that, according to the Earth Policy Institute, a doubling of the world's US$15 billion annual spending is required to reach the goal. However, this is nothing compared to the US$100 billion spent on bottled water annually.

Sonevas Resorts decided to do their part and have since October 2009 dedicated 50 per cent of their water sales to provide clean water for people without access to this vital resource. Two projects providing safe drinking water and basic sanitation services have been implemented, which will last at least 10 years. The funds are distributed through Soneva SLOW LIFE Trust, which funds partner organizations. The main partner organizations have been Water Charity and Thirst-Aid.

As of January 2012:

* 562,787 people have been helped through projects either in progress or completed.
* 432 projects (402 completed) in 51 countries have been initiated.

The aim is to expand on the results achieved through Soneva SLOW LIFE Trust. Currently two consultants has been engaged to establish an industry-wide Hotel Water Campaign to get other hospitality companies to follow suit by banning imports of water, banning plastic bottles and to give a small percentage to clean water projects to help people without access to clean water. The Hotel Water Campaign is due to be launched in 2012 and the hope is to get some of the big hotel chains to join. This will enable the industry to make a huge difference and to help millions of people.

Water Charity

Water Charity is a registered charity in the USA and operates in more than 60 countries (Asia, Africa, Central America, Europe, etc.). It has 8,000 volunteers through a network of **NGOs**, mainly Peace Corps volunteers. The volunteers ensure sustainability in the projects by training locals to do maintenance, which creates jobs/micro business that looks after the finished project. They provide systems depending on needs: complete systems, catchments, reservoir, water filters, repair of existing systems, etc.

Water Charity was chosen because of its ability to implement clean water projects with great impact, fast. They have divided their projects into two categories:

- *Water Charity projects*: these projects implement practical solutions to provide safe water, effective sanitation and meaningful health education to those in need for the long term.
- *Appropriate project initiative*: these projects are designed to undertake small water and sanitation development all over the world in the immediate future, which will cost no more than US$550 and use appropriate technology and will be completed in 30 days.

As of January 2012:

- 306 projects have been completed and 28 are in progress.
- 486,291 people have been helped.
- Locations:
  - Asia: Thailand, Cambodia, the Philippines, Mongolia, Vietnam, Japan
  - Central America: Guatemala, El Salvador, Panama
  - Caribbean: Jamaica, Dominican Republic, Togo
  - South America: Paraguay, Peru, Bolivia, Ecuador, Brazil, Suriname
  - Africa: Senegal, Malawi, Rwanda, Gambia, Morocco, Mali, Swaziland, Tanzania, Burkina Faso, Cameroon, Liberia, Botswana, Ghana, Benin, Zambia, Kenya, South Africa, Namibia, Ethiopia, Madagascar, Togo, Uganda
  - Europe: Georgia, Moldova, Ukraine, Armenia
  - Oceania: Micronesia, Fiji, Samoa, Western Samoa.

Thirst-Aid

Thirst-Aid is a registered charity in the USA and operates in Myanmar. They have established five ceramic water filter (CWF) factories in Myanmar, which employ 143 people – three other factories were established privately. They work with other NGOs, such as UNICEF, who fund the purchase of CWFs, which Thirst-Aid quality control install and provide education on their use. Furthermore, they provide local partnerships and education programmes. In Myanmar, 16 million people rely on ponds, lakes and rivers as drinking water, and they do not know if they are polluted or not. Hence education and CWF are necessary to make the water safe.

As of January 2012, in Myanmar:

- 79 projects have been completed and 2 are in progress.
- 46,440 people have been helped.
- 5,000 ceramic water filters have been distributed.

Source: Soneva Resorts, http://www.soneva.com/.

EXERCISES

1   GROUP DISCUSSION, GROUP PROJECT OR WRITTEN ASSIGNMENT

Simple water management checklist

- Create an activity checklist which could be used at a hotel to manage water.

  Minimum requirements:
  - one managing activity regarding water storage
  - one managing activity regarding water distribution network
  - three activities to reduce water use in housekeeping
  - three activities to reduce water use via retrofitting
  - three activities to reduce water via refurbishment
  - one activity to reuse treated water
  - one activity to use rainwater.

2   GROUP DISCUSSION OR GROUP PROJECT

Water waste

- Find examples of water waste, either in your region or in another country. The focus of the research can be on agricultural, industrial or domestic usage of water. Summarize your findings and discuss.

3   GROUP PROJECT OR WRITTEN RESEARCH

Water stewardship

The United Nations predict that by 2030, 50 per cent of the world's population will live in water-stressed areas.

- Should a hotel find out where, when and how it will be affected by water scarcity?
- What should a hotel water management strategy look like?

4   GROUP RESEARCH AND DISCUSSION

A question of water

Provide answers and critically discuss the following questions:

- What are the issues surrounding water availability in tourism and hospitality developments?
- What are the environmental problems caused to communities and tourist developments when water becomes scarce?
- Describe the process of desalination.
- Describe how hospitality managers can reduce water consumption through the use of technology.

References

Rainforest Alliance (2010) *Allies in Sustainability*. Available at: http://www.rainforest+-alliance.org/sites/default/files/publication/pdf/AR10_web.pdf.

UNEP (2009) 'New UN report warns of increasing pressure on water', press relese, 16 March 2009. Available at: http://www.unep.org/ecosystemmanagement/News/PressRelease/tabid/426/language/en-US/Default.aspx?DocumentID=573&ArticleID=6101&Lang=en7.

Webster, K. (2000) *Environmental Management in the Hospitality Industry*, New York: Cassell.

Resources

Energy Saving Trust: http://energysavingtrust.org.uk.

International Tourism Partnership: http://www.tourismpartnership.org/.

Saving Water: http:// savingwater.org/business_hotels.htm.

US Environmental Protection Agency: http://www.epa.gov/.

Additional material

Go to www.routledge.com/cw/sloan to find PowerPoint slides of all the figures and tables from the book, additional case studies, a test bank of questions and extra links to useful videos.

Eco-design in hospitality architecture

CHAPTER OBJECTIVES

The objectives for this chapter are:

- To explain the impacts buildings and hotels have on the environment
- To describe the waste created and the resources used in the construction of a hospitality operation
- To describe the principles of sustainable architectural design
- To explain the priorities of sustainable design
- To explain the theory of embodied energy
- To describe sustainable certification and rating systems for buildings

COMPANION @ WEBSITE

The **hospitality industry** constitutes one of the most energy- and resource-intensive branches of the **tourist** industry. Energy efficiency in facilities designed for hospitality is frequently low and the resulting **environmental impacts** are typically greater than those caused by other types of buildings of a similar size. The negative effects on the **environment** during the construction phase are caused by the excessive consumption of non-renewable resources, e.g. water, electricity and fuel, as well as by emissions into the air, groundwater and soil.

Many hospitality travellers demand a lot from hospitality facilities. They expect a high level of comfort and service in accommodation and food and beverage operations, they also desire experiences that cater to their needs and wants. In addition, the modern guest wishes to feel that his or her actions are environmentally responsible, they want an earth-conscious experience that will ensure their hospitality stay caters both to them and the world in which they live. The concepts of service and ecology once appeared to be polar opposites in the hospitality industry. The traditional idea shared by both the consumer and the property was that, in introducing more **sustainable** and environmentally friendly alternatives, the property would sacrifice ambience, comfort and the guest's enjoyable experience. Thanks to technological advancements and greater environmental knowledge, this is no longer so. In the majority of cases, major energy saving can be achieved by adopting a common-sense approach, requiring neither advanced expertise nor excessive investments. This is particularly true when the concepts of energy efficiency and resource **conservation** are already accounted for when planning and designing a hotel facility. In recent years this process has become known as **eco-architecture**, eco-design, green design or sustainable design.

Impacts of buildings on the environment

The construction industry is one of the most conspicuous forms of economic activity and has enormous environmental impact. During a building's existence, it affects the local and global environments via a series of interconnected human activities and natural processes. At the early stage, site development and construction influence the local ecology and landscape. The procurement and manufacturing of building materials impact the global environment. Construction materials are responsible for tremendous damage through mining, **deforestation** and other **impacts** resulting from their production and supply. Without major changes in practices, at some point in this century we will simply run out of some of the key resources required to keep up with the explosive growth in building demand. Resources are exploited at a much greater rate than the planet can sustain. As a society's economic status improves, its demand for architectural resources – land, buildings or building products, energy and other resources – will increase. This in turn increases the combined impact of architecture on the global **ecosystem**, which is made up of inorganic elements, living organisms and humans. Once built, the building inflicts a long-lasting impact on the environment. For instance, the energy and water used by its inhabitants produce toxic gases and sewage; the process of extracting, refining and transporting all the resources used in the building operation and maintenance also have numerous effects on the environment. From a climate perspective alone, **greenhouse gas** emissions from buildings are significant and growing fast. While most current efforts in sustainable construction projects are put into energy efficiency, **sustainability** is not limited to this aspect. Another apparent trend is that still too often thoughts on how to make new buildings 'green' are only addressed in the final stages of construction. The vast majority of successful sustainability elements in a construction project have to be integrated into the initial design. While the practice of **retrofitting** is relevant to older buildings, it is the wrong approach for new buildings.

Climate change

The construction industry is one of the most highly energy-intensive of all industries. It creates large amounts of CO_2 emissions, **pollution** and waste and uses most non-energy-related resources. The UK Association for Environment Conscious Building (AECB, 2009) estimates that building use in the UK contributes about 50 per cent of the UK's CO_2 emissions and the construction industry contributes about another 7 per cent. The AECB has shown that the government figures on energy performance of houses grossly underestimate the CO_2 gains that could be made by building energy-efficient buildings and refurbishing existing buildings.

Construction waste

According to the UK Department for Environment, Food and Rural Affairs (DEFRA, 2011), the waste going to landfill from the construction industry in 2009 was about 120 million tonnes or more than three times the amount of domestic waste collection. More than 25 million tonnes of this is sent straight to landfill without any form of recovery or re-use. In many situations this is equivalent to one house being buried in the ground for every thirs house built. This is an important consideration when the **embodied energy** of a building is being calculated. Usually such calculations do not take into account an extra 25 per cent energy for waste. This is obviously more serious for higher embodied energy products than low embodied energy products.

There are increasing regulations on waste disposal after construction and many products, even common products like gypsum plasterboard and mineral wool insulation, are now labelled as hazardous and require special disposal. In addition, there are many projects to find new uses for waste construction materials (through the UK government bodies such as WRAP). However, here, as with waste disposal, the less processed and hazardous a material is, the easier re-use, **recycling** or healthy disposal (for example, through composting) will be.

Resource use

Some 90 per cent of all non-fuel minerals consumed and a large proportion of timber are used by the construction industry. Many of the materials come from countries with weak environmental control or little labour justice. The global community exceeded sustainable levels of consumption of building materials in the mid-1980s, so from both the point of view of human survival and of justice and equity; it is not feasible or desirable to continue at current levels of resource use in the construction industry. Some material used in the industry is sustainable, i.e. renewable resources, particularly those that are grown in short time cycles, such as certain kinds of timber and plentiful resources such as clay, chalk and sand. In addition, materials which can be indefinitely re-used or recycled easily are to some extent sustainable. Copper wiring and lead flashing fall into this category, although supplies are rapidly diminishing. Sustainability in terms of building material is a relative term. Items built with sustainable material such as bricks, soft wood flooring and ceramic tiles, etc.

often travel long distances from the point of production to the building site, incurring a substantial **carbon footprint** in the process. Non-sustainable resources are those where total global supply is limited such as many minerals, oil and some exotic slow-growing timber. It is perhaps interesting to reflect on traditional building techniques where only the material that could be carried by a horse and cart or on a boat would be used for buildings.

Many essential materials are now in short supply. These include materials such as copper, which is largely mined in South America, where whole mountains have been taken down and landscapes altered in the search for ever more rare resources. They include materials like titanium ore, which is used for the production of titanium dioxide, which is one of the main ingredients of paint, among other things. This is often mined in rare habitats such as Madagascar with consequential and inevitable dangers to the ecology.

Of course, it is possible to mine and extract materials from habitats without destroying them. However, there will always be consequences to this benign form of extraction in terms of cost, speed and quantity. It is therefore imperative that we radically reduce our demand on such materials in order to allow this process to happen benignly. At present, the whole world is heading in the opposite direction, and we will lose huge areas of unique habitat forever in the coming years unless we change the way we consume such materials. This is particularly true with regards to construction work. It means using less of these materials by building more simply, with more local and plentiful (i.e. sustainable and renewable) materials and with less waste.

While the three greatest and most imminent threats to the survival of our civilization are **global warming**, peak oil (the growing energy gap between supply and demand), and resource depletion, habitat destruction can have a more immediate and disastrous effect on certain localized areas and species. Sometimes, these can also have a global impact (for example, the impact of the deforestation of the Amazon rainforests).

It is hard to keep track of the number of species made extinct every year, and of the further erosion of **biodiversity** and rare habitats. It is equally hard to relate this destruction to construction use in the UK. However, the fact that the construction industry is such a huge consumer of materials, particularly of imported chemicals, minerals, metals and organic materials such as timber, inevitably means it has a huge impact, and obviously has the greatest impact of any sector in the UK, on habitat erosion and destruction globally.

Concrete could almost be considered to be sustainable since most of its ingredients can often be sourced locally. Portland cement is one of the many constituents of concrete, the glue that holds the other materials together. Concrete is made by mixing cement, sometimes supplementary cementitious materials, water, fine aggregate (sand), coarse aggregate (gravel or crushed stone) with or without other fibres or pigments. As a result of its ubiquity, functionality and flexibility, it has become by far the most popular and widely used construction material in the world. The yearly cement production of 1.6 billion tonnes accounts for about 7 per cent of the global loading of **carbon dioxide** into the atmosphere. Portland cement is not only one of the most energy-intensive materials of construction but is also responsible for a large amount of greenhouse gases. Producing a tonne of Portland cement requires about 4 giga-joules of energy (approximately three-quarters of a barrel of oil, when combusted).

Concrete typically contains about 12 per cent cement and sand, gravel and crushed rock, equalling around 10 to 11 billion tonnes every year. Mining such large quantities of raw materials often results in extensive deforestation, top-soil loss and permanently damages river beds and shorelines when aggregate is extracted. The industry also uses large amounts of fresh water; approximately 1 trillion litres every year. Numerous chemical and mineral admixtures are incorporated into concrete that also represent huge inputs of energy and materials into the final product. After all these inputs, it should be remarked that concrete structures are generally designed for a service life of only 50 years, but examples abound of buildings deteriorating after 20 or 30 years in urban and coastal environments.

Pollution from the construction industry

Finally, the environmental impact of construction is also felt in terms of pollution. This is not in the extraction but in the processing of materials for construction. And again, not surprisingly, the construction industry has the biggest effect of all sectors because of the quantity of materials used in construction. In the past, there was a simple general equation between the amount of pollution and the amount of energy in a process. On the whole the more energy required and processes required, the more waste and the more pollution generated.

Although the processing of many products like plastics, the manufacture of titanium dioxide and the galvanizing of metals are all potentially very polluting, many of these processes are now controlled by legislation in Western nations. Most basic materials and components are now often processed elsewhere. The loss of control of manufacturing processes therefore has a considerable environmental impact. As with habitat destruction, it is difficult to track or control it. Until there is a clear global legislation or **certification**, the construction industry needs to stick with what is inherently non-polluting.

Sustainable architectural design

The goal of **sustainable architectural design** is to find architectural solutions that guarantee the well-being and coexistence of society, the environment and profit-ability. Not only does sustainable architectural design attempt to reduce negative effects on the humans and on the environment, but it also attempts to create greater resource efficiency than found in conventionally constructed buildings. Efficiency means that these buildings save costs in terms of energy and water, while providing at least the same ambient quality. Sustainable architecture starts with sustainable planning. This means that before construction the planners, architects must consider all environmental and **social** impacts. Social impacts can be health, safety, comfort, productivity or quality of life. To assess these impacts, the so-called Social Impacts Assessment (SIA) has been developed. In order to assess the environmental impacts, an **environmental impact assessment (EIA)** is made. Conducting an EIA includes identifying **direct** and **indirect impacts**, assessing the significance of these impacts, identifying measures in order to avoid or reduce them, and establishing strategies for **monitoring** the success of impact avoidance and reduction.

The principles of sustainable architectural design

There are seven principles of sustainable architectural design:

1.   Preserving local vegetation cover.
2.   Energy and resources independence.
3.   The effect of the sun.
4.   Maximizing natural lighting.
5.   The **stack effect**.
6.   Sustainable construction materials.
7.   Embodied energy.

Each principle is described in detail below.

Preserving local vegetation cover

Trees, especially when fully grown, are valuable in terms of biodiversity, whole ecosystems rely on them. They are like sponges absorbing rainwater and releasing it slowly into the environment in drier times. They are also natural mitigators of CO_2 like all vegetation in the process of photosynthesis, converting it into energy with the help of the sun. All too often, construction project managers still choose to clear trees and all vegetation from a construction site. These trees take a long time to re-grow and often the bird and animal life is lost or diminished forever. It makes more sense to preserve them on site and adapt the construction design in consequence. Unfortunately, there are few examples of constructions which have successfully managed to preserve trees and build around them, or even incorporate them within the structure. Sustainable construction means at least displacing trees and re-planting them rather than cutting them down.

   This point becomes increasingly important for locations of natural beauty, rich in biodiversity or untouched forested terrains that are very often preferred for the development of resorts. Resort development projects should then work towards replanting numerous new trees and plants on site. Creating biotopes on buildings is not a fantasy, extensive use of the now well-proven technologies for rooftop gardens and vertical green walls should be made where possible by construction engineers.

Energy and resources independence

Most locations still rely on fossil fuel-based heating in cooler climates. There seems to be no logic for a sustainable building to source its energy from non-renewable supplies that put a heavy load on the environment. There are now options to build construction projects that are completely off-grid and rely on a combination of **renewable energy** sources such as solar, wind and geothermal. With a good design, it is easy to produce more energy than a building actually needs. The same independence concept applies to other resources. In fact, any so-called sustainable building should now seriously look at ways of closing resource loops through projects now proven as feasible and profitable, through initiatives such as:

• collecting and filtering rainwater and re-distributing the excess to the grid;
• producing electricity from renewable sources and redistributing the excess to the grid;
• collecting waste and valuing it by reusing certain types in a closed-loop model or reselling or distributing unwanted items, which in many cases can be seen as valuable resources for other businesses.

Pushing the concept further, some hotels and restaurants are starting to explore the idea of producing part of their food supplies on site or nearby the structures. Vertical farming and eliminating the reliance on external sources are key for the buildings of the future.

The effect of the sun

A fundamental principle of solar design is that the warming effects of the sun's rays should be maximized in the winter and minimized in the summer. This can be achieved in three ways: glazing, orientation and **thermal mass.**

Controlled glazing is the vital component of environmental design. Although glass allows 90 per cent or more of the energy in the sun's rays to pass through, it is a very poor insulator. Double glazing is twice as good (or half as bad) because the small air gap between the sheets of glass is a good insulator. Even so, double glazing still only has the insulating power of a single layer of bricks.

Glass has to be used with precaution, having enough glass to benefit from the free heat of the sun and let in plenty of daylight, but not so much that the house overheats during sunny days and freezes at night.

There are two solutions to this problem: orientation and thermal mass.

Orientation

Correct orientation of the building is crucial for determining the amount of sun it receives, because the direction and height of the sun in high northern latitudes and low southern latitudes change dramatically throughout the year.

- Only surfaces facing south receive sun all year round. For this reason, solar panels and windows that will capture solar warming in winter should face as close to south as possible.
- Surfaces facing north are in the shade all year round. For this reason solar design concentrates insulation and minimizes glazing on this side of a house.
- The winter sun is low, the summer sun is high. Vertical south-facing windows work best to maximize solar heating in the winter as they capture the low winter sun.
- The high summer sun makes it easy to design shading for vertical windows. Only a small overhang is needed to completely shade vertical south-facing windows in summer. This is another strong argument for maximizing south-facing glazing.

Thermal mass

The way in which a building can store and regulate internal heat is known as thermal mass. Buildings with a high thermal mass take a long time to heat up but also take a long time to cool down. As a result, they have a very steady internal temperature.

Buildings with a low thermal mass are very responsive to changes in internal temperature – they heat up very quickly but they also cool down quickly. They are often subject to wide variables in internal temperature.

Brick, concrete and stone have a high thermal mass capacity and are the main contributors to the thermal mass of a building. Water has a very high thermal capacity, so it is well suited to central heating systems. Air has a very low thermal capacity – it warms up fast but cannot stay warm for long. Only when the walls and floors in a building have warmed up will the air stay warm.

Sustainable buildings are designed to have a high thermal mass for several reasons:

- to retain daytime solar gain for night-time heating;
- to keep houses cool during the day in summer;
- to increase the efficiency of the central heating system. A small boiler working at maximum efficiency will slowly and steadily raise the temperature of a building with high thermal mass before turning itself off for a long period. Buildings with a low thermal mass tend to have much wider fluctuations in temperature, and the boiler is constantly switching itself on and off to compensate. The positioning of exterior wall insulation can affect the thermal capacity of a house significantly.

Maximizing natural lighting

Maximizing natural light not only saves light but also creates a better working and relaxing internal environment. The best way to achieve this is once again through good design that takes into account aspects such as building orientation, open concept and the type of material used. Whatever can be done to naturally brighten indoor spaces will reduce the need for artificial lights at a later stage. The vast majority of buildings use artificial lighting during daytime, simply because nobody considered lighting during the design process.

The stack effect

In warm climates, it is very important during the design stage to plan for maximizing the use of natural air flow and cooling. This can be achieved in a range of ways, starting from the orientation of buildings and how they are conceived to amplify and capture air breezes. There are also passive techniques to capture wind and create air flows within buildings through the stack effect or chimney effect.

Air expands and rises when it warms, in a process called convection. In this way, heat moves around rooms and entire buildings. Ventilation with fresh air is vital and convection plays a leading role. Hot air rises and escapes through small gaps in the building fabric at the top of the house. Escaping warm air draws in new cold air through similar gaps at the bottom of the house, this is called the stack effect, or sometimes the chimney effect because it is the same process that draws smoke up a chimney. If badly controlled, the stack effect can produce unwanted cold drafts. However, when carefully controlled, it can produce a low and effective level of natural ventilation. The stack effect is by far the most effective way of keeping a building ventilated in summer. Over the past ten years, sustainable architecture has paid increasing attention to generating the stack effect in order to create natural ventilation, especially in large buildings like hotels. Excessive use of air conditioning (which is a major source of energy usage in warm countries) is the less desirable alternative and often due to poor cooling efficiency design.

Sustainable construction materials

Most construction companies use unsustainable materials such as conventional concrete for their core construction. There are now a number of alternatives, including modified cement that contains a high percentage of recycled material (e.g. fly ash from incineration plants), materials from more sustainable sources (e.g. bamboo, hemp and soft woods from well-managed plantations) or raw materials from natural sources such as clay (e.g. adobe or mud bricks). Moreover, certain construction techniques can significantly reduce the use of structural steel (e.g. Ferro-cement and composite wooden beams) and the amount of material used (e.g. geodesic designs like domes and partial underground structures). Sustainable construction is about integrating a much greater proportion of reused materials in new construction projects (e.g. demolition site rubble, even old automobile tyres have many uses in sustainable construction).

Embodied energy

Sustainable design encapsulates the principle of embodied energy or hidden energy, i.e. the quantity of energy required to manufacture and supply to the point of use, a product, material or service. In the case of sustainable architecture, the extraction, processing, manufacture and transport of the materials needed in the construction of the building must be examined. The embodied energy in the structure of a new hotel is considerable, exceeding the total energy required to heat that hotel for the next 20 years. No hotel can claim to be an eco-hotel if it is constructed from materials that had a major environmental impact elsewhere.

The principle of embodied energy divides new eco-buildings into two distinct groups. The first group of eco-buildings, which at present account for those hotels built along the principles of sustainable architecture, aims at low energy consumption with the most efficient available technology, such as solar water heating panels and photovoltaic panels that produce electricity. Such buildings have a high embodied energy which they try to justify with large savings in their energy consumption, or even by becoming a producer of surplus energy that they can supply to others. The other group of eco-buildings, such as some eco-lodges, aims to achieve the lowest possible embodied energy by using salvaged building material or simple local materials (straw bales, compacted earth bricks, wood-fibre boards, sheep wool, wood frames with wattle and daub) (see Table 6.1). Such buildings usually have higher annual energy consumption and are less durable, but often have a lower overall environmental impact over the course of their lifespan.

TABLE 6.1 Coefficient of embodied energy of building materials (energy needed to produce a given material)

Material	Coefficient
Wood	1
Brick	2
Cement	3
Glass	4
Fibre glass	7
Steel	8
Plastic	30
Aluminium	80

Embodied energy in existing hotel properties

Renovating an existing building will always use less energy than building a new hotel. Even if a new hotel is extremely energy-efficient, it will be many years before it can pay off the energy embodied in its structure. Alternatively, an existing building only has to account for the embodied energy of the materials used for the renovation in its environmental impact analysis. Renovating existing buildings can also positively reinforce conservation and preservation of buildings with cultural or historical value. In comparison to using new buildings it can sometimes be more challenging to use redesign techniques and technology when renovating. Especially when the building has evolved over time, there are often restrictions due to historic status, making an environmentally friendly approach more complicated to implement. However, 'greening' existing buildings provides a great opportunity to cut down on energy consumption and carbon emissions. There are always some technologies available that can be used to improve the environmental performance of old buildings, such as more efficient heating, cooling or ventilation systems.

Other ways to reduce the cost of embodied energy in renovations include:

- *Use local raw building material*: where possible, use local raw building material such as local stone or wood from environmentally managed forest.
- *Avoid materials that have the highest embodied energy*: such as laminated beams, chipboard and hardboard that are bonded with formaldehyde, especially materials coming from far away that embody transport generated energy costs.
- *Use salvaged materials*: using salvaged materials obtained locally from demolition sites or salvage yards effectively cuts down on embodied energy loss other than energy used in transport.

Sustainable design priorities

Economy of resources

By economizing on resources, sustainable architecture reduces the use of non-renewable resources in the construction and operation of buildings. Economizing energy has highest priority in any eco-hotel because the use of non-renewable energy resources has the greatest environmental impact on the average building. So, when there is a limited budget and a conflict of interest, **energy conservation** should be prioritized. As an added bonus, money is saved in the process. The eco-hotel aspires to self-sufficiency and the more it can meet its own needs, the less of a demand it is making on the wider environment. Examples of self-sufficient technologies include: solar space water heating; using waste greywater and rainwater; saving and reusing waste heat; and electricity generation from windmills and photovoltaic solar panels. A hotel that reduces its consumption is a highly efficient low-cost building. It is when the hotel starts meeting its own needs that it becomes a true eco-hotel.

Life cycle design

Traditionally, building materials were reused in times gone by. When a house came to the end of its natural life, the stones, bricks, wood and sometimes fittings were used to make new houses and other useful buildings. The conventional building **life cycle** is now a linear process consisting of four major phases: design; construction; operation and maintenance; and demolition. Environmental issues related to the procurement and manufacturing of building materials or **waste management** are not addressed. A 'cradle-to-grave' approach recognises the environmental consequences of the entire life cycle of architectural resources, from procurement to return to nature. Life cycle design is based on the idea of reusing and recycling architectural materials with no end to their potential usefulness.

Design for humanity and the environment

Design for humanity and the environment is concerned with providing harmony for all parts of the global ecosystem, including mankind, the **flora** and the **fauna**. This humanitarian principle is founded on the belief that mankind should respect his neighbours and the planet. It is deeply rooted in the need to preserve the ecosystems that allow human survival. Building construction must be limited to improving human life within the **carrying capacity** of the planet's resources and ecosystems. Sustainable architecture is about providing built environments in hospitality operations that provide guests with comfort and provide workers with optimal conditions for productivity.

In the context of sustainable development, hospitality ventures must strive to create optimum relationships between people and their environments. Sustainable development should have the absolute minimal impact on the local, regional and global environments.

Management and leadership

Sustainable buildings can only really have a future when all the people who work, live and relax in them follow the ethos of sustainability; the human factor still plays an important role in how resources are used. Management following a clear sustainable management system is essential. Before any building is completed, there is a chain of people involved in the development, including architects, civil servants, developers and designers. All need training in the fundamentals of environmental protection, and the tools to design and construct more sustainably. Consumers, **lifestyle** choices and government support through stricter legislations and incentives will drive the movement forward.

The ultimate aim in sustainable construction is to develop **zero-energy buildings** that have a zero net energy consumption and zero carbon emissions. Zero-energy buildings produce their own energy that is harvested on site and any surplus can be fed back into the grid. The zero-energy design principle is becoming more practical to adopt due to the increasing costs of traditional fossil fuels and their negative impact on the planet's climate and ecological balance. A number of countries and regions have already established long-term targets and regulations that will require zero-energy building construction that will come into effect over the coming years, some as soon as 2016. As a result, the construction industry as a whole, led by Heating, Ventilation and Air-Conditioning (HVAC) vendors, real estate developers, construction companies, as well as renewable energy developers, are in the process of developing products and service lines that will meet demand for zero-energy building and ensure compliance with new regulations.

Rating systems for sustainable buildings

LEED

The United States Green Building Council (USGBC) created the Leadership in Energy and Environmental Design (LEED) programme in the late 1990s. The aim of this green building-rating programme is to certify and rate buildings on their environmental performance. The LEED system rates the building construction, design, the use of materials and the use and consumption of energy. Of all the sustainability categories under review, energy resources account for the largest block. When a company or organization applies for certification, it has to follow a set of guiding principles. Over the years, LEED has become one of the most accepted and best-known international green building rating systems with more than 2500 rated properties worldwide in more than 30 countries all over the world.

CASE STUDY 6.1 Cocoon Boutique Hotel: towards LEED
certification

The Cocoon Boutique Hotel, situated in the heart of Quezon City, the biggest and most progressive city in Metro Manila, claims to be the Philippines' first truly Green Hotel in Quezon City.

With each stay and use of the deluxe amenities at Cocoon, its guests can share the hotel's commitment to environmentally sustainable luxury. The Cocoon endeavours to make significant contributions to save the environment with the goal of achieving LEED (Leadership in Energy and Environmental Design) certification. In addition, the hotel is a venue for community integration, such as youths with disability at the hotel's back-of-house operations. The following list of Cocoon's sustainable facilities and services gives a good overview what hotels can do in order to become more sustainable.

PICTURE 6.1 Front view of the Cocoon Hotel in Manila, the Philippines

The building

- **Rainwater harvesting (RWH)** and groundwater harvesting for toilet flushing, plant irrigation and general house cleaning;
- 100 per cent use of LED lighting;
- all wood, metal roofing and steel grills reclaimed from structures demolished on site;
- use of reclaimed materials for the construction process and re-use to form part of the structure;
- passive cooling through building orientation;
- use of insulation on metal roofing.

The lobby

- Use of natural and renewable materials such as woodstone;
- use of used lighting fixtures;
- front stairwell has natural lighting and ventilation.

The hallway

- Fresh cool air generated from a heat recovery system;
- use of used lighting fixtures;
- use of CCTV and addressable fire alarm systems for security;
- limited traffic access by use of RFID key card system.

PICTURE 6.2 Hotel lobby with sustainable
design features
Source: Daniel Gerber.

PICTURE 6.3 Deluxe room with sustainable
design features
Source: Daniel Gerber.

The rooms

- Inverter type air-conditioners using non-ozone-damaging R410A refrigerant;
- art wall from individual scrap wood pieces;
- large windows for natural lighting;
- fixed windows for sound insulation;
- lower operable awning window to allow fresh air;
- fresh air circulation in guestrooms through natural positive–negative air pressure;
- waste segregation programme;
- linen reuse programme;
- built-in desk and floors using reclaimed solid hardwood.

The bathrooms

- Towels reuse programme;
- eco-certified 100 per cent organic bathroom amenities;
- packaging of toiletries made from plasticized cornstarch, stone, paper and soy ink;
- dual piping system for separate grey water and potable water;
- water-saving taps with aerators and Siphonic jet toilet flushing.

The ballroom

- Low-E laminated glass and insulated double-glazed glass for windows and doors;
- use of eco-friendly cleaning materials throughout the hotel.

Source: Cocoon Boutique Hotel, www.thecocoonhotel.com.

BREEAM

The Building Research Establishment Environmental Assessment Method (BREEAM) is a voluntary measurement rating system for green buildings that was established in the UK by the British Research Establishment. BREEAM is similar in conception to LEED in the USA, Green Star in Australia, DGNB in Germany and HQE in France. Until now, BREEAM has certified more than 100000 buildings.

At previous times used as a pub, restaurant, hotel and originally a coaching house, the Angel Building in Islington, London, has been awarded an Excellent rating by BREEAM for its sustainable features, which include rainwater harvesting, biomass boilers and low-velocity water fittings. The renovated building uses half as much energy per unit area as an existing building of a similar size and function. Also, by retaining much of the original concrete structure, approximately 33,000 tonnes of concrete in the building were diverted from going to landfill and some 7,400 tonnes of carbon dioxide were prevented from being emitted. Other tangible benefits included reduced demolition time, less risk on site, less pollution from dust and lower transport costs. Lastly, the new building was 15 per cent cheaper to create than it would have been, had the previous structure been razed to the ground.

The most stringent form of certification is the German Passivhaus standard, which applies to buildings that reduce their energy requirements so dramatically – by 90 per cent compared with standard construction – that they can forgo heating and cooling systems altogether.

Is hospitality luxury compatible with the environment?

Hospitality luxury and the environment once appeared to be poles apart in the hospitality industry. The traditional idea shared by both the consumer and the property was that environmental friendliness was akin to flickering neon lights in the bedroom and vegetarian nut cutlets in the restaurant. Thanks to technological advancements and creative ideas, this is no longer so. An increasing number of major hotel brands have realized and accepted that the changing luxury market demands that their hotels offer both environmental accountability and a true high-class experience. New, specifically branded, environmentally friendly, five-star properties are now opening. Starwood Capital Group's announcement regarding its new 1 Hotel and Residences brand is a notable entry into this eco-luxury category. Eco-luxury starts with sustainable design and architecture. Hospitality architects and designers are now integrating environmental design into their practices. Whether by developing LEED-certified buildings through the US Green Building Council or just carefully inspecting materials and employing a holistic design strategy, the hospitality industry is moving forward.

Sustainable design does not reduce the guest experience; on the contrary, it can be seen often to enhance the ambience and comfort of the property through, for example, natural light and ventilation. Furthermore, many environmental design solutions are completely invisible to guests and have no sensory impact on the perceived luxury experience. These behind-the-scenes solutions include lower energy use and power consumption, innovative wastewater technologies and natural paints and building materials.

Eco-luxury branding is about the basics: sustainable materials and processes; a conscious knitting together of resources; and the empowerment of everyone, from employees to local artisans and businesses. In the case of new buildings, greener construction and design practices that range from the carpeting and external ceiling systems to the light bulbs and washing machines can all come to define eco-luxury. Not only is eco-luxury common sense, it's also now a common expectation.

CASE STUDY 6.2 Accor's PLANET 21 programme

Accor, the world's leading hotel operator and market leader in Europe, is present in 90 countries with more than 4400 hotels and 530,000 rooms.

With 145,000 employees worldwide, the group has a great leverage effect on fostering sustainable development. In 2011, Accor launched a shared knowledge platform on sustainable development in the hospitality industry that is both free and open to all (http://www.accor.com/en/sustainable-development/planet-21-research.html). In 2012, Accor implemented a new sustainable development strategy: PLANET 21. It defines 21 commitments and ambitious goals looking to 2015 and includes a programme to inform guests and employees and encourage them to contribute to reinventing hotels, sustainably (Figure 6.1).

The new PLANET 21 strategy includes a programme for informing customers and encouraging them to contribute to the hotel's actions and achievements. From booking to room stay and restaurant service, customers will discover a rich and diverse array of educational messages encouraging them to contribute actively to the hotel's action by means of a few simple gestures. The tone of the messages will be friendly and thoughtful, aimed at encouraging customers to participate without ever making them feel guilty.

To guarantee the credibility of this programme, hotels can only use the PLANET 21 messages if they comply with a certain level of performance in terms of sustainable development, assessed according to a list of 65 check points or recognised external certification.

Source: Accor, http://www.accor.com/.

7 pillars 21 commitments	21 quantifiable objectives for 2015
1. Ensure healthy interiors	85 per cent of hotels use eco-labelled products
2. Promote responsible eating	80 per cent of hotels promote balanced dishes
3. Prevent diseases	95 per cent of hotels organize disease prevention training for employees
4. Reduce our water use	15 per cent reduction in water use between 2011 and 2015 (owned/leased hotels)
5. Expand waste recycling	85 per cent of hotels recycle their waste
6. Protect biodiversity	60 per cent of hotels participate in the Plant for the Planet reforestation project
7. Reduce our energy use	10 per cent reduction in energy use between 2011 and 2015 (owned/leased hotels)
8. Reduce our CO_2 emissions	10 per cent reduction in CO_2 emissions between 2011 and 2015 (owned/leased hotels)
9. Increase the use of renewable energy	10 per cent of hotels use renewable energy
10. Encourage eco-design	40 per cent of hotels have at least three eco-designed room components
11. Promote sustainable building	21 new or renovated hotels are certified as sustainable buildings
12. Introduce sustainable offers and technologies	20 per cent of owned and leased hotels offer green meeting solutions
13. Protect children from abuse	70 per cent of hotels have committed to protecting children
14. Support responsible purchasing practices	70 per cent of hotels purchase and promote products originating in their host country
15. Protect ecosystems	100 per cent of hotels ban endangered seafood species from restaurant menus
16. Support employee growth and skills	75 per cent of hotel managers are promoted from internal mobility
17. Make diversity an asset	Women account for 35 per cent of hotel managers[1]
18. Improve quality of worklife	100 per cent of host countries organize an employee opinion survey every two years
19. Conduct our business openly and transparently	Accor is included in 6 internationally-recognised socially responsible investment indices or standards
20. Engage our franchised and managed hotels	40 per cent of all hotels are ISO14001 or EarthCheck-certified[2]
21. Share our commitment with suppliers	100 per cent of purchasing contracts are in compliance with our Procurement Charter 21

FIGURE 6.1   PLANET 21: 7 pillars, 21 commitments and quantifiable objectives for 2015

Notes: 1 Outside Motel 6/Studio 6. 2 Excluding economy segment.

EXERCISES

1 **GROUP PROJECT**

   Checklists

   Develop checklists for environmentally sound:

   • siting

   • building design and orientation

   • renewable energy use

   • construction and selection of building materials.

   Consider these checklists for each of the following hospitality businesses:

   • a 1,000-room city hotel

   • a 25-room mountain guest house

   • a 100-room beach hotel

   • a 15-room holiday village bordering a rainforest

   • a desert campsite for approximately 35 people on desert safari, located 1 kilometre from an oasis.

2 **GROUP PROJECT OR WRITTEN ASSIGNMENT**

   Implementing green technology

   • 'Technology will save the planet' or will it?

   • What is meant by 'green innovation in technology' and what are the consequences for the hospitality industry?

   • What green technology should be implemented by hotels now?

3 **WRITTEN ASSIGNMENT**

   • Are there trials and demonstration projects for environment-friendly building design in your country or region? (These need not be tourism or hospitality businesses.) Arrange a field visit to one of these properties. Include a question-and-answer session with the developers and managers.

   • Write a report of 1500 words on the sustainable design features used and the benefits they are bringing to the property.

4 **GROUP PROJECT OR WRITTEN ASSIGNMENT**

   • Develop an interior decorating and furnishing checklist for:

     − a 500-room city hotel

     − a 25-room rural guest house

   • Use materials produced within your region/country, and in keeping with your region/country's typical and traditional designs and styles.

5 **GROUP RESEARCH AND DISCUSSION**

   A question of eco-design

   Provide answers and critically discuss the following questions:

   • What are the environmental impacts especially of hotels on the environment?

- How can the building construction process said to be polluting?
- Describe the principles of sustainable construction.
- Why are there fewer environmental impacts during the renovation of a building than in construction?
- Explain the sustainable design priorities.

Acknowledgments

The exercises proposed for Chapter 6 (except Exercise 2 and Exercise 6) were originally created by the International Association of Hotel Schools (EUHOFA), the International Hotel & Restaurant Association (IH&RA) and the United Nations Environment Programme (UNEP) in a document entitled *Sowing the Seeds of Change: An Environmental Teaching Pack for the Hospitality Industry* published in 2001 and updated in 2008. Thank you to EUHOFA (http://www.euhofa.org/), IH&RA (http://www.ih-ra.com/), UNEP (http://www.unep.org) and François-Tourisme-Consultants (http://www.francoistourismeconsultants.com).

References

Association for Environment Conscious Building (AECB) (2009) cited in *Natural Buildings, Environmental Impact*. Available at: http://www.natural-building.co.uk/environmental_impact.html.

Department for Environment, Food and Rural Affairs (DEFRA) (2011) *Waste Data Overview*. Available at: http://www.defra.gov.uk/statistics/files/20110617-waste-data-overview.pdf.

Resources

Association of Environment Conscious Builders (AECB): http://www.aecb.net/index.php.

Association pour la Haute Qualité Environnementale (HQE): http://www.assohqe.org/.

Building Research Establishment Environmental Assessment Method (BREEAM): http://www.breeam.org.

Department for Environment, Food and Rural Affairs (DEFRA): http://www.defra.gov.uk/.

Green Building Council of Australia (GBCA): http://www.gbca.org.au/.

Leadership in Energy and Environmental Design (LEED): http://www.usgbc.org/DisplayPage.aspx?CategoryID=19.

United States Green Building Council (USGBC): http://www.usgbc.org/.

World Wildlife Fund (WWF): http://www.panda.org.

Additional material

Go to www.routledge.com/cw/sloan to find PowerPoint slides of all the figures and tables from the book, additional case studies, a test bank of questions and extra links to useful videos.

CHAPTER

7

Food security

CHAPTER OBJECTIVES

The objectives for this chapter are:

- To analyse the world food crisis
- To describe the challenges with conventional agriculture
- To discuss genetically modified food
- To analyse the links between food production and food scares
- To define the Western diet
- To describe the agricultural inputs to support the Western diet
- To discuss issues of animal welfare

COMPANION @ WEBSITE

Sustainable food and beverage management infers a holistic approach respecting the planet, **biodiversity** and all people in equal measure. The subject of sustainable food cannot be ignored by the **hospitality industry** although its meaning is complex. The provision of nutritious food that maintains a healthy and active life and respects the **environment** is known as **food security** and **sustainable** agriculture is at its heart. All too often, conventional agricultural systems are unsustainable due to extensive reliance on fossil fuels and negative **impacts** on biodiversity. Agriculture in developing countries is the largest employment sector, around 70 per cent of their population work on the land. Trade liberalization can arguably reduce a country's food security by reducing agricultural employment levels. In the West, we put pressure on the planet's finite resources in our food and **lifestyle** choices. Land that could be used for growing cereals for people is used to grow food for animals and for producing bio-fuels. Employment conditions for some workers producing cash crops like cocoa, bananas and coffee are sometimes precarious. The conditions that many farm animals are kept in defy the rules of humanity. The result of consuming cheap food and especially meat in these conditions is a population in the West suffering from ever increasing levels of obesity and food-associated health problems.

According to the Worldwatch Institute (2009), the major problem in the global food production system is in the unsustainable inputs that are used. As a result, many forms of environmental **degradation** occur: falling water tables, deterioration of pasture, soil erosion. The **Western diet**, with its high consumption of fish, meat and dairy products, is endangering the environment; croplands are diminishing and the ocean's fish stocks are in decline. These grim warning signs are matched with some positive signs of awareness in society for health, **environmental stewardship** and animal welfare.

The world food crisis

In 2011, the UN Food Price Index hit an all-time global high and is set to go even higher with more predicted shortfalls in harvests and more mouths in the world to feed. Food shortages are now high up on the public agenda and governments around the world are becoming more nervous at what is to come. 2011 saw wheat prices, like many other cereal prices, increase by as much as 75 per cent. In the West this means a few more pence on the price of a loaf of bread but in countries where cereal is the staple diet, such an increase can be the difference between life and death. For the world's 2 billion people living in absolute poverty where more than half their meagre income goes on food, such a price increase spells disaster.

In the past, food price increases tended to be almost exclusively driven by drought weather conditions. Such events were always disruptive but eventually came to an end. Unfortunately, today droughts are exacerbated by trends that are both elevating demand and making it more difficult to increase production: among them, a rapidly expanding population, crop-withering temperature increases and irrigation wells running dry. Each night, there are 220,000 additional people to feed at the global dinner table.

Alarmingly, the world no longer has the ability to soften the effect of shortages. Until the beginning of the twenty-first century, grain surpluses in the USA or Russia could make up the shortfalls in other parts of the world. The USA, along with countries like Brazil, now converts any surplus grain into fuel for cars. In fact, now the USA converts one-third of its grain harvest into bio-fuels. In 2010, the United States harvested nearly 400 million tonnes of grain, of which 126 million tonnes went to the ethanol fuel distilleries. Hence, the price of grain is now tied to the price of oil. When oil hits US$150 per barrel or more, the price of grain will follow it upward as it becomes more profitable to convert grain into oil substitutes.

Rising temperatures can be equated to lowering grain harvests, as witnessed by Russia during the 2010 heat wave when the country's harvests were reduced by 40 per cent. Falling water tables are another cause of lowering harvests as farmers are handicapped by less water for irrigation. The World Bank reports that 175 million Indians and an estimated 130 million Chinese are currently fed by over-pumping aquifers. Less water, more heat and poor land management are creating soil erosion at an alarming rate. Satellite picture images show two huge new dust bowls: one over northern and western China and stretching over western Mongolia; the other across central Africa. Civilization can survive the loss of its oil reserves but cannot survive the loss of its soil reserves.

The much heralded technology boom in agriculture does not appear to be delivering its promises. Decade after decade, advancing technology underpinned steady gains in raising land productivity producing a tripling of world grain yield per acre between 1950 and 1995. In China and Japan, which account for one-third of the world's rice harvest, rice yield per acre is now levelling off and wheat yields have plateaued across Western Europe's three largest wheat-producing countries: the UK, France and Germany.

Some countries are scrambling now to secure their own food needs at the expense of poorer nations. Saudi Arabia, South Korea and China, took the unusual step in 2008 of buying or leasing land in other countries on which to grow grain for themselves. Most of these land acquisitions are in Africa where some governments lease cropland for less than US$1 an acre per year. Among the principal destinations were Ethiopia and Sudan, countries where millions of people are being sustained with food from the UN World Food Programme. These 'land grabs' totalled nearly 140 million acres in 2010 and typically involve water rights, according to the World Bank, meaning that countries downstream are affected as well. Any water extracted from the Upper Nile River basin to irrigate crops in Ethiopia or Sudan, for instance, will now not reach Egypt, upending the delicate water politics of the Nile by adding new countries with which Egypt must negotiate. Local hostility toward such land grabs is the rule, not exception. In 2007, China signed an agreement with the Philippines to lease 2.5 million acres of land. A public outcry ensued from the Filipino farmers and the Manila government was forced in this instance to suspend the agreement. Food nationalism may help secure food supplies for individual affluent countries but the developing countries that host land grabs or import grain will likely see their food situation deteriorate.

The solution for increasing global food yields could lie in the hands of the world's smallholder farmers. Smallholder farms are often very efficient in terms of production per hectare, and they have tremendous potential for growth. Helping smallholder farmers can contribute to a country's economic growth and food security. For example, in Vietnam, 73 per cent of the population live in rural areas, and agriculture has always been their main source of income. Vietnam has gone from being a food-deficit country to being a major food exporter, and is now the second largest rice exporter in the world. It achieved this largely through development of its smallholder farming sector. In 2007, the poverty rate fell below 15 per cent, compared with 58 per cent in 1979.

In many parts of the world, smallholder farmers are struggling to live and to feed their families on less than US$2 a day. Most have not been able to respond to increased demand for food globally and locally because they lack access to **assets** and capital. Often their great problem is getting the food they produce to their markets. At a local level, transport infrastructures are often poor and the higher prices paid for agricultural products do not always filter down to the farm-gate, where poor farmers often have to sell their produce.

The increased global appetite is being met by large commercial farmers in developed and food-exporting countries. Supporting smallholder farmers would not only enhance world food security, but would make a significant dent in poverty. Leaving them out of the equation will push many into greater poverty and hunger and, incidentally, force them to move to overpopulated urban areas and increase the numbers of the urban poor. In order to buck this trend, smallholder farmers need a long-term commitment to agriculture from their own governments and the international community, backed up by greater investment.

Today, there is no organized effort to ensure the adequacy of world food supplies. However, specialized agencies within the UN system such as the World Health Organization and the Food and Agriculture Organization (FAO), play major roles in the world today. But while the FAO collects and analyses global agricultural data and provides assistance, food policy-making on a global scale is lacking. All too often, governments and international bodies are happy to stand back and bask in the glories of the short-term goals of the multinational food giants.

Issues with conventional agriculture

Conventional agriculture, as we know it today, has only existed since about the late 1940s. A series of successful research initiatives on plant breeding and the use of agrochemicals (i.e. artificial nitrogen fertilizers and plant protection agents such as herbicides, fungicides and pesticides) resulted in a tremendous boom in agricultural productivity. This new development reached its peak in the 1960s and later became known as 'the Green Revolution'. One major breakthrough was the development of high-yielding wheat, rice and corn varieties – the world's staple foods – that made it possible to yield far more grain per hectare of arable land. The Green Revolution is frequently credited with saving millions of lives through increasing agricultural productivity in times of an ever-rising world population. However, it is also increasingly blamed for its detrimental effects on both human welfare and environmental quality. In this regard, the system of modern agriculture is more criticized than its individual parts. In sum, most criticism revolves around conventional agriculture's dependence on unsustainable inputs, which in turn is caused by its reliance on large-scale monocultures.

Genetically modified food

Even the widely publicized endeavours of scientists trying to develop higher crop yields through genetic modification have met with little proven success. Many people see genetically modified food as a worrying technology. Advocates of GM food products see them as a near-perfect solution to reduce the environmental impacts, improve human health and create new products with enhanced long-term health benefits. They argue that these higher-yielding crops are urgently needed in order to deal with rising global hunger and under-nourishment. Opponents argue that biotechnology interferes with the forces of evolution and could bring about unpredictable outcomes. The long-term environmental risks and impacts on human health have not been analysed sufficiently (IFOAM, 2008). Fears also include upsetting the balance of nature, losing biodiversity and the development of unmanageable plant characteristics. In addition, the ethical question can be asked whether humans have the right to interfere with nature on such an enormous scale. Genetically modified rice strains with higher yields have not been developed and wheat crops see only small gains. According to the environmental group Friends of the Earth, genetically modified soya, maize and cotton make up 95 per cent of the total acreage of GM and none of the crops introduced so far has increased yield, enhanced nutrition, drought tolerance or salt-tolerance. Because they are genetically engineered to be tolerant of pesticides, they allow farmers to spray herbicides more frequently which in turn encourages the growth of herbicide-resistant plants. Friends of the Earth claim widespread acceptance of GM crops resistant to the herbicide glysophate and the emergence of weeds tolerant to the chemical have caused a 15-fold increase in the use of the herbicide between 1994 and 2005. GM crops are primarily used in North and South America for animal feed and bio-fuel production instead of tackling poverty in developing countries.

Food production issues and food scares

The main preoccupation of the food economy is to increase production in order to feed the growing world population and fulfil the culinary desires of the developed nations. Unfortunately, issues such as the quality of products, nutritional value and health implications are sometimes neglected. People are becoming increasingly concerned about the quality and safety of the food they consume. The recent food scares and the outcry over genetically modified foods have heightened consumer awareness over the quality, safety and source of foods. The US Centers for Disease Control and Prevention claim food-borne illnesses, many from fresh produce, send 300,000 Americans to the hospital every year. Food-borne pathogens are responsible for 76 million illnesses in the US every year, 90 per cent of which are due to seven known pathogens: *Salmonella*, norovirus, *Campylobacter*, *Toxoplasma*, *e. coli*, *Listeria* and *Clostridium perfringens*. According to 2010 estimates, the norovirus pathogen is the most common, and is responsible for 5.4 million illnesses and 149 deaths each year. The World Health Organization reports that the global incidence of food-borne diseases is difficult to estimate, but nearly 2 million people in developing countries die from diarrhoeal diseases every year. A great proportion of these cases can be attributed to contamination of food and drinking water. Additionally, diarrhoea is a major cause of malnutrition in infants and young children. While most food-borne diseases are sporadic and often not reported, food-borne disease outbreaks may take on massive proportions. For example, in 1994, an outbreak of salmonellosis due to contaminated ice cream occurred in the USA, affecting an estimated 224,000 persons.

Many food-borne pathogens contaminate food due to poor hygiene and are only rarely the fault of farmers and food companies. However, the safety of food derived from biotechnology requires careful surveillance. To provide the scientific basis for decisions regarding human health, new methods and policies to assess such foods need to be developed and agreed upon internationally. Cost/benefit assessments should be considered in order to prevent possible negative health implications, but potential risk analysis has been lacking in the past. All crops modified to combat pests, food allergens or foods constructed with increased essential nutrients require careful scrutiny. The weighing of potential risks and benefits is an important aspect of the assessment of foods derived from biotechnology that has not received much attention in the past. If not properly monitored and assessed, changes in animal husbandry practices, including feeding, may have serious implications for food safety. In the 1990s bovine spongiform encephalopathy (BSE, or 'mad cow disease') associated with the human variant Creutzfeldt-Jakob (vCJD) hit the headlines. The disease was caused by the manipulation of the natural diet of ruminants who normally consume only grass and in some cases cereals. Animals suffering from BSE had been fed the remains of other dead animals.

Modern intensive agricultural practices have contributed to the increased availability of affordable foodstuffs. Low-priced food additives can improve the quality, quantity and safety of the food supply but careful attention must be paid to avoid human intoxication. Naturally occurring toxins, persistent organic compounds and metals are found in the food industry. Mycotoxins, such as aflatoxin and ochratoxin A, are found at measurable levels in many staple foods, but the health implications of long-term exposure of such toxins are poorly understood.

Exposure to persistent organic compounds such as dioxins can lead to a wide variety of adverse effects in humans, such as increased cancer risk, reproductive disorders, alteration of the immune system, neuro-behavioural impairment, endocrine disruption, genotoxicity and increased birth defects. Dioxins are unwanted by-products of some industrial processes such as manufacturing herbicides and pesticides and waste incineration. Although formation of dioxins is local, they spread at a global level. High levels of these compounds are found in some soils, sediments and food, especially dairy products, meat, fish and shellfish. Very low levels are found in plants, water and air. In late 2008, the Republic of Ireland recalled many tonnes of pork meat and pork products when up to 200 times more dioxins than the safe limit were detected in samples of pork. The contamination was traced back to contaminated feed. In 2011, *The Ecologist* magazine reported that dioxin-contaminated eggs came from Germany where the hens had been fed oils designed for refining into bio-fuels. From there, the eggs were sent hundreds of miles to Holland for treatment and then transported by sea and road to two companies in Cornwall and Cardiff, which in turn supplied supermarkets. The UK Food Standards Agency (FSA) was quoted as saying that the eggs posed 'no food safety risk'. But the question must be asked, since when has digesting potent poisons and pollutants been good for us? Dioxin-contaminated eggs are no different from previous food contamination incidents, such as antibiotic nitrofurans in prawns in 2002 and the infamous Sudan

1 dye, an industrial dye used in floor polish and solvents, which found its way into convenience foods like pasta sauces and ready-meals in 2003. They have in common obscure, illegally used ingredients that had originated thousands of miles from these shores, all of them known carcinogens.

Heavy metals are natural components of the Earth's crust that cannot be degraded or destroyed. To a small extent they enter our bodies via food, drinking water and air. As trace elements, some heavy metals (e.g. copper, selenium, zinc) are essential to maintain the metabolism of the human body. However, at higher concentrations they can lead to poisoning. Heavy metal poisoning could result, for instance, from drinking water contamination (e.g. lead pipes), high ambient air concentrations near emission sources or intake via the food chain. They are dangerous because they tend to bio-accumulate, i.e. they increase in the concentration of a chemical in a biological organism over time. Heavy metals can enter a water supply through industrial and consumer waste, or even from acidic rain breaking down soils and releasing heavy metals into streams, lakes, rivers and groundwater.

The three most pollutant heavy metals are cadmium, lead and mercury. Cadmium is produced as an inevitable by-product of zinc (or occasionally lead) refining, and long-term exposure to humans is associated with renal dysfunction. High exposure can lead to obstructive lung disease and has been linked to lung cancer, although data concerning the latter are difficult to interpret due to compounding factors. Cadmium may also produce bone defects (osteomalacia, osteoporosis) in humans and animals. In addition, the metal can be linked to increased blood pressure and effects on the myocardium in animals, however, most human data do not support these findings.

Lead in the environment comes from both natural and anthropogenic sources. Exposure can occur through drinking water, food, air, soil and dust from old paint containing lead. For infants up to 4 or 5 months of age, air, milk formulae and water are the significant sources. High levels of exposure may result in damage to the kidneys, the gastrointestinal tract, joints and the reproductive system and acute or chronic damage to the nervous system. It is thought that the Mad Hatter in Lewis Carroll's *Alice in Wonderland* probably suffered from lead poisoning since lead was used in the felting process necessary for making hats.

World-wide mining of mercury leads to indirect discharges into the atmosphere and its use is widespread in industrial processes and in various products. Mercury poisoning is associated with tremors, gingivitis and/or minor psychological changes, together with spontaneous abortion and congenital malformation. Mercury is found sometimes in shallow water fish feeding near discharges and has lead to neurological damage in infants and children in Japan.

The Western diet

The obesity epidemic and the rise in weight-related conditions like heart disease, diabetes and certain cancers can be directly linked to the food eaten in the West.

Cheeseburgers, French fries, super-sized sodas, deep-dish pizza – all of these foods are part of the Western diet also referred to as the Meat–Sweet Diet. Moreover, the negative health consequences associated with this diet are worsened by the lack of portion control coupled with the trademark Western sedentary lifestyle. Lack of fresh fruits and vegetables, its strong reliance on fast-food, high sugar beverages, high-fat dairy, refined carbohydrates and red meat characterize this way of eating. While these foods can be eaten as part of a healthy diet in moderation, the Western diet is characterized by its extremely large portion sizes, often large enough to feed two or more individuals. Ingredients commonly found in these foods include high fructose corn syrup, trans-fat or partially hydrogenated oils, sugar, bleached, enriched flours, food dyes, artificial flavours and many other chemical additives that strip foods of any and all nutritional value. Worryingly, the Western diet is being adopted in countries like India and China with new middle-class citizens numbering around 300 million. Their rates of weight-related health conditions are starting to soar in direct relation to the increased amount of meat and calorific foods they consume.

The number of young people who had a food or digestive allergy increased 18 per cent between 1997 and 2007, according to the same organization. In 2010, the US Centers for Disease Control and Prevention claimed that food allergies affect an estimated 6–8 per cent of children under the age of 5, and about 3–4 per cent of adults compared to just over 2.3 million (3.3 per cent) in 1997.

While there is no cure, some children outgrow their food allergy as they get older. It is easy to confuse a food allergy with a much more common reaction known as food intolerance. While bothersome, food intolerance is a less serious condition that does not involve the immune system.

For many, health problems, such as heart disease and obesity, are due to inadequate diets; or over-consumption in developed countries and under-nutrition in developing countries. Cancer and cardiovascular diseases, including heart disease and stroke, are the major causes of death. About one-third of cancers can be attributed to poor diet and nutrition. Unhealthy diets, along with physical inactivity, have also contributed to the growth of obesity. Some 22 per cent of men and 24 per cent of women in the UK are now obese, a trebling since the 1980s, and 65 per cent of men and 56 per cent of women – 24 million adults – are either overweight or obese. It is a growing problem with children and young people too. Around 16 per cent of 2–15-year-olds are now obese (DEFRA, 2006). Interestingly, people are eating less saturated fat, trans-fat (hydrogenated fat) and added sugar than they were 10 years ago. However, in 2009/10, almost a quarter of adults (24.3 per cent of respondents) in England reported that they had taken part in sport on 11–28 days within a four-week period. Obesity brings its own health problems, including hypertension, heart disease and Type 2 diabetes. Obesity is responsible for an estimated 9,000 premature deaths per year in England. It is estimated that the treatment of ill health from poor diet costs the National Health Service (NHS) at least £4 billion each year (Department of Health West Midlands, n.d.). Huge health costs are associated with poor diet, in 2007, US$174 billion was spent in the USA caring for people with diabetes.

Agricultural inputs to the Western diet

The intensive conventional agriculture practised in the West to feed the enormous appetite for the Western diet is characterized by high inputs of pesticides, chemical fertilizers and huge acreages. These chemical additives are manufactured from non-renewable resources which provide generally high-yielding crops but can have an adverse effect on biodiversity and on the health of the workers on the farms.

In the USA alone, more than 9 billion animals are maintained to supply the animal protein consumed each year. Poultry only consume grain whereas cattle and sheep, although naturally grass eaters, consume both grains and forage. The amount of grains fed to US livestock is sufficient to feed about 840 million people who follow a plant-based diet. However, in the West we consume on average 77 grams (g) of animal protein per day in addition to about 35 g of available plant protein, totalling 112 g of protein. The World Health Organization recommends a daily protein allowance of 56 g from a mixed diet. Therefore, Westerners consume more protein than they need and about 1000 kcal in excess per day per capita.

Top quality beef cattle require around 10 kilos of cereal and soy for each kilo of protein produced. Broiler chickens require about 4 kilos of grain for each kilo protein produced. In conventional livestock production systems, fertilizers, herbicides and other inputs are fossil fuel in origin, thus, non-renewable. The average fossil energy input for all the animal protein production systems studied is 25 kcal fossil energy input per 1 kcal of protein produced. This energy input is more than 11 times greater than that for grain protein production, which is about 2.2 kcal of fossil energy input per 1 kcal of plant protein produced.

Environmental impacts of fossil fuel pesticides and herbicides

Much of the cheap meat and dairy produce sold in supermarkets across Europe is arriving as a result of serious human rights abuses and environmental damage in developing countries. Recent research by Professor Leslie Dennis from the University of Iowa looked at more than 55,000 pesticide sprayers working in Iowa and North Carolina and asked them to detail their exposure to 50 pesticides. It was found that repeated exposure to pesticides can increase the risk of developing skin cancer. Using the data collected, researchers were able to compare their cancer rates with their use of certain pesticides and it turned out that six chemicals in all, including two fungicides and two insecticides, were found to double the risk of developing skin cancer with repeated exposure of more than 50 lifetime days. In another study undertaken by the European Parliament's Committee on the Environment, Public Health and Food Safety, increased cancer rates were found among children of farm workers and children living on farms. Film-maker Fredrik Gertten had made a documentary following the story of banana workers in Nicaragua as they brought lawsuits against the Dole fruit company for the adverse health effects they suffered as a result of the use of the pesticide DBCP. The pesticide was banned in the USA in 1977 for causing male sterility but Standard Fruit – now Dole – continued to use the pesticide in its plantations outside the US until 1982. Workers reported being unable to father any children and women reported losing children. They are now involved in an on-going legal battle in the USA to seek compensation.

Soy is prized for use in animal feed as it provides a cheap source of protein for poultry, pigs and other intensively reared animals that require fast growth in order to produce large meat, egg and milk yields. Globally, it has been estimated that as much as 97 per cent of soymeal produced is now used for animal feed. Attracted by cheap land prices, poor environmental regulations and **monitoring**, widespread corruption and low taxation on agricultural export commodities, agribusinesses mainly use GM soya in industrial production in developing countries, thus, avoiding the ban imposed in some European countries. These farmlands are often dependent on the frequent application of powerful pesticides and other agrichemicals which have been linked to environmental degradation and a host of negative health impacts on people living nearby. In Paraguay, crop spraying has polluted important water sources in many rural regions, say campaigners, poisoning both domestic and wild animals, threatening plant life and resulting in a number of health problems in people, including diarrhoea, vomiting, genetic malformations, headaches, loss of sight and even death.

The environmental organization Greenpeace has compiled a report using government records, company documents and trade data from Brazil, China, Europe, Vietnam and the USA to piece together the global movement of meat, leather and cosmetics ingredients made from Brazilian cattle. They claim that clearing tropical forests for agriculture is estimated to produce 17 per cent of the world's greenhouse gas emissions – more than the global transport system. Cattle farming is now the biggest threat to the remaining Amazon rainforest, a fifth of which has been lost since 1970.

Raj Patel claims in his 2009 book, *The Value of Nothing*, that the 'true' economic cost of a hamburger in the USA would be around US$200. This calculation is from research done by The Center for Science and Environment in India, assuming that the meat for the hamburger came from an animal raised on pasture that was once rainforest. Considering the ecological services provided by that rainforest, the loss of diversity, carbon sequestration, water cycling, fuel and tropical product sources, among many other things, the cost would come to US$200.

Animal welfare

Concentrated animal feeding operation (CAFO) is an industrial farming model that the USA has perfected and is now being exported to the rest of the globe as meat consumption is on the rise. By concentrating farm animals in the smallest space possible, to gain weight as quickly as possible and at the least cost, CAFOs deny the most basic rights of an animal as a living being. The following are some examples:

• All but 5 per cent of the 280 million hens in the US egg-laying flock are raised in battery cages – each bird has a living space smaller than a single sheet of letter-sized paper.

- The gestation stalls that pregnant sows are confined in has been described by animal rights campaigner Dr Temple Grandin as, 'like being stuffed into the middle seat of a jam-packed jumbo jet for your whole adult life, and you're not ever allowed out in the aisle'.
- Veal calves are kept in small crates which prevent movement, inhibiting muscle growth so their flesh will be tender. They are also fed a diet deficient of iron to keep their flesh pale and appealing to the consumer. Veal calves spend each day confined alone with no companionship and are deprived of light for a large portion of their four-month lives.
- Half of the cows in the US dairy herd are raised in intensive confinement, where they suffer emotionally from being socially deprived and being prohibited from natural behaviour. Dairy cows produce milk for about 10 months after giving birth so they are impregnated continuously to keep up the milk flow.

Food security is considered a hygiene factor by many in developed countries: abundant food is available and food security is taken for granted. It is only if and once food security is lost that one recognises the importance of it.

EXERCISES

1 **GROUP DISCUSSION, GROUP PROJECT OR WRITTEN ASSIGNMENT**
   Outline the major agricultural challenges facing the world today
   - How are the challenges surrounding agriculture impacting upon your country or region?
   - Critically examine how the resulting changes in agricultural outputs are affecting the tourism and hospitality industry in your country or region.

2 **GROUP DISCUSSION OR GROUP PROJECT**
   Conventional versus organic
   - What are the major advantages and disadvantages of conventional agriculture?
   - What are the major advantages and disadvantages of organic agriculture?
   - Find a hotel or restaurant that offers products based on organic agriculture and interview the manager/owner. Find out more on the motivating factors for offering organic food.
   - Make a 10–15-minute presentation of your findings.

3 **GROUP PROJECT**
   Genetically modified food
   - Research all food that has been genetically modified and sold in your local supermarket. Present the findings to the class.
   - Discuss whether special labelling designating the food as 'Genetically Modified' should be required or not.

4　GROUP PROJECT OR WRITTEN ASSIGNMENT
Animal welfare

Choose and answer one of the following questions:

- Many vegetarians believe that factory farming is a cruel and unnecessary practice and that a diet would be healthier if less meat was eaten. Do you agree? *Or*

- If there are so many problems today with food scares and general food safety, it is because animals are not being treated properly in the first place. Do you agree? *Or*

- Many countries spend a great amount of money on household pets. Some argue that money spent on helping poor and hungry people instead would be wiser. Do you agree? *Or*

- Hotels and restaurants should regularly pay a visit to the slaughterhouse in order to check and control the suppliers of meat, the same meat which eventually ends up on plates in the dining room. Do you agree?

References

Department for Environment, Food and Rural Affairs (DEFRA) (2006) *Food Industry Sustainability Strategy*. Available at: http://www.defra.gov.uk/publication/files/pb11649-fiss2006-060411.pdf.

Department of Health West Midlands (n.d.) *Quality, Innovation, Productivity & Prevention: Food*. Available at: http://www.obesitywm.org.uk/resources/FOOD-MAIN-REPORT-jule retyped.doc.

International Foundation for Organic Agriculture Movements (IFOAM) (2008) *Organic Standards and Certification*. Available at: http://www.ifoam.org/about_ifoam/standards/index.html.

Patel, R. (2009) *The Value of Nothing*, London: Portobello Books.

Worldwatch Institute (2009) *State of the World: Into a Warming World*. Available at: http://www.worldwatch.org/node/5984.

Resources

American Hotel and Lodging Association (AHLA): http://www.ahla.com.

Conservation International (CI): http://www.conservation.org/Pages/default.aspx.

Convention on Biological Diversity (CBD): http://www.cbd.int/convention/text/.

Greenhotels: http://www.greenhotels.com.

Greenpeace: http://www.greenpeace.org.

International Hotel & Restaurant Association (IH&RA): http://www.ih-ra.com.

National Restaurant Association (NRA): http://www.restaurant.org.

United Nations (UN): *Millennium Development Goals*. Available at: http://www.un.org/millenniumgoals.

Additional material

Go to www.routledge.com/cw/sloan to find PowerPoint slides of all the figures and tables from the book, additional case studies, a test bank of questions and extra links to useful videos.

CHAPTER

Sustainable food issues and food sourcing

CHAPTER OBJECTIVES

The objectives for this chapter are:

- To understand the link between food and beverage operations and agriculture
- To explain issues related to conventional agriculture
- To describe the various forms of sustainable agriculture
- To explain issues and limitations of organic agriculture
- To understand the concept behind 'food miles' and its implication for sustainable hospitality operations
- To develop a differentiated approach to the concept of 'regional food systems' and its useful applications

Organic labelling

Various voluntary **certification** programmes and standards for **organic agriculture** have been developed in the past 20 years. In addition to numerous private organic standards worldwide, more than 60 governments have already codified organic standards into technical regulations (IFOAM, 2008). The United States Department of Agriculture (USDA) has established a set of national standards for any food-handling organization that wants to sell organically produced foods (USDA, 2008). In the European Union, all organic products must be certified by an approved organization such as the Soil Association, based in the UK, Sweden's KRAV or Australian Certified Organic. The aim of these national standards is to assure consumers that 'the organic foods they purchase are produced, processed and certified to be consistent with national organic standards' (USDA, 2008).

Under EU Eco regulations, products certified under organic certification schemes cannot be labelled as 'organic' if they contain genetically modified plant cells. Food labelled as '100% organic' must contain only organically produced ingredients. Food labelled 'organic' has to contain a minimum of 95 per cent organically produced ingredients. If labelled to be 'made with organic ingredients' the food must contain at least 70 per cent of organic ingredients.

CASE STUDY 8.1   Bio seal in German gastronomy and hospitality

Since 2003, in Germany, restaurants and other retailers can label food products, dishes or whole menus on their menu with the bio seal. In order to get this organic certification, they need to take part in the control procedure of the 'EG-Öko-Verordnung'. All levels of production and processing of the food products as well as their final preparation in the kitchen are controlled. If a whole dish is labelled with the bio seal, at least 95 per cent of the ingredients have to be organically produced. Control in restaurant kitchens becomes very complicated as the origin of all the ingredients used in a recipe has to be identified. Depending on the size of the restaurants, a price of between 150 and 600 euros has to be paid to obtain the organic certification for one year.

Source: DEHOGA, www.dehoga-bundesverband.de.

Organic agriculture: the main principles

A wise US farmer once proposed that eating is essentially an agricultural act (Berry, 1990). But how can that be? The truth is: *good cooking starts with good agriculture.* The food any restaurant serves can only be as good as the agricultural practices of the farm where the raw food products used for a dish originate. Even the most sophisticated chef will not be able to turn a steak sourced from a super-fast grown bull, overfed with concentrated feed, growth hormones and antibiotics, kept in the minimum amount of space in large herds, transported over long distances to be slaughtered under high stress levels, and left to age only in a vacuum pack, into the soft, juicy, flavoursome and nourishing piece of meat you would expect. And this problem counts by no means only for meat. Yet, agricultural practices do not affect only the quality of its produce. Moreover, depending on the farming practice, *there are substantial environmental and **social** effects* on soil fertility, **biodiversity**, groundwater quality or rural livelihoods' welfare, to name just a few.

In a report entitled 'Organic agriculture and the global food supply' (Badgley *et al.* 2007), it was shown that it is possible to meet the needs of the world's rapidly growing population without planet-wrecking factory farms and bio-fuels – by eating healthier lower-meat diets, replacing imported soy with home-grown feed. The International Federation of Organic Agricultural Movements (IFAOM, 2008) argues that many of these problems can be solved by conversion to more **sustainable** forms of agriculture. According to the UK Soil Association, **organic farming** results in multiple environmental benefits such as a higher level of biodiversity, lower **pollution** from pesticides, lower energy use and carbon emissions, and a lower level of waste. Various social and economic benefits are derived from organic farming as well.

Organic agriculture standards

It is tempting to talk about organic food and agricultural practices as if the world had already agreed to a single set of standards. However, the opposite is the case. There is an endless array of available certifications and seals to identify 'organically' (or even 'sustainably') produced foods and each may stand for a different definition of the term 'organic'. Standards for organic food production can be set up by a multitude of associations and institutions; however, in most countries, a governmental body defines the minimum required standards. Since the 1990s, many countries have implemented national rules and regulations for their farmers and food processors in terms of production, processing and labelling. Most prominent examples are the European Union's Council Regulation (EC) No. 834/2007 and the United States Department of Agriculture's National Organic Program (USDA NOP). For example, the EU has defined 'organic production' as:

> an overall system of farm management and food production that combines best environmental practices, a high level of biodiversity, the preservation of natural resources, the application of high animal welfare standards and a production method in line with the preference of certain consumers for products produced using natural substances and processes. The organic production method thus plays a dual societal role, where it on the one hand provides for a specific market responding to a consumer demand for organic products, and on the other hand delivers public goods contributing to the protection of the environment and animal welfare, as well as to rural development.
>
> (Council Regulation (EC) 834/2007, p. 1)

Both the US and the EU rules and regulations differ slightly and given the fact that they apply to about 90 per cent of the global market for organic food, they provide a good example of the universal understanding of organic food. In essence, the following key points differentiate their understanding of organic in contrast to conventional food production:

- Most *synthetic plant* protection agents and mineral nitrogen fertilizers should not be applied.
- The use of *genetically modified organisms* and ionizing radiation is strictly prohibited.

- *Crop production* should take place within a suitable crop rotation, including nitrogen-fixing plants, such as legumes (e.g. peas, clover, broad beans).
- *Plant and animal species* should be chosen according to their suitability to given environmental conditions and farming practices; biodiversity and the use of traditional and sturdy species are strongly encouraged.
- In *plant and animal production*, preventive measures to ensure plant and animal health (e.g. a balanced diet for ruminants) should always be preferred, before opting for curative measures.
- *Antibiotics* are not allowed in livestock farming.
- All animals should be fed on 100 per cent *organic feed*, which should not contain any animal by-products or growth hormones.
- Animals must have *access to outdoor roaming* areas and be kept in circumstances that allow them to show natural behaviour and guarantee animal welfare.
- *Processed products*, such as convenience foods, must contain 100 per cent certified organic ingredients.

Generally speaking, organic farmers are encouraged to increase soil fertility through conservational farming systems, establish matter and nutrient cycles on their premises, use as few as possible products from non-renewable resources, take advantage of crop rotation, and produce as much of the needed animal fodder on the farm as possible. Further, farms should provide natural habitats for endangered species or other beneficiaries and promote general biodiversity.

Biodynamic agriculture

Governmental bodies set minimum required standards, but several farmers' associations have taken organic agriculture a step further: **biodynamic agriculture**. Farmers working in a so-called 'biodynamic' manner are arguably most rigorous with respect to true sustainable agricultural practices. These farmers are widely represented by their international association 'Demeter'. They see the entire farm as an organism, where plants, soil, animals and humans interact and depend on each other. In fact, you will hardly find a biodynamic farm that produces only one or two commodities. There will most probably be a variety of livestock, fruit, vegetables and field crops. The farmers apply a complex farm management system, homeopathic sprays, herbal preparations and the lunar cycles in order to increase soil fertility and protect plants and animals from pests and diseases that foster their natural resilience. The Organic Wine Company (2012) describes this method of agriculture as 'ultra-organic' and states that it was developed at the beginning of this century, based on the theories of the social philosopher, Rudolf Steiner. Biodynamic farmers plant their crops according to the belief that plant development is guided by cosmic energy that radiates from the moon, stars and the planets.

Integrated agriculture

Integrated agriculture can be very much in line with organic agriculture. Farms that work in an integrated manner try to minimize external farm inputs, such as fertilizers or pesticides, and take advantage of the synergies between a variety of livestock and plant production systems. For example, cattle may be kept on grassland not suitable for the production of field crops. Their manure from the stables could be used as a nutrient- and organic matter-rich fertilizer for growing maize. In return, part of the maize harvest could be turned into silage and used as additional cattle feed during the winter. However, in most countries 'integrated agriculture' is neither a clearly defined nor protected term, unlike 'organic', which is protected by law in many countries. There are institutions that offer up-to-date guidelines according to the latest research, such as the Center for Integrated Agricultural Systems at the University of Wisconsin-Madison. However, they are certainly not binding. In this sense, food claimed to be produced by means of 'integrated farming' may have been produced just like its organic counterpart or just in a conventional way.

Fair prices for local farmers

The immense reduction in transport costs, cheap food production in developing countries as well as the increase in large food companies and supermarket chains are responsible for dramatically reducing farm-gate prices in industrialized nations. Local shops are increasingly disappearing and effects on rural economies and farming communities are detrimental (DEFRA, 2006).

The Soil Association (2008) sees organic meat production in the UK in real danger unless pricing structures are reconsidered. Organic producers of beef and lamb are being paid prices that do not meet the cost of production, hence, increasing the likelihood of them reducing their organic stock or discontinuing organic production. Additionally, new regulations, forcing organic farmers to use 100 per cent organic feed are putting even higher pressure on them. The average organic beef price in 2006 in England was £2.88 per kilo, compared to average costs of production of £3.32 per kilo (Soil Association, 2008). A significant increase in farm-gate prices seems to be the only way to ensure short- and long-term organic beef farming. Due to the distribution systems now in place, more and more money is going to supermarket chains or large food corporations instead of to the local farmers. Now in Germany, for example, only about 20 per cent of the price of food goes to the farmer, whereas they received 75 per cent of the share in the 1950s. New sustainable systems of distribution need to be developed that pay local farmers a fair price reflecting the real costs of production.

Limitations and current issues of organic agriculture and food processing

With respect to the US and EU regulations, there are next to no regulations for packaging, transporting or production according to seasonality. It is therefore perfectly 'organic' to produce strawberries in the middle of winter in heavily heated greenhouses in Spain, have them harvested by poorly paid migrant workers, packed in plastic boxes and shipped to hotel kitchens all over the world. These regulations are therefore frequently criticized for being just production-oriented. Additionally, competent authorities overseeing the certification of organic agriculture and processing may grant exemptions from the binding regulations in particular cases. In sum, the current regulations in place may provide loopholes for anyone not willing to work 100 per cent according to the organic **sustainability** paradigm.

On a more general note, the entire idea of organic agriculture being a truly sustainable system of food production is debatable. For example, organic farming can only work well on soils that show a minimum amount of organic matter content and available nutrients. If, however, soils are utterly depleted or eroded, the use of mineral nitrogen fertilizers can help restore soil fertility and organic matter contents to a point where the organic system could then take over. Yet the idea that organic practices alone can safeguard soil fertility indefinitely may also be misleading. Besides nitrogen and potassium, phosphorus is one of the most essential nutrients

CASE STUDY 8.2 Human excreta in agriculture?

One of the most important, yet challenging aims of sustainable agricultural practices is the closing of nutrient cycles. Nutrients leave a farm's soil in the form of vegetables, fruits, milk, meat, etc. This loss of nutrients can partially be replenished by the use of nitrogen-fixing plants or the return of dung and liquid manure from the stables to the fields. However, such practices can only partially make up for the loss of nutrients. Particularly in developed countries, a large share of farm products ends up as food for human consumption, which eventually passes through toilets and the waste water systems, no longer retrievable for agricultural purposes. This is a major issue, as the annual amount of toilet waste equals about 520 kg per person, which contains enough essential nutrients, such as nitrogen, phosphorus and potassium, to grow about 230 kg of grain – on average, the amount a person consumes per year. Maybe it is time for modern societies to reconsider the value they attach to one of their least-appreciated, yet highly valuable products!

Source: Wolgast, M. (1993) *Recycling System*. Stockholm, Sweden: WM-Ekologen ab.

plants need to grow. It is found only in certain areas of the world, mostly within rocks, and cannot be produced by plants themselves. **Conventional agriculture** depends heavily on phosphorous input, but organic agriculture does, too. If the natural resources of rock phosphate are depleted, agriculture will face an extremely serious challenge. The whole idea of 'nutrient cycling', which is already an integral part of organic agricultural, needs to be taken to another level to safeguard agriculture's future.

According to the Food and Agricultural Organization (FAO), the current global level of meat consumption, the predictions as to its future development and its related **environmental impacts** pose yet another serious issue. In the second half of the twentieth century, the global population roughly doubled from 2.7 billion to just above 6 billion. The world hunger for meat, however, increased fivefold, from 45 billion to 229 billion kg. Projections show that by 2050 about 9.1 billion people will demand about 465 billion kg of meat annually. Today, most animals farmed for meat production are fed with grains (e.g. barley or triticale) or soy beans, so-called 'concentrated feed' and not with what they would naturally feed on, such as grass or hay. As a matter of fact, meat production in this quantity and under factory-farming conditions may not be possible without concentrated feed and it is exactly this demand for feed that has had severe **impacts** on **ecosystems**, biodiversity, the health of the livestock and the **environment** at large. In sum, this system is against the organic paradigm, leading to the assumption that future conversion towards organic agriculture may only be possible, if human meat consumption does not decrease in favour of more vegetables and grains.

Last, but not least, organic agriculture is frequently challenged to be unable to produce as much food as conventional farming, which would be a strong counterargument in the face of an ever-growing world population. Now, the question arises: can organic agriculture feed the world? In a ground-breaking attempt to produce a universal answer to this bold question, Badgley *et al.* (2007) have come up with a much-debated answer: yes, it could! Organic agriculture may produce lower yields in the developed world in comparison to conventional yields, but in the developing world yields could be increased. Given the global market place, this could balance out while at the same time have tremendous positive environmental effects. This answer, however, remains highly debatable and with less than 1 per cent of the world's agricultural land being managed organically, such an assumption cannot be put to the test.

The Sustainable Agriculture Initiative was created by major transnational food corporations in 2002. Although not performing the responsibility of certifying agricultural practices, it has become a useful platform for the development of sustainable agricultural practices that are harmonized along the food chain through activities centred on knowledge-building, awareness-raising, **stakeholder** involvement and technical support. Sustainable agriculture attempts to internalize external environmental and social costs in addition to biodiversity. The promotion of sustainable agriculture has important repercussions in developing economies where small farmers cannot always compete with large corporations.

The Coffee Platform is part of the Sustainable Agriculture Initiative and aims at improving the quality of coffee, reducing the over-supply of coffee and protecting the environment, thus improving the livelihoods of sustainable coffee producers. The initiative draws on financial support from large firms and the international community: Ecom, Efico, Kraft, Nestlé, Neumann Kaffee Gruppe, Sara Lee, Tchibo and Volcafe.

Organic agriculture = sustainable agriculture?

To answer to this question completely a whole book would be required. In sum, even though current organic agricultural practices have their shortcomings, they perform better when considering the environmental bottom line. Furthermore, the reduction of negative **externalities** when switching to organic agriculture may in turn lead to *de facto* net savings. A study by Pretty *et al*. (2005) claims that the actual costs of externalities from the UK's conventional agriculture totalled £1514.4 million per year in 2000. If the entire agricultural sector converted to organic management, externalities could be reduced to £384.9 million per year.

Other issues, such as social welfare, are not considered within most organic certification schemes, as opposed to products sold under Fair Trade certification. And, again, the organic principles explained above constitute just one understanding of organic farming. There may be others and in fact, maybe even some conventional farmers, or non-certified farmers for this matter, may work almost organically. Governmental rules and regulations represent only a minimum required standard in most countries. There are sometimes loopholes and ways to avoid strict adherence. Furthermore, there are only very few regulations about seasonality, packaging and transport. For example, much of the organic meat production in developed countries depends heavily on feed imports from developing countries, not without detrimental effects on their environment. In contrast, many farmers' associations, such as the Soil Association (the UK) or Bioland (Germany), have implemented their own set of rules, which tend to be stricter and try to incorporate a more holistic approach to 'organic' food production and respective certification, including social welfare and fair trading aspects. Hence, the answer to the question 'is organic food sustainable?' depends, on the one hand, on what type of organic agriculture is being referred to, and, on the other, from where, how and when the product in question is sourced. Restaurateurs and kitchen chefs trying to turn their premises into a truly sustainable eatery should be well aware of this fact.

Fair Trade food

The Fair Trade system seeks to pay producers an agreed minimum price that covers the costs of sustainable production in decent working conditions and living conditions. The development of the global agri-business has meant that smallholders in developing countries have found that they could not compete on purely economic terms. Fair Trade initiatives are often in tandem with local economic development, and this sustainable approach benefits the community at large.

In 2001, FINE, the umbrella organization for Fair Trade networks, set out the following definition:

> Fair Trade is a trading partnership, based on dialogue, transparency and respect, which seeks greater equity in international trade. It contributes to sustainable development by offering better trading conditions to, and securing the rights of, marginalized producers and workers – especially in the South. Fair Trade organizations (backed by consumers) are engaged actively in supporting producers, awareness raising and in campaigning for changes in the rules and practice of conventional international trade.

Fair Trade can be seen as a new way of capitalism but is definitely part of the market economy. A criticism levied at Fair Trade is that it does not seek to increase the market; it simply distributes profits in a more equitable manner. Producers and farmers not only benefit from guaranteed prices, there is also a stricter enforcement of labour law and social welfare. These benefits may not be as great as many of the proponents of Fair Trade imply. Although prices are guaranteed, the quantities purchased are not. Fair Trade also comes with a cost. There is a levy on the wholesaler as well as a certification charge for producers. In 2010, the certification charges started at £1570 in the first year, a sum of money that many producers in poor developing countries cannot pay. In fact, Fair Trade does not focus on the poorest countries, preferring instead middle-income nations. Globally, the market share for Fair Trade products only accounts for about 2 per cent. Some large agricultural companies criticize Fair Trade for distorting market prices, which is exaggerated, given its current level of penetration.

Fair Trade has a particularly strong potential role to play in poverty alleviation. The FINE states that it finances wider community projects such as health clinics, schools, roads, sanitation and other social services. According to the Fairtrade Labelling Organization (FLO), in 2009, around US$65 million was provided as a social premium to Fair Trade producers and their communities above and beyond the Fair Trade price.

Fair Trade is not the only initiative that labels products that claim to ensure particular 'social' or 'ethical' standards. Loosely defined, ethical trading means the trading of a product where there is particular concern in the supply chain over a particular ethical issue such as human rights, the environment, labour conditions and animal well-being. For-profit and non-profit organizations are engaged in ethical trading issues along with governments and international organizations. This new interest in what are essentially non-economic interests is a response to a growing demand from consumers. Businesses tend to classify these considerations under the general rubric of **corporate social responsibility**.

The 'Rainforest Alliance' and 'Bird Friendly' are initiatives with a main focus on compliance with environmental standards. The Bird Friendly label is the most rigorous environmental certification scheme in the coffee sector, since it combines organic standards with shade cover and species richness. The Rainforest Alliance is a comparatively looser certification scheme for coffee, cocoa, ferns, lumber, cut flowers, fruits and tea, which integrates environmental and social concerns. Strictly speaking, neither can be described as **eco-labels** offering a guarantee of organic produce, instead both promote 'good practice' for the management of agrochemicals and wastes, and promote a minimum cover of trees. The market share of both initiatives is still very small though rapidly growing as global corporations such as Lavazza, Kraft, Procter & Gamble and Chiquita Brands International have recently started to buy Rainforest Alliance certified coffee and bananas for some of their product lines.

Good African Coffee has positioned itself as a 'trade and not aid' ethical product steering away from the illusion of charity conveyed by Fair Trade. Starbucks developed socially responsible coffee buying guidelines by evaluating the economic, social and environmental aspects of coffee production. **Monitoring** of Starbucks' criteria is carried out by third parties and the costs are covered by producers. Producers participating in the programme, however, normally earn price premiums above the market price.

Consumer demand has also sparked specific certification for farms that have an ethical approach to animal welfare. The Animal Welfare Approved Program, the Validus Animal Welfare Review and the American Humane Association all monitor and certify farms raising animals humanely, outdoors on pasture. Their **auditing** cover a range of farming practices: humane animal handling and management, food and water quality standards, and housing that promotes animal comfort and cleanliness.

Sourcing

In the twenty-first century, the food that Westerners eat generally does not follow seasonal rhythms and can be characterized as coming from nowhere in particular. The food industry has been significantly affected by **globalization** and modern supply chain management practices and capabilities. Private and institutional consumers buy foods that are grown or produced far away from the consumption location. **Food miles** have become a synonym for this globalization of the food sector.

Food miles

The food miles or, more accurately, the 'food transportation' debate is concerned with the environmental and social costs associated with food transport, from where it is produced to where it is processed, to the wholesaler, to the retailer or catering outlet and to the consumer (DEFRA, 2005). DEFRA identified the major cultural, structural and commercial reasons for the increase in food miles as coming from:

- An increase in consumption of food that cannot be grown in the country, for example, oranges for juicing.
- Consumer demand for year-round food resulting in importation of out-of-season produce.
- Lower prices of imported food products.
- Increases in leisure travel and consequent exposure to and demand for exotic food products.
- Growth of out-of-town shopping centres and the resulting increase in travelling by shoppers.
- Growth of prepared and processed foods leading to the centralization of processing and, consequently, increases in travel to and from factories and processing centres.
- Simplified procurement processes, reduction of a supplier base and a resulting tendency not to purchase from small-scale local producers.
- Changes in consumer **lifestyle** and demographics leading to an increase in preference for ready-made food and food consumed outside the home.
- Growth in numbers of logistics service providers and their tendency to offer an ever increasing range of services.

The interest in food miles is based on its effects on the environment, sustainable agricultural development, local food systems and socio-economic development.

Food miles are significant and growing in number. They accounted for 33 billion vehicle kilometres globally in 2002 and they gave rise to around 20 million tonnes of CO_2. Air freight of food accounts for only 0.1 per cent of the vehicle kilometres. However, air freight accounts for 10 per cent of the food miles CO_2 equivalent emissions (DEFRA, 2005). The external costs of food miles are high in terms of **greenhouse gas** emissions, air pollution, noise, congestion and accidents. The necessary infrastructure in the United Kingdom associated with food miles is estimated at just over £9 billion each year.

Importing organic Argentinean beef to Europe leads to about eight times the transport emissions compared to a similar joint of Welsh beef, being sold in South-east England. When consumers want to be environmentally friendly, it is not necessarily the best solution to purchase imported organic produce from far away. The proximity of the food plays an important aspect as well. Additionally, fresh food products start to lose their nutritional content in storage: as time increases between harvesting and consumption, the nutrient value decreases. For example, spinach, if kept at room temperature, loses between 50 per cent and 80 per cent of its Vitamin C content within 24 hours.

According to some more critical sources, the concept of food miles in regards to sustainability is not as simple in reality. As argued in the study 'The validity of food miles as an indicator for sustainable development', conducted by DEFRA (2005), a 'single **indicator** based on total food kilometres is an inadequate indicator of sustainability'. Differences in food production systems need to be taken into consideration, for example. If imported food has been produced more sustainably than local food, the impact of food transport can be offset to some extent. Hence, it could be more energy-efficient to import tomatoes from Spain than producing them in heated greenhouses near the end consumer. As the amount of greenhouse gas emissions also depends on factors such as the transport mode or transport efficiency, further research into these issues is necessary. Socio-economic issues and environmental impacts other than CO_2 emissions have to be taken into consideration. The sole focus on food miles and related carbon emissions may be misleading when trying to tackle the issue of **sustainable food** sourcing. Since the subject is high on the public agenda, 'local food' has developed as a major trend throughout the food sector.

Local food

The terminology used is diverse: local food, regional food, re-localized food systems, home-grown – all aiming at the concept of producing, marketing and consuming food products within a certain geographic area. 'From farm to fork' is a common phrase used to describe the general paradigm of local food systems – bringing together primary producers and final consumers, cutting out middlemen and long supply chains, thus decreasing the environmental impact from travel (food miles) and helping to support the local economy. The localization of food systems could therefore be seen as a countertrend to some of the detrimental effects of globalization. However, it would be naïve to believe that regional food as such or regional sourcing for this matter is inherently desirable, despite the widespread belief that localization of food systems equates to sustainability. Such claims tend to be criticized as **greenwashing**, as they thrive on consumer demand for fresh, safe and eco-friendly goods, but lack a thorough and holistic approach to responsible food sourcing. Yet, it is the agenda of the given system, not its scale that makes it more or less sustainable. There is a growing understanding of the connectedness of sustainable (rural) development and local food systems. Key points are:

- closing matter and nutrient cycles;
- reduction of traffic and carbon emissions;
- maintaining economic activities and jobs in rural areas;
- environmental protection and landscape care;
- promotion of 'soft' **nature-based tourism**;
- increasing of regional value chains;
- fostering regional cultures and rural livelihoods.

Accordingly, benefits for the farmers/producers can be:

- higher net prices (or farm-gate prices) as products are mostly not distributed through wholesale channels or other middlemen;
- higher variety of sales channels and more economic self-determination;

- possibility to also market products which would not match wholesalers' product specifications or quantities demanded, which holds particularly true for producers of low-yielding, rare or traditional species, which often cannot live up to international market regulations (e.g. vegetables have to have a certain shape and size in order to fit into transport and storage facilities);
- generally more flexibility as to how, when, where and to whom to sell, which could at the same time also pose a challenge to producers, depending on their proficiency in marketing.

Benefits for consumers can include:

- access to fresh seasonal food from neighbouring farms without negative impacts from food miles;
- access to more diverse food, as farmers can choose more independently which species to grow;
- better prices for seasonal products;
- the potential to build personal trust relationships to food producers and maybe even to influence or take part in farming activities.

In the restaurant industry, this has received broad public attention. The U.S. National Restaurant Association has recently published its 'What's Hot in 2012?' survey of nearly 1800 American chefs. The mentioned top ten trends speak an unmistakable language:

1. Locally sourced meats and seafood
2. Locally grown produce
3. Healthful kids' meals
4. Hyper-local sourcing (e.g. restaurant gardens)
5. Sustainability
6. Children's nutrition
7. Gluten-free/allergy-conscious food
8. Locally-produced wine and beer
9. Sustainable seafood
10. Wholegrain items in kids' meals

The whole idea of local food sourcing is certainly gaining momentum. An increasing awareness among chefs of issues related to food sourcing and changing consumer behaviour have been followed by the initiation of several non-profit organizations promoting local and sustainable food procurement in the catering industry worldwide. A prominent example is the US-based 'Chefs Collaborative', founded in 1993 and boasting about 12,000 members, which has set out a clear mission:

> Chefs Collaborative works with chefs and the greater food community to celebrate local foods and foster a more sustainable food supply. The

About Fairmont Hotels & Resorts

Located in world-class destinations around the globe, Fairmont Hotels & Resorts is a celebrated collection of hotels that includes landmark locations like London's The Savoy, New York's The Plaza and Shanghai's Fairmont Peace Hotel. With more than 60 hotels, Fairmont is known as much for its warm, engaging service and culturally rich experiences, as its classic hotels that imbue a sense of **heritage**, sophistication and social importance and are often considered destinations in their own right. A community and environmental leader, Fairmont is also regarded for its **responsible tourism** practices and award-winning Green Partnership Program. Fairmont is owned by FRHI Holdings Limited, a leading global hotel company with over 100 hotels under the Fairmont, Raffles and Swissôtel brands. The company also manages Fairmont and Raffles branded estates and luxury private residence club properties: www. fairmont.com.

Toronto, 22 September 2011. Going local is so 2009. Upping the ante when it comes to sustainable food sourcing is Fairmont Hotels and Resorts, which has broadened the 'go local' mantra by adopting local goats and chickens, allowed diners to catch their own dinner and gone out of its way to create homemade tofu. Long an advocate of green, fresh and healthy cuisine, the brand's properties were some of the first to add onsite herb gardens and honeybee apiaries, and have pioneered myriad innovative projects that have brought farm and fork closer than ever.

Across the portfolio, Fairmont's Green Cuisine programme includes initiatives that cater to specific local and regional needs. In Quebec City, Executive Chef Jean Soulard of Fairmont Le Château Frontenac recently added five hens, who are the newest neighbours of the hotel's resident honey bees. Chantecler hens, the only 100 percent Québec breed, have been carefully selected by Chef Soulard and have been placed in a coop equipped with a copper roof that matches the architecture of the hotel. Fed only organic grains, each hen produces about one egg per day with the collected eggs served up to guests dining within the hotel.

Fairmont Newport Beach in California is constantly in pursuit of the best local produce, and the recent adoption of seven goats is the hotel's latest culinary initiative. In collaboration with Drake Farms Goat Dairy, where the female goats reside, the animals are cared for by dedicated farmers and staff and receive regular visits from the hotel's Executive Chef. The farm uses the goats' milk to produce organic and sustainable goat cheese, which the chef collects and brings back to use in dishes for the restaurant and lounge as well for in-room guest amenities. Fairmont Newport Beach follows in the footsteps of Fairmont The Queen Elizabeth in Montreal, which adopted two goats, one affectionately named Blanche Neige (Snow White), in 2010. While living at the local Fromagerie du Vieux St-François, the goats produce cheese for the menu at The Beaver Club, as well as for sale at the Fairmont Store.

At Fairmont Pittsburgh, Executive Chef Andrew Morrison of Habitat restaurant not only offers eggs from local heritage chickens, but has a side of grass-fed beef from

Burns Angus Farm delivered each week so the culinary team can specially prepare every cut to their liking. The team butchers their own steaks, roasts and grinds beef, utilizing every piece of the meat down to the bones, which are used to make stock. The hotel's signature home-made soap is made using the leftover tallow (rendered beef fat) along with coconut oil, lye and natural scents. Beef is a staple in Kenya, where Chef Hubert Des Marais continually seeks out the area's best to help support local farmers and serve sustainable cuisine. Chef Hubert recently debuted a special 'platinum steak' from local Morendat Farm, which comes from selecting and breeding particular Angus/crossbred steers just for Fairmont's East Africa properties. The cows have a specially crafted 180-day feeding programme and are taken through a process of dry ageing for approximately 21 days, which further enhances the delectable flavor and texture of the cuts.

Many of the brand's properties, from China to Washington, DC, have added honeybees to their onsite herb gardens or partnered with local parks and organizations to source local honey for cocktails and menu items. Fairmont Yangcheng Lake in Kunshan, China, has developed 200 acres as a private, organic herb and vegetable garden along the resort's namesake lake, and has recently added 10 beehives housing 2500 honeybees, which produce around 40 kg of honey in Spring. In Seattle, The Fairmont Olympic Hotel plans to install five rooftop hives, while in nearby Victoria, The Fairmont Empress has installed 10 hives in the hotel's Centennial Garden. With close to 20 active Fairmont bee programmes in place around the world, new hives have also recently been installed at The Fairmont Jasper Park Lodge, Fairmont Southampton in Bermuda, Calgary's Fairmont Palliser and Fairmont Newport Beach in California.

Toronto's Fairmont Royal York has cultivated rooftop beehives for a number of years, and has recently partnered with nearby Mill Street Brewery to create a unique honey beer, called 'Royal Stinger'. To make the beer, brewers add the rooftop honey at the end of the aging process, immediately before sealing it in kegs for distribution. But, Fairmont chefs are taking advantage of more than just local honey – in Vancouver, chefs at Fairmont Pacific Rim go the extra mile to make their very own tofu. Homemade tofu allows the guests to taste the nuances and flavor profile of the soy bean, and is used in a dish with braised daikon, gai lan and shiitake mushrooms.

Some Fairmont properties have even taken their search for hyperlocal cuisine under the sea, such as Fairmont Battery Wharf, which offers access to the only lobster boat tour in Boston. Guests can arrange a private excursion with a Fairmont Chef aboard an authentic down-east-style lobster boat to learn firsthand how to bait, drop and haul in lobster traps. After a day at sea, guests return with their catch and stop in at the hotel's restaurant, Aragosta, where the chef will prepare the lobster to their liking.

In Toronto, The Fairmont Royal York's EPIC Restaurant has recently introduced the new Thisfish lobster tagging programme, which involves tagging and tracing lobster from ocean to plate. When fishermen land their catch, they tag individual fish or entire fish lots with a distinctive code. Information about the fish – who caught it, where, when and how – is linked to the code and uploaded to http://www.this fish.info/, where diners can retrieve details about how their lobster was handled and processed through the supply chain.

Collaborative inspires action by translating information about our food into tools for making knowledgeable purchasing decisions. Through these actions, our members embrace seasonality, preserve diversity and traditional practices, and support local economies.

Essentially, it is about networking – connecting chefs (consumers) and farmers (producers) for the sake of information exchange, establishing business relations and broadening awareness – and education through farmer–chef interactions or **best-practice** examples and turning them into tools, which then can be accessed by all members of the collaborative. One example of such a tool is the Green Chefs Blue Oceans programme, jointly set up by Chefs Collaborative and the Blue Ocean Institute. Chefs can learn about responsible seafood choices and how to source them, benefit from a range of recipes and stay up to date on issues in the seafood industry.

CASE STUDY 8.4 Regional sourcing and tourism: a sustainable partnership?

In 2008, an 850 km^2 part of the Swabian Alb, a hilly and rural area close to Lake Constance, in south-west Germany, was officially recognised as a 'biosphere reserve' under UNESCO's Man and Biosphere Program. The Swabian Alb has thus been recognised as a place that seeks to reconcile **conservation** of biological and cultural diversity and economic and social development through partnerships between people and nature, proposed to test and demonstrate innovative approaches to sustainable development from local to international scales. This award, however, came with obligations: vast areas of woodland may not be utilized or changed in any way by human activity. Agricultural practices (farming, animal keeping and hunting) are encouraged, but may only take place if done in environmentally sound and sustainable ways (e.g. no use of pesticides and herbicides) and only on land, which was utilized for agricultural production before. In other words: the Swabian Alb has become thoroughly sustainable, presenting the region with a so far unmatched chance to present itself as an attractive tourism destination to regional, national and even international tourism.

Until now, the Swabian Alb has been struggling to position itself successfully in the tourism market as three publicly funded tourism agencies promoted their view of the region, each claiming to be 'the one and only' tourism gateway to the land and people. Nevertheless, most tourism attention was given to the neighbouring region of the Black Forest, internationally recognised for its lively cultural heritage, unique crafts and fine cuisine (featuring some of the most highly Michelin-decorated hotels and restaurants in Germany). Now it seems as if times are about to change. In 2010, a group of five restaurateurs have joined together to bring to life the 'Biosphere hosts' association. Their aim is to jointly promote their efforts to cultivate a regionally grounded cuisine, featuring food products sourced from the biosphere area, or at least from within the state and at the same time to support the Swabian Alb's touristic attractiveness. At present, the initiative accounts for 21 certified restaurants.

Being a member of this association comes with two major obligations:

1. Within two years after certification the restaurant needs to source 50 per cent of its food products from within the biosphere area. However, such sourcing may only take place from producers, which have been recognised as 'Partners of the Biosphere Area'. Additionally, more than 50 per cent of its beverages (wine, spirits and juices) and the ingredients of more than six dishes need to be sourced from within the state of Baden Württemberg.
2. The restaurants (and adjacent hotels) need to become **EMAS**-certified (the **European Union Eco-Management and Audit Scheme**). This certification entails a thorough review of all potentially environmentally harmful activities/ facilities within the business (e.g. use of detergents, **waste management**, energy consumption), the replacement of hazardous activities/substances/ facilities by eco-friendly ones, and the introduction of an auditing scheme.

Sources: Biosphären Gastgeber, http://www.biosphaerengastgeber.de; Biosphärengebiet Schwäbische Alb, http://www.biosphaerengebiet-alb.de; EMAS, http://www.emas.de/meta/english/.

Regional sourcing: a strategic approach for restaurants

Sourcing food regionally can have many positive impacts on a restaurant's triple bottom line. However, restaurant owners looking at increasingly sourcing food locally should consider the larger managerial implications.

The expressions 'regional' or 'local' are by no means strictly defined terms. There is currently no such thing as a universally accepted label for regional products. Perceptions as to what constitutes a regional food item may vary greatly among guests, employees and other restaurant stakeholders. Restaurant managers must therefore carefully consider how they can define their specific region and how this definition can be communicated to their clientele in order to avoid mistrust.

*   *Defining the scope*: once a restaurant has agreed on its perception of its region, chefs should consider to what extent ingredients should be sourced locally. Some regions offer more options for local sourcing than others. This decision depends on geographic and climatic conditions and the available agricultural infrastructure. In some regions, it may not be a good idea to source wine locally – in others it may be a must. Additionally, some areas may boast great products

during summer, but none during winter. This should not keep chefs from sourcing locally, but customers must be made aware of this fact.

- *Build a strategic partner network*: to successfully engage in local sourcing restaurateurs need to look for suitable strategic partners. Ongoing relationships with several providers of key ingredients can decrease the risk of running dry on key supplies. Partners, such as local farmers or processors, need to be reliable, flexible, show a constant level of quality and have transparent pricing policies. In turn, restaurants may offer a good opportunity for farmers and processors to promote themselves. Other strategic partners can be chefs' collaboratives and other stakeholder organizations, such as consumer interest groups like Slow Food or the food media. They can play a key role in promoting a restaurant's activities as well as provide training and education for team members.

- *Always strive for quality*: 'just' serving local food will neither benefit the restaurant, nor will it have any sustainability implications. Local food products should always be of superior quality. The taste of products tends to be an underestimated factor in the localizing food debate. Always opt for the best available product and spare no effort to source it. Great taste in tandem with regional sourcing can be a real USP for a restaurant.

- *Decide on the communication strategy*: some guests might like to know where your food comes from and they may be looking specifically for a restaurant serving local food. Service staff and chefs should be well trained and able to provide information about the particular food item: how, where and from whom it was sourced, and what its particular characteristics are. Other guests may not perceive 'local' as a favourable attribute for the type of restaurant they are after. Decide on whether or not local is something that adds value to your overall restaurant strategy and how to communicate it accordingly – or not.

CASE STUDY 8.5 Fairmont roofs abuzz with honeybees: honey is on the menu as chefs add offsite apiaries across the brand

Fairmont Hotels and Resorts has been committed to the protecting the environment for over 20 years, and as a part of that commitment is always brainstorming creative ways to enhance the brand's eco-focused Green Partnership Program. With growing concerns about Colony Collapse Disorder in North American honeybees, Fairmont saw an opportunity to help by placing hives in some hotels' rooftop gardens. Not only will this help the local environment by providing plenty of bees to pollinate area gardens and parks, but, by harvesting the honey, chefs can offer delicious, local and sustainable honey for use in onsite bars and restaurants. Proving to be a success, the programme has now extended beyond North America, with onsite hives thriving in Kenya and China as well.

Below is a list of Fairmont's properties that have joined the programme. Guests can also check in with Fairmont's bee programmes online at: http://www.fairmont.com/promotions/fairmontbees.

United States

The Fairmont Washington, DC has guests buzzing after welcoming thousands of Italian honeybees in summer 2009 to their new home: three beehives on the roof, affectionately named Casa Bella, Casa Blanca and Casa Bianca. The bees will enhance the hotel's culinary programme along with its interior courtyard garden, which already provides fresh herbs and flowers such as edible pansies, as well as plants, trees and flowers. The Fairmont bees came from Larry and David Reece in Germantown, Maryland, and the first honey was harvested in fall 2009.

Vital Stats: 105,000 Italian honeybees living in three beehives produce about 100 pounds of honey per year.

As part of The Fairmont San Francisco's effort to serve local, organic and sustainable cuisine, in June 2010, the iconic hotel installed four beehives in its 1,000-square-foot onsite culinary garden. The bees came from nearby Marshall Farms and now dine on the hotel's lavender and herbs to create delicious honey, with each hive boasting 50,000 bees when fully mature. Executive Chef J.W. Foster uses the harvested honey at afternoon tea service and in cocktails, entrées and desserts at the hotel's three restaurants.

Vital Stats: 50,000 honeybees living in four beehives produce 120–150 pounds of honey per year.

The storied Pyramid Restaurant and Bar at The Fairmont Dallas focuses on seasonal and local ingredients and has cultivated a beautiful rooftop garden since 2008 with a greenhouse added in 2009. Beehives are the newest addition to the rooftop, having been installed in 2010. Executive Chef André Natera and the Texas Honeybee Guild harvest the honey several times a year, which is used to complement the flavors of Chef Natera's fresh cuisine on dishes such as the local cheese plate, Blueberry Clafoutis, Baby Beets and Watermelon Brûlée.

At The Fairmont Olympic Hotel in Seattle, the culinary team is installing five rooftop honeybee hives and plans to have local honey on the menu at The Georgian restaurant in Spring 2012. Executive Chef Gavin Stephenson spearheaded the programme, and Ballard Bee Company's Corky Luster, an urban apiarian, serves as a project consultant.

Vital Stats: It is hard to say how much honey the bees will produce, but a healthy hive can typically yield 30–40 pounds. At full capacity the five hives will house 500,000 bees.

In 2011, Fairmont Newport Beach in California saved their current hive of honeybees from extermination when they were found 'swarming' in the hotel's ground-level parking lot. The hotel's beekeeping partner, Backyard Bees, rescued the bees before relocating them to a safer home on the rooftop. Executive Chef Chad Blunston personally helps the beekeepers cultivate and extract the honey for use in Bambu Restaurant, banquet menus and in room dining menus as well as for specialty VIP welcome amenities.

Vital Stats: 30,000 bees live in three hives.

In partnership with Marshall's Farm, Executive Chef Bruno Tison of the Fairmont Sonoma Mission Inn & Spa will be installing honey beehives on the resort's perimeter in order to help support the Valley's bee population, which has decreased in number by 90 per cent since the 1980s. Hotel honey will be used in soups, salad dressings, pastries, ice cream and showcased on the Michelin-starred Santé menu. Soon to be spotlighted on the Santé dessert menu: Canelés – a heavenly decadent, custardy treat baked in a traditional fluted mold coated with beeswax.

Vital Stats: When the beehives mature, they will each house up to 50,000 bees and are estimated to produce approximately 250 pounds of honey.

Canada

The Fairmont Royal York in Toronto expanded its own rooftop apiary from three to six hives in summer 2009. Later in the year, the hotel's honey placed third in the Dark Honey category at the 2009 Royal Agricultural Winter Fair, following up their second place finish in 2008. Since June 2008 over 378 pounds of honey have been harvested from the 14th story apiary, with much of it going into the hotel's mouthwatering cocktails and cuisine. The rooftop apiary was established in partnership with the Toronto Beekeepers Cooperative and FoodShare as a way to deliver fresh local honey to hotel guests in a sustainable way, and is a natural extension of the flourishing, decade-old rooftop herb garden.

Vital Stats: In summer, 350,000 honeybees living in six beehives produce about 480 pounds of honey per year.

Special Products: A unique beer, called 'Royal Stinger,' is made by local Mill Street Brewery and features honey from the hotel. This draught can only be found in the hotel's restaurants and at Mill Street Brewery.

The Fairmont Algonquin in St. Andrews by-the-Sea, New Brunswick, has welcomed royalty spanning two centuries, but in 2008 welcomed a queen of a different kind. That's when their own Queen Bee took up residence in the hotel's lavish gardens. Since then she and her hive have feasted on nearby Kingsbrae Gardens, a 27-acre horticultural masterpiece, as they produce fresh honey. The honey is on sale for guests, but is also showcased in Chef Ryan Dunne's culinary masterpieces at the hotel's three diverse restaurants, and as a complement to Fairmont's traditional afternoon tea.

Vital Stats: 200,000 honeybees living in four beehives produce 150 pounds of honey per year.

Special Products: The resort's honey is on sale for guests in the gift shop.

The Fairmont Waterfront in Vancouver is proud to share its 2,100 square foot herb garden with six honeybee hives on the hotel's third-floor terrace. The hotel's inaugural honeybee season in 2008 produced a harvest from three hives, while in 2009 the hotel captured a fourth hive of wild bees that outgrew their original home in nearby Stanley Park. Summer 2011 will bring an additional hive, bringing the apiary to just over 500,000 honey bees. Guests of the hotel are invited to join the weekly garden and hive tours conducted by Director of Housekeeping and resident Beekeeper, Graeme Evans.

Vital Stats: 500,000 honeybees living in six beehives produce 600–800 pounds of honey per year.

Special Products: The hotel's honey truffles, the 'Bee's Knees', are created in partnership with British Columbia's legendary chocolatier, Rogers' Chocolates. Offered in milk and dark chocolate, they feature flavor notes of butterscotch, vanilla and cinnamon and a package of six is available for $15 CAD.

At Fairmont Le Château Frontenac in Quebec, four Queen Bees recently made their debut from hives in the Chef's rooftop garden. Each hive contains about 70,000 bees that will produce enough honey for the entire hotel, with the extra being sold in the Fairmont Store. The honey is harvested three times a year (Spring, Summer and Fall) and used in special honey-based menus (for banquets) and select dishes in the fine dining restaurant, Le Champlain.

Vital Stats: 70,000 honeybees living in four beehives produce 650 pounds of honey per year, depending on the weather.

Special Products: The hotel jars and sells its own honey for guests.

The Fairmont Vancouver Airport is always thinking outside the box when it comes to sustainable initiatives and its commitment to the environment. With 52 colonies happily residing in their new homes at McDonald Beach Park, located just five minutes from the hotel, the hotel bee specialists have their hands full tending to a million busy honey bees. In partnership with the Honeybee Centre, The Fairmont Vancouver Airport is anticipating a tonne of the liquid gold at harvest and twice the amount the following year. The culinary team is planning a signature line-up of honey harvest offerings as well as a multitude of uses such as sweeteners for teas, coffees, yogurt, waffles, pancakes, dressings, garnishes, cocktails and more.

Vital Stats: One million honey bees living in 52 beehives produce one tonne of honey per year.

Special Products: The hotel offers a 500 gram bottle of their Canada #1 Amber honey for $16.99 CAD.

The Fairmont Empress in Victoria, British Columbia, has been privileged to welcome kings and queens, but this queen's arrival is a first. On 26 May 2011, the hotel welcomed a Queen Bee and 400,000 honey bees. The bees reside in the hotel's Centennial Garden and will pollinate Victoria's most lavish hotel gardens. In total, ten hives of European Carniolan and Italian bees will produce over 1,000 pounds of honey which will be featured in the hotel's restaurants, including the world-renowned Afternoon Tea service. The hives are provided by apiarist, John Gibeau, of the Honeybee Centre in Surrey, BC, who has managed beehives at Vancouver's Fairmont hotels. The mastermind behind the honey bees is the hotel's new Executive Chef, Kamal Silva, who initiated the honey bees at The Fairmont Vancouver Airport.

Vital Stats: About 800,000 Carniolan and Italian bees living in 10 beehives produce approximately 1,000 pounds of honey per year.

The Fairmont Jasper Park Lodge's Executive Sous Chef Cory Ledrew, is getting ready to launch an in-house beehive initiative that will debut this spring. Construction for the beehive began on the roof in late May, and Cory and his apprentices will be the beekeepers. They will lead the kitchen team in providing fresh honey for the Pastries department to use in many delicious baked goods, which are used for the resort's breakfast buffets and room amenities.

The Fairmont Palliser's culinary team in Calgary imported its very own honeybees from New Zealand for a new rooftop apiary in April 2011. The two hives, affectionately named the 'Bees N' Honey Hotel' and 'Miss Bee Haven', are set in DeWinton, Alberta, in the corner of a Saskatoon field, and will produce the majority of their honey from surrounding dandelions and the Saskatoon berry blossoms. The delicious honey is used by Executive Chef, Greg van Poppel and the hotel's culinary teams and pastry shop to enhance fabulous desserts throughout the property.

Vital Stats: About 100,000–120,000 honey bees living in two beehives produce over two hundred pounds of harvestable honey per year.

Asia

The Fairmont Yangcheng Lake in Kunshan, China, recently installed beehives that will produce fresh honey on the hotel's namesake lake. The resort has brought in a local expert, who has been in beekeeping business for 15 years, to tend the beehives and bring wild bees from the West Mount in Suzhou. Meanwhile, the hotel provides serene surroundings with plenty of trees and flowers in its 200 acres of private organic herb and vegetable garden. Each day the resident bees can produce around 40 kg honey in Spring, which allows chefs to offer guests a natural taste for desserts and entrées throughout the resort.

Vital Stats: More than 2,500 honey bees living in 10 beehives produce 40 kg of honey per day in peak season.

Fairmont Beijing is devoted to using products from local purveyors wherever possible. Currently the hotel purchases honey from several parts of China, with the majority of honey coming from Shangri-La farms. These farmers have been given free technical support, tools and training opportunities which have allowed them to grow and bottle pure, organic honey.

Africa

Fairmont Mount Kenya Safari Club has partnered with local beekeeper Stephen Macharia, who has been in the beekeeping business for over 17 years, to bring fresh honey to guests. Stephen started out collecting wild honey from the slopes of Mount Kenya, but by June will have eight hives on the property to help pollinate African flowers and the nearby Mount Kenya Forest. Each beehive will host approximately 4000 bees and produce an average of 30 kg of high quality honey, with the resort expecting their first mountain honey harvest by September. Also in June, the resort will offer lectures for guests with Stephen so they can learn about bees and honey production, in addition to indulging in a delicious tasting.
   Vital Stats: 32,000 honey bees live in eight beehives.

Mexico and Bermuda

Fairmont Mayakoba in Mexico's Riviera Maya uses their local honey in a way that is unique at Fairmont. In 2010, the United Nations Foundation acted as a liaison between the resort and the 'Flor de Tajonal' community which resulted in the installation of an onsite apiary. The 'Melipona' bees are a rare species from the area that is in danger of extinction, but which also produces a type of honey that is known for its medicinal purposes. The bees, known as Xunan Cab in Mayan, are native to the Yucatan Peninsula and are stingless. This bee is smaller that European bees and its honey is thinner and not as sweet. The Melipona has remained an important part of the Mayan culture and religion for over one thousand years and, in modern times, the honey has been used medicinally as a natural antibiotic, to eliminate cataracts, to prevent throat infections and to soften a mother's muscles during childbirth. In addition to incorporating Melipona bee honey in many recipes and beverages, the honey is being used in treatments at the luxurious Willow Stream Spa.
   Vital Stats: About 5,000 Melipona bees living in one beehive produce approximately 2 pounds of honey per year. The resort will be adding a second hive in the near future.

The Fairmont Southampton in Bermuda is committed to preserving and protecting Bermuda's natural resources, and as part of this commitment, has begun the delicate process of establishing a beehive at the South Shore resort in partnership with local beekeepers. As Bermuda's bee population has dwindled dramatically in recent years, this project will contribute to ongoing efforts to increase the number of healthy bees on the island. In time, tours will be conducted to the hive where locals and visitors alike can learn about the significant role played by bees in the island's agricultural industry, the sustainable development of the island and **food security**. The honey produced by the bees will be utilized by chefs in kitchens throughout the resort's eight restaurants.

EXERCISES

1 **GROUP DISCUSSION, GROUP PROJECT OR WRITTEN ASSIGNMENT**
   Calculating the miles
   - Take a typical meal (e.g. a holiday meal or a daily meal at the cafeteria), identify the ingredients, the sourcing of those ingredients and calculate the food miles for one dish. Share your results with classmates and discuss ways to reduce the miles.

2 **GROUP DISCUSSION OR GROUP PROJECT**
   Agricultural challenges and hospitality
   - A crisis in global agriculture is emerging. How should the hospitality industry prepare for these challenges which will inevitably affect daily operations?

3 **GROUP ACTIVITY**
   Visit supermarkets, organic markets and local farmers' markets
   - Visit a local supermarket and make a list of key fresh ingredients (produce, fruits) including the purchasing prices. Follow the same procedure at an organic store and at a local farmer's market. Compare your results with the class.
   - Conduct a comparative tasting of various ingredients (blind tasting). Identify the 'better-tasting' ingredients.

4 **GROUP RESEARCH AND DISCUSSION**
   A question of food
   Provide answers and critically discuss the following questions:
   - What are the different types of agriculture and how do they differ with respect to their sustainability profile?
   - Why should hospitality managers bother about agricultural practices and food sourcing?
   - What are the key principles of organic agriculture?
   - What issues do you see with sourcing certified organic food for your restaurant and at the same time claiming to be a fully sustainable eatery?
   - Explain the implications and limitations of regional food sourcing with respect to a restaurant's triple bottom line.
   - What is the concept of 'food miles' and how does it relate to globalization?

References

Badgley, C., Moghtader, J., Quintero, E., Zakem, E., Chappell, M.J., Avilés-Vázquez, K., Samulon, A. and Perfecto, I. (2007) 'Organic agriculture and the global food supply', *Renewable Agriculture and Food Systems*, 22: 86–108.

Berry, W. (1990) 'The pleasures of eating', in W. Berry, *What Are People For?*, New York: North Point Press. Available at: http://www.ecoliteracy.org/essays/pleasures-eating.

Department for Environment, Food and Rural Affairs (DEFRA) (2005) 'The validity of food miles as an indicator for sustainable development'. Available at: archive.defra.gov.uk/evidence/economics/food/farm/.../foodmile.pdf.

Department for Environment, Food and Rural Affairs (DEFRA) (2006) 'Food industry sustainability strategy'. Available at: http://www.defra.gov.uk/publications/files/pb11649-fiss2006-060411.pdf.

International Foundation for Organic Agriculture Movements (IFOAM) (2008) *Organic Standards and Certification*. Available at: http://www.ifoam.org/about_ifoam/standards/index.html.

Pretty, J.N., Ball, A.S., Lang, T. and Morison, J.I.L. (2005) 'Farm costs and food miles: an assessment of the full cost of the UK weekly food basket', *Food Policy*, 1: 1–19.

Soil Association (2008) *Organic Food and Farming Report*, Bristol: Soil Association.

The Organic Wine Company (2012) *Organic Wines 101*. Available at: http://www.theorganicwinecompany.com/owc/pages/organic_101.shtml.

United States Department of Agriculture (USDA) (2008) *National Organic Program*. Available at: http://www.ams.us.da.gov/AMSv1.0/getfile?dDocName-STELDEV3004446.

Resources

Blue Ocean Institute: http://www.blueocean.org.

Center for Integrated Agricultural Systems: http://www.cias.wisc.edu.

Chefs Collaborative: http://chefscollaborative.org.

Department for Environment, Food and Rural Affairs (DEFRA): http://www.defra.gov.uk.

European Commission on Organic Agriculture: http://ec.europa.eu/agriculture/organic.

International Assessment of Agricultural Knowledge, Science and Technology for Development (IASSTD): *Synthesis Report*. Available at: http://www.agassessment.org/.

International Federation of the Organic Movement (IFOAM): http://www.ifoam.org.

National Restaurant Association: 'What's Hot in 2012?'. Available at: http://www.restaurant.org/foodtrends.

Soil Association: http://www.soilassociation.org.

United States Department of Agriculture National Organic Programme: http://www.ams.usda.gov/AMSv1.0/nop.

Additional material

Go to www.routledge.com/cw/sloan to find PowerPoint slides of all the figures and tables from the book, additional case studies, a test bank of questions and extra links to useful videos.

Sustainable food and beverage management

CHAPTER OBJECTIVES

The objectives for this chapter are:

- To explain what sustainable food is
- To describe the issues around food security and genetic engineering
- To define the categories of sustainable food
- To explain the issues of nutrition and health
- To explain the challenges of modern food production
- To describe organic food and organic food labelling
- To explain the concept of 'food miles'
- To explain how sustainable wine can be sourced

The emergence of the sustainable food movement

The movement for **sustainable food** has its origins in the 1970s as a result of increasing public awareness about environmental issues that impact on the global economy. Sections of society realized that the health of the planet and of people depended on innovations that would save the **environment** for the present as well as future generations. Sustainable food has its roots in the prevailing liberal climate of the time and in the 'back to nature' movement that stressed the importance of integrity of foods derived from natural agricultural systems in the locality, following the seasons. Even before this period, during the early stages of the food industry that developed in the 1850s thanks to new food processing techniques, groups were founded across Europe that sought a more natural and authentic nutrition. People following this **lifestyle** were aware of the necessity to protect nature and the problems of animal welfare which together sparked the establishment of the vegetarian movement and healthy lifestyles.

The last three decades of the twentieth century saw the development of diverse food movements, in addition to *vegetarians* who only eat vegetables and dairy products. Restaurants that cater for *vegans* who follow a vegetarian diet without dairy products, *macrobiotics* who avoid meat but sometimes eat fish and seaweed, *crudivores* who only eat uncooked food and *locavores* who only eat food that comes from predetermined local areas, can be found everywhere. All these food movements are based upon a strong interest in the nutritional content of food. Health food is a term notoriously difficult to define and a vast panoply of natural food and drinks and food supplements can be found in health food restaurants and shops. The goal of leading a healthy life is nothing new but the origin of eating specific foods and food extracts goes back to the turn of the nineteenth century when scientists discovered and analysed nutrients in foods. Scientific breakthroughs were made by scientists such as Eijkman (1896), who detected that thiamine deficiency causes Beriberi, Fischer (1902), who discovered the protein and amino acids requirements for human beings, and Burr and Burr (1929) who discovered the importance of essential fatty acids. These discoveries lead to the 'analyses of nutrients in food' movement, a group which later became the 'health food' movement.

Unfortunately 'health food' has no clear definition and is used as a general term encompassing natural foods, organic foods, vegetarian foods, etc. and the use of dietary supplements. However, one thing is clear: health food can be seen as the opposite of junk food. Common junk foods include salted snack foods, chewing gums, candies, sweet desserts, fried fast food and carbonated beverages. All of them typically contain high levels of calories from sugar or fat with little protein, vitamins or minerals.

Research by Johnson and Kenny at the Scripps Research Institute in 2010 suggests that junk food consumption alters brain activity in a manner similar to addictive drugs like cocaine or heroin. Working with rats in laboratory conditions, they found that after many weeks of unlimited access to junk food, the pleasure centres of rat brains become desensitized, requiring more food for pleasure. A 2007 *British Journal of Nutrition* study found that mothers who eat junk food during pregnancy increased the likelihood of unhealthy eating habits in their children. A 2011 report published in *The Federation of American Societies for Experimental Biology Journal* suggests infants whose mothers eat excessive amounts of high-fat, high-sugar junk foods when pregnant or breastfeeding are likely to have a greater preference for these foods later in life.

Opposed to the culture of junk food or 'fast food', the movement known as Slow Food seeks to encourage the enjoyment of regional foods representing cultural traditions. It is a defender of the organic movement and supports initiatives to set up seed banks to help protect fruit and vegetable species which are no longer farmed. It aims to defend agricultural **biodiversity** and opposes agricultural policy issues such as the use of chemical herbicides and pesticides and most forms of genetic engineering. The organization sees itself as having an educational role and is generally opposed to commercial agribusiness, factory farms and the monoculture system.

Slow Food can be best summed up as an ethical, anti-fast-food, anti-industrial-agriculture movement. It was first started in 1986 by Carlo Petrini, an Italian journalist. In 2010, there were over 100,000 members worldwide, mostly in English-speaking countries. Slow Food was originally launched to deal with a crisis in Italian food, as traditional produce seemed to be disappearing in the face of global fast-food chains. The organization is financially supported by its members' subscriptions and sponsorship from corporations such as Lavazza.

The Slow Food organization has been accused of being tilted more toward high-class gastronomy and being less interested in public health issues. Although the organization states that it aims to bring about environmental **sustainability**, economic equality and **social** justice, it does not state its strategy for achieving these goals. Indeed, Slow Food has been criticized for providing something for everyone without any real focus.

The movement away from junk food by the health conscious towards 'slow food' and 'health foods' has been seen as a way to avoid serious health problems. In the 1980s the term 'functional food' first begun to appear. Functional food believes in the all-fixing power of food, one that promises solutions to health, fitness, indulgence and prestige. Functional food can be defined as a health food in as much that it is a food where a specific ingredient has been added to promote better health or prevent disease. Fortified foods with health-promoting additives, like 'vitamin-enriched' products are in this category, iodine added to table salt or the fatty acid, Omega 3, added to margarine to prevent heart disease are examples of functional food.

Unsustainable consumption patterns of food

The range of food products available to Western consumers is greater now than at any other period in history. Since the 1950s the percentage of disposable income spent on food has continued to decline as food products have become more affordable and available all the year round, and food seasonality has lost its meaning to the modern-day consumer. The constant global trade in food has resulted in consumers who have become increasingly estranged from the production of their foodstuffs and their local food traditions. Despite the recent revival of interest in regional food and organic produce, consumer knowledge on seasonality or regional supply has been lost by the general public.

Food habits and preferences are shaped by cultural traditions, norms, fashions and physiological needs, as well as by personal food experience. Such preferences and tastes, together with finances, time and other personal constraints, influence food consumption patterns. Country-specific and household-specific characteristics such as age, income, education and family type all influence food consumption levels and make the job of promoting more sustainable food consumption harder.

Over the past 60 years consumers have become used to cheap food and, if given the choice, will spend their money on other consumer products rather than purchasing more expensive foodstuffs. Hence, price in particular has become a major decision criterion. Consumers are constantly tempted by a range of convenience foods, ready meals and affordable restaurants. In fact, for many, eating fast food has become the norm. Time spent on food purchasing and cooking, as well as time spent on eating, has decreased significantly over the past few years. One habit that has not changed much is that women still spend more time on food purchasing and cooking than men. The role of communal food eating is being lost; families eat less often together around a table than ever before. This is regrettable since food consumption is furnished with symbolic meaning and hedonistic experiences.

Hence, the rationale for sustainable food has many strands; respect for nature, authenticity, well-being, economics and health.

The concept of sustainable food

At present, there is no international legal definition of 'sustainable food', although some aspects, such as the terms 'organic' or 'Fair Trade', are clearly defined (see Chapter 8). Sustainable food is defined by the UK Government Sustainable Development Commission as food that is:

- *Safe, healthy and nutritious*, for consumers in shops, restaurants, schools, hospitals, etc. and can meet the needs of the less well-off people.
- *Provides a viable livelihood* for farmers, processors and retailers, whose employees enjoy a safe and hygienic working environment, whether in the UK or overseas.
- *Respects biophysical and environmental limits* in its production and processing, while reducing energy consumption and improving the wider environment. It also respects the highest standards of animal health and welfare, compatible with the production of affordable food for all sectors of society.
- *Supports rural economies* and the diversity of rural culture, in particular through an emphasis on local products that keep **food miles** to a minimum.

All the evidence suggests that sustainable food and beverages are good for business in restaurants and hotels. Consumers are asking for it, and its availability has vastly improved over the last few years and it is good for the environment and society as well. Educating and retaining customers is the essence of good hospitality management. Being able to tell customers an engaging story about where the ingredients come from can give competitive advantage, helping to attract new customers and making sure they come back. Training staff to be able to talk to customers about the origin and quality of the ingredients used can also result in increased staff pride and loyalty. Incorporating local and seasonal food into the menu can turn sustainability into a unique selling point by making clear the company's commitment to improve its environmental performance.

Figures in the retail sector show that around the world consumers are increasingly demanding 'ethical foods' such as organic and Fair Trade produce. Recent surveys comparing organic food consumption in EU countries have also found little difference between countries in what motivates consumers to buy organic produce. It is likely, therefore, that the barriers to buying organic stem more from the structural characteristics of the context, that is to say, the access, availability and affordability of the supply. Other research shows that less than 10 per cent of organic purchases are motivated by environmental concerns. Health aspects are the main driver in about 60 per cent of all cases of purchasing situations.

Despite strong growth in all major European markets and the USA, in 2011, sales of organic products fell by 3.7 per cent in the UK, as consumers continued to reduce their spending in the face of ongoing tough economic conditions. Internationally, organic sales grew by 8 per cent in 2011 when global sales were valued at €44.5 billion. The USA was the biggest organic market with sales climbing by about US$2 billion to US$26.7 billion, followed by Germany, where sales rose by about €200 million to €6.02 billion. Data published by the Switzerland-based Research Institute of Organic Agriculture showed that France ranked third in organic food popularity as sales increased by about €340 million to €3.39 billion. Per capita consumption of organic products was highest in Switzerland, Denmark and Luxembourg, according to the report. Sales of fairly traded products have grown everywhere, including the UK, where sales grew by 12 per cent in 2011. The latest figures from the Fairtrade Foundation revealed that the value of Fair Trade products sold through shops reached £1.32 billion in 2011, compared with £1.17 billion in 2010.

Constituents of sustainable food

Ethical aspects

Fundamental to the sustainable food movement is the idea of ethically responsible food production, practices and conditions in the food chain, i.e. animal welfare, the respect of biodiversity, fair working conditions and social justice for farm workers and the environment. It should be noted that these are goals that restaurants wishing to be more **sustainable** should aspire to. Possible key terms in this area are:

- *Food safety*: food should not endanger the health of consumers. All new developments in nutritional research and technology, such as functional foods and genetically modified foods should always pass stringent health checks by competent authorities. The core issue is the 'ethical traceability' of key consumer concerns.
- ***Food security***: food security is the just and fair supply of food and drink to human beings encompassing a multiplicity of aspects, ranging from food and water security to meeting the needs of a growing world population.

- *Free range*: this is defined in European law, but only for poultry. Free range poultry farming systems must allow poultry to have access to the open air and vegetation, mimicking a more natural environment. Rules governing the amount of space that the birds have and the type of shelter provided are stipulated. Other animals such as pigs are often described as 'free range' or 'outdoor reared', but these terms are not legally defined.
- *Fair Trade products*: these are conceived to improve the well-being and livelihoods of agricultural producers and labourers in poorer countries. Improved trading relationships ensure better working conditions and Fair Trade projects work with local people to create greater access to healthcare and a higher standard of living.
- *Organic* **certification**: as well as upholding environmental standards of agriculture protecting the environment and restricting the use of chemical additives and antibiotics, organic certification tends to require higher standards of animal welfare. Various voluntary certification programmes and standards for **organic agriculture** have been developed in the past 20 years (see Chapter 8 for details).

Reduce consumption of food derived from animals

A major strategy in encouraging more sustainable food consumption is to eat less meat and meat-derived products since a meat-intensive diet is associated with the inefficient use of water, energy and grain. Eating less meat can contribute to a healthier diet, support the provision of more vegetable foods for a growing world population, and help reduce **environmental impacts** especially **greenhouse gas** emissions. One potential solution is to promote the purchase of higher quality meat and dairy products and to eat smaller portions less frequently.

There is plenty of scientific evidence to suggest that eating a greater proportion of foods of plant origin (fruits, vegetables, pulses, nuts, seeds and cereals) can reduce the risks of serious diseases such as heart disease and certain cancers. Foods of plant origin tend to be naturally low in fat and salt and also contain high levels of other useful nutrients such as vitamins, minerals, antioxidants and dietary fibre. Some research suggests there are 4 million non-meat eaters in the UK alone, while this number has remained relatively stable over recent years, evidence suggests that more and more people are looking for alternatives to eating less meat. Indeed, research suggests that 'meat reducers' account for 45 per cent of the population. Although in the minority, just one non-meat eater in a group of people going out to eat can influence the group's choice of restaurant.

Animal welfare remains a primary motive for choosing a vegetarian diet; over 2 million animals are killed every day for food in the UK alone, according to the Vegetarian Society. In their research, they state that one hectare of land, producing vegetables, fruit and cereals can feed up to 30 people. The same area, if used to produce meat, could feed between only 5 and 10. It is becoming harder to be an ethical meat-eater, with factory farming being the predominant means of meat production, the Vegetarian Society estimates that at least 80 per cent of the EU's farm animals are factory-farmed animals often dosed up on a host of antibiotics and kept in cramped conditions.

Avoid fish from unsustainable sources

Fish is a preferred dish for many people as it has lots of variety in taste and texture, it is versatile and low in saturated fat and high in protein, essential minerals and vitamins. Oily fish such as mackerel, herring and sardines are sustainable and contain Omega-3 fatty acids, a type of polyunsaturated fat which can help to reduce blood cholesterol, protect the heart and may reduce the risk of certain cancers. These fatty acids also help maintain healthy nerve tissues, strong bones and teeth and a glowing complexion. Fish eating has always been popular throughout history though until the invention of modern cooling, freezing systems and fast transport infrastructure, it was mainly limited to coastal areas. The increasing industrialization of the fishing industry, along with far more opportunities for the consumer to buy fish, has led to a serious over-exploitation of sea fish. Globally, 85 per cent of fish stocks are fully or partly over-fished; only eight out of 47 fish stocks in the European, Atlantic fishing waters are currently in a healthy state.

Many other problems are associated with fishing including the loss of marine biodiversity, not only from declining fish stocks but also from 'by-catch', i.e. the non-targeted and often commercially useless species such as whales, sharks, dolphins, sea birds and young fish being accidentally killed by fishing gear. More than half the fish served in restaurants come from fish farming, or aquaculture which on the surface can seem like the solution to many of these problems. The aquaculture industry has boomed in recent years, with farmed species including salmon, trout, sea bass and prawns. However, aquaculture is often very intensive and is associated with a host of social and environmental problems. The fish-feed to fish protein conversion ratio is low. The fish meal and oils used in fish farming come from fish such as sand eels. Their removal in massive quantities by industrial fishing vessels has had a devastating effect on the marine **ecosystem**. Many farmed species are carnivorous and some are migratory by nature, for example, salmon that need around 3 kg of wild caught fish to produce 1 kg of farmed salmon. Diseases and parasites such as sea lice affect fish farmed in pens and **pollution** of the marine environment can occur due to fish faecal matter, antibiotics and toxic chemicals such as 'anti-foulants' used to keep cages and netting free of seaweed and barnacles. Unfortunately, as in other cash crop farming activities in developing economies, environmental and social **impacts** are prevalent.

In a 2012 report by the New Economics Foundation, it is claimed that restoring fish stocks to health would create jobs and increase the income of Europe's fishing fleets by over €3 billion per year but the short-term focus of fisheries policy at present means that stocks are not allowed to recover. A new, restored European fishing industry would support more than 100,000 new jobs in the sector with increased catches of about 3.5 million tonnes greater than at present.

There are two key issues determining whether or not a fishery is sustainable. The first is how healthy the population or 'stock' is and the second, the method used to catch the fish. Some methods are clearly very destructive (like bottom trawling, which ploughs up the sea floor) or indiscriminate (like pair trawling that catches non-target species such as dolphins). There are very few sustainable fisheries. In Europe, the best are line-caught mackerel, line-caught sea bass, and farmed mussels and

CASE STUDY 9.1 Shangri-La announces sustainable seafood policy and discontinuing use of all shark fin products in 72 hotels and resorts

Shangri-La Hotels and Resorts announced its 'Sustainable Seafood Policy' including the commitment to cease serving shark fin in all of its operated restaurants as well as accepting new orders for shark fin products in banqueting, with immediate effect. Future banquet bookings made prior to this date will be honoured as per the signed contractual agreement. At the same time, Shangri-La announced that it will phase out Bluefin tuna and Chilean sea bass in all its operated restaurants within the year. In December 2010, the company initiated the process with the removal of shark fin products from its restaurant menus. The new policy is a continuation of Shangri-La's journey towards environmental support.

The company launched its first **CSR** initiatives in 2005 which were streamlined and formalized in 2009 in the three main areas of Sustainability, Embrace and Sanctuary towards a strategic commitment to **corporate social responsibility** (CSR).

Sanctuary, Shangri-La's 'Care for Nature' project, was introduced specifically to ensure consistency in biodiversity, **conservation** and habitat protection across all resorts. Projects include the development of marine sanctuaries to ensure reef protection and stability of the underwater and marine life. Two years later, in May 2011, the company published its first Sustainability Report, outlining the company's progress in the areas of environment, health and safety, employees, supply chain and **stakeholder** relations.

Shangri-La's ethos and core values show a commitment to the environment that the company does business in. As part of the CSR efforts, Shangri-La has been working on a number of projects related to sustainability for several years. The sustainable seafood campaign has been at the forefront as the initiative will deliver immediate results.

Shangri-La will continue to review and refine its overall programmes including environmental and sustainability issues.

Source: Shangri-La Hotels & Resorts, http://www.shangri-la.com/en/corporate/press/pressrelease/57020.

oysters. Rod and line-caught tuna and herring practised by the Spanish and Portuguese fishing fleets are also considered to be sustainable fishing techniques.

Fortunately there are sustainable options. Surveys show that a very significant 77 per cent of European consumers are already concerned about seafood sustainability. A particular seafood is sustainable if it comes from a fishery with practices that can be maintained indefinitely without reducing the target species' ability to maintain its population and without adversely impacting on other species within the ecosystem by removing their food source, accidentally killing them or damaging their physical environment. With some species, this is not easy to achieve and it is advised to always ask the fish supplier for assurances that the fish they supply has been ethically and sustainably farmed or caught. Look for fish that is certified as being sustainable by such organizations as Marine Stewardship Council (MSC).

Use local, seasonally available ingredients as standard

Consuming local food above all supports the local economy and regional food products can save energy when distributed efficiently due to the reduction in energy needed in transportation. Bulk purchasing is less likely to be needed and so energy used in storage can be reduced as well. Regional distribution structures make it, in principle, possible to harvest fruits and vegetables that are fresh and ripe, thus increasing their taste and nutritive values, e.g. soluble vitamins like vitamin C. In the conventional system, fruit especially is harvested unripe and arrives in front of the restaurant guest ripened in transit. Although not scientifically proven, the sensory quality of local fruit and vegetables seems to be more appetising, local strawberries smell, feel, look and taste better! Local processing of meat products like sausages means that chemical preservatives like phosphates can be left out. Where permitted by law, highly nutritious unpasteurized milk can be purchased locally. The pasteurization process not only increases the shelf life but it also decreases the nutrients.

Seasonal food is local food and designing menus around it saves energy directly and indirectly. Asparagus flown into Europe from South America or green beans flown in from Kenya seem to have no place on a sustainable restaurant menu. However, Europeans find it difficult to live without oranges, bananas, pomegranates and passion fruit. Good advice would be to enjoy these fruits in moderation in the winter, at a time of year when European fruit is relatively sparse.

Planning a menu 365 days of the year around imported food can be to the detriment of local food traditions and local fruit and vegetable varieties. Literally hundreds of varieties of carrots exist, suited to different climates and soil. A restaurant in Stockholm would be doing a disservice to local horticulturists by buying imported carrots from Spain. It is not only energy that is saved by consuming local, seasonal produce but also water. It is often water-scarce regions of the world that grow cash crops like coffee, bananas and even wheat in the plains of the USA.

The passing of the seasons brings a never-ending choice of foods to the restaurant kitchen. Whenever a particular locally produced ingredient goes out of season, it can be guaranteed that another delicious food will come back into season to tempt customers. Ultimately, eating the seasons is about enjoyment, not abstinence. All restaurateurs who seek to offer the best food quality and have an awareness of when certain ingredients are at their best will, quite naturally, end up serving more foods in season and less of those shipped half-way around the world.

Local food grants consumers greater knowledge about its origins and sometimes the possibility of getting a better price. Farm-gate shops and local markets give the opportunity to customers to fully understand the growing or production process. Confidence in the sustainable authenticity of a product is much easier to have when the cows can be seen in the field. The term 'traceability' or 'provenance', taken from the French, is now popular parlance. Traceability means the ability to track any food, feed, food-producing animal or substance that will be used for consumption, through all stages of production, processing and distribution. Traceability is a way of responding to potential risks that can arise in food and feed, to ensure that all food products are safe to eat. In sustainable food supply chain management, traceability is more of an ethical or environmental issue. Environmentally friendly and ethical retailers may choose to make information regarding their supply chain freely available to customers, illustrating the fact that the food and drink products they sell are produced on farms and in factories where non-authorized chemical additives are not used and in safe working conditions, by workers that earn a fair wage, using methods that do not damage the environment.

Of course, even when a food is in season, its quality can vary dramatically. Food produced locally, e.g. bought from a farmers' market, is likely to be a lot fresher than central distribution system equivalents. Meat produced with respect for the animals concerned will inevitably be far superior to intensively-reared animals that are likely to have spent pitiful lives in abhorrent conditions.

Purely calculating food miles as a barometer for making purchasing decisions can be criticized for over-simplifying and neglecting relevant factors related to the environmental and social impacts of food. The environmental impacts of food transportation depend on a variety of factors, including the means of transportation (e.g. aircraft, train, ship or lorry), loading capacity and distance. Needless to say, the environmental impact of some foods transported by air can be substantial. Vegetables and fruits that have low production environmental impacts have high transport environmental impacts and vice versa for meat, due to its bulk. For instance, transportation's share in greenhouse gas emissions for food eaten in Europe is about 15 per cent for fresh vegetables coming from South Africa and about 2 per cent for Argentine beef.

Regionally produced food is not always more environmentally friendly than food transported over long distances. However, local food is always better if local production conditions exactly match those overseas since greenhouse gas emissions from transportation are avoided. Internationally produced foodstuffs may be better if superior production conditions compensate for the impacts of longer transportation. For instance, tomatoes cultivated in the south of Spain during the winter months without the use of fossil fuel heating can have a lower environmental impact than the Dutch equivalent. Environmental impacts vary from product to product, depending on a variety of factors, including specific production conditions, means of transportation and efficiency of logistics. On balance, buying locally grown, seasonal, fresh fruit and vegetables and regionally produced food and beverage products is better in terms of taste, ethics and local culinary traditions, since it helps support local economies and cultures.

Avoid bottled water

Bottled water is a huge commercial activity which has little to do with sustainability. It is expensive for the consumer, wasteful and has many environmental impacts while boasting dubious health benefits. Estimates of worldwide bottled water sales vary between US$50 and US$100 billion each year, with a 7 per cent annual global market expansion. Bottled water produces up to 1.5 million tonnes of plastic waste per year, requiring up to 180 million litres of oil per year to produce. Plastic waste is now at such a volume in the world's oceans that it represents a great risk to marine life, killing birds and fish which mistake garbage for food. This plastic waste will be around for a long time yet since its decay rate is very slow.

In general, people do not drink enough water, even though it is good for hydration, digestion and all-round well-being. For health, bottled water is certainly better than high-calorie sugary fizzy drinks, but most of the health benefits of bottled water are unfounded. There are no known health benefits from drinking bottled water instead of tap water. In developed nations, tap water is governed by strict rules and is tested to even more stringent standards than bottled water so it is safe and palatable to drink. In the USA, for instance, municipal water falls under the control of the Environmental Protection Agency, and is regularly inspected for bacteria and toxic chemicals.

Recent surveys of restaurant customers show that restaurant customers resent being made to feel 'cheap' if they ask for tap water, and also resent the mark-up on bottled water. A simple, cost-effective way of demonstrating opposition to bottled water is for restaurant customers to routinely ask for tap water. Many people drink bottled water because they do not like the taste of their local tap water, or because they question its safety. Blind taste tests confirm that, particularly if the water is chilled, most people cannot tell the difference between tap water and still bottled water. Alternatively, restaurants could consider the use of simple carbon filters in areas where there is a high concentration of chlorine in the tap water. A fancy indulgence that can please some customers is for restaurants to carbonate water themselves, meaning no one has to use fossil fuels to ship a bottle filled with water across the world. A similar initiative is for restaurants to offer wine on tap.

Reduce processed food

Demand for high quality, safe, nutritious processed foods continues to increase and can consequently impose an enormous burden on the environment. Industrial food processing can affect food and consequently health even more than agriculture does because it not only adds various industrial ingredients but also significantly alters foods, most often at very basic levels. Processed foods tend to be high in fat and refined sugars and low in minerals and vitamins. In any sustainable diet, it is important to maintain the wholesomeness and integrity of food and to avoid where possible the alteration of fatty acids and amino acids that can happen during processing. Minimizing food processing translates into minimizing inputs of energy and water. Moreover, it means supporting local food and agricultural structures.

In attempts to become more sustainable, the food processing industry is taking an integrated approach to the whole food supply chain including farm and post-processing operations. **Life cycle assessment (LCA)** facilitates this approach and can enable meaningful environmental messages to be communicated to consumers. Food manufacturers and processors have discovered opportunities to execute a wide range of environmental initiatives. Thermal food processing plants (for freezing and cooling) can benefit from reuse of water and waste heat from their processes. Cooling water can be reused and alternatively, by co-generation, surplus steam and heat can be converted to electricity. Another significant potential for reducing water consumption is replacing the use of low-pressure wash systems to clean food processing equipment with high-pressure wash systems on shorter cycles. Heat exchange systems have been designed to take residual heat off the top of boiler stacks, using condensing stack economizers to recapture the latent heat in water vapour and use it in the manufacturing process. Recently, engineers have identified opportunities to redesign vacuum cooling operations utilizing steam pumps, the end result being a significant reduction in natural gas usage. Lastly, the installation of metres gives a clear indication of how much it costs to run individual production lines, facilities and operations as a whole.

Although technological advances have been made enabling the reduction of the environmental **footprints** of processed foods, the best advice for restaurants is to use less. A truly sustainable restaurant should only purchase processed foods produced with minimal fossil energy inputs that do not use industrial chemical ingredients. Although all cooking is nothing else but a form of food processing, delicious food can be made with minimum of fuss; the less processed it is, the better.

Reduce packaging

Buying food products with reduced packaging is more sustainable. Although the wrappings, boxes and containers that food is delivered in only play an ancillary role in the environmental impacts of food production along the value chain, any small reduction helps the planet. In general, packaging's share in greenhouse gas emissions is higher in goods whose production causes lesser greenhouse gas emissions (e.g. vegetables, fruit) and lower in goods whose production causes many greenhouse gas emissions, e.g. meat. Generally, environmental impacts from packaging are less than 10 per cent of a products' **life cycle**.

Sustainable restaurants cut down on the amount of excess packaging that comes with food and beverages. Wholesalers should be required to source products with minimum packaging or buy in bulk. Weight for weight, larger boxes, cartons and bags use less packaging materials than smaller ones. Restaurant service-ware should be chosen that is preferably re-usable i.e. washable plates jugs, cutlery and other goods are far better than those that get used only once and then thrown away. Cut down food waste by making the very best use of the food purchased and try **composting** any leftovers.

The sustainable and the unsustainable kitchen

Defining 'junk food' is fairly easy for most people but recognizing unsustainable foods is sometimes difficult. Sampling the local cuisine is a big part of travelling but in some destinations, it may not be the taste or texture that travellers have a hard time stomaching; it may be the ethics that lie behind the food on the plate that cause concern. Here are some examples:

Whale meat

Despite a decades-old worldwide moratorium on commercial whaling, whale meat is still eaten in Japan, Iceland and Norway. Many species of whale are endangered. Catching them is done in the name of scientific research but some of the meat still ends up on restaurant tables. In the USA, and in most of the EU, the sale of the whale meat is illegal; a California sushi restaurant faced federal charges in 2010 for serving whale meat to customers.

Turtle eggs

Turtle eggs might not sound appetising to Westerners but they are eaten in several Central American countries, particularly Nicaragua and Guatemala. The practice has put in peril the work of researchers working to save endangered and vulnerable turtle species, like the olive ridley, by poachers, who snatch the eggs from nests.

Ortolan buntings

The consumption of this now-endangered bird whose habitat is in the south-west of France is now outlawed. Traditionally it is roasted and eaten whole, bones and all, by diners who shield their faces with napkins for the gourmet's aesthetic desire to absorb the maximum odour with the flavour. The EU has also banned large-scale capture of the birds in places like Malta and Italy where there is widespread poaching. François Mitterrand's last meal included this specially prepared bird which was illegal to prepare and eat at that time.

Bluefin tuna

The Bluefin is prized and very costly, and its fatty flavour is especially popular in sushi. Thanks to four decades of over-fishing, due to the massive commercial demand, it has been driven to just 3 per cent of its 1960 numbers, a decline of 97 per cent. According to the US National Oceanic and Atmospheric Administration, the Atlantic Bluefin is a 'species of concern' and is subject to sometimes ignored quotas set by the International Commission for the Conservation of Atlantic Tunas.

Foie gras

Many lovers of this duck-liver dish do not like to talk about how the buttery delicacy ended up on their plates. The ducks are confined inside dark sheds and force-fed enormous amounts of food several times a day. In just a matter of weeks, the ducks become grossly overweight and their livers expand to up to 10 times their normal size. In response to this treatment the state of California has decided to ban foie gras from menus. However, Europeans are free to continue to eat this favourite delicacy.

Tips for the sustainable kitchen

Eating and drinking are two of the most intensive actions between mankind and nature. The term sustainable kitchen may not sound exciting as a description but there are several important principles behind it:

- *Think flavour and texture*. In the **Western diet** it is not only protein consumers crave, it is also rich complex flavours. Layering flavours involves cooking techniques that add depth of flavour. Proper cooking ensures the diner experiences foods of interesting flavours and textures. Grilling, smoking and roasting foods concentrate and add more flavour notes to lean vegetables and protein foods. Also, caramelization, toasting, poaching and slow cooking all have their place in the sustainable chef's armoury. Flavours combined enhance richness and more subtleness in the finished dish. Since we eat with our eyes first, an artful plate presentation ensures that the meal launches on a positive note.
- *Use up leftovers, and be creative!* Tasty soups and stews can be made from offcuts. Always use vegetable trimmings and meat and fish leftovers for making delicious stock.
- *Don't be fooled by the cosmetic appearance of fruit and vegetables*. Use blemished fruit and vegetables and riper fruits that might otherwise go to waste.
- *Diverse food should be supported and one should not be against local biodiversity and local resources*. Consider 'wild food', our ancestors were fishermen, farmers, hunters and gatherers. Now, some restaurants are attracting customers with mushrooms, flowers, nuts and seeds coming straight from the wild.

- *Think nutrition.* Preparation techniques should always maintain maximum nutrient retention. Exposing foods to light or air, cooking on high temperatures, using too much liquid or cooking for long periods may reduce nutrient levels. Traditional foods and cooking methods are well suited to healthy cooking. Here are some examples:
  - *Wild berries* grown without pesticides have high levels of antioxidants. One Canadian study found that wild blueberries can counteract inflammation and insulin sensitivity, two factors that, when abnormal, can contribute to arthritis and diabetes. Wild mulberries, huckleberries and blackberries, all have higher antioxidant content than cultivated berries.
  - *Natural honey* is full of living hormone-like qualities, which makes it a valuable adjunct to the diet. It is rich in antioxidants and is often used as an antiseptic treatment on wounds. It contains phyto estrogens, and studies on Greek honey have found that they can slow down the growth of breast, prostate and endometrial cancers. Honey also has a low glycaemic index, so using it to sweeten tea or coffee will not lead to energy-sapping blood sugar drops later in the day. The best honey is raw, local honey from a nearby farmer, preferably with an organic seal. A recent test by Food Safety News revealed that more than 75 per cent of the honey sold in the USA is so heavily processed and filtered that none of the original pollen put there by the bees is still found in it. Buying honey helps support biodiversity as well. In the past ten years 40 per cent of the European bee population has been lost as a result of conventional agricultural practices.
  - *Seaweed* has been a traditional food in China, Japan and the Republic of Korea and in other coastal regions of the world for several centuries. On the Atlantic coast of Europe, eating dulse, wrack, kelp and sea lettuce might sound like extreme modern culinary weirdness but in fact, seaweed can be delicious. Toasted Japanese nori, steamed hijiki or kombu, the basis for dashi, the broth that is a keystone to many Japanese soups, all make up flavoursome, nutritious dishes. Seaweed is rich in amino acids, which give it a deep savoury flavour known as *umami* in Japanese. Use of seaweed is based on historical or cultural traditions and as such is used as a medicine. It is thought to reduce the risk of cancer, diabetes and strokes, while staving off age-related degeneration of the brain and nervous system.
  - *Lactic acid-fermented foods* including dairy products like buttermilk, cheese and yogurt, have been around throughout recorded human history. Do-it-yourself food preservation has been making its way back into restaurant kitchens during the past few years. While homemade jam and tomato sauce have always been popular, fermented foods like raw sauerkraut, kimchi and pickles have found a new popularity away from their regions of origin. Miso, a fermented or probiotic form of soy bean, is particularly rich in amino acids which are believed to be cancer-preventative. Enzymes produced in the soya fermentation process dissolve blood clots that can lead to heart attacks, strokes and senility. Vitamin K2 and isophrabon found in miso and natto help

prevent diseases such as osteoporosis and breast cancer and slow down the aging process.

– *Insects* have served as a food source for people for tens of thousands of years, although this type of food is still rare in the developed world. Insects remain a popular food in many developing regions of Central and South America, Africa and Asia. With the demand for steak and hamburgers rising dramatically in fast-developing nations like China and India, and bio-fuel production competing for land, it is clear that meat as we know it is quickly going to become a precious commodity. Farming insects as miniature livestock is a smarter, more efficient and ultimately environmentally safer means of sustaining a healthy and convenient food supply. Some of the more popular insects eaten around the world are: crickets, grasshoppers, ants, a variety of species of caterpillar, also referred to as worms, such as the mopani worm, silkworms and waxworms. Beef contains more protein but far less fat and calories than crickets per gramme.

– *Offal* refers to any of the internal organs and entrails of an animal. Every time people eat sausages or pâté, they are usually eating offal unwittingly. As well as being economical, not throwing anything away demonstrates a certain respect to the animal and is more environmentally friendly. Traditional British offal dishes include brawn (a sort of terrine that uses up the pig's head),

CASE STUDY 9.2 Demeter: a brand for biodynamic products and procedures

About Demeter

As an international brand, Demeter is represented in 38 countries worldwide, and their working procedures are implemented by 3200 farms. Each year Demeter products have a sales volume of about €220 million. Only approved partners, who are strictly controlled and contractually bounded, are allowed to use the brand name. There is a continuous control mechanism, beginning with the cultivation and ending with the distribution. Through every single step the Demeter partners have to fulfil the production and process standards of the organization. In addition to opposing the use of synthetic fertilizers and pesticides, the Demeter organization focuses on the protection of natural resources. According to Demeter publicity, 'Demeter farmers and procedures actively contribute towards the shaping of a future worth living for and creating healthy foods with distinctive taste "Foods with Character" – Demeter – the Brand you can trust.' The Demeter product range also includes natural cosmetics and textile products from wool and cotton.

Source: Demeter-International, http://www.demeter.net/.

chitterlings (pigs' intestines that are sometimes plaited before cooking and serving) and faggots (made with pork offal, such as liver, lungs and spleen, and wrapped in caul fat, the membrane found around internal organs). Sheep's brains are a specialty in France and the Japanese happily eat grilled cow stomach, tender slices of *tetchan* (large intestines) or *hatsu* (beef heart) and sesame-oil-marinated tongue.

Sourcing wine

Currently, there are several recognised sustainable schemes for wines available, such as Agriculture Raisonée in France, Sustainable Winegrowing in New Zealand, Integrated Production of Wine in South Africa and the California Integrated Winemaking Alliance. Sustainable Winegrowing New Zealand, for example, aims to help companies to work towards improving performance in regards to environmental, social and economic sustainability in the vineyards. Some of these organizations are independently audited, others are **self-audited** and each of the schemes has different criteria for judging and giving **accreditation**.

Wines deemed to be sustainable normally fall into three categories; organic, biodynamic and vegan wines.

- *Organic wines*: as wine is extremely fragile by nature, winemakers have added sulphites for centuries. However, wine carrying an 'organic' label must be made from 100 per cent certified organic grapes, without any added sulphites. Around 200 different chemicals have been found in conventionally produced wines. Without the use of chemical fertilizers, herbicides or insecticides, a healthy and biologically active soil can be maintained for growing grapes. Instead of applying herbicides in the vineyard, the soil is cultivated and cover crops are planted. Natural fertilizer, such as composted animal manure, is used and biodiversity of plants is promoted in order to naturally regulate the vineyard soil. Because more manual operations are involved, organic wines are normally more expensive than conventional ones. There is no doubt that organic wine is better for the environment and the people that work in the vineyards are protected from effects of chemicals. There is a distinction between wine labelled 'produced from organically grown grapes' and wine simply labelled 'organic'. In contrast to the latter, wine labelled as 'produced from organically grown grapes' is allowed to contain up to 100 parts per million (ppm) of added sulphites per litre (Organic Wine Company, 2012).
- *Biodynamic wines*: **biodynamic** farmers also focus on establishing a healthy soil but take the organic approach a step further. They use homeopathic sprays, herbal preparations and the lunar cycles in order to increase soil fertility and protect vines from pests and diseases (Organic Vintners, 2002). The Organic Wine Company (2012) describes this method of agriculture as 'ultra-organic' and states that it was developed at the beginning of this century, based on theories

of the social philosopher, Rudolf Steiner. Biodynamic farmers plant their crops according to the belief that plant development is a flow of chemical energy that radiates from the moon, stars and the planets.

- *Vegan wines*: both organic and conventional winemakers frequently use animal products during the clarification and fining process. These animal products include egg white to brighten red wine, milk proteins to make wine taste softer and gelatine to remove bitterness. A wine classified as a 'vegan wine', on the other hand, does not use any animal-derived products.

CASE STUDY 9.3 Fairmont Hotels & Resorts: Green Cuisine Programme

In 2004, Fairmont Hotels & Resorts launched a brand-wide commitment to offer menus that focus on what they could do for the Earth, as well as the customers' taste buds. The first hotel company to formally commit to using, wherever possible, sustainable, locally sourced and organically grown products as part of everyday food service operations, Fairmont took the lead in the green culinary revolution. As part of an ongoing process, Fairmont continuously assesses where it can make a difference through responsible food purchasing practices and menus across the chain reflect this focus on fresh, clean cuisine.

Fairmont's Green Partnership, the company's award-winning environmental programme, encourages guests to think green when travelling, and offering healthful and delicious menu choices that highlight organic wines, local purveyors and on-site herb gardens is a natural extension. Fairmont proactively reviews its purchasing and food sourcing practices to see in which areas more sustainable choices can be incorporated, both at a hotel and a corporate level. For example, all their hotels worldwide offer guests the choice of menu items prepared with organic eggs.

Consumers today are increasingly interested in where their food is sourced and how it is produced, and Fairmont menus provide those sources by highlighting local, organic ingredients and the purveyors who produce them. Like-minded partners on a brand level currently include The Metropolitan Tea Company Ltd., North America's first member of the Ethical Tea Partnership where products are sourced through Fair Trade organizations (in the countries where available), and most of the line features organic production. Hotels also offer organic or biodynamic wines from producers such as Bonterra Vineyards, the world's leading producer of wines made from certified organically grown grapes.

Fairmont's approach makes it easy for guests to make individual, sustainable food choices as part of a global effort. Guests who dine at Fairmont can count on the very best, freshest ingredients and that there will always be a range of sustainable options for them to consider.

Fairmont hotels' culinary brigades commit to sourcing, wherever possible, menu items that are:

- *Local*: food grown or raised as close to hotels as possible, particularly in the season in which it is grown. 'Food miles' refer to the distance a food item travels from the farm to its destination.
- *Organic*: items produced without the use of antibiotics, chemicals, fertilizers and pesticides, and which are certified by a third party organization, such as the USDA's National Organic Program, after rigorous examination.
- *Sustainable*: production enables the resources from which it was made to continue to be available for future generations. A sustainable product can be created repeatedly without generating negative environmental effects, without causing waste products to accumulate as pollution, and without comprom- ising the well-being of workers or communities.
- *Biodynamic*: **biodynamic agriculture** is a holistic approach. In addition to organic practices such as crop rotation and composting, biodynamics uses special plant, animal and mineral preparations and the rhythmic influences of the sun, moon, planets and stars to create a thriving agrarian ecosystem.
- *Fair Trade*: products that are Fair Trade Certified confirm that they were sourced from operations that emphasize fair prices, fair labour conditions, community development and environmental sustainability. Fair Trade em- powers farmers and farm workers to lift themselves out of poverty by develop- ing the business skills necessary to compete in the global marketplace.

In addition to highlighting these choices on menus, many Fairmont properties also offer innovative guest experiences such as winemaker's dinners, Shop with the Chef excursions, cooking classes and trips to the farms where guests can learn where the food is sourced. Meeting planners can also incorporate sustainable choices into their events through Eco-Meet, the company's environmentally friendly conferencing programme which features local and organic food, appropriate handling of food waste and donations of leftover untouched food to local groups and shelters.

To date, 28 Fairmont properties have herb and/or vegetable gardens on their rooftops and patios, using the harvested produce in their restaurant menus.

- Nearly 20 Fairmont hotels have bee-keeping operations, incorporating the collected honey into menu items and even an award-winning micro-brew at The Fairmont Royal York.
- Fairmont properties such as Fairmont Le Château Frontenac in Quebec raise organically fed hens, whose eggs are served daily to restaurant patrons.
- Hotels, including Fairmont Newport Beach and Fairmont The Queen Elizabeth, have adopted goats that are cared for at local farms and produce cheese for their restaurants.

- Fairmont properties in Kenya debuted a 'platinum steak' which comes from steers selected and cross-bred specifically for the East Africa properties by local Morendat Farms.
- Additionally, Fairmont properties worldwide have removed threatened fish species like Chilean sea bass and Bluefin tuna from their restaurant menus and aligned themselves locally with reputable seafood watch organizations, ensuring guests continue to be provided with a comprehensive selection of sustainable seafood choices. Fairmont's seafood purchases are made with the guidance and consultation of these well-respected groups and in consortium with local suppliers.

Put into practice, Fairmont's commitment to ocean sustainability means working with reputable suppliers who purchase fish that are resilient to fishing pressure and harvested in ways that limit damage to marine or aquatic habitats. Specifically, Fairmont identified two seafood choices that are most at risk and has eliminated them from its food service operations. They include:

- Chilean sea bass – also called Patagonia Tooth, this is a long-life fish, meaning it does not reproduce quickly. Due to worldwide popularity of this menu item, their numbers have been dwindling dramatically from illegal and aggressive fishing.
- Bluefin tuna – heavily over-fished in international waters, the plight of this species is so serious that the World Conservation Union lists Southern Bluefin Tuna in its grouping of most threatened wildlife. Their numbers have declined by 97 per cent over the past four decades.

In the face of these findings, Fairmont does not serve these two fish varieties on menus and also makes it easier for guests to make informed food choices by identifying responsible seafood choices on its restaurant menus. The end result: healthier practices flowing down to suppliers, who then offer better choices to restaurants. In addition, by promoting awareness and sustainable alternatives among its guests, Fairmont will play a role in influencing and shaping the tastes and preferences of guests who care about the future of the planet.

Fairmont Hotels & Resorts' dedication to the protection of the environment goes well beyond helping conserve species that reside in the sea. On a wide-ranging basis, the luxury hotel brand maintains a comprehensive commitment to purchasing local, organic and sustainable food items whenever possible. But it is important to note that good environmental practices do not mean guests at Fairmont restaurants miss out on world-class cuisine. Instead, they feast on various fish caught or sourced in ways that ensure their continued survival.

EXERCISES

1 INDIVIDUAL PROJECT AND DISCUSSION

My food habits

- Make a complete listing of food, food types and food ingredients that you consume over a complete week. Develop a categorization system for the food (e.g. organic, local, processed, etc.) and share and discuss your results with classmates.
- How much effort would it take to ensure a sustainable food sourcing?

2 GROUP DISCUSSION OR GROUP PROJECT

Working with restaurateurs

- Visit a local restaurant and find out where the food comes from (sourcing). Develop an action plan for the manager or owner of the restaurant to increase the sustainability of the food offerings. Present the results to the manager or owner and classmates.

3 GROUP RESEARCH AND DISCUSSION

A question of food management

Provide answers and critically discuss the following questions:

- How would you describe sustainable food?
- What types of food can be considered sustainable?
- Describe some common health problems that can result from poor eating habits.
- What is organic agricultural production?
- What is understood by the term 'food miles'?
- Describe three types of sustainable wine.

References

Bayol, S.A., Farrington, S.J. and Strickland, N.C. (2007) 'A maternal "junk food" diet in pregnancy and lactation promotes an exacerbated taste for "junk food" and a greater propensity for obesity in rat offspring', *British Journal of Nutrition*, 98(4): 843–51.

International Foundation for Organic Agriculture Movements (IFOAM) (2008) *Organic Standards and Certification*. Available at: http:// ww.ifoam.org/about_ifoam/standards/index.html.

Johnson, P.M. and Kenny, P.J. (2010) 'Addiction-like reward dysfunction and compulsive eating in obese rats: role for dopamine D2 receptors', *Nature Neuroscience*, 13(5): 635–41.

New Economics Foundation (2012) *Jobs Lost at Sea*. Available at: http://www.new economics.org/node/1968.

Ong, Z.Y. and Mulhausher, B.S. (2011) 'Maternal "junk-food" feeding of rat dams alters food choices and development of the mesolimbic reward pathway in the offspring', *The Federation of American Societies for Experimental Biology Journal*, published online

22 March 2011. Available at: http://www.fasebj.org/content/early/2011/03/20/fj.10-178392.full.pdf+html.

Organic Vintners (2002) *Glossary*. Available at: http://www.organicvintners.com/glossary.htm.

The Organic Wine Company (2012) *Organic Wines 101*. Available at: http://www.theorganic winecompany.com/owc/pages/organic_101.shtml.

United States Department of Agriculture (USDA): http://www.usda.gov/wps/portal/usda home.

Resources

Amodio, M.L., Colelli, G., Hasey, J.K. and Kader, A.A.A. (2007) 'A comparative study of composition and postharvest performance of organically and conventionally grown food', *Journal of the Science of Food and Agriculture*, 87(7): 1228–36.

Chef's Collaborative: http://chefscollaborative.org/.

The Co-operative: http://www.co-operative.coop/.

Darden Environmental Trust: http://www.dardenusa.com/com_ff_preservation.asp.

Department for Environment, Food and Rural Affairs (DEFRA): www.defra.gov.uk.

Global Partnership for Safe and Sustainable Agriculture (EUREGAP): http://www.eurepg ap.org/.

Fairtrade Labeling Organizations International (FLO): http://www.fairtrade.net.

Food Standard Agency (FSA): http:// www.food.gov.uk.

The Global Partnership for Good Agricultural Practice (GLOBALGAP): http://www. globalgap.org/.

Gordon, W. (2002) *Brand Green: Mainstream or Forever Niche?*, London: SOS Free Stock.

Institute of Grocery Distribution (IGD): http://www.igd.com/index.asp?id=0.

International Foundation for Organic Agriculture Movements (IFOAM) (2008): *Organic Standards and Certification*. Available at: http:// ww.ifoam.org/about_ifoam/standards/ index.html.

National Health Service (NHS): http://www.nhs.uk/.

Organic Trade Association (OTA): http:// www.ota.com/organic.

Organic Wine Company: http://www.theorganicwinecompany.com.

Seafood Choices Alliance: http://www.seafoodchoices.com/home.php.

Shiva, V. (2000) *Stolen Harvest: The Hijacking of the Global Food Supply*, Cambridge, MA: South End Press.

Soil Association (2008) *Organic Food and Farming Report*, Bristol: Soil Association.

Sustainable Development Commission UK (SDC): http://www.sd-comission.org.uk/.

Sustainable Wine Growing New Zealand: http://www.nzwine.com.

United States Department of Agriculture (USDA): http://www.usda.gov/wps/portal/ usdahome.

U.S. Centers for Disease Control and Prevention (CDC): http://www.cdc.gov/.

Worldwatch Institute: http://www.worldwatch.org/.

Additional material

Go to www.routledge.com/cw/sloan to find PowerPoint slides of all the figures and tables from the book, additional case studies, a test bank of questions and extra links to useful videos.

Green marketing and branding

CHAPTER OBJECTIVES

The objectives for this chapter are:

- To define sustainable marketing
- To identify the principles of responsible marketing for hotels and restaurants
- To provide an understanding of the importance of openness, honesty and credibility in the responsible marketing context
- To provide an understanding of the concept of sustainable development in relation to external communications and responsible marketing
- To examine responsible marketing as part of a company's ethical strategy
- To discuss the four new Ps reflecting a green concept
- To comprehend the concept of branding in relation to green operations

Green marketing and branding

Today's services marketplace is characterized by the convergence of forces such as **globalization** of markets, the escalating pace of technological change and increasing economic turbulence. Adding to this tumultuous mixture is the added pressure on companies to show responsibility. This is nothing particularly new. Traditionally, companies have held various levels of responsibility towards their shareholders and employees. These responsibilities may range from profit making to providing correct working conditions. However, since the start of the new century, the sense of company responsibility has broadened to include responsibility to local communities, the local **environment** and the planet. In business management, these new responsibilities are part of a larger concept labelled as Corporate Social and Environmental Responsibility. In hospitality management practices, these responsibilities are mirrored by hands-on operational initiatives that may include supporting local charities, partnering community development projects or purchasing food from local organic farmers. These new responsibilities may be perceived as added burdens to some while others clearly see an opportunity to enhance their overall image. Arguably, today's ferocious competitive pace does not allow firms to sit back and hope that the well-worn differentiating strategies will do the trick and enable them to stay ahead of the competition. Thus, in order to avoid the commoditization of certain sectors of the hospitality and tourism industry, innovative brands are looking for new ways to build relationships with their customers. This is where companies enter the realm of **green marketing** and branding.

From cause-related marketing to green marketing

The perception and impact of marketing vary from person to person. In some cases, people feel that the objective of a marketing organization is to serve the greater good of society through **social** marketing efforts. In other instances, marketers' activities are experienced in negative ways and are open to criticism on ethical grounds, particularly for being responsible for glamorizing consumption. Producing goods and services does use up resources, which generate waste and **pollution**. Restaurants have a direct contact with customers and sustain their business level by ensuring a constant flow of customers through the doors. The focus of the marketing efforts is then directed at attracting more customers, enabled through the conventional marketing theory views. The traditional marketing mix with the four Ps, being product, price, place and promotion, conventionally has played a leading role in influencing customers' purchasing decisions.

The emphasis on satisfying customers beyond the four Ps and managing the customer experience play an increasing central role in the marketing effort. Customers have grown out of being simple buyers, to being – with the help of information technology – informed buyers. In most cases, a business undertaking a strict environmental protection conduct or actively supporting the community's social activities will want to communicate its engagement to its customers. Marketers, as influencers, communicators and shapers of culture, can ensure that they make a significant difference to their customers, the planet and to the bottom line. In practice, it is about assessing and minimizing the **impacts** products and/or services produced have on the environment. In this chapter we will consider what **sustainable** marketing means by looking into the principles of responsible marketing for the hospitality business. Through ethical promotion, publicity and branding techniques, the hospitality business can develop a customer base built on quality and trust. Customers are influenced by the four new Ps of **sustainable development**: people, planet, profit and progress.

The concept of sustainable development is now on the agenda of most governments around the globe. Citizens of many nations have adapted certain modes of consumption coherent with a sustainable development. Some companies have in turn adapted their marketing strategies to capture this new consumer. We will define and review **cause-related marketing**, green marketing and sustainable marketing. We will then propose a set of principles for a new marketing paradigm: responsible marketing.

Cause-related marketing appeared in the United States in the middle of the 1980s till the 1990s, where binding the sale of a product to a particular cause would lead to increased revenue streams and public recognition. The multiplication of such initiatives, however, led certain companies to a higher bid in making the cause-related marketing a central element of their strategy. The payment of a fraction of the sales price of a product or a service to a charity organization has become a marginal element of the cause-related marketing over the years. The implication of a company in a cause now takes on several forms and often consists of a combination of monetary gifts, premiums for the voluntary activities of the employees and gifts in the form of equipment, products or services. Certain companies may engage in strategic partnerships with ecological charity organizations or social welfare associations.

Cause-related marketing is closely linked to emotional branding, which aims at creating an emotional bond between the customer and the brand. One of the major criticisms of cause-related marketing strategy is the fact that all marketing activities, even if attached to a particular cause, are aimed at straight consumption and tend to be narrowed in focus.

The changing natures of brands

In the world of marketing, branding is the synonym of quality assurance, recognition and prestige for some, while for others branding has become ubiquitous and intrusive. Branding stirs passions, and, arguably so it should. The start of the twenty-first century is marked by a change in consumption and purchasing habits. Consumers appear to be better informed and expect companies to embrace environmental and societal values. Parallel to this trend are the consumer's new emotional needs. Emerging from the treadmill of continuous product consumption, consumers increasingly search for brands driving images and emotions. However, the era when consumers would let themselves be manipulated by crafty brand messages seems to be coming to an end. Consumers are sensitive to brand messages and they demand authenticity, transparency and ultimately responsibility.

In a world of choice, product differentiation is a fundamental feature but with growing competition, it can be argued that brands should transcend product-line promotion to encompass corporate identity and embrace company philosophy.

To summarize, a brand permanently articulates two existing modes: the first can be defined as the expression, whereby the various material aspects of a brand fit, such as the physical or tangible dimension of a brand, as captured by the consumer through sensory perception. The second mode could be defined as the content which corresponds to the multitude of ideals and messages portrayed by a brand. A brand is like a coin with two sides, individual but intrinsically united.

Defining green marketing

One of the very first challenges to consider when attempting to define green marketing is the question of semantics. A plethora of alternatives to the traditional meaning of marketing has emerged in boardrooms, university lecture halls and consultancy language. These include: (1) ethical marketing; (2) responsible marketing; (3) cause-related marketing; (4) environmental marketing; (5) sustainable marketing; (6) ecological marketing; (7) societal marketing; (8) social marketing; and, of course, (9) green marketing. One can easily understand why many business leaders and consumers alike tend to disregard any alternatives to the traditional meaning of marketing as mere fads.

The American Marketing Association (AMA) offers a definition of green marketing which serves as the basis for understanding green branding. The AMA definition entails three parts (American Marketing Association, 2009):

1. The marketing of products that are presumed to be environmentally safe.
2. The development and marketing of products designed to minimize negative effects on the physical environment or to improve its quality.
3. The efforts by organizations to produce, promote, package and reclaim products in a manner that is sensitive or responsive to ecological concerns.

The main message arising from the AMA's definition of green marketing is not to incite consumers to consume less, but to consume better. If employed wisely, marketing can be one of the best ways to change spending patterns, redefine quality standards and sustain a company's brand position in the marketplace.

Reconciling green marketing and sustainability

The origins of green marketing can be traced back to the Bruntland Commission's definition of sustainable development, found in the Commission's landmark report, *Our Common Future* (WCED, 1987). A company's decision to adopt this course lies in its desire to establish, maintain and enhance customer relationships. The company and its customers need to agree on a kind of trade that does not compromise the ability of future generations to meet their needs and deplete the Earth's non-renewable resources or cause **environmental deterioration.**

Marketing is a crucial aspect of daily business operation and can be put to the service of sustainable development. Indeed, marketing is often perceived as the engine of our modes of consumption. It is also undoubtedly one of the best tools to change our spending patterns and to make progress in a market by redefining quality standards. A growing number of marketing professionals and companies are enthusiastic about reinventing marketing, starting with ethical responsibilities and with one particular goal in sight: to encourage consumers to adopt responsible consumption. And that can only start with a proper product and service stewardship.

However, this may prove to be more challenging than first anticipated. Companies are faced with double objectives that go alongside all forms of marketing: (1) the traditional task of stimulating consumption in order to generate profit, on one hand, and (2) the ambition and desire to regulate or perhaps redress the imbalances and fluctuations generated by previous generations' consumption modes, on the other. This state of imbalance needs to be solved. Sustainable business practices are the only alternative to current forms of business practices that can remedy the imbalances. Economic profitability should therefore be perceived not as an end in itself but as a mean of development. The essence of green marketing is based on the premise of sustainable business practices.

During the past two decades, management buzzwords have crawled into corporate boardrooms. From crazes to fads and trends, from One-Minute Management to Total Quality Management, one must decide whether the many management approaches are useful and whether they can contribute to organizational effectiveness. To prevent the current green movement from fading into obscurity over the next few years, executives must sign up and commit their organizations to sustainable business practices. The commitment of an organization starts with leadership. Figure 10.1 shows the importance of communication between all the different areas to implement green marketing in business.

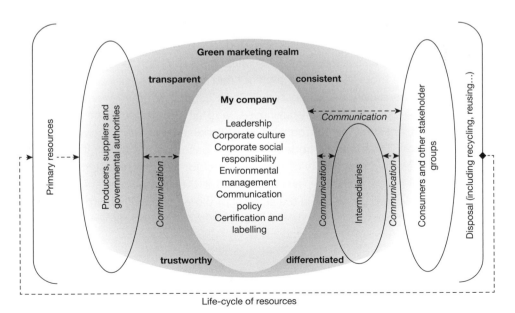

FIGURE 10.1 Green marketing and the business environment

Green marketing requires business leaders and managers to reconsider traditional marketing principles in the following eight areas:

1. Initial positioning of the company within a market.
2. Image perceived by the consumers, suppliers and other **stakeholders**.
3. Legitimacy of environmental positioning by the company.
4. Acceptability of green products and services by consumers.
5. Suitability of suppliers to engage in a green supply chain.
6. Readiness of intermediaries to support green initiatives.
7. Consumer expectations.
8. Consumer perceptions of benefits that green products and services offer.

The concept of green marketing shows several characteristics:

1. *Short-term actions for future generations.* One characteristic is defined as being a short-term action aiming at improving the long run; this is to say that it is imperative to start with the thoughts of future generations' needs to understand the necessity not to exhaust all natural resources today.
2. *Businesses are just as responsible as individuals.* The second characteristic of green marketing pertains to the durable action to maintain a positive image of the company related to the protection of the environment. Indeed the goal of a company, which bases its communication and its publicity on the respect of the environment and the safeguarding of the planetary resources, demonstrates a human side to its operation and being. The human side of a company distinctively demonstrates the implication in the survival of the planet to the same level as each individual. This idea supports the neo-classic theory saying that nature is a capital because it is an amalgam of indirect goods which, by production, increase the production of direct goods. Neo-classic thought did not consider nature as a reserve of inexhaustible resources and today one consumes 5 to 10 times more than what the planet can offer.
3. *Ethical responsibility of businesses.* A third aspect of green marketing is the creation of a bridge between businesses and all stakeholders, including competitive businesses, on the base of ethical behaviour. The key word here is cooperation. The common **code of ethics** is based on the fact that every generation is entitled to a quality of life at least as good as the preceding one. This aspect of green marketing also shows that the companies are not solely interested in their profit but in the survival of planet and its inhabitants. What is needed is a holistic approach to marketing in order for sustainable development to progress.

From green to sustainable marketing?

Marketing has a tremendous influence on the environmental and social impacts of businesses and their products, policies and production processes. Indeed, in most businesses, marketers play an important part in developing a corporate strategy and it is considered that the boundaries between 'corporate' and 'marketing' strategies are often blurred. Marketers are then well placed to exert positive influence in helping businesses to become sustainable. Sustainable marketing utilizes traditional marketing methods to understand the values, emotions and buying behaviour of the potential customer with the goal of establishing a sustainable, restorative relationship. Sustainable marketing can be defined as the establishment, maintenance and enhancement of customer relationships so that the objectives of the parties involved are met without compromising the ability of future generations to achieve their own objectives.

Consequently, rather than a simple extension of traditional marketing, sustainable marketing represents a discontinuous shift in corporate philosophy. Sustainable marketing is ethical, ecological and compatible with sustainable development. It is a holistic approach to marketing where the impacts of all activities, from cradle to grave, are considered. This is simply the way companies should conduct business in the twenty-first century – being responsible. We will therefore simply label sustainable marketing as *responsible marketing* which is the contribution that the marketing profession can make to sustainable development.

The marketing environment revisited

While a detailed explanation of the marketing analysis is beyond the scope of this chapter, we will look at one important aspect of the marketing analysis: the marketing environment. The marketing environment constitutes all the external actors and issues that affect the marketing decisions and practices of a business (Kotler *et al.*, 2002). The marketing environment is split in two. The micro-environment, where customers, competitors, suppliers and distributors impact the way a business performs its day-to-day tasks. The macro-environment includes broader influences, such as politics, economics, technology and social trends that usually have long-term and irregular influences on a business.

Two aspects of the conventional macro-environment analysis are missing. First, the *physical environment* is not considered a part of the marketing environment, even though the planet ultimately underpins all that a business achieves. Second, analysis of the marketing environment is set in the present with sole consideration of today's generation of customers, shareholders, employees and other stakeholders.

The marketing Ps revisited

The sustainable development paradigm, founded according to three axes of social equity, environment and economy, provides the base for the augmentation of the classic four Ps of marketing (product, price, place and promotion) with the new three Ps of sustainable development – people, planet and profit, as depicted in Figure 10.2.

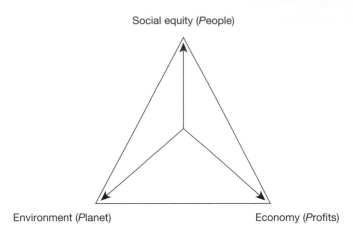

Social equity (People)

Environment (Planet)   Economy (Profits)

FIGURE 10.2 The new three Ps in relation to the pillars of sustainability

This added form of the three Ps (people, planet, profits) quickly was enriched by a fourth P: progress. This inclusion of progress acts as a driver for a business to integrate ethics and long-term commitment to a better world within the company mission statement (see Figure 10.3). Thus, the concept of responsible marketing is intimately bound up with the three axes of sustainable development.

Businesses do not operate in bubbles. The activities of competitors, suppliers, distributors and consumers all play a role in the impact a particular company will have – whether it is environmental, social or economic. Looking inwardly at a company's own products, services, processes and working at reducing the negative impacts and improving the society's welfare is all very good, but here again, it calls for a more holistic approach. This will have **direct impacts** on the responsible marketing activities.

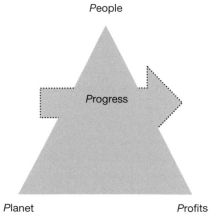

People

Progress

Planet   Profits

FIGURE 10.3 The new four Ps

Life cycle assessment

A **life cycle assessment (LCA)**, also known as life cycle analysis, eco-balance and cradle-to-grave analysis, is the investigation and valuation of the **environmental** impacts of a given product or service caused or necessitated by its existence. The goal of LCA is to compare the full range of environmental and social damages assignable to products and services, to be able to choose the least burdensome one. LCA offers clear links to marketing functions.

Hospitality businesses may decide to look at the whole **life cycle** of their products. The term life cycle refers to the notion that a fair, holistic assessment requires the assessment of raw material production, manufacture, distribution, use and disposal, including all intervening transportation steps necessary or caused by the product's existence. The sum of all those steps – or phases – is the life cycle of the product. From growing and farming methods, food mileage accumulated, purchasing and distribution activities, preparation, service and sales techniques, the life cycle of a product offered provides the hospitality managers with a clear insight on what energy, time and money are being spent and the activity's impact on the planet.

The food sector is often considered one of the three most resource-demanding and polluting sectors, together with the building and road transport sectors. Because the **hospitality industry** relies on the steady food supply for its own operations (sourcing and sustainable supply chain management is covered in Chapter 8), the sustainable management of the supply chain becomes a key factor in **sustainability** operations. The typical questions addressed by the food chain LCA include the packaging and transport options, the choices of conventional versus **organic agriculture**, the fresh versus cold versus preserved food as well as the agricultural stage versus the processing and transport. The impacts associated with the food chain are especially those related to the agricultural phases, energy, water, nutrient and land consumption.

Few hotel companies have yet undertaken full life cycle assessment. This is in part due to the cost and complexity in completing a full-scale life cycle assessment, especially in an industry such as the hospitality industry where multiple products, processes and services are integrative components of the so-called hospitality product. In general, service industries, to which the hospitality industry belongs, tend to generate less environmental impact at the point of use than throughout their extensive supply chain.

Despite the service economy accounting for a significant share of the Gross Domestic Product of most industrialized countries, LCA models and case studies for services in countries have only recently appeared. Indeed, services present unique challenges for LCA. The various definitions of services and boundaries are complicated and varied. While LCAs in hospitality are still uncommon, a few case studies have been identified. The LCAs of hospitality service by Italian hotels (University 'G. G. d'Annunzio', and FEBE and FEBE EcoLogic) were performed using the GaBi software (http://www.gabi-software.com/) tool to model life cycle systems and to process the data.

Marketing research

Marketing decision-making depends upon the systematic gathering, analysis and interpretation of data on customers and competitors, markets and industries and the broader environment. Numerous agencies specialize in researching the ethical, social and environmental concerns of consumers. Sustainable Motivation is an example of a project focusing on research into consumer behaviour and attitudes toward sustainable production and consumption undertaken by MPG International on behalf of the United Nations Environment Programme (**UNEP**). Ultimately, the more quality information a business possesses, the better it can adapt and formulate its offer.

CASE STUDY 10.1 Strategies advocating green concepts

Joie de Vivre Hospitality is a hotel and restaurant company in San Francisco, California. It is considered the second largest operator of boutique hotels in the USA. Given that rising gasoline prices have continued to hamper the travel agenda of vacationers who intend to take the car as a transportation mode to the destinations of interest, Joie de Vivre Hospitality introduces a Keep the Green or Give the Green programme. This programme advocates the use of mass transportation and offers hotel guests a reward to boost the guest's awareness of green issues: The reward entails either a US$20 gas-card from Chevron or a US$20 **carbon offset** credit. The carbon offset credit refers to the reduction of **carbon dioxide (CO_2)** supported by Carbonfund.org. The US$20 credit will be used to support a variety of carbon-reduction-related projects to conserve the environment wisely. The programme allows Joie de Vivre to gain a name as green operator.

Hotel Royal Hsinchu, a premier business hotel in Hsinchu, Taiwan, belongs to the Hotel Royal Group of Taiwan and was officially opened on 15 January 1999. It is located in the northern part of Taiwan, which is famous for its high-tech industry. This region is called the Silicon Valley of Taiwan by the locals. Owing to its access to mass transportation and a centralized location, Hotel Royal Hsinchu has been the top choice of accommodation for business travellers staying overnight in Hsinchu. Hotel Royal Hsinchu won an award in the 2008 National Green Hotel Contest. The hotel sets up various goals which are measureable and achievable in response to the reduction of energy usage and a friendly environmental practice. Like most green hotels, it has implemented different kinds of initiatives responsible to the environment. For example, the room cleaning service will not be provided as long as the guest hangs out an 'environment card' on the door knob. Complementary transportation is offered by the hotel to reduce the travelling effect on the eco-system. In addition,

recycling programmes can be visibly seen in the hotel. At the onset of deliberating green initiatives, the hotel attempted to encourage its guests to follow green practices by inventing a novel pricing strategy since green hotels were not a familiar service model in the mind of most business travellers. The hotel reduced the room rate for guests staying more than one night and did not ask the housekeepers to clean the room. In conclusion, this pricing strategy helps raise the awareness of business travellers in relation to issues of energy usage and **waste management**.

Sources: *Energy & Ecology Business* (4 August 2008); http://www.vacationagent magazine.com/Editorial.aspx?n=43331.

Principles of responsible marketing

Responsible marketing ought to represent a shift in emphasis away from traditional approaches focused on a certain aspect of a product towards an ethical approach, which takes a holistic view of the product from cradle to grave and considers the context in which it is produced. Responsible marketing is about the provision of information about the product, service and providers to the consumer along with advice on how best to handle the product and service until final disposal. It is about product and service stewardship.

Every day the concept of 'the average consumer' loses its relevance in a world where personalized, one-to-one marketing, plays an important role. Responsible marketing finds its legitimacy here. It answers indeed to the consumers' increased request aimed at *better consumption*. If this tendency is confirmed, to target these responsible consumers will become one of the key success factors of a product. With responsible marketing the marketing mix has changed and while the environment must be integrated into the policy of the company, a new variable has been added in the management of a company: production. It is indeed essential that the product or service, along with its manufacturing or transformation and the components which it uses, respect the engagements announced in the policy of communication. The distribution can thus be adjusted and the product or services distributed with special eco-labelling. The price will have to take into account the possible surplus or decrease caused by the sustainable making of a product or service. And obviously, marketing communication could be centred on the ecological dimension of the product. However, a company should not lose sight of the fact that other values such as quality, durability or service and sustainable development must equally be defended.

Within the marketing mix, and in the development of a responsible marketing strategy, there are a number of priorities, which need to be addressed.

Corporate social responsibility and environmental policy

Responsible marketing is as much about marketing the organization as any of its products and services. Commitment to sustainability does not stop at the product or service level but rather starts at the corporate level. Prior to making practical and operational changes, a business needs to develop a **corporate social responsibility** and environmental policy which go on to become cornerstones in developing a positive corporate culture (see Figure 10.1). Policy-makers develop a mission statement examining the rationale for going green. A plan and a timeline are also included, defining and tracing the path towards the implementation of practical green initiatives. It is recommended to start by detailing any green initiatives the company has already adopted and then go on to describe the actions that will be taken to improve sustainability within the company. The hospitality industry is rapidly becoming aware of both the risk of standing still and of the opportunities for greening operations. Going green is part of the process of continuous improvement and not a goal in itself. Remodelling operations to become sustainable requires a holistic approach by hospitality managers that implies a thorough industry analysis to include:

- reviewing logistics and supply chain activities;
- developing a caring approach to stakeholder relationships;
- understanding markets and the changes in consumers demands;
- analysing how climate change and environmental **degradation** affect food supply and service delivery;
- embracing green design that can avoid environmental impacts.

Product/service policy

Products and services offered in a hotel or restaurant should minimize the use of non-renewable resources and be designed for recyclability. If the manufacturing, or in this case the provision of products and services, is deemed not sustainable, the credibility of the product, the communication and the company are at stake. The best way to sell a product is to be honest about the offer, the sourcing, the production methods and the ingredients.

Packaging policy

Although, generally speaking, the hospitality industry makes minimal usage of packaging, hotels and restaurants depend on sourcing of food, furniture and fixture which in turn are massive users of packaging material. Careful analysis of packaging from the supplier side should be made and preference should be given to materials which do less damage to the environment and for which the supplier may arrange for recycling or re-usage. For promotional purposes, a hotel using excessive packaging of brochures and guides is considered unethical.

Promotion policy

Hospitality firms improving their environmental and social credentials are often eager to capitalize on this by communicating with customers and other stakeholders to improve the perception of their offer and company. Of course, it is crucial for restaurant owners and managers to remember that everything communicates. The actions – or inactions – of a business communicate as much as deliberate campaigns. Ultimately, promotions should highlight the credentials of both the company and its products and services. Moreover, promotions should merge with education and campaigning in a strategic move towards sustainable development.

Pricing policy

If environmental or social measures costs a company more than if the status quo were observed, the extra costs can be passed on to the consumers as long as it is clearly explained that the price difference results in the sustainability improvements. If, however, costs are reduced following environmental initiatives, such as the traditional hotel towel scheme, it is then ethical to provide a reduction in the final consumer prices.

Transportation and distribution

Similar to the packaging issue, the hospitality industry does not directly make heavy use of transportation and distribution, but both these activities are essential to the daily operations of any hospitality businesses. The act of travelling to and from a destination represents a considerable **carbon footprint**. Some hotels have decided that once customers have checked in, daily public transport passes are included in the room rate for use by guests during their stay in a particular town or city. Some restaurants are sourcing food locally, working with regional suppliers in order to reduce food mileage in the distribution channel.

Quality and effectiveness

Sustainable management requires a shift from quantity towards quality. Quality is part of the environmental profile of a product as high quality goods last longer, are worth repairing and use less energy.

Education and personnel policy

Awareness of the importance of sustainability in business practices should be enhanced by training and education. Ultimately, the entire workforce is responsible for improvements in sustainable development.

When implementing a green business programme, a company needs to keep itself informed about green issues and undertake a series of activities which increase the credentials of a green brand (see Figure 10.4). In doing so, a company becomes a

FIGURE 10.4 Parallel activities to implementing a green programme

resource for customers, suppliers and all stakeholders bringing them within the company's sphere of influence (see Figure 10.1). By embracing sustainable practices, a company can start the process of branding itself as a forward-thinking and environmentally conscious organization. The change in company image becomes an effective tool in boosting not only the company's morale but in creating marketing opportunities. Taking time to train employees, sales representatives and business partners about the green business programme is an inexpensive and effective way to create momentum and interest for green initiatives.

Environmental information system

Monitoring the changes in environmental management is essential to identify potential challenges and real problems, but also to ensure that suppliers are aligned with the corporate requirements and consistent with the environmental policies.

Responsible communication strategy

Communication is one of the key tasks within the marketing mix as it establishes a link between a company and its environment. In addition, communication conveys a certain image of a company to the outside world. Responsible communication, internal or external, must relate to all stakeholders.

Commercial communication

Commercial communication is a communication form directed particularly at the customers of the company. This is the economic aspect of communication. That is, the positive effect of commercial communication should be a growth in turnover or an increase in market share, etc. It is this communication, which will help the company to sell its products and services.

However, responsible communication towards the general public cannot be accomplished using a similar method. The focus is broadening to include the entire company. We then refer to corporate communication. The actions of a company are communicated rather than a sole focus on a product or service claim. Publicity will have the role of informing the customer, sensitizing and educating the customer. The product and service, the brand and the company will then build a unique image of a company engaged in sustainable development.

Internal and external communication strategy

Businesses use communication means to reach other targets than the final consumer. Internally, the employees and shareholders form a group and externally, the political institutions, associations, suppliers or distributors form another group.

Internal communication

The image of a company is not based solely on the various external communication actions, which are carried out. The life within a company and the involvement of employees also shape the image projected by a company. A company's success in a market is the direct result of the work and success of its employees. The same applies regarding sustainable development. Environmental initiatives will be as successful as the level of involvement from the employees. There are several means based on internal communication to implement the application of environmental protection within the company. A company's internal newspaper, annual reports, postings in the buildings, videos and seminars are all ways to communicate internally.

In many cases, hospitality establishments are changing their operations in various ways, such as adding solar panels and water-saving devices to promote the concept of sustainable management. Often employees and managers do not have a clear picture about what the green concept is and do not know how to implement it effectively. On-the-job training via seminars, workshops and conferences becomes vital and a channel in communicating with staffs of hospitality establishments pertaining to augmented services friendly to the environment. Retrospectively, for new hospitality businesses which embrace greener concepts at the onset, the attempt to promote the idea of sustainable operations to all levels of service staff may be easier as long as the firm stipulate their green service standards and strategies toward future practices in their mission statement.

External communication

External communication is the key to all marketing development, particularly in the branding process. Accurate information should be communicated to all stakeholders including customers to ensure transparency (see Figure 10.1). The central message must be clear, understandable, relevant, consistent and honest. Claims must be truthful, accurate and explicit. Clear and understandable credentials such as approved **eco-labels** may help the positioning of the brand as green. However, many including the common standards developed by the International Standard Organization (ISO) or the **European Union eco-management and audit scheme (EMAS)**, are not always fully understood by the general public and potential customers. Words such as *leading*, *healthiest* or *environmentally friendly* are. Coupling strong credentials with catchy wordings help the brand to gain attention. While real quality is important in consumers' minds, perceived quality plays a more important role. If a hotel company decides to launch a complete organic breakfast, it might be suffering from a lack of perceived quality unless it is partnered by a certified system such as Demeter which stands for strict organic agricultural standards. Consumers must be able to associate a brand to a category which also applies when branding green. A green brand such as the German-based Bionade has managed to establish itself as an organic and healthy drink in the minds of consumers within the carbonated beverages range. Name, shape and colour need to stand out among competitors to make impact.

A company involved in sustainable development will gain new types of cooperation with distributors and suppliers, will engage in discussions with environmental organizations and will ensure positive relations with the public authorities.

A responsible company can form agreements stipulating that partners, whether suppliers or distributors, commit themselves to limit the use of non-renewable resources as well as ensuring ethical work conditions upstream and downstream.

A responsible company may find it very beneficial to communicate its environmental engagements with regard to the public authorities, thus avoiding potential fines or taxation regarding environmental protection.

CASE STUDY 10.2 Internal communication towards green practices

The City Hotel Shanghai in China has stipulated that the green concept should be collectively implemented by all functional departments. Thus, each hotel department sends delegates to participate in educational sessions to learn green ideas, concepts and practices from industry experts. Moreover, executive managers are required to attend international conferences focusing on the issues confronting green hotels. Consequently, green initiatives have successfully been deployed within all the hotel departments. For example, its catering department offers a take-out service and stores the bottles of wine that are not empty. In a so-called 'green napkin' programme, the hotel restaurant supplies its customers with cloth napkins as opposed to paper napkins. Hotel guests can take the 'green napkin' with them as a souvenir. Those green projects have received positive feedback from the hotel's guests; meanwhile, the hotel is planning to give away reusable shopping bags to encourage its guests to reduce the consumption of plastic or paper bags.

Finally, a responsible company will communicate with non-governmental organizations or other consumer protection associations in order to guarantee the sincerity of the claims made. Those organizations and associations tend to maintain a close relationship with the media which can either be very positive or can quickly damage the image of a company if the latter does not live up to its promises in terms of sustainable development. While carrying out a partnership with an environmental protection, a company will acquire a certain credibility and legitimacy in its engagement.

Competitive advantages from responsible marketing

A responsible marketing strategy does the following:

- differentiate the brand;
- mitigate risks and identify opportunities;
- increase customer retention and brand loyalty;
- drive innovation and creativity;
- protect reputation and build strong brands;
- motivate employees;
- retain the best staff;
- delight customers;
- save costs;
- attract investment.

The fine line between green marketing and greenwashing

The danger businesses always face is of being accused of **greenwashing**. Greenwashing describes the efforts by companies to portray themselves as environmentally responsible in order to cover up environmental misdemeanours. A company promoting a product as 'organic' without proper **certification** or a company claiming to be energy-efficient but causing pollution could justifiably be accused of greenwashing. Environmental friendliness is in vogue, shareholders and stakeholders exert a great amount of pressure. Some companies unfortunately come up with a series of good adverts but with little sustainable merit in their operations. Some get caught out, some not. Companies must meet the demands of customers and promote authentic products and services that lead to a sustained positive image.

Greenwashing can have fatal effects on a company's trustworthiness. Not only a firm's customers are being deceived, but greenwash can ruin relationships with any stakeholder of a business such as suppliers, investors, politics and the media. And while a competitive advantage can be obtained from sustainable practices and responsible marketing, companies that operate in a sustainable way but do not communicate this to its external environment, face the risk of being overtaken by competitors. Businesses have to manage different forms of pressure.

Pressures exist to promote products or services that have little or no negative effect on the environment (shareholder and market pressure) or to demands to create a positive image (stakeholders and market pressure) or simply the demands to capture a growing market for green products and services (stakeholder pressure) (Figure 10.5). The temptations to greenwash are great. Consumer demand for green products and services, largely unregulated corporate social and environmental responsibility, lack of compulsory **environmental communication** standards are all drivers for greenwashing. This course is perceived to be a relatively simple escape strategy with direct short-term financial benefits (capture more sales by portraying a green image) (Figure 10.5). The drivers for green business actions include increased scrutiny from non-governmental organizations into the day-to-day operations of businesses in relation to environmental impacts, demands from society at large and consumers for transparency and for more governmental regulations to be put in place, carbon tax being one example. Responsible companies enact well-thought-out green business strategies over the long term.

Various methods and marketing tools are used to communicate a green image, ranging from simple adverts and advertising posters to the use of green jargon and alibi cooperation with environmental associations. Effective greenwashing campaigns are able to mislead consumers and communicate a positively distorted company image. The most popular instrument of greenwashing is the advertising campaign. For example, companies use pictures of a green and pleasant countryside with a blue sky overhead to suggest environmental compatibility and sustainability. The simple use of wording can illustrate yet another example of greenwashing. **Energy management** systems are implemented in many hotels. The term energy management system implies improved energy management and consequently lower energy consumption. This belief is misleading, as energy management systems do not actually reduce the energy consumed but only spread the hotel's energy

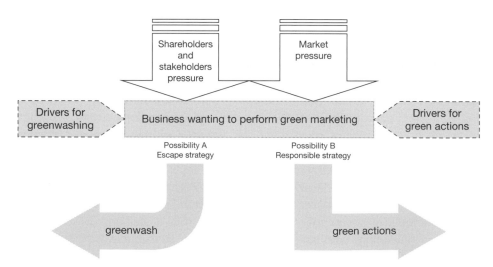

FIGURE 10.5 Pressure, drivers and exit strategies

consumption in a more sophisticated way. If a hotel promotes their energy management systems as environmentally friendly, they could be accused of greenwashing.
Greenwashing companies will fail to gain competitive advantage and may even
experience competitive disadvantage when their actions are made public. Marketing
communication about environmental friendliness has to be consistent and truthful.

Corporate Social Reports or Sustainability Reports have been used to create
misleading company images. While in essence, reporting on activities pertaining to
sustainability is commendable, some companies do not hesitate to use reporting as
the sole tool for demonstrating the green profile of the company. Such reports are
currently not accredited by any international binding guidelines, a clear difference
from accounting and financial reporting. A company is thus able to shine the light
on its positive actions while leaving questionable practices in the dark.

The widespread use of eco-jargon has had the effect of diluting the true meaning
of words such as sustainability, environmentally friendly and eco-responsibility. A
well-known example in German is the switch from using the word *Gentechnologie*
(genetic technology or engineering) to *Biotechnologie* (bioengineering) in the drive
by the chemical industry to establish a greener image.

Some companies have gone one step further in greenwashing techniques by
setting up pseudo-citizen groups and grassroots movements designed to create
positive publicity around products, services and green actions. This practice is called
astroturfing.

While greenwashing may appear to be the simple way to reap short-term profits,
companies caught greenwashing suffer serious brand damage. The general problem
resulting from widespread greenwashing is the loss of consumer confidence.

Sustainable claims and communications

Communications will be a key element in any marketing process. Accurate
information should be communicated to all stakeholders and particularly customers.
The central message should always be visible, understood, relevant and honest.
Companies that are promoting an environmentally friendly image, products and
services must be precise in the claims they make.

In short, the claims must embody the following traits:

- *Truthfulness and accuracy.* Although there are not yet requirements to have
  information independently verified, many hospitality companies work with various
  agencies developing sustainable standards and certification programmes.
- *Relevance.* It is important to explicate the green products or services delivered
  and the potential impacts associated with them.
- *Clarity.* The providers should clearly state which environmental issue or aspect
  of the product the claim refers to. A restaurant may claim to be environmentally
  friendly because the kitchen processes only organic food. However, the claim
  may be irrelevant if, in order to process only organic products, the foodstuff must
  be sourced in other countries, necessitating air transportation.

- *Explicitness.* It is wise to add background information concerning any green-related symbol used in the claim, unless the symbol is required by law, or is backed up by regulations or standards, or is part of an independent certification scheme.

Responsible marketing: a driver to loyalty

The principal objective of companies, with the goal of creating loyal customers, is then to make the latter feel concerned by all the issues related to environmental protection, social equity and economic benefits by promoting responsible consumer behaviour. Thus, a company already committed to environmental protection and sustainable development strategies requires that their customers are equally responsible actors in order for these strategies to bear fruit. Logically, the relationship is not one only of buyer and seller in a monetary transaction, but rather one of partnership for the common and greater good.

On branding green services

Concepts of brand in tourism

As stated earlier in the chapter, a brand is in general considered to be the commodity of name, sign, symbol and logo in relation to products or services offered in the market place. In a broader sense, brand could deal with images of artefacts, species, persons or locations that have no relation to consumption. Further, in tourism settings, some regions with unique climate, scenery or culture could be treated as brands which could well resonate with travellers who are inclined to experience distinct characteristics in connection with the region, such as the case of Tahiti which is viewed as a paradise for exotic culture in Pacific.

Factors influencing brand values in the hospitality business

In a highly competitive environment, it is imperative to comprehend the potential factors which could directly impact the consumer's perception of the value of brand. experience in addition to the attempt to lessen the potential threats to the natural environment.

- *Visiting experiences.* Prior service experiences often alter the perception of a brand in either a more positive or negative fashion. However, the levels of influence rooted in service experiences may vary, depending on the subjects of service and the frequency of service encountered. Hotel guests, for instance, may not change their attitude toward a property using alternative energy when such service is not presented in the face of technological meltdown. Importantly, services integrating green notions should emphasize the quality of the visit.

- *Reputation*. A positive perception of a brand in the mind of consumers shapes a brand value. In the hospitality business, service reputation encompasses various aspects, ranging from the quality of service to the deployment of marketing strategies such as pricing. Frontline employees are directly in control of service quality. Thus, the attitude of service staffs toward customers as well as the staff's reaction to service failures, in some cases, could significantly damage the overall reputation of the brand. Also, the quality of hospitality amenities provided is a defining factor impacting the reputation of a brand.
- *Green manifestations*. To construct a brand associated with environmentally friendly practices which are respectful to the host community, the evidences of service should be saliently unveiled. Otherwise, this may be misconceived as greenwashing. Since at this moment green management is not considered the prevailing model of operation in the hospitality business, it is imperative to communicate with consumers concerning those practices unique to the protection of the environment and with an appreciation of community harmony.
- *Service innovation*. Hospitality firms have long built an image as an industry constantly in search of excellence in delivering optimal lodging, meal and service experiences via product innovation. Although implementing green technologies and initiatives in a property is considered an innovative mode of operation, it is wise to consider securitizing the pitfalls confronting green initiatives and exploiting novel technologies and creative solutions to engage the customer to reduce energy consumption and dispose of waste in an appropriate manner as recommended by the firms. Certainly, this innovation is necessarily linked with customer experience. Innovation may also entail logistic items affecting daily operations, for example, staff uniforms could be made of recyclable fabric which causes less harm to the environment.
- *Loyalty programme*. A loyalty programme for frequent visitors should not only centre on financial incentives. It should also communicate with extant customers about the current green practices implemented by hospitality firms. The patron's evaluation of the services should be diligently reviewed since the group of green consumers, who appreciate the effort made in promoting **environmental stewardship**, are more knowledgeable about environment practices than customers from **mass tourism**. Their input to service performance is very valuable. In sum, a loyalty programme could be regarded as a vital communication link reassuring the concerns of customers as well as manifesting the mission of the firm.

Building green hospitality brands

In the hospitality industry, the subject of branding is high on the agenda of many marketing executives. In the field of green branding, hospitality businesses have chosen either an expansion of their brand or a contraction (Figure 10.6). A green brand expands by including a green product brand in an existing product line.

Green brand expansion

(e.g. InterContinental Hotels Group launch the Hotel Indigo brand)

Green brand contraction

(e.g. Fairmont Hotels and Resorts efforts to green its operations since 1990 by setting up the Green Partnership programme)

FIGURE 10.6 Green branding strategies

A green brand contraction becomes stronger when the focus is narrowed. Companies achieve powerful branding by starting with contraction.

Like any other business, it requires a sheer version to be successful in venturing product innovation. Those private entities attempting to consummate their environmentally friendly delivery ought to construct relevant action plans to effectively achieve the mission of the firm. Since the implementation of environmentally minded hospitality services is still at the embryonic stage, well-crafted branding strategies could successfully assist the firms to cope with the challenges that may undermine service experiences offered to green consumers. The following illuminate the key considerations in branding green services and products:

- *Image creation*. In the image formation process, consumers first evoke their perception of a brand organically. In this stage, the consumers have no prior knowledge about the brand. However, the image of brand may quickly change once the consumers explore the information of the brand. Advertising is the typical method of communication to enhance the consumer perception of products/services. Word-of-mouth is often viewed as an effective channel to create a brand image; however, this can only reach a smaller number of consumers. Traditionally, radio, TV, the printed media and the internet have influenced a large number of consumers and conveyed communicative messages to core customers, thereby enhancing the process of image building. Recently, web-based social networks, such as Facebook and Google+, have become viable channels for image creation.
- *Product positioning*. In a competitive market environment, understanding the strengths and weaknesses of a particular brand help a firm vigorously position its brand in the market place. When analysing its relative position in the market, a firm needs to develop a list of attributes associated with its current services and products. Then, the firm should compare all the brand attributes of the firm and its competitors. This analysis helps the firm to develop the most appropriate marketing strategies to reach its goals. For example, Hotel XYZ finds that the

overall guests' perception of its green practices is high compared to that of its close competitor, however, its room rate is considerably higher than that of its competitor. Hotel XYZ may position itself as a premier green hotel which has constantly worked on new solutions to reduce energy usage without compromising the quality of guests' stays.

- *Segmentation*. Hospitality firms in general attempt to serve the needs of diverse groups of customers. In reality, a business establishment is not likely to fulfil the needs of all its customers. In the hospitality business, the concept of segmentation aims to attract demand from core groups of customers who are likely to purchase hospitality services and products. In deploying branding strategy, it is important to evaluate who the potential customers are. Are they homogeneous in terms of their socio-demographic characteristics? Do they have a similar type of **lifestyle** or not? If they are not homogeneous, which groups of customers are more likely to purchase the goods and services? Moreover, for a loyalty programme, the marketers have to find out which groups of customers are apt to buy more or come back, as distinguished by their socio-demographic, lifestyle or psychological traits.

- *Brand connection*. Nowadays, with the advances in information technology, service firms can learn how to better serve their customers. A firm could obtain further critical market insights regarding its competitors' augmented or added services, that would allow the firm to replicate those new service concepts, if necessary. However, the customer may regard these service concepts as the norm for those firms in a certain competitive range. Since services are almost the same in all that range, when making a purchase decision, customers may focus on the price, apart from the service quality, which is unknown if the customer has never used or heard about the service previously. Thus, price becomes the defining factor manipulating the buying decision in the absence of product loyalty. In order to win the customer base, a firm ought to devote time and energy to building a customer relationship and broadening customer loyalty.

- *Value co-creation*. In a fast-track economy, hospitality consumers are constantly confronted with new ideas or services and may not be fully aware of the underlying benefits connected with these services. As a result, customers may not appreciate those services specifically catering to their needs and hesitate to use the service. In theory, customers are not inclined to buy services if the benefits of those services are not explicitly disclosed in marketing materials and service menus. Hence, it is imperative that service staff and managers provide educative information on the anticipated benefits of novel service concepts unfamiliar to the consumers. Further, a hospitality firm should arrange necessary support to enable its customers to have the optimal service experience. As customers fully enjoy the benefits of service provided to them by the staff, they may use the service more and promote the service via positive word-of-mouth. Indeed, customers and the service team are capable of co-creating the brand value as the service staff enhance the customers' experience.

- *Service evaluation*. Not all services or products are likely to meet customer expectations at every point in time. Product designers and service providers should find out the obstacles detrimental to the growth of the brand. To boost service quality in response to customers' needs and wants, various evaluative mechanisms on service performance should be built up in a systematic way. Through the results of customers' evaluation of services, a provider is able to identify the problems causing the failure of service. The service evaluation not only involves the customers but also other service stakeholders such as service staff and designers. Personal interviews, observations, focus group surveys and questionnaire surveys can be exploited to collect the necessary information on service performance.

Responsible marketing outlook

For companies manufacturing products or rendering services, it is no longer enough to focus on the functional benefits alone. In order to follow responsible marketing, businesses must think and act holistically and should start by asking questions such as:

- What are we making?
- How are we making it?
- Is it sustainable or not?
- Who are we working with?

The next step is to build relationships with consumers and turn them into advocates by sharing the passion and the vision intrinsic to the company products or services. Communication is essential in order to build trust and ensure transparency. The message must be consistent and carry an aura of authenticity. The principal objective of companies is to create loyalty among customers. The relationship created through green branding strategies should evolve from that of buyer–seller to a relationship of equals striving for the greater good of the environment.

EXERCISES

1   **GROUP DISCUSSION, GROUP PROJECT OR WRITTEN ASSIGNMENT**
    Marketing green initiatives in hospitality
    The history concerning the deployment of green initiatives in the hospitality business is brief. Possibly, some consumers are not aware of the implementation of green initiatives by hospitality firms.
    - If you know a particular hospitality establishment practising green management, describe the specific marketing strategies used by the firm that brought its green initiatives to your attention.
    - Suggest how the firm could increase its visibility in green operations from a marketing perspective.

2 GROUP DISCUSSION OR GROUP PROJECT

Being green online

- Evaluate the websites of five different hotels undertaking green initiatives and compare the differences and similarities of the green-related messages posted on the web.
- Discuss if there is any issue preventing the successful delivery of the online communicative messages.

3 GROUP PROJECT

Communicating the four new Ps

- Write a short essay that could be used for a press release, incorporating the concepts of the four new Ps (people, planet, profit and process). Choose the hospitality entity you are interested in and report its green performance.

4 GROUP PROJECT OR WRITTEN ASSIGNMENT

Brand image and green hospitality

- Identify an establishment involving green hospitality management and find out how the specific service/product attributes affect the image of the brand.

5 GROUP PROJECT AND PRESENTATION

Market analysis

- Conduct a market analysis on the major players among green hotels from a particular city, region or country. The analysis should reveal the strengths and weaknesses of each player in regard to service quality and pricing structure.

6 WRITTEN (AND RESEARCH) ASSIGNMENT

Loyalty programmes

- Compare the loyalty programmes of three green hotels of interest. In the diagnosis, state the similarities and differences in reward provision among those three programmes.

References

American Marketing Association. Resource Library: Dictionary (2009) Available at: http://www.marketingpower.com/_layouts/Dictionary.aspx?dLetter=G.

World Commission on Environment and Development (WCED) (1987) *Our Common Future*. Available at: http://www.un-documents.net/wced-ocf.htm.

Resources

Ayuso, S. (2006) 'Adoption of voluntary environmental tools for sustainable tourism: analysing the experience of Spanish hotels', *Corporate Social Responsibility and Environmental Management*, 13(4): 207–70.

Baker, W.E. and Sinkula, J.M. (2005) 'Environmental marketing strategy and firm performance: effects on new product performance and market share', *Journal of the Academy of Marketing Science*, 33(4): 461–75.

Bohdanowicz, P. (2005) 'European hoteliers' environmental attitudes: greening the business', *Cornell Hotel and Restaurant Administration Quarterly*, 46(2): 188–204.

Brown, M. (1996) 'Environmental policy in the hotel sector: "green" strategy or stratagem', *International Journal of Contemporary Hospitality Management*, 8(3): 18–23.

Carmona-Moreno, E., Cespedes-Lorente, J. and Burgos-Jimenez. J.D. (2004) 'Environmental strategies in Spanish hotels: contextual factors and performance', *The Service Industries Journal*, 24(3): 101–30.

Chan, E.S.W. and Hawkins, R. (2010) 'Attitude towards EMSs in an international hotel: an exploratory case study', *International Journal of Hospitality Management*, 29(4): 641–51.

Claver-Cortes, E., Molina-Azorin, J., Jorge, P. and Lopez-Gamero, M.D. (2007) 'Environmental strategies and their impact on hotel performance', *Journal of Sustainable Tourism*, 15(6): 663–79.

Dief, M. and Font, X. (2010) 'The determinants of hotels' marketing managers' green marketing behaviour', *Journal of Sustainable Tourism*, 18(2): 157–74.

Dinan, C. and Sargeant, A. (2000) 'Social marketing and sustainable tourism: is there a match?', *International Journal of Tourism Research*, 2: 1–14.

Fuller, D.A. (1999) *Sustainable Marketing: Managerial-Ecological Issues*, Thousand Oaks, CA: Sage.

Gustin, M.E. and Weaver, P.A. (1996) 'Are hotels prepared for the environmental consumer?', *Journal of Hospitality & Tourism Research*, 20(2): 1–14.

Kasim, A. (2009) 'Managerial attitudes towards environmental management among small and medium hotels in Kuala Lumpur', *Journal of Sustainable Tourism*, 17(6): 709–25.

Kirk, D. (1998) 'Attitudes to environmental management held by a group of hotel managers in Edinburgh', *International Journal of Hospitality Management*, 17(1): 33–47.

Kotler, P., Roberto, N. and Lee, N. (2002) *Social Marketing: Improving the Quality of Life* 2nd edn, Thousand Oaks, CA: Sage.

Kotler, P., Bowen, J. and Makens, J. (2003) *Marketing for Hospitality and Tourism*, 2nd edn, Englewood Cliffs, NJ: Prentice Hall.

MacDonald, C. and Whellams, M. (2007) 'Greenwashing', in Robert W. Kolb (ed.) *Encyclopedia of Business Ethics and Society*, Thousand Oaks, CA: Sage.

Middleton, V.T.C. and Hawkins, R. (1998) *Sustainable Tourism: A Marketing Perspective*, Oxford: Butterworth-Heinemann.

Peattie, K. and Crane, A. (2005) 'Environmentally responsible marketing: legend, myth, farce or prophesy?', *Qualitative Market Research: An International Journal,* 8(4): 357–70.

Williams, E. (n.d.) *CSR Europe's Sustainable Marketing Guide*, Brussels: CSR Europe.

Additional material

Go to www.routledge.com/cw/sloan to find PowerPoint slides of all the figures and tables from the book, additional case studies, a test bank of questions and extra links to useful videos.

Consumer typology and behaviour

CHAPTER OBJECTIVES

The objectives for this chapter are:

- To examine the changes in consumer behaviour in relation to sustainable development
- To identify the various types of consumers
- To provide an understanding of the concept of sustainable development in relation to external communications and responsible marketing
- To appreciate the development of a new consumption model
- To understand behavioural variances toward consumption

Consumers and responsible consumption

The consumers are the main actors of responsible consumption. Today's consumers, as global citizens, can influence companies and public authorities in various ways. As simple consumers with their purchase practices, as investors, by choosing to invest in companies engaged in environmental protection, and as citizens by electing a government and influencing policies. A significant – and growing – proportion of consumers are deeply concerned about the sets of themes surrounding **sustainable development**. Consumers are increasingly vigilant in regard to ethical behaviour of businesses. The sole emphasis on the economic result and the race to profits has given way to a new business paradigm. The general public, as citizens and consumers, is increasingly interested in businesses strategies in regard to **social** welfare and environmental protection.

The engaged consumer

Consumer behaviour and attitudes have changed over the past three decades in regard to environmentally **sustainable** products and services. Consumers, not governments, are the driving force behind the environmental orientation of companies. Firms that neglect consumers' attitudes will fail to satisfy their needs. Hotel chains' customers can basically be divided into two groups: corporate and leisure guests. This basic split has its roots in the economic model of hospitality. Both groups show very distinct booking and spending behaviour. But the major change is not taking place in the economic segment, but rather in the environmental and social equity awareness of these two groups. The change in green thinking will demand hoteliers respond to altered needs and wants.

First of all, let us recall that a consumer is an individual who acquires a product or service for personal usage. A new era of consumption is developing. Indeed, consumption is no longer a matter of freedom of choice, but is closely related to issues of responsible citizenship. We are seeing the emergence of a new type of consumer: the engaged consumer. This consumer engages his/her individual responsibility in the state and economic systems and more particularly in the fields of social equity and the environmental protection. Moreover, this engaged consumer wants to drive his/her values and in particular tries to ensure favourable pricing for the end consumers by reducing the length or complexity of the distribution system. There are two types of consumers that have emerged from the evolution of the engaged consumer: the activist consumer and the informed consumer.

1. *The activist:* on the one hand, activism is all the more important as it represents the voice and the force of the consumers vis-à-vis that of the producers and the distributors. The activist consumer strongly engages in favour of sustainable development. Sorting waste, safeguarding energy by simple gestures, buying biodegradable products, using public or human-powered transport, consuming organic, local food, **composting**, participating in **ecotourism** projects and volunteering for an environmental or local social association are simple examples which are considered *common sense* by the activist consumer. The activist will prefer to organize weekly organic food distribution in cooperation with local farmers rather than purchase organic product in supermarkets. Some activists will visit farmers' markets at closing time to buy all the fruits and vegetables left over from the day, often deemed as not *sellable* because of minor faults. Finally, the activist consumer organizes large gatherings to discuss experiences, contemplate new ideas and generally to promote an open exchange within the community of activists. A community of activist consumers will organize a day of non-consumption.

2. *The informed:* on the other hand, and in spite of the rise of the activist consumer, we can see the first sign of the slowing down of this collective movement. Indeed, there have been changes in the way we perceive our **environment** and

thus in the way we consume. The trend seems to be going in the direction of consuming less, but better, with a slight preference towards useful products and services. The consumer is more inclined to spend time searching for information rather than taking part in actions. The informed consumer requires a personalized service with a special requirement: intelligibility and traceability of the labels found on products. This informed consumer supports a return of reasonable agriculture, hence organic production, and keeps a close eye on where and how are products are manufactured. The informed consumer tends to act less on the political level, which is different from the activist consumer, but will focus on raising the level of social equity and environmental awareness within a community at large.

CASE STUDY 11.1 Hoteliers' attitudes and behaviours toward green operations

In the entire tourism business, the hotel sector is regarded as the most energy-consuming and energy-intensive one (Bohdanowicz, 2005). Thus, in pursuit of green management, the attitude of a hotelier is as critical as that of a consumer. A survey of European hoteliers indicates that managers in franchised hotels are more likely to pay attention to environmental issues than independently-operated accommodation (ibid.). Further, initiatives on the part of the government could influence the attitude and behaviour of hoteliers. Bohdanowicz (2006), in a survey of Swedish and Polish hoteliers, finds that hotel facilities have an **environmental impact** on the natural environment. The Swedish and Polish hoteliers consider that 'the environmental impacts of their hotels were medium to significant' (ibid., p. 669). However, few studies identify whether hoteliers from developing countries show a different attitude towards environmental protection and **corporate social responsibility**. A case in Ankara, Turkey (Erdogan and Baris, 2007), reveals that hoteliers' policies and practices often ignore the significance of environmental protection. Further, hotel managers might lack knowledge and motivation to meet the fundamental obligation of **environmental stewardship** (ibid.). In an investigative effort embracing small and medium-sized enterprises (**SMEs**) in the hotel business, Kasim (2009) describes behavioural barriers in incorporating green operations as coexisting endogenous influences (e.g., lack of knowledge about environmental-friendly practices) and exogenous effects (e.g., consumer demand for green services).

The consumer and sustainable development

As we have seen, the activist but also the informed consumer is involved in the safeguarding of the environment and more particularly in sustainable development. Indeed, a sort of *collective awakening* was necessary to be able to reflect rationally on the place and the modes of consumption and the importance of our needs in our lives. It is important to differentiate between basic needs such as eating, drinking, dressing and the more transitory, infinite, subjective and changing desires. According to the phenomenon of zero or negative growth, to consume is not considered a pleasure in its current form, but rather an act of despair. Indeed, in most developed countries, the basic needs may not be considered as particularly important and the majority of consumption is based on compulsive wants. However, those wants are infinite and as soon as they are appeased, reappear again. It can be visualized as a vicious circle with no end, but a feeling of discouragement. However, for various reasons, including the increase in natural disasters, the emergence of films on the environment and the increase in the price of natural resources, a larger audience of consumers around the globe has joined the activist and informed consumers with a particular interest in sustainable development. As a direct result of catastrophes or price fluctuation, some consumers decide to dedicate themselves to self-production on a small scale. There is a return to authenticity in products and services and an increased interest in the local soil. Alternative forms of energy sourcing and the purchasing of equitable products are other signs of growing interest in sustainable development.

The unpredictable consumers

A new profile of consumers has made an appearance with a clear tendency towards mass consumption. This is the unpredictable consumer. This incoherent consumer is not an activist, not particularly informed and rather unaware of the impact of choices made when purchasing products and services. This consumer's wants are unforeseeable, and consequently without coherent references. In this context, to predict the behaviour of this consumer is complicated and highly dependent on the situations of consumption. Such a consumer may be wearing a very expensive watch, driving a luxury car, but do the weekly food purchases at the mass discounter. The awareness of issues surrounding sustainable development is limited. This will be the chance for a business to use wise responsible promotion and instructive tools to inform and educate.

The greening of tourists

Tourists' interest in the environment has gradually increased over the past decades with the majority of travellers preferring to choose environmentally friendly hotels.

The ecotourists

For many people, tourism has already gone too far. Ecotourism, a new phenomenon, has developed over the past decade in the tourism field. Although ecotourism accounted for 4–5 per cent of all international travel expenditure, it is the fastest growing and a lucrative segment of tourism. Ecotourists are tagged as 'high spending, nature-loving, responsible tourists [and] are undoubtedly an attractive option for governments looking for ways of earning foreign exchange'. The word ecotourism has a good ring. Finally, a form of tourism is taking account of the need of the environment in addition to the needs of the tourist. Finally, a form of tourism which does not contribute to the crowding issue and all the (environmental) problems it brings with it. Finally, a new model of destination development engages the communities in (sustainably) designing their future. But soon, problems arise in considering whether four-wheel-drive vehicles racing round Africa's renowned game parks constitute ecotourism or not! Is trekking considered ecotourism when authorities are building a road through an ancient forest to reach a trekking lodge? Is ecotourism a marketing ploy for tour operators rather than a statement of true commitment? Are struggling nations around the world able to safeguard their environment and culture and meanwhile lure affluent foreigners and their tourist dollars? Probably, ecotourism is the most over-used and misused word in the tourism business.

Swarbrooke and Horner (2007) define ecotourists as largely motivated to see the natural history of a destination typically with the purpose of observing wildlife and learning something about the environment. It is argued that environmental awareness is different between individuals and the 'shades of green tourists' consider the broad range of environmental concerns. It is also argued that a tourist's attitudes regarding environmental issues are highly dependent on where they originally come from (Ivarsson, 1998; Swarbrooke and Horner, 2007). Furthermore, a hotel's performance on environmental issues is highly dependent on where its core guests come from. Greek hoteliers, for example, have greatly improved their environmental performance because the majority of their guests come from Germany, where people's environmental protection and awareness are relatively high. In Europe, the Scandinavian countries, Germany, France and the Netherlands are far more concerned about environmental issues than the eastern or southern member countries. Internationally operating hotel chains accommodate guests from various countries and cultures. This variety creates an issue in the way that different guests have different environmental perceptions and standards. Each guest has his or her own perception of sound environmental management. Additionally, there are different opinions as to what extent guests should be involved in environmentally sustainable initiatives. By promoting research and especially by defining ecotourism, producing guidelines to tour operators and codes for travellers, the hopes are that ecotourism can gain the place it deserves in the future of tourism development.

The responsible tourists

The concept of **responsible tourism** is based on the relationship between the tourist and the tourism actors which involve the providers of tourism experiences, hotel employees and local inhabitants. The tourist travels with his own culture, practices and attitudes and financial capacity but also brings along curiosity and a desire for exchanges. The welcoming communities are more than a simple campsite, hotel or beach. Rather, they are a space, a village, a soil, with its population, its social rules, its economy, its environment and its landscape. The meeting – a mixture of curiosity and respect – between the welcoming and the welcomed constitutes the first steps of responsible tourism.

Beyond the basic tourism offers which may include transport, lodging and activities at a destination, responsible tourism finds its roots and falls under the logic of sustainable development. Indeed, responsible tourism is located at the intersection of three fields: economic, social and environmental. Responsible tourism, in its design, mobilizes the local population, stimulates local agricultural and cultural production and generates income, contributing to the financing of new projects (e.g., education, health, environment, production) for community living. The responsible tourist is an element of social dynamics and a factor of open cultural exchanges, respect, listening and cultural exchanges. The responsible tourist embodies a new solidarity between individuals of different cultures. Finally, the responsible tourist treats the environment and **heritage** in a transmitting logic (to future generations) not in a destructive logic. The responsible tourist actively participates in a mini-laboratory of sustainable development.

Motives for responsible consumption: some theoretical considerations

If an individual regards their potential contribution to the human and environmental balance as effective, the relationship between their attitudes and their behaviour regarding green consumption tends to be strong. If, on the contrary, the same individual does not recognise the effect of his own behaviour, attitude and behaviour will diverge. The ratio contribution to remuneration is not perceived similarly between individuals and justifies different behaviours. The theoretical consideration of consumer behaviour presumes that the degree of influence of attitudes on behaviour depends on the consumer's perceived effectiveness or of their convictions of control. Individuals can be distinguished according to the degree with which they think they are able to control themselves, the events and the circumstances of their lives. If a person believes that his own actions are the cause of a given situation, this is characterized as an internal control mechanism. On the other hand, if the same person explains his own situation by other social factors such as the influence of other people, powerful groups or by other non-controllable environmental factors (chance, luck, destiny), this is characterized as an external control mechanism. We will now consider the motivations for responsible consumption:

- attitudes, intentions and actual consumption behaviour;
- the tourists' intentional and actual consumption behaviour;
- the cost-saving dilemma;
- a new market segment;
- the influence of labels and **certification** schemes on consumer buying and purchasing behaviour.

Attitudes, intentions and actual consumption behaviour

These theoretical considerations make it possible to explain the shift between attitudes, intentions and actual behaviour of consumers. The more consumers estimate that they are responsible for societal or environmental problems, the more they feel that their actions – even in small amounts – can have a direct benefit, which is recognised by their peers. However, the more consumers believe in a responsible evolution of society, the more their behaviour will reflect their attitudes. In addition, human beings constantly attempt to make their behaviour coherent. If an individual believes that external factors control his behaviour, the more his consumption will be out of line with his attitudes. Attitudes toward consumption are influenced according to the values of the individual with, at the end of the chain, products, services and actions.

An internally controlled individual will see a higher utility in the attributes of products, which correspond clearly to his attitude. Consequently, an individual may want environmental protection, believe in social justice or again wants to support local economies, and then the products that have corresponding characteristics will be favoured and purchased. To encourage consumption in line with environmental protection and social equity, for example, individuals must be convinced that their actions are positively supporting these issues. The study of consumers' consuming and purchasing behaviour provides businesses with a framework of analysis likely to increase their performance on the three **sustainability** pillars.

The tourists' intentional and actual consumption behaviour

The travel and tourism industry is not only the largest industry, it is also still growing and competition is fierce. Businesses that assume they are riding some automatic growth escalator invariably descend into stagnation (Levitt, 1960). Consumers, partly due to their increasing bargaining power, have a growing influence on the development of sustainable investments in the hotel industry. Contradictory results have been published about consumers' buying behaviour regarding sustainability in this industry. For example, Miller's research showed that 'consumers are already making decisions based on environmental, social and economic quality for day-to-day products and are keen to transfer these habits to the purchase of tourism products' (Miller, 2003, p. 17). Miller's research shows that 78 per cent of respondents either always or sometimes looked for environmental information about their intended holiday destination (ibid., 29). Furthermore, the Italian Environment Protection Agency reported that sensitivity to the **eco-label** has increased and that 73 per cent of their interviewees preferred eco-labelled tourist accommodations (ANPA, 2001). On the other hand, Reiser *et al.* reported recently that 'tourists' decision making is still only marginally influenced by such [eco] labels and it appears that sustainability does not feature much in tourists' general consumption behaviour' (Reiser *et al.*, 2005, p. 590). It is clear that an important difference exists between consumer buying intentions and actual consumer behaviour.

The cost-saving dilemma

Ford *et al.* (2001) introduce a very sensitive topic, namely, promoting environmentally sustainable initiatives to hotel guests. They argue that guests are aware that environmentally sustainable initiatives, like towel reuse or energy-efficient technology, often result in vast cost reductions. Therefore, hoteliers hesitate to promote environmental initiatives, especially those that result in reduced costs. Stipanuk (2002, p. 112) adds that 'Some hospitality managers believe that certain environmental actions may result in negative customer reaction.' At the same time, he suggests a solution to this dilemma. He proposes that test marketing as well as educating guests on environmentally sustainable behaviour could reduce the negative feelings among guests.

Many hotel guests argue that the money saved goes directly into the pockets of hoteliers but room rates remain the same. Grove *et al.* (1996) argue that the negative effect on guest satisfaction is even worse if guests perceive that environmentally sustainable initiatives reduce the level of comfort. If that happens, they will look for new service providers where they do not experience lower quality at their expense. This issue might be of interest for luxury hotel brands. If those hotels promote cost savings, their guests will soon criticize the hotel's pricing policy.

A new market segment

LOHAS is an acronym for Lifestyles of Health and Sustainability – a US$227 billion market segment in the USA alone but worldwide in its extent. It aligns with those who espouse New Age beliefs but extends also into the environmentalist movement and complementary and alternative medicine. It describes a market place for goods and services which appeal to consumers who value health, the environment, social justice, personal development and sustainable living.

These consumers are variously referred to as culturally creative, conscious consumers or LOHAS consumers, and represent a sizeable group in the United States: 32.3 per cent of adults, or 68 million consumers. In other countries these consumers form an important sector as well because this **lifestyle** well suits the commercial interests of the organic food industry. Although there is, for example, a tendency to change from fast food to slow food and an increase in ecologically produced food, it is doubtful whether this post-modern trend can equate to true sustainability.

The opposite of LOHAS is the LOVOS which represents the Lifestyle of Voluntary Simplicity. This consumer is not post-modern oriented but consistently post-materialistic and contrasts with consumerism. From the point of view of marketing, the LOVOS is a marginal phenomenon which is often neglected, but the LOVOS comprises a future potential change in consumption in society.

The influences of labels and certification schemes on consumer buying and purchasing behaviour

In the **hospitality industry**, as in all industries, it is very important to have a good reputation, an image which conveys values matching those of the targeted consumers. This image has four dimensions: *financial, commercial, social* and *societal*:

- The *financial dimension* concerns the owners (shareholders). It speaks for transparency, clarity and reliability of the information.
- The *commercial dimension* concerns the consumers' wallets. It presents the fair trade, fair value of products and service rendered.
- The *social dimension* concerns the motivation of the employees. It relates to the conditions, the remuneration aspect and the working climate.
- The *societal dimension* concerns all other partners (suppliers, distributors, associations, public authorities). It confers a professional and responsible image and thrives in developing cooperation.

The image contributes directly to the sustainability results and the viability of the business. A business deciding to invest fully in environmental and social responsibility can find massive rewards in terms of image. In the same way, proper and recognised certification or labelling would enhance the marketing presence of this company in the market and gain respect from consumers.

However, opinion is divided on whether a certified product or service is automatically a better quality product than its traditional counterpart. Consumers may perceive certified products as being too expensive, in part due to the **accreditation** processes. Consumers tend to pay greater attention to labelling and certification schemes in the food market than in other types of industries. This is partly due to the high level of media coverage of food and health issues. Consequently, consumers may pay more attention to the organic labelling of food bought at the local store compared to the ISO14001 accreditation, obtained by the hotelier around the corner. It is finally partly due to the fact that consumers find it difficult to personally check whether the standards prescribed within the certification scheme are actually respected. Thus, consumers must trust the certification scheme to believe in the quality of the product or service purchased.

A proper information and transparency strategy needs to be put in place in the field of environmental certification in order to obtain the impact desired regarding consumers.

CASE STUDY 11.2 Green strategies toward consumers

Encountering some serious environmental issues harmful to human life and an escalating energy cost, a growing number of businesses are amending their current strategies to be more responsible to the environment so as to reassure the concerns of vigilant environmentally friendly consumers. The extant literature (Grundey and Zaharia, 2008; Menon and Menon, 1997) reveals three types of strategies habitually undertaken by organizations to showcase their green operations: tactical, quasi-strategic and greening strategic approaches. The tactical approach refers to a minimal change in the existing operations. The quasi-strategic approach, a more proactive thinking, entails broader modifications of the operations. Furthermore, the strategic greening approach aims to extensively and intensively follow a systematic framework in integrating environmental measures across all operations. Grundey and Zaharia (2008) describe several integrated strategies for **green marketing** which includes green design, green positioning, green pricing, green logistics, marketing waste, green promotion and green alliance. In addition to the aforementioned strategies, Ginsberg and Bloom (2004) offer different tactics such as carefully cultivating a green corporate culture and building credibility in green marketing. Moreover, from a holistic viewpoint, Cronin *et al*. (2011), in their review of consumer literature, summarize the major types of green strategies into three domains: (1) green innovation; (2) greening the organization; and (3) green alliance. A strategy study (Claver-Cortés *et al.*, 2007), touching on environmental management as a source of competitive advantage for hotels in southern Spain, discovered three distinct groups (pro-active, intermediate and reactive) of hotels according to the attitude toward environmental practice. This study clearly shows that variance exists among the hotel groups concerning the effort of quantifying the cost and saving associated with environmental practices. Interestingly, there is no significant difference in financial performances, such as room occupancy rate, among the three groups of hotels. Finally, Ottman, Stafford and Hartman (2006) discuss the buzzwords *green marketing myopia*. They argue that green marketing must meet two goals, including: (1) improved environmental quality; and (2) customer satisfaction. Over-achieving or under-achieving either aim will result in green marketing myopia. Consequently, they recommend three approaches to prevent green marketing myopia: consumer value positioning, calibration of consumer knowledge and credibility of product claims.

Responsible consumer behaviour: the consumption model

Personal purchase choices can be structured around individual determinants including physiological state, preferences, knowledge, perceptions and other psychological factors. However, while individual determinants are necessary, they are not sufficient to explain a responsible purchasing behaviour. Collective determinants refer to interpersonal influences on **responsible purchasing** behaviour, the environmental, the physical, economic and social environment as well as public policies. However, there is a complex set of interactions and influences characterizing the purchasing decision. Numerous frameworks have been developed to analyse consumption whereby the consumer, in making a choice, is influenced by numerous factors. Those factors can be categorized into person-related factors (socio-demographics, biological, psychological), environmental factors (cultural, economic, marketing) and the properties of the product or service purchased (physiological effects, sensory perception). However, the motivations of responsible consumerism can be summarized in four factors as described in Figure 11.1, namely, personal health, ecology, ethics and lifestyle.

The decision process can be described as a fairly linear progression starting with the recognition of a need, followed by a search for information, the evaluation stage and the choice (Traill, 1999). However, there are a series of influencing factors that play a critical role before, during and after the decision process. These, portrayed

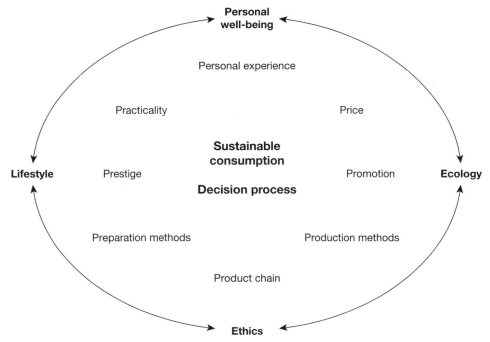

FIGURE 11.1 Persuasive influences model on responsible consumer purchasing behaviour

in Figure 11.1, form the eight Ps of the responsible customer choice influencing factors. Personal experience can be described as the sensory attributes of the products, maybe the food and tasting experience in a restaurant or individual preferences. While personal experiences play an important role, price influences when considered within the concept of value. The promotion through media coverage of rating and ranking of hotels and restaurants and news on the latest popular or exotic destination are also an influencing element. The production methods from the transformation processes of food in hotel kitchens to the type of equipment used and the energy consumed play a role in the final choice of the responsible consumer. The product chain, hence the sourcing, has become an extremely important aspect of sustainable development. The use of fertilizers and pesticides in growing foodstuff, as well as processing, packaging and distribution – and particularly **food miles** – become critical influencing factors in the responsible decision process.

The remaining three Ps of the persuasive influences model in Figure 11.1, namely preparation methods (cooking and **waste management**), prestige (following social trends and norms) and practicality (purchasing convenience, cost and other constraints) are also considered important constituents affecting consumption choice.

The inherent dynamic structure of the model allows the decision process to be modelled according to the various life stages and strength of one influencing factor over another over time.

Future generations: born as responsible consumers

Physiological changes take place as childhood passes to the early years of adult life. As a result of emotional and social development, young people are exerting more control over purchasing choice than ever before. It is especially the younger generation that is likely to respond to environmental issues. Today's children are growing up in times when environmental, economic and social issues are converging. It is likely that those future generations will consider responsible consumerism the only possibility or method of consumption.

Behavioural variances toward consumption

For consumers, a decision-making process regarding a purchase could be compli-cated and perplexing, reflecting the influences of various psychological traits. In some perspectives, individuals' purchasing behaviour could be seen as irrational. In a bid to successfully forecast consumer demand for goods and services, providers ought to understand the behavioural consequences shaping consumers' purchasing decisions as well as consumption experiences. In consumer behaviour literature, those psychological connotations are distinguished by the stages of consumption, including pre-purchase and post-purchase. Pre-purchase elements, for instance, may be described by motivation, perception, attitude and decision-making. Retrospectively, satisfaction and re-purchase intention are reviewed as post-purchase psychological attributes. The following sections explain the significance of the above key psychological influences in relation to product innovation and service delivery.

- *Motivation*: this is a psychological construct coinciding with individuals' needs and wants. From managers' perspectives, in the stage of product development, it is important to know what the motive influencing consumer purchase intention is. In tourism settings, motivation can simply be described as either escaping from daily routines or seeking something new. Certainly it may be further elaborated to a much broader context such as togetherness with families and friends, novelty seeking, socialization, etc. In the hospitality sector, services are often presented in a miscellaneous fashion. As a result, marketers are interested in assessing service-specific purchase motivations, as opposed to a general motivation for a visit. Further, consumers' purchase motivation could be multifaceted and complex. Nevertheless, an effective marketing champion always embraces persuasive messages, moderating consumption behaviour, appealing to the mainstream consumers who are likely to be induced by the marketing communication.
- *Perception*: in the decision-making process, individuals tend to form an evaluative platform according to their perceptions of a particular product or service in relation to their perceptions of other products or services under purchase consideration. The formation of product/service perception is evoked via influences from various informational sources. It could come from the interaction with others in conversation. The mass media in print (e.g., newspapers and magazines) and in motion (e.g., movies and TV programmes) are another powerful source of information, affecting individuals' perceptions. In consumer psychology, scholars often discuss individuals' perceptions from two viewpoints. The first deals with the cognitive component and the other pertains to the affective domain. Individuals develop cognitive images of products/services via a process of knowledge learning. However, the affective image is associated with the levels of emotional attachment to the product and service under evaluation. For example, an affective image of a green hotel could be labelled very exciting or less exciting.
- *Attitude*: in Icek Ajzen's theory of planned behaviour (1985), attitude is regarded as one of the three determinants that have a **direct impact** on behavioural intention (e.g., motivation). As a result, a positive attitude toward products and services under consideration may further encourage an individual's purchasing decision for the product considered. Since attitude constitutes a critical stimulus to the purchasing decision, it is important to know which

psychological attribute could mediate the intention. In consumer literature, various studies report that individual's behavioural beliefs could alter his behavioural intention. Behavioural belief reflects an individual's belief about the outcome of a particular behaviour. In theory, if an individual could benefit from the outcome of a particular behaviour, he is likely to be motivated by such a belief to act on the particular behaviour. For example, if a consumer believes that purchasing environmentally friendly products is highly beneficial in terms of personal health, this initiates a positive attitude to buy environmentally friendly products at some point.

- *Decision-making*: when individuals make a purchase decision, they may go through different stages of evaluation and consider a host of standards for the evaluation. Information search is considered a valuable factor in the decision process. Certainly, in some cases, individuals may not look for any further information as long as they can recall the product information from their memory bank. However, when individuals sense they are missing information on the product under consideration, they may start the process of an information search. In their search, individuals may go through various information channels that may entail personal consultation, printed media, the internet, TV and radio. Once the acquired information is deemed to be sufficient, the decision-makers may construct distinct criteria for evaluation. In the process, the individual may begin with a set of products for consideration that is referred to as the evoked set, according to the literature. Once an individual evaluates the products, he may put some undesirable products into the inert set while including interesting products in the consideration set which the marketers are apt to influence by using advertisements.

- *Satisfaction*: a feeling toward a particular product or service may quickly emerge as soon as consumers purchase the product/service. Such a feeling, in a positive or negative way, may only last for a short time before it changes to a different emotional direction according to usage experiences, product characteristics and some environmental factors (e.g., the weather). Consequently, dis/satisfaction is a temporary, emotional evaluation of a product/service purchased. When consumers are dissatisfied with the product or service purchased, their evaluative perception of the product and service may change if the providers address the problems associated with the product/service. Consequently, service recovery is viewed as a decisive strategy in winning consumer satisfaction in the event that the deficiency of product/service exists. If the providers cannot sufficiently cope with the deficiency, it is likely that those dissatisfied consumers will no longer purchase the same product/service. However, if consumers are highly satisfied with the acquired product/service, they tend to come back and recommend the product and service to others. In consumer literature, researchers often refer to the positive reactions concerning *repurchase intention*, *willingness to buy more* and *willingness to recommend to others* as the key **indicators** of consumer loyalty. Nevertheless, in a tourism setting, consumers have a propensity for novelty seeking that may include experiencing a new service and product each time. In effectively assessing consumer loyalty toward tourism goods and services, unlike *intention to purchase again* and *willingness to buy more*, *willingness to recommend to others* is a more appropriate indicator of loyalty.

CASE STUDY 11.3 Green consumer behaviour

In the consumer behavioural literature, research pertaining to green practices in the hotel and restaurant business is rather sporadic and insignificant. However, behavioural studies on environmentally friendly practices in the area of ecotourism are well established. Recently, aspiring to the concept of sustainable development, some hospitality researchers have started evaluating consumer perception, attitude, decision-making and loyalty. Lee *et al.* (2010), in their online study of green hotel guests in the USA, state that the cognitive images embracing value and quality attributes positively affect the affective images (e.g., arousing, pleasing, exciting and relaxing) and the overall images. Subsequently, all three kinds of images could mediate hotel guests' intention to revisit, word-of-mouth practice and **willingness to pay** more. Further, Schubert *et al.* (2010) investigated attitude, belief, willingness to pay more and behaviour intention toward environmentally sustainable practices in green restaurants. This study concluded that there is a market for green restaurants because consumers cherish the environmentally friendly practices. Approximately 85 per cent of respondents show that they are willing to pay a premium for the reduction of waste and energy usage; the use of recycled products is considered the most important green practices. Han *et al.* (2009) investigated the role of consumers' eco-friendly attitude on consumer behaviour and report that consumer attitudes toward green behaviours play a critical role in the overall image of a hotel. They find that the hotel image influences the revisit intention, word-of-mouth and willingness to pay a premium. Han *et al.* (2011) confirm that hotel customers' environmentally friendly attitude positively affects the intention to stay at a green hotel, the intention to spread word-of-mouth praise and the willingness to pay extra. In a cross-cultural study, Choi *et al.* (2009) examined consumers' environmental attitudes and their behavioural intention toward environmentally responsible practices between Greece and the United States. Their study exhibits that respondents in both countries demonstrate a high level of willingness to pay more for the hotels involving green practices. Meanwhile, hotel guests in Greece are likely to pay more than those in the United States. In another cross-culture research, Dutta *et al.* (2008) reviewed consumer attitudes towards green practices and willingness to pay. The study shows that consumers in the United States are more inclined to engage in green practices in restaurants than those in India; further, the green attitude significantly influences the willingness to pay a premium of up to 10 per cent or higher over the standard menu. Further, a study of India's green hotels (Manaktola and Jauhari, 2007) demonstrates that if two hotels provide the same level of service quality, the hotel which shows favourability to environment-friendly practices would stand out. Moreover, this research also validates a positive relationship between consumers' attitude and their behaviour towards green practice. Touching on **renewable energy**, Dalton *et al.* (2008) assessed tourists' attitudes toward micro-generation renewable energy supply (RES). Some 86 per cent of respondents support RES while 74 per cent are in favour of decreasing their energy consumption (e.g., a moderate use of air-conditioning in their rooms). Interestingly, 52 per cent of respondents claim that they are not willing to pay an additional premium for hotel accommodation due to the use of RES. Furthermore, Mair and Bergin-Seers (2010) investigated the effect of four different kinds of in-room messages in relation to towel reuse behaviour. Concerning the in-room messages, *information plus request* generates the stronger influence on towel reuse behaviour whereas *information with incentive (a donation)* has the lowest impact on towel reuse. Finally, in their examination of the relationship between visitor response to eco-labels and their environmental values, Fairweather *et al.* (2005) note that 61 per cent of respondents express a biocentric attitude toward the environment while 39 per cent exhibit an ambivalent attitude. The biocentric tourists illustrate more recalling exposure to tourism eco labels than ambivalent tourists, in addition to the willingness to choose an eco-labelled accommodation. A decision-making study by Jang, Kim and Bonn (2011) discovered that *values/services reliability*, *resultant reputation* and *food quality* highly affect the selection of a green restaurant among the young generation. Meng (2011), evaluating consumer attitudes toward green products, divulges a tremendous market potential for hospitality goods and services. Price, product quality and social responsibility are reported to have a significant impact on consumers' decision-making behaviour. It is likely that individuals may reveal a different environmental attitude moderated by the activity pursued. For example, an environmental consciousness survey (Andereck, 2009), conducted in a visitor centre, outlines that visitors' perceived importance of incorporating environmental practices at a destination is strongly correlated with sightseeing, natural area activities, cultural/arts/heritage activities and adventure activities among all sorts of tourist engagement. Most recently, consumer behaviour researchers (Chen, Hsu and Lin, 20111) also have found that socio-demographic traits (e.g., education level) could moderate travellers' attitude toward environmental practices.

CASE STUDY 11.4 Overnight stay with a minimum CO_2 footprint: 'Sleep Green' is a new European green hotel network

April 2012, Salzburg, Austria. Five dedicated hoteliers and forerunners in terms of climate protection in hospitality, have joined forces, to market their cutting-edge operations to environmentally conscious guests. The five hoteliers, located in Vienna and Salzburg in Austria and Freiburg, Munich and Bad Aibling in Germany have gathered years of experience in operating low environmental impacts hotels and always striving for holistic sustainability where hospitality is an essential cornerstone of business strategy.

The 'Sleep Green' Hotel Network founders are:

Boutique Hotel Stadthalle in Vienna (80 rooms);
Hotel zu Post in Salzburg (37 rooms);
BandO Parkhotel in Bad Aibling (70 rooms);
Best Western Premier Hotel Victoria in Freiburg (66 rooms);
Derag Livinghotel, Campo dei Fiori in Munich (43 rooms).

It is planned that other environmentally friendly hotels will join the hotel network in the future.

The small group of innovative hoteliers are providing information to fellow industry professional on tactics to offer green overnight stays, and strategies in the successful implementation of 'green hospitality'. The founders are providing a clear example of how experience, know-how and expertise can be transferred between hoteliers.

Source: 'Sleep Gren Hotel Network', www.sleepgreenhotels.com.

EXERCISES

1 GROUP DISCUSSION, GROUP PROJECT OR WRITTEN ASSIGNMENT

Green consumer typology

- This book introduces the typologies of green consumers. Find out if socio-demographic traits can influence the typology.

2 GROUP DISCUSSION OR GROUP PROJECT

- Since 'green hotel' is a refreshing new business jargon, write down your idea of a green hotel from the perspective of product/service offerings and management schemes.

3 **GROUP PROJECT**

Motivation to purchase green

- Interview your friends or colleagues to discover what are the potential factors motivating them to stay at a hotel practising green operations.

4 **GROUP PROJECT OR WRITTEN ASSIGNMENT**

Perception of green hotels

- Conduct a behavioural study by interviewing a few individuals who are regarded as frequent travellers, to understand their awareness and perceptions of green hotels.

5 **GROUP PROJECT AND PRESENTATION**

Communication of green efforts

- Browse three hotel websites which contain information on their green practices. Then, elaborate if those green-related communicative messages affect your choice of hotels. If so, why are they so effective?

6 **WRITTEN (AND RESEARCH) ASSIGNMENT**

- If you were a marketing manager in a green hotel, suggest three innovative marketing ideas which could increase room sales, so as to secure consumer loyalty (e.g. giving a discount to those staying at a room consuming energy below the average usage of energy per room).

References

Ajzen I. (1985) 'From intentions to actions: a theory of planned behavior', in J. Kuhl and J. Beckmann (eds) *Springer Series in Social Psychology*, Berlin: Springer Verlag.

ANPA (Agenzia Nazionale Per La Protezione Dell'Ambiente) (2001) *Tourism Accommodation EU Eco-Label Award Scheme*. First Activity Report.

Andereck, K.L. (2009) 'Tourists' perceptions of environmentally responsible innovations at tourism businesses', *Journal of Sustainable Tourism*, 17(4): 489–99.

Bohdanowicz, P. (2005) 'European hoteliers' environmental attitudes: greening the business', *Cornell Hotel and Restaurant Administration Quarterly*, 46(2): 188–204.

Bohdanowicz, P. (2006) 'Environmental awareness and initiatives in the Swedish and Polish hotel industries: survey results', *International Journal of Hospitality Management*, 25(4): 662–82.

Chen, F., Hsu, P. and Lin, T. (2011) 'Air travelers' environmental consciousness: a preliminary investigation in Taiwan', *International Journal of Business and Management*, 6(12): 78–86.

Choi, G., Parsa. H.G., Sigala, M. and Putrevu, S. (2009) 'Consumers' environmental concerns and behaviors in the lodging industry: a comparison between Greece and the United States', *Journal of Quality Assurance in Hospitality and Tourism*, 10(2): 93–112.

Claver-Cortés, E., Molina-Azorín, J.F., Pereira-Moliner, J. and López-Gamero, M.D. (2007) 'Environmental strategies and their impact on hotel performance', *Journal of Sustainable Tourism*, 15(6): 663–79.

Cronin, J.J., Smith, J.S., Gleim, M.R., Ramirez, E. and Martinez, J.D. (2011) 'Green marketing strategies: an examination of stakeholders and the opportunities they present', *Journal of the Academy of Marketing Science*, 39(1): 158–74.

Dalton, G.J., Lockington, D.A. and Baldock, T.E. (2008) 'A survey of tourist attitudes to renewable energy supply in Australian hotel accommodation', *Renewable Energy*, 33: 2174–85.

Dutta, K., Umashankar, V., Choi, G. and Parsa, H.G. (2008) 'A comparative study of consumers' green practice orientation in India and the United States: a study from the restaurant industry', *Journal of Foodservice Business Research*, 11(3): 269–85.

Erdogan, N. and Baris, E. (2007) 'Environmental protection programmes and conservation practices of hotels in Ankara, Turkey', *Tourism Management*, 28(2): 604–14.

Fairweather, J.R., Maslin, C. and Simmons, D.G. (2005) 'Environmental values and response to ecolabels among international visitors to New Zealand', *Journal of Sustainable Tourism*, 13(1): 81–98.

Ford, M., Fair, M., Govan, J. and Byrd, J. (2001) 'Managing environmental perceptions', *Green Hotelier*, 21(1): 16–17.

Ginsberg, J.M. and Bloom, P.N. (2004) 'Choosing the right green marketing strategy', *MIT Sloan Management Review*, 46(1): 79–84.

Grundey, D. and Zaharia, R.M. (2008) 'Sustainable incentives in marketing and strategic greening: the cases of Lithuania and Romania', *Technological and Economic Development of Economy*, 14(2): 130–43.

Han, H., Hsu, L. and Lee, J. (2009) 'Empirical investigation of the roles of attitudes toward green behaviors, overall image, gender, and age in hotel customers' eco-friendly decision-making process', *International Journal of Hospitality Management*, 28, 519–28.

Han, H., Hsu, L.J., Lee, J.S. and Sheu, C. (2011) 'Are lodging customers ready to go green? An examination of attitudes, demographics, and eco-friendly intentions', *International Journal of Hospitality Management*, 30: 345–55.

Ivarsson, O. (1998) 'Going green: is it important?', *Green Hotelier*, 12: 11.

Jang, Y.J., Kim, W.G. and Bonn, M.A. (2011) 'Generation Y consumers' selection attributes and behavioural intentions concerning green restaurants', *International Journal of Hospitality Management*, 30: 803–11.

Jensen, S., Birch, M. and Fredriksen, M. (2004) 'Are tourists aware of tourism ecolabels? Results from a study in the county of Storstrom in Denmark', paper presented at 13th Nordic Symposium in Tourism and Hospitality Research, Aalborg, Denmark, 9 December.

Kasim, A. (2009) 'Managerial attitudes towards environmental management among small and medium hotels in Kuala Lumpur', *Journal of Sustainable Tourism*, 17(6): 709–25.

Lee, J., Hsu, L., Han, H. and Kim, Y. (2010) 'Understanding how consumers view green hotels: how a hotel's green image can influence behavioural intentions', *Journal of Sustainable Tourism*, 18(7): 901–14.

Mair, J. and Bergin-Seers, S. (2010) 'The effect of interventions on the environmental behaviour of Australian motel guests', *Tourism and Hospitality Research*, 10(4): 255–68.

Manaktola, K. and Jauhari, V. (2007) 'Exploring consumer attitude and behaviour towards green practices in the lodging industry in India', *International Journal of Contemporary Hospitality Management*, 19(5): 364–77.

Meng, N.K. (2011) 'The potential of hotel's green products in Penang: an empirical study', in *Proceedings of 2nd International Conference on Business and Economic Research*, pp. 741–57.

Menon, A. and Menon, A. (1997) 'Enviropreneurial marketing strategy: the emergence of corporate environmentalism as market strategy', *Journal of Marketing*, 61: 51–67.

Ottman, J.A., Stafford, E.R. and Hartman, C.L. (2006) 'Avoiding green marketing myopia: ways to improve consumer appeal for environmentally preferable products', *Environment*, 48(5): 22–36.

Schubert, F., Kandampully, J., Solnet, D. and Kralj, A. (2010) 'Exploring consumer perceptions of green restaurants in the US', *Tourism and Hospitality Research*, 10(4): 286–300.

Resources

Bohdanowicz, P. (2005) 'European hoteliers' environmental attitudes: greening the business', *Cornell Hotel and Restaurant Administration Quarterly*, 46(2): 188–204.

Dolnicar, S., Crouch, G.I. and Long, P. (2008) 'Environment-friendly tourists: what do we really know about them?', *Journal of Sustainable Tourism*, 16(2): 197–210.

France, L. (1997) *Earthscan Reader in Sustainable Tourism*, London: Earthscan.

Grove, S.J., Fisk, R.P., Pickett, G.M. and Kangun, N. (1996) 'Going green in the service sector', *European Journal of Marketing*, 30(5): 56–66.

Honey, M. (1999) *Ecotourism and Sustainable Development: Who Owns Paradise?*, Washington, DC: Island Press.

Honey, M. (2008) *Ecotourism and Sustainable Development: Who Owns Paradise?*, 2nd edn, Washington, DC: Island Press.

Levitt, T. (1960) 'Marketing myopia', *Harvard Business Review*, 38: 45–56.

LOHAS (2009) 'LOHAS background', Louisville, CO: Lifestyle of Health and Sustainability. Available at: http://www.lohas.com/.

McDonald, S., Oates, C.J., Young, C. and Hwang, K. (2006) 'Towards sustainable consumption: researching voluntary simplifiers', *Psychology and Marketing*, 23(6): 515–34.

McLaren, D. (2003) *Rethinking Tourism and Ecotravel*, 2nd edn, Sterling, VA: Kumarian Press.

Miller, G. (2003) 'Consumerism in sustainable tourism: a survey of UK consumers', *Journal of Sustainable Tourism*, 11(1): 17–39.

Reiser, A. and Simmons, D.G. (2005) 'A quasi-experimental method for testing the effectiveness of ecolabel promotion', *Journal of Sustainable Tourism*, 13(6): 590–616.

Richards, G. (ed.) (2001) *Cultural Attractions and European Tourism*, Wallingford: CABI Publishing.

Stipanuk, D.M. (2002) *Hospitality Facilities Management and Design*, Lansing, VA: Educational Institute of the American Hotel and Lodging Association.

Swarbrooke, J. and Horner, S. (2007) *Consumer Behaviour in Tourism*, 2nd edn, Oxford: Elsevier.

TIES (2002) *Definitions and Principles*, Washington, DC: The International Ecotourism Society. Available at: http://www.ecotourism.org/webmodules/webarticlesnet/templates/eco_template.aspx?articleid=95andzoneid=2.

Traill, B.W. (1999) 'Prospect for the future: nutritional, environmental and sustainable food production considerations: changes in cultural and consumer habits', *Proceedings from the Conference on International Food Trade*, Melbourne, 11–15 October.

Weaver, D. (2005) *Sustainable Tourism*, Oxford: Butterworth-Heinemann.

Additional material

Go to www.routledge.com/cw/sloan to find PowerPoint slides of all the figures and tables from the book, additional case studies, a test bank of questions and extra links to useful videos.

Corporate social enterprises

CHAPTER OBJECTIVES

The objectives for this chapter are:

- To identify the underlying principles of sustainable business management
- To define corporate social responsibility
- To identify the relevance of corporate social responsibility to the hospitality industry

A business charter for sustainable development

For many hospitality managers, the daily agenda still focuses on priorities seen to be more important than **sustainable** business management, including cost control, profit maximization and shareholder value. But in the context of **globalization**, emerging **sustainable development** concerns and priorities increasingly cut across all areas of management interest and responsibility.

Environmental protection, **social** accountability, ethics and education, sustainable development and think global – act local proposals are examples of intertwined matters redrawing the rules: doing business in the twenty-first century is different. Owners, general managers and line managers cannot ignore these developments. They need to understand and respond to changing societal expectations of business. And they must effectively communicate what they consider to be realistic expectations of what business can – and cannot – achieve. In this chapter, we will be looking at one particular aspect of doing business in the new century. **Corporate social responsibility (CSR)** is concerned with a company's obligations to be accountable to all its **stakeholders** when operating and undertaking activities.

The world business **environment** is on the move. The past 50 years have been a real whirlwind in terms of management. What defined business requirements for success and competitiveness yesterday may be quite different today. Indeed, various trends and forces are challenging the conventional views of competitiveness and of the success factors for prosperity. This is particularly true for hospitality and food-and-beverage operations, which depend on a complex supply chain and on an intricate delivery network. Generally speaking, the following trends and forces affect businesses in general:

- globalization of markets;
- globalization of supply chains and financial flows;
- intensification of competition;
- quantum leaps in technological development;
- advances in information technology;
- demographic changes;
- environmental challenges;
- changing **lifestyles** and value systems.

There is widespread recognition in the **hospitality industry** that environmental protection must be among the highest of priorities. The industry generally favours a self-regulation system, while governments often prefer to legislate. The **International Chamber of Commerce (ICC)** created a Business Charter for Sustainable Development comprising 16 principles for environmental management (see Table 12.1).

TABLE 12.1 Business Charter for Sustainable Development by the International Chamber of Commerce

Principle	Explanation
1. Corporate priority	To recognise environmental management as among the highest corporate priorities and as a key determinant to sustainable development; to establish policies, programmes and practices for conducting operations in an environmentally sound manner.
2. Integrated management	To integrate these policies, programmes and practices fully into each business as an essential element of management in all its functions.
3. Process of improvement	To continue to improve corporate policies, programmes and environmental performance, taking into account technical developments, scientific understanding, consumer needs and community expectations, with legal regulations as a starting point; and to apply the same environmental criteria internationally.
4. Employee education	To educate, train and motivate employees to conduct their activities in an environmentally responsible manner.
5. Prior assessment	To assess environmental impacts before starting a new activity or project and before decommissioning a facility or leaving a site.
6. Products and services	To develop and provide products or services that have no undue environmental impact and are safe in their intended use, that are

	efficient in their consumption of energy and natural resources, and that can be recycled, reused or disposed of safely.
7. Customer advice	To advise, and where relevant educate, customers, distributors and the public in the safe use, transportation, storage and disposal of products provided; and to apply similar considerations to the provision of services.
8. Facilities and operations	To develop, design and operate facilities and conduct activities taking into consideration the efficient use of energy and materials, the sustainable use of renewable resources, the minimization of adverse environmental impact and waste generation, and the safe and responsible disposal of residual wastes.
9. Research	To conduct or support research on the environmental impacts of raw materials, products, processes, emissions and wastes associated with the enterprise and on the means of minimizing such adverse impacts.
10. Precautionary approach	To modify the manufacture, marketing or use of products or services or the conduct of activities, consistent with scientific and technical understanding, to prevent serious or irreversible environmental degradation.
11. Contractors and suppliers	To promote the adoption of these principles by contractors acting on behalf of the enterprise, encouraging and, where appropriate, requiring improvements in their practices to make them consistent with those of the enterprise; and to encourage the wider adoption of these principles by suppliers.
12. Emergency preparedness	To develop and maintain, where significant hazards exist, emergency preparedness plans in conjunction with the emergency services, relevant authorities and the local community, recognizing potential trans-boundary impacts.
13. Transfer of technology	To contribute to the transfer of environmentally sound technology and management methods throughout the industrial and public sectors.
14. Contributing to the common effort	To contribute to the development of public policy and to business, governmental and intergovernmental programmes and educational initiatives that will enhance environmental awareness and protection.
15. Openness to concerns	To foster openness and dialogue with employees and the public, anticipating and responding to their concerns about the potential hazards and impacts of operations, products, wastes or services, including those of trans-boundary or global significance.
16. Compliance and reporting	To measure environmental performance; to conduct regular environmental audits and assessments of compliance with company requirements, legal requirements and these principles; and to periodically provide appropriate information to the Board of Directors, shareholders, employees, the authorities and the public.

Source: http://www.iccwbo.org/policy/environment/.

A company deciding to endorse the charter will follow the principles to improve environmental management within the organization and determine which principles should be included in the company's own **environmental management system (EMS)**. The principles then act as a guidance tool. Detailed standards should be listed and explained in the EMS and companies are usually measured against an industry standard or **code of practice**. Consequently, the challenge for hospitality managers is to regularly demonstrate and document their actions and achievements. A restaurant seeking to engage actively with its staff and communities, referring to Principle 14, needs to define the parameters in order to report the outcome of the activities undertaken in both financial and social terms. The ICC developed the charter in 1991 when environmental management by businesses was only starting to gain importance. By today's standards, it is necessary to add the social dimension of sustainable development.

Shareholders' value and interests

Maximization of shareholders' value is at the core of corporate strategy, but not exclusively. It is often at the moment of collision between the interests of the shareholders and that of the community that corporations usually come under extreme pressure. Indeed, very few companies can still allow themselves to choose the narrow interests of the shareholders over the broader interests of the community. Kenneth Boulding's essay (1966) entitled 'The Economics of the Coming Spaceship Earth' boldly suggested that problems result from acting like cowboys on a limitless open frontier, the cowboy economy, when in truth we inhabit a living spaceship with a finely balanced life-support system. Via communication technology, communities are linked together. Thus, a growing number of consumers are aware of the cowboy attitude of some businesses and are demanding more information about how products are made, how food-and-beverage operations are run or how employees are being treated. A number of companies have been caught doing what was considered wrong by civil society and have paid a high price in terms of reputation and future sales. In short, these companies have failed to meet the demand for social responsibility.

Suppliers

As stated earlier, it is most important to treat all suppliers in a fair way, including fair payment terms, etc. As these aspects will be further discussed in the next sections on 'Fair Trade', 'Fair Prices' or already have been discussed in previous chapters such as in Chapter 8, they will not be discussed again at this stage.

Customers

According to the Green Hotelier (2007a), social responsibility includes being honest and transparent with customers. Additionally, customers need to understand the links between healthy local economies, an attractive and balanced environment and food products. Hence, some background information about the restaurant and its actions, initiatives and programmes should be given. Especially in regard to food and beverages, affecting the guests' health directly, information has to be provided. Guest education as well as labelling on the menu is important, inspiring the customers to adopt healthier nutrition as well as more environmentally friendly choices. The herb and vegetable garden of the restaurant should be used to educate the guests on the quality of local and seasonal produce, taste and cooking in a pleasurable way. Guests could, for example, be invited on a guided tour through the garden where local herbs and flavours are pointed out and their use explained. If possible, cooking classes with local produce could be held in the herb and vegetable gardens. Initiatives to bring local farmers and customers together, and hence benefit the local economy, could include some 'local market' events, where local farmers offer their 'food from the land' in the restaurant establishment.

Such actions increase awareness among guests in regard to local produce and increase demand for it. The restaurant's website also should be used to provide information about the restaurant's initiatives and policy and thereby educate guests regarding local produce, local suppliers, etc.

The easiest way to educate the customer is to include the message of **sustainability** in the overall atmosphere of the restaurant. The decoration, furniture, landscaping around the building and food presentation could be used and therefore enhance the idea of sustainability. The goal could be to make the customer feel the local distinctiveness and diversity of the respective region. Additionally, it should be possible for guests to take part, on a voluntary basis, in some community development projects and environmental programmes (Green Hotelier, 2007a). Optionally, money for social community development projects could be raised through a donation box with information on the supported project. To have some dishes on the menu where it says 'one dollar of the price of this dish is donated to a local charity project' could be another option (Green Hotelier, 2007b).

All in all, attention has to be paid to not overwhelming the customer with information, as this can negatively affect their restaurant experience.

The community

Ways to make the local community benefit from the presence of an establishment have to be identified. Support through development projects with time, money or other needed resources could be options (Green Hotelier, 2007a). Waste furniture and fittings resulting from refurbishments could be reused by local charities and other businesses, and food leftovers could be given to homeless people or charities. Being sensitive to the needs of the local community also includes respecting their cultural **heritage** as well as their traditions (Green Hotelier, 2007a). Therefore, local, traditional techniques and skills such as art and crafts, and also fishing, etc., should be respected and supported. Purchasing local artists' or crafts items and displaying them for sale in the restaurant could be an option. Garden pots and ornaments could also be selected from local producers, used for decoration or offered for sale as 'locally made' products (Green Hotelier, 2006a). Initiatives like these would make the restaurants' customers interact with parts of the wider community, a very important aspect with regard to social sustainability.

Government

The role of a business in the modern global economy is not only to maximize profits and shareholder value, but also to be accountable to stakeholders and to contribute to a better world. What were once guiding principles of governments have become the responsibilities of enterprises. Because humans do not live in one restricted area, nor are countries under only one type of supranational governance, at least not in practice, all forms of corporate governance face the global challenge of adapting to the local situation. What Germany may consider corporate social responsible behaviour is most probably very different from that of Nigeria, for example. From environmental protection to child labour, employment practices and labour standards, national governments often determine what is considered the basic law by which every organization within the national borders must abide. Are there any obligations beyond the law? This is a very important question raised over the last decade.

Non-governmental organizations (NGOs)

Non-governmental organization (**NGO**) is a term that has become widely accepted to refer to a non-profit-making, voluntary, service-oriented or development-oriented organization, either for the benefit of members (a grassroots organization) or of other members of the population (an agency). An NGO can be a non-profit group or association organized outside of institutionalized political structures to realize particular social objectives (such as environmental protection) or to serve particular constituencies (such as indigenous people). NGO activities range from research, information distribution, training, local organization and community service to legal advocacy, lobbying for legislative change and civil disobedience. In the cases where NGOs are funded totally or partially by governments, the NGO maintains its non-governmental status insofar as it excludes government representatives from membership of the organization. NGOs have played a crucial role in sustainable development. This is partly the result of the restructuring of the welfare state system in many Western countries and the drive toward globalization. International treaties and international organizations such as the World Trade Organization were perceived as being too centred on the interests of capitalist enterprises. NGOs have developed to push forward humanitarian issues, developmental aid and sustainable develop-ment. A prominent example of this trend is the World Social Forum, which is a rival convention to the World Economic Forum held annually in January in Davos, Switzerland. NGOs today play often a consultative and lobbying role in pushing for stricter governmental legislations and business obligations on all sustainability issues.

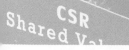

Employees

In order to give most benefit to the local community, local workers should be hired wherever possible. When necessary, local workers should be trained for employment opportunities. Being sensitive to the needs of the employees and treating them in a fair manner is also of great importance. This includes ensuring a safe working environment, paying fair wages, etc. (Green Hotelier, 2007a).

The best environmental policy does not help much if employees do not understand the philosophy and the goals behind it and do not know how to achieve the goals. Employees, who are expected to achieve and implement certain things, need to have proper skills, knowledge, motivation and awareness (Green Hotelier, 2007b). Hence, environmental training should be regularly conducted to motivate staff in order to achieve the best results. Once environmental data on special projects is available, targets for staff should be set in special training sessions and feedback should be given. Environmental training could include topics such as **waste management** and the importance of reducing, reusing and recycling. To improve training results, a copy of the restaurant's sustainability policy could be given to each employee and information could be displayed on staff noticeboards. A small library with books, journals and additional information on recent environmental topics could be established for all employees (Green Hotelier, 2006c, 2007a). Allocating money saved through environmental initiatives to a special staff fund could be an option to motivate staff even more to implement certain practices. In order to get creative ideas from employees, suggestion boxes, competitions or special rewards could be used (Green Hotelier, 2007a).

Unions

All employees have the right of freedom of association, collective bargaining and the right to adequate complaints procedures. A labour union is an organization run by and for employees who have joined together to achieve common goals in key areas such as wages, working hours and working conditions. The most common objective of these organizations is to maintain or improve the conditions of employment.

Over the past 300 years, many trade unions have developed into a number of forms, influenced by different political and economic regimes. The immediate objectives and activities of trade unions vary, but usually include the provision of benefits to members, collective bargaining, industrial action and political activities.

- Benefits may include insurance against unemployment, sick leave and retire-ment. In many developed countries, these functions have been assumed by the state. The provision of professional training and legal advice is an important benefit of union membership.
- Collective bargaining takes place when unions negotiate with employers over wages and working conditions.

- Industrial action may take the form of strikes or resistance to lockouts when negotiations are unfruitful.
- Political activities include campaigning and lobbying to promote legislation favourable to the interests of their members.

Partnership and industry associations

According to the **Millennium Development Goals (MDGs)**, cross-sector partnerships are encouraged in order to develop practical solutions with regard to sustainable development (United Nations, 2008). Cross-sector partnerships mean governments, non-governmental organizations, the public and private sectors as well as local communities work together (Green Hotelier, 2005). In addition, industry members need to work together as well as with other stakeholders in order to break down barriers to progress and to better address issues with regard to sustainable practices (Green Hotelier, 2006b). As stated by David Roberts, General Manager of the Fairmont Château Whistler Resort, 'We all have the power of one', and, collectively, 'individuals can move mountains' and 'corporations can make single decisions to shift policy that in time will produce major cultural and behavioural change' (Harris *et al.*, 2002, p. 269). International and national **certification** schemes, such as **Green Globe 21**, provide tools and support for sustainable practices for tourism businesses (Green Hotelier, 2007a). Joining organizations such as Slow Food also could help a restaurant in particular to establish ties to local producers and obtain information about regional produce and tastes. In addition, getting involved in associations or partnerships keeps one up to date, provides new ideas and enhances the critical view regarding sustainability. Therefore, participation and engagement in such associations or partnerships are highly recommended.

Corporate social responsibility (CSR): definition and dimension

Corporate social responsibility (CSR) – also referred to as business ethics, corporate citizenship and corporate accountability – is a concept by which companies integrate the interests and needs of customers, employees, suppliers, shareholders, communities and the planet into corporate strategies. In short, businesses need to be good corporate citizens. The social pillar in sustainability is the third key element in sustainable hospitality and socially responsible corporate governance is at its heart. CSR is intrinsically linked to the concept of sustainable development. This interaction is one of the key methods companies employ to adapt to the challenges of sustainability. The central hypothesis is that without moral and ethical values a company is incapable of embarking on a strategy of sustainable management. The general idea is that CSR is the vehicle for integrating social and environmental objectives into its managerial decisions, meaning that the expectations of all the stakeholders are taken into consideration in strategic decision-making. CSR can result in meaningful improvements to society and the environment.

The International Organization for Standardization, as part of its work on the new ISO 26000, defines CSR as:

the responsibility of an organization for the impacts of its decisions and activities on society and the environment, through transparent and ethical behaviour that:

- contributes to sustainable development, including the health and the welfare of society;
- takes into account the expectations of stakeholders;
- is in compliance with applicable law and consistent with international norms of behaviour;
- is integrated throughout the organization and practised in its relationships.

The environment in which companies assume CSR is depicted in Figure 12.1. CSR is all about managing these dimensions and responsibilities.

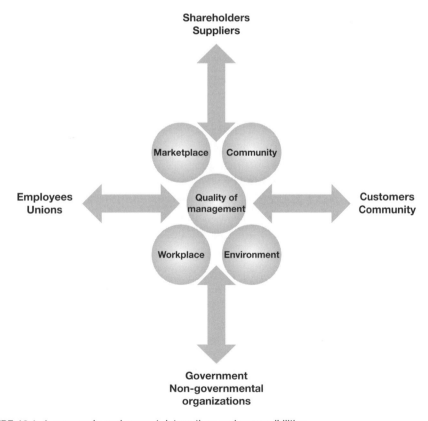

FIGURE 12.1 A company's environment, interactions and responsibilities

Similar to CSR is corporate philanthropy, sometimes known as corporate giving. Here, the hotel company donates some of its profits, or resources to charity organizations. These charitable acts are either handled by senior management or, in large corporations, through a foundation. Cash is most commonly donated but sometimes companies also donate the use of their facilities or give advertising support. In some cases, employee volunteer groups are set up that then donate their time. Commonly, companies donate to environmental, cultural and human support organizations.

CSR results in donations to charitable organizations as well and as part of its sustainability strategy hotels make promises to lower **environmental impacts** which are fortunately, increasingly being realized. Hospitality businesses use their charitable efforts either in the name of CSR or corporate philanthropy to reinforce their reputation, image and positioning. In the longer term their competitive position is consequentially improved.

CSR can be quite ambiguous and is sometimes difficult to separate from corporate philanthropy which is easier to comprehend. Donations and interventions that companies make in the name of CSR are often limited charitable endeavours that are similar to their core business. This is at least partly understandable since their knowledge base makes it easier for them to formulate initiatives in a concept they can easily understand and that are cost-effective for them. An example would be a resort hotel that donates money to the local nature reserve and call this their CSR project, but in reality it is still very similar to corporate philanthropy.

CSR in hospitality also means that the business declares its position as a good neighbour and part of society and the larger community. Therefore, in its decision-making, it must take account of society as a whole and serve the direct and indirect interests of the environment. CSR is a type of business behaviour that goes beyond the legal requirements. Voluntary codes of practice are adopted that businesses believe will be in their long-term interest. Companies should not see CSR as an optional addition to their core business activities, it should be the guiding principle about the way in which business is managed.

CSR is purely voluntary. It is worth noting that in the UK the Confederation of British Industry and the Institute of Directors have both opposed all attempts to make CSR in any way mandatory and have lobbied against the UK government's Corporate Responsibility Bill. Companies are free to start and finish with CSR when and if they please.

Despite the positive declarations companies make about CSR, it has recently come under much criticism. It is doubtful that society and the environment really gain from CSR, it seems that the primary beneficiary is the company who gains branding benefits. Whether it is because the company is associating with a cause, exploiting a cheap means of advertising or countering the claims of pressure groups, there is always an underlying financial motive, so the company benefits more than the NGO. Unfortunately it is not always market-based solutions that will solve social and environmental crises. CSR can even create a veil of integrity for a company that is infringing environmental or employment legislation. It can be a means of deflecting blame or problems caused by corporate operations while hampering efforts to find just and sustainable solutions. It can effectively help to **greenwash** a company's image. Bearing in mind that most CSR policy in companies is created in the Marketing and PR departments, it is not surprising that it is criticized as being a PR stunt. CSR is often portrayed as the elixir of all evils, i.e. if a problem in society or the environment exists, then market forces will solve the problem with each actor acting selfishly in its own best interests.

CSR and company performance: greenwash versus accountability

CorpWatch is an organization located in San Francisco dedicated to watch, as its name implies, corporations around the globe. It reports on unethical behaviour in corporations and disseminates its findings through the internet. CorpWatch has set up a greenwash contest. The awards are given to companies that publicize good actions undertaken to cover up either environmentally damaging operations or various unscrupulous activities. The food-and-beverage industry is under tight scrutiny and many large restaurant organizations do not escape independent reviews and critics. Numerous corporations spend more on corporate image advertising boasting their humanitarian programmes than on their own activities (be it charities, donations or contributions). This is the so-called *greenwash effect*. Hence, the troublesome issue is that CSR can easily become just another public relation exercise! Independent organizations often created by various stakeholders are cropping up everywhere, reminding businesses of the need to be accountable for their actions. For many owners and managers, CSR is still driven more by the concern about the negative consequences of ignoring reputation with regard to CSR performance than by the potential benefits of embracing a responsible behaviour.

Profits are only one measure of benefits, based on quantitative data. Companies have experienced a range of bottom-line benefits. Table 12.2 depicts the overall benefits from CSR at the business level, supported by short examples or added information.

CSR business strategy: internal issues and global challenges

Important aspects of a successful CSR programme are:

- clear policies;
- commitment and agreement on objectives;
- resources made available;
- no conflicts with other policies;
- coordination of efforts and communication by a committee or problem-solving group.

Therefore, one of the first steps toward integrating CSR within the hospitality industry is to develop business-wide policies, recognizing the importance of the business to

TABLE 12.2 Corporate social responsibility overall business benefits

CSR benefits	Example/explanation
Improved financial performance	Several academic studies have shown a correlation between CSR and improved financial performance
Reduced operating costs	Environmentally oriented programme: Energy efficiency reducing utility bills, recycling reducing waste disposal costs.
	Human Resources programme: Work–life scenario reducing absenteeism and increasing retention, thus reducing employee turnover costs
Enhanced brand image and reputation	Brands greatly benefit from positive public relation campaign linked to CSR activities
Increased sales and customer loyalty	Growing demands from customers on value-based criteria: sweatshop-free clothing, child-labour free running shoes and reduced environmental impact type of products. Ethical conduct and environmental and social consciousness of companies make a difference in purchasing decisions
Increased productivity and quality	Improved working conditions equal to a greater employee involvement in decision-making processes, increasing productivity and reducing failures
Increased ability to attract and retain employees	Strong CSR commitment facilitates recruitment of highly qualified candidates, boosts morale and results in higher retention rates
Reduced regulatory oversight	CSR translates itself into a self-regulatory system, thus reducing the involvement of local or national governments on various compliances
Access to capital	A great number of assets under management in investment portfolios are linked to ethics, the environment and corporate social responsibility

Source: Adapted from the Business Social Responsibility Organisation.

the economic development of regions and the responsibilities toward the community and the surrounding environment. In short, the policy should cover the following aspects:

- develop a written policy statement covering all areas;
- incorporate the mission statement;
- incorporate codes of practices as minimum standards;
- set realistic and measurable targets, including key performance targets and periodical audits compatible with its trading partners (suppliers).

A company incorporating CSR must revise its internal practices regarding governance, core ideology, organizational alignment, audits and accounting practices as well as education for social responsibility.

Corporate governance is concerned with planning, organizing and directing policy-making, and **monitoring** the long-term strategy and direction of the business. Core ideology defines the values a company espouses, describing a sense of purpose well beyond profit or shareholders' wealth maximization. Day-to-day decisions, human resources policies and the physical environment (buildings, layouts) are a few areas where organizational alignment to the core ideologies occurs. Organizational alignment is achieved when all departments within a company understand and work toward the same vision, goals and objectives. Traditional audits are formal examinations of the company's financial situation and accounting practices. **Environmental auditing** and social audits report how a firm has performed in terms of its specific CSR objectives or action programmes.

Finally, a critical element lies in the education for social responsibility. In order to integrate responsible business practices into the day-to-day operations, the involvement, commitment and knowledge of employees, from the general manager to the front-line server, are essential. Spreading the word about the crucial importance of revising how business is being conducted is the key to the adoption of CSR behaviour.

Other models of corporate governance

Unfortunately many pressing social and environmental problems have their origins in the market system and their solutions lie in reducing consumption or paying a price that reflects true external costs. The perversity of market mechanisms is exemplified by carbon trading whereby companies can pay to pollute by buying **carbon credits**. Market-based solutions to complex societal and environmental problems tend to focus on the power of the consumer to create the necessary shift towards more sustainable markets. Few consumers make their purchasing decisions on purely ethical grounds; price is more often the barometer that controls spending. In any case, the power of advertising is so strong that it is questionable whether the consumer has unbiased access to correct information. Business commentator Noam Chomsky writes that the consumer's desires and lifestyles are moulded through the use of advertising to the consumer's own detriment. He says, 'The ideal is to have individuals that are totally dissociated from one another . . . whose sense of value is "Just how many created wants can I satisfy?"' CSR demonstrates how many public functions can become privatized. Companies sponsoring health care, libraries, school playgrounds are common practice, businesses are able to demonstrate their 'caring' attitude to society. Such actions blur the responsibilities of business and the state, in fact, by doing good turns companies are adopting the role of governments and of the regulator without the individual having any say. Milton Friedman's adage that 'the business of business is business' is proving untrue. Increasingly the business of business is power and control. The question then arises 'What does a socially and environmentally responsible business look like?' Here are some issues that responsible companies have at the heart of their business strategy:

- *Make efforts to address climate change* by reducing **greenhouse gas** emissions, by using **renewable energy**, by cutting energy consumption and by cutting reliance on oil and fossil fuels.
- *Stop selling harmful products*. For some companies this would mean curtailing activities. It is questionable whether fast food companies that profit from obesity and ill health should exist.
- *Internalize all costs*. Too often industry passes on the true environmental costs to society. A responsible company would cover these costs rather than seeking to externalize them.
- *Adopt socially responsible labour practices*. Responsible companies employ local people at fair rates of pay near their markets and do not exploit cheap labour and poverty in developing countries.
- *Stop lobbying against the public interest and pay taxes in full.* Always operating in the interests of the general public and complete financial transparency are essential for a truly socially responsible company.
- *Reduce consumption and limit growth*. The present capitalist model requires constant economic growth, consumers should not be manipulated into spending beyond their means and to over-consume beyond levels the planet can tolerate.

Creating shared value

The goal of business sustainability has bred new corporate governance models recently that might be better equipped to integrate all three pillars of the **triple bottom line**. In 2011, Professor Michael Porter claimed to have produced a formula for reinventing capitalism: **creating shared value (CSV)**. For a long time, traditional capitalists have focused too narrowly on profits, he claims. Creating shared value involves value creation for business that simultaneously yields more profit and greater positive social impact. The concept of creating shared value focuses on developing partnerships between people and economic progress. Shared value offers companies a way to keep their shareholders happy while also protecting the environment. In the January–February 2011 issue of the *Harvard Business Review*, Porter and his co-author say:

> We create economic value in business while creating value for society as well, responding to social needs and challenges. The concept of shared value can be defined as policies and operating practices that enhance the competiveness of a company while simultaneously advancing the economic and social conditions in the communities in which it operates. Shared value creation focuses on identifying and expanding the connections between societal and economic progress.
>
> (Porter and Kramer, 2011)

CSV came about as a reaction to the financial crisis at the end of the first decade of this century when economic development and social development came into conflict. It stems from the frustrations embedded in capitalism where corruption and short term greed are rife in many businesses.

CSV focuses on three innovative strategic tools:

- *the creation of market 'ecosystems'*, especially when doing business with developing countries requiring companies to make partnerships with NGOs and governments;
- *expanding their value chains* to include unconventional partners such as non-profit organizations and business start-ups;
- *creating new industrial clusters*.

During the financial crisis in the late 2000s, confidence in the business world was shaken. In Porter's view, most companies had stuck blindly to CSR where social welfare is a voluntary addition rather than being the focus. With CSV, companies can use their management ability to simultaneously bring about social progress while making financial profits. CSV recognises the social and environmental costs that for centuries companies have externalized and left the rest of society to pay for. CSV takes a long-term view on company objectives, aiming to train employees, and in developing countries, educate workers as an investment in the future.

Although no examples of CSV exist in the hospitality industry yet, there are examples from elsewhere. Walmart has saved a fortune by addressing packaging procedures with operatives and reducing waste. Five per cent of Unilever's sales in India now come from an army of underprivileged women entrepreneurs. CSV is opposed to charity donations that companies make under the banner of CSR; it regards Fair Trade as a charity organization since its primary objective is a redistribution of revenues and not increasing market share. A scheme to support small cocoa farmers in Côte d'Ivoire supported by the Rainforest Alliance which raised workers' incomes by over 300 per cent by improving yields, product quality and procurement is a better example of CSV.

Social entrepreneurship

Taking inspiration from the Brundtland Report's definition of sustainable development (WCED, 1987), sustainable enterprises are defined as organizations that have business strategies, activities and products and services that meet the needs of the enterprise and its stakeholders in the short term while protecting and enhancing human and natural resources for future generations.

Examples of social entrepreneurship exist in many industries, the hospitality industry being no exception. The social entrepreneurial organization Le M.A.T. has developed a hotel franchising system for potential social entrepreneurs wishing to help underprivileged sections of society gain employment. The organization has success stories right across Europe. In Hamburg, the Stadthaushotel employs mentally handicapped individuals. Similarly, the family atmosphere of the Inout Hotel in Barcelona helps handicapped people through the therapy of salaried employment. The Hotel Tritone in Trieste, Italy, was created to give meaningful employment to socially dislocated people on the edge of society. The organization also provides employment opportunities for ex-prisoners, war veterans and ex-drug addicts.

Current theory suggests social purpose organizations emerge when governments no longer provide solutions, and where social need exists, social entrepreneurs can be seen to sometimes fill this gap. According to management consultant Peter Drucker, entrepreneurs exploit the opportunities that change creates, for example, in technology, consumer preferences and social norms. He says, the entrepreneur always searches for change, responds to it and exploits it as an opportunity. Thus, **social** entrepreneurs are one of such a species, they are entrepreneurs with a social mission and have the following characteristics:

- *creation and consolidation of social value*, not just returns for investors;
- *using entrepreneurial principles* to organize and manage a venture to make social change possible;
- *assessing success in terms of the impact on society* the venture has instead of measuring performance in terms of profit and financial return.

Social entrepreneurship aims to ensure that the very purpose of these businesses changes from one of maximizing returns to investors to optimizing returns to all stakeholders. Though the concept of social entrepreneurship has gained popularity in recent years, it can mean different things to different people which sometimes leads to confusion. Social entrepreneurship is often associated exclusively with not-for-profit organizations. Others use it to refer to business owners who integrate social responsibility into their operations. Although this is not wholly inaccurate, there are many new hybrid business examples of for-profit sustainable revenue-generating enterprises with a social value-generating structure.

CASE STUDY 12.1 Chumbe Island Coral Park Ltd in Zanzibar/Tanzania

This case study on Chumbe Island Coral Park focuses on sustainability initiatives established by the hotel and a marine research centre. It strives to work with the local people on issues of education, sustainable fishing, preservation of coral-rag forests and of course the coral reefs in Zanzibar, Tanzania.

Chumbe Island is registered with the World Conservation Monitoring Center and has exceeded its anticipated goals in community aid and in the protection of **biodiversity**. Chumbe Coral Park organizes excursions for local schools offering educational programmes on the reef and forest habitat as well as classes in children's snorkelling and swimming. Village fishermen, who previously practised fishing in all areas of the reserve, now respect the boundaries of the coral park, and fish only outside the protected areas. Previously the coral reef was not valued by the local people and the relationship between the resort developers and the fishermen was strained. The fishermen did not want to accept that this was not their fishing territory. They agreed to learn from former fisherman turned park rangers and slowly began to understand that the fish would slowly migrate outside the boundaries, which would be to the fishermen's benefit.

Through providing fishermen with the opportunity to become park rangers, a form of social entrepreneurial tourism has developed. The park rangers now manage the Coral Reef Sanctuary. In supporting the local economy, Chumbe purchases local food produce from spice and fish markets which provide around 90 per cent of their needs in their hotel lodge restaurant. Buying locally grown produce supports farmers in the region, local women are employed to cook and serve meals based on local traditions. These women are also employed as operatives in the Chumbe Lodge Hotel. Job opportunities are also offered by international research institutions that have set up a highly reputable marine research centre. Profits from the hospitality operations are re-invested into **conservation** area management and free island excursions for local school children through environmental educational programmes.

The **environmental stewardship** objectives of the Chumbe Island Coral Park are to educate local people, the government, school children and employees on the importance of the forest and coral reefs, that is not only beneficial to the environment, but to the lodge as well. The reserve helps to restock locally depleted fisheries. The Chumbe Lodge Hotel is completely sustainable with solar water heating, solar energy and waste management protocol that carefully benefit the local environment and produce no **carbon footprint**. The kitchens in the Chumbe hotel are virtually 100 per cent sustainable due to major efforts through new state-of-the-art **passive solar design** and greywater technology. At the beginning of the project, Chumbe had serious problems obtaining environmentally friendly technologies and local partners who understood the principles of sustainability.

Source: Riedmiller, S. (2012). 'Can ecotourism support coral reef conservation? Experiences of Chumbe Island Coral Park Ltd in Zanzibar/Tanzania', in Sloan, Simon-Kaufmann and Legrand (eds), *Sustainable Hospitality and Tourism as Motors for Development*, Abingdon: Routledge.

CASE STUDY 12.2 The Case of Inkaterra: pioneering ecotourism in Peru

This case study focuses on Inkaterra Amazonica and how they have over the years pioneered a new form of social entrepreneurship and environmentally friendly tourism in Latin America. The project has given much-needed support to local cultures through staff trained to develop a sustainable retreat resort. All have expert knowledge of the surrounding **ecosystems** and the immense regional biodiversity. Inkaterra has successfully created a market for high quality, luxurious, sustainable hospitality and tourism.

Jose Koechlin, the owner and founder, has created three sustainable hotel complexes in the jungles of the Peruvian rainforest. His priority was to form a team capable of offering new knowledge and skills to local indigenous communities who could combine the benefits of tourism dollars with environmental stewardship and care for local people. The first hotel project was in the Ese'eja-Sonene community where travellers were introduced to local communal traditions exemplified by hunter-gatherer lifestyles. Another benefit to the communities is the training given to locally educated personnel to represent the interests of Inkaterra in local governments. Benefits such as accommodation, food, airfare and insurance are provided to the local staff of Inkaterra. This, along with educational support, health campaigns, agro-forestry workshops raising the awareness of biodiversity, are just some of the activities of Inkaterra in their contact with local communities. However, there have been problems with national legislation that prevents local people being employed as guides who do not have five years previous experience. There are also concerns at hiring locals from the Amazonian communities in the hotels since their culture is not easily adapted to Western accommodation expectations.

Inkaterra works to achieve 'authentic nature travel' and is behind several research projects on biodiversity, natural resource management and conservation of natural reserves. They are also presently supporting a rescue centre for spectacled bears. Due to the rich local biodiversity requiring specialized knowledge, some tours are led by members of indigenous communities who have intimate knowledge of the **flora** and **fauna**.

In addition to providing an example to all social entrepreneurs and environmental stewards, Inkaterra is now a financial profit-making organization. Starting from humble beginnings in the Amazonian rainforest where services were non-existent, the organization overcame enormous difficulties in obtaining equipment and employing an indigenous population who, although they were more than happy to cooperate, required extensive training. This conversion to the principles of **sustainable tourism** and hospitality has been achieved in such a way as not to endanger the cultural heritage.

Source: Richter, U. and Sigbjorn, T. (2012) 'The case of Inkaterra: pioneering ecotourism in Peru', in Sloan, Simon-Kaufmann and Legrand (eds), *Sustainable Hospitality and Tourism as Motors for Development*, Abingdon: Routledge.

CASE STUDY 12.3 The Periyar Tiger Reserve, Kumily, in Kerala, India

The Kumily ecotourist lodge in Kerala, India, is home to important ecosystems sustaining roughly 30 per cent of India's plant, animal and freshwater species. However, like many areas in the country, the environment faces issues such as **deforestation**, paddy field conversions and disruption of blackwater ecosystems.

The social entrepreneurial mission of the Kumily project leaders reveals the importance of linking community development with biodiversity conservation within protected areas, without harming the livelihood of local people or degrading the natural environment by means of tourism. The Periyar Tiger Reserve in Kumily is now on the brink of being a major tourism destination due to its immense natural beauty, reflected by its rich flora and fauna. The challenge faced by the leaders of this community-based sustainable tourism and hospitality venture is to protect the site from environmental **degradation** and social upheaval.

This form of **responsible tourism** is now successfully being used not only to sustain but also to regenerate the environment while providing a livelihood for local people and tribes. Originally funded by the India Ecodevelopment Organization Project, the Periyar Tiger Reserve produces not only benefits for the environment and well-being for local people but also revenue for the local economy that funds improvements to local infrastructure such as roads and schools.

One of the key benefits is the integration of **tourists** in the life of the villages by introducing them to local activities based on traditional knowledge. Tourists lodge with local people in so-called 'homestays' where the villagers open up their homes to the Westerners who both gain valuable insights into local culture and provide financial support to a traditional way of life. Locals also work as guides, rickshaw drivers and plantation farmers, who in turn provide food products to their visitors. They also have the opportunity of working in the local hotels where they make no secret about learning the trade while harbouring the hope to one day have their own accommodation operation. Fortunately local tribes have a very tightly knit community spirit and strong culture that withstands the sometimes obvious Western, consumer behaviour.

Source: Sebastian, L.M. and Rajagopalan, P. (2012) 'Tourist destinations with planned interventions: the success of Kumily in Kerala, India', in Sloan, Simon-Kaufmann and Legrand (eds), *Sustainable Hospitality and Tourism as Motors for Development*, Abingdon: Routledge.

CASE STUDY 12.4 The Ritz Carlton Community Footprints programme

Engage. Contribute. Inspire. These are the guiding principles of The Ritz-Carlton social responsibility programme, Community Footprints. This philosophy has served us well since 1983, when our first mission statement was inked and we vowed that all Ritz-Carlton hotels would be 'positive, supportive members of their communities and sensitive to the environment'.

To integrate social and environmental responsibility into our business operating model, we have developed comprehensive processes to support the creation, deployment and measurement of our community engagement strategies. To have maximum impact, our properties around the world focus their efforts in three areas:

- hunger and poverty;
- well-being of children;
- environmental conservation.

We tackle poverty by providing food, building homes, and offering education and training services to those who otherwise would not have options to secure competitive jobs and break the cycle of poverty.

We support disadvantaged children who lack access to opportunity and education, and are at risk of exploitation. We are committed to working towards a more sustainable future by protecting and preserving natural resources and integrating environmental responsibility throughout our operations.

To support these efforts, our Community Footprints programme is integrated into The Ritz-Carlton Service Values and Key Business Success Factors, and is the second strategic pathway of our company's Long-Range Plan.

On an annual basis, our hotels, resorts, residences and destination clubs complete a comprehensive Community Footprints Annual Plan, which outlines

PICTURE 12.1
Engaging staff in community activities

strategic non-profit and NGO partnerships, projected volunteer hours, cash and in-kind donations, guest voluntourism offerings, Succeed Through Service youth engagement modules and overall community impact projections. Each property's Community Footprints Annual Plan is evaluated throughout the year to ensure it is fully executed and the Plan ratings are integrated into our Brand's overall Business Priority Metrics.

Succeed Through Service programme

An example of The Ritz-Carlton Hotel Company's commitment to social responsibility can be seen through the extensive deployment of The Ritz-Carlton Succeed Through Service programme. Through this Community Footprints Youth Engagement programme, our 77 Ritz-Carlton properties around the world partner with local schools and children's organizations that serve low-income communities.

PICTURE 12.2 Succeed Through Service: a Community Footprints Youth Engagement programme

Taught by Ritz-Carlton employees, the lesson plans engage and inspire young students through career exploration, life-skills training and community projects. Succeed Through Service is designed to help youngsters focus on a future that unlocks their potential and overcome the challenges of life. Our aim is simple – to nurture inspiration.

Succeed Through Service was developed to support America's Promise Alliance's Grad Nation campaign to address the school drop-out crisis in the United States and help all young people in the USA graduate from high school ready for college, work and life. The programme is also deployed internationally at our properties in Asia Pacific, Europe and the Middle East. Around the world, sadly there is an overarching and common theme that children from low-income surroundings often do not have access to positive role models, cannot visualize a career path and do not feel connected to their communities. There is nothing worse than the scale of this lost potential. In the United States, Succeed Through Service is deployed primarily at Title 1 (low-income) middle schools (average student age 11–13) while our international properties deploy the programme with a broad array of children's organizations including SOS Children's Villages, centres for children with learning disabilities and organizations addressing the needs of homeless children and children of migrant workers. Working closely with children facing economic and social challenges, the programme is now in its third year with over 8,000 young students around the world having benefitted from the programme. Succeed Through Service has been recognised by General Colin Powell (Ret.), the Founder of America's Promise Alliance, who said at the programme's launch, 'We thank you so much because you're not only investing in kids, you are investing in the future of our country and the other countries where you are located.' As the name suggests, Succeed Through Service is all about helping young people thrive and flourish.

Succeed Through Service overview

Succeed Through Service was developed based on the learning outcomes from multiple Community Footprints pilot programmes between 2008 and 2010 in wide-ranging locations including New York, Jakarta, Phoenix, St. Thomas, Berlin, Atlanta and Singapore. The pilot programmes had successfully provided young students with access to positive mentors, introduced them to the fundamentals of life skills and engaged them in Community Footprints projects.

The Succeed Through Service concept is straightforward, with three components: career exploration; life-skills training; and community service-learning projects, all designed to help young students flourish:

- *Engaging through career exploration*: in the first phase of Succeed Through Service, the students visit their partner Ritz-Carlton hotel, tour the front and 'heart of house' areas, interact with the ladies and gentlemen in their work environment and participate in an Introduction to the Hospitality Industry presentation from the General Manager and local team. Employees from the various departments introduce the young students to the roles, responsibilities and broad-ranging career opportunities available to students if they remain in school to graduate.
- *Inspiring students through life skills training*: throughout the school year Ritz-Carlton employees deliver life-skills training modules to the students, both in the classroom setting and at the hotel. Aimed at boosting self-confidence, the comprehensive, multi-lingual lesson plans introduce the children to essential skills, including the following modules:
  - *How to Make a Successful Presentation* is designed to introduce the students to basic presentation skills, educate them on ways to overcome anxiety and practise the delivery basics of a presentation (eye contact, facial expressions, gestures, movement, appearance and voice).
  - *Safe Food Handling Skills* educates the students on how to safely handle and store raw and cooked food; the appropriate use of cutting boards or working surfaces to avoid cross-contamination; and how to properly work with cutlery and appropriate disinfecting techniques used around the kitchen and in refrigerator and cabinet spaces. The module also educates students on food storage techniques.
  - *Eat Healthy* is designed to introduce the students to healthy eating habits by educating them about grains, vegetables, fruits and proteins, discussing the importance of staying hydrated and showing them how to prepare easy-to-make nutritious dishes, as part of The Ritz-Carlton commitment to First Lady Michelle Obama's 'Let's Move' campaign.

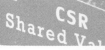

PICTURE 12.3
Hart Middle School
vegetable garden

- *Environmental Conservation* educates the students about their 'environmental footprint'. Children learn how to assess some of their daily actions and identify simple things they can do to lessen their environmental footprint, including **recycling**, **composting** and gardening.
- *The Power of Teamwork* introduces the students to why teams are essential to success and what makes a winning team. Concepts include partnerships, conflict resolution, empowerment and encouragement of others, and a winning attitude.
- *Social Skills and Dining Etiquette* provides the students with a basic understanding of the personal skills and manners needed to create a good first impression and professionally interact with others.
- *Contributing through community projects*: the community service component of Succeed Through Service teaches students civic responsibility as they work together to identify and help address a need in their community. During the first semester of the school year, students work with their teachers and our Ritz-Carlton employees to develop a Community Footprints project. During this segment of Succeed Through Service, students select a meaningful community project that focuses on hunger and homelessness, child literacy or environmental conservation. The projects take place during the Spring semester (the Semester of Service). Examples of 2011 projects include:
  - *The Ritz-Carlton Corporate Office* team joined forces with the students at their Succeed Through Service partner school, Hart Middle School, to create a vegetable garden to benefit the students and their family members at the local Title 1 Ferebee Hope Elementary School.
  - In partnership with *The Ritz-Carlton, Amelia Island*, older students at the Boys and Girls Club of Fernandina Beach helped local second-grade students improve their literacy skills by working with them one-on-one in reading and writing classes, and offering help on hard-to-understand language skills and comprehension.
  - At *The Ritz-Carlton, Guangzhou*, employees and students have worked together to create a vegetable garden with produce to be donated to a local hunger relief organization.

- In Singapore, young students at the Northlight School worked with *The Ritz-Carlton, Millenia Singapore* employees to remove invasive kudzu from a local park and provide a clean play environment for local kids and families.
- Students at Kenmore Middle School in Arlington, Virginia, partnered with *The Ritz-Carlton, Pentagon City* and created a service project to support Arlington Food Assistance Center. The 40 students each repackaged the contents of 50-pound rice sacks into 1-pound bags for donation and cut, sewed and assembled the empty rice bags into grocery tote bags for AFAC recipients.
- *Global Youth Service Day*: in April of each year, all Ritz-Carlton properties around the world host an annual Career Exploration and Service Learning Celebration Day to coincide with Global Youth Service Day. The young students participate in a wide range of Career Exploration and Job Shadowing projects, and celebrate the outcome of their service-learning project. The Global Youth Service Day Celebration event honors the young students that our Ritz-Carlton employees mentor each year, and the countless hours devoted to inspiring them to do their very best in school and for their future. This global celebration wraps together the rich tapestry of activities at our hotels and resorts around the world into one threaded global story, reinforcing The Ritz-Carlton Hotel Company's commitment to social responsibility through Succeed Through Service.

Succeed Through Service programme impact

The record of The Ritz-Carlton 'Succeed Through Service' programme can be seen through the countless comments from youngsters who have participated in workshops, listened to life skills discussions from hotel mentors and now look forward to reaching their potential with encouragement from this volunteer outreach campaign. Not only students, but teachers and principals have extolled the impact Succeed Through Service has made on their students.

Conclusion

In recognition of the achievements of Succeed Through Service, in 2011 Herve Humler, President and COO of The Ritz-Carlton Hotel Company, joined a gathering of senior private and public sector leaders invited to attend The White House Educational Roundtable hosted by President Barack Obama. Mr. Humler was proud to have the opportunity to share the 'Succeed Through Service' initiative with the group, and the impact it is making on the lives of children around the world.

The Ritz-Carlton Hotel Company is proud to help children shape and define their own future through Succeed Through Service.

Source: The Ritz-Carlton, http://www.ritzcarlton.com.

CASE STUDY 12.5 Kempinski and Stop TB Partnership

In 2010, 8.8 million people became ill with tuberculosis (TB) and 1.4 million people died from the disease. Each minute, three people die from TB. In a single day, TB causes the equivalent in lives lost of 15 jetliner crashes. People with TB often suffer from **discrimination** and stigma, rejection and social isolation. And the disease is a major cause of poverty because people with TB are often too sick to work, and they and their families may have to pay for treatment. TB is the number four cause of death among women worldwide, according to the Stop TB Partnership.

Kempinski Hotels S.A employs around 20,000 employees across more than 25 countries and hosts on average more than 3 million guests per year. The company sells hotel management know-how regulated under a long-term management contract to owners of hotels for a fee.

Vision

To be renowned as hoteliers offering the European art of luxurious hospitality, favoured by people who expect excellence and value individuality.

Mission

By gathering the most luxurious hotels, pairing them with distinctive and unique services delivered through our management know-how under the Kempinski brand, while ensuring financial performance for our owners.

Overall aim and objectives of the Stop TB programme

Mobility is a fundamental component of the hospitality industry, as we are mainly a people business, and this may introduce infectious diseases in many ways, affecting customers, employees and the local community. Health is without a

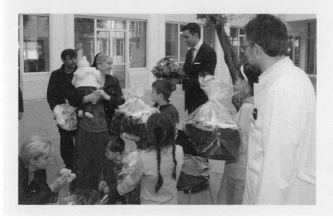

PICTURE 12.4 Activities on World TB Day at the Hotel Adlon Kempinski in Berlin, Germany

doubt a shared value between the company and the local community. For that reason, Kempinski feels responsible for its guests and employees' health and is committed to fight against tuberculosis by becoming an active partner of the Stop TB Partnership.

With the above in mind, Kempinski decided to conduct a grass-roots awareness campaign within all their hotels with the following objectives:

- change knowledge, educate on and de-stigmatize tuberculosis among staff worldwide as well as raise awareness and encourage hotel guests to donate. Staff were encouraged to become responsible for their health and seek diagnostic treatment if they were worried, with the underlying commitment of the company to support them through treatment and convalescence and re-integrate them if possible.
- reach an international market of high potential donors for the Stop TB Partnership.

The target population was defined as:

- 20,000 employees worldwide (Europe, Africa, the Middle East and Asia);
- hotel customers worldwide (around 3 million per year).

The programme's activities

In order to raise awareness and educate employees and reach customers, Kempinski started its communication campaign to promote the Luis Figo Stop TB Campaign in 2008 and 2009 in all Kempinski's hotels by the following means:

- distributing the Luis Figo postcards during the turndown service in each guest room on each guest's pillow; the postcard included facts and information

PICTURE 12.5 World TB Day at the Emirates Palace Hotel, Abu Dhabi, UAE

about tuberculosis, how tuberculosis can be cured and how the Stop TB campaign aims to eliminate TB, plus information on how to make a donation;

- educating all employees at the hotel, regional and corporate levels on what TB is through an in-house training programme delivered to all staff worldwide; how prevalent it is in their country; what the early signs of TB are; and what to do if they are worried they are infected (the tools included were specifically designed for the training module by Kempinski, and the Stop TB Partnership's PSA, such as the Luis Figo movie and posters, the poster campaign, TB quiz days for staff, their families and in some cases for local business community as well);
- internal information campaigns included printed magazines and e-newsletters;
- external information campaigns included a press release about Luis Figo's involvement distributed in the UK, a feature article with Luis Figo in Kempinski's guest magazine distributed to all guest rooms worldwide;
- active participation of hotels worldwide during World TB Day 2009, 2010, 2011 (2012 is planned) with various activities (sports activities, staff picnics, drawing competitions, TB training and quiz, etc.);
- Management Board members' personal support for the entire programme resulted in TB being put on the agenda for the first time in many hotels.

PICTURE 12.6 World TB Day in Ajman, UAE

PICTURE 12.7 World TB Day at the Hotel Adlon Kempinski in Berlin, Germany

External partnerships which contributed to the success of the programme

1. The Stop TB Partnership (WHO) provided with the related Luis Figo PSA (currently Craig David PSA).
2. Eli Lilly financed the production and delivery of the Luis Figo postcards in 2008 and 2009.

Funding of the programme

The costs of Kempinski's activities and time to support the Luis Figo campaign were calculated in terms of availability of human resources and donated time, both on a corporate and hotel level. Travel expenses were absorbed by corporate and regional offices.

Measurement and evaluation of the programme's performance

1. No specific tool able to measure how many customers may have donated how much money to the Stop TB Partnership was put in place; therefore, there are no accurate figures regarding the total amount of donations via Kempinski customers.
2. No start–end surveys were put in place to measure staff's change in knowledge about TB, therefore, measuring the campaign's impact was limited. Nevertheless, feedback from both staff and customers was positive. Hotels in countries where TB prevalence is high continue actively to support Stop TB Partnership's new communication campaign with Craig David.
3. Incidental evidence, however, shows the magnitude of 'newly' reached 'high potential' people, who stay in our hotels and who have not previously been touched by TB messaging. Craig David, the new goodwill ambassador of the Stop TB partnership, learned about TB through this Figo campaign when he picked up a Luis Figo postcard available in one of the Kempinski hotels. He has now already dedicated much of his time and shared his name and brand to raise awareness for Stop TB as a global ambassador. He is just one of the new 'high potentials' whom we believe have been reached through our campaign (and in line with our objective mentioned under question no 1, to 'Reach an international market of high potential donors for the Stop TB Partnership').

The difference the programme is making

- A five-star hotel is not the usual environment to promote an awareness campaign about TB, moreover, customers may have been surprised to find a TB postcard on their pillow.
- More than 13,044 guest rooms have acted as an open door to TB awareness and donation during the last three years.
- Raising awareness among 20,000 staff members directly, and indirectly, and their families, especially in countries where family members do not always have access to health care prevention services.
- The message dissemination filled an information gap about TB among young staff, particularly in the European countries where tuberculosis is commonly considered to have been eradicated. Young staff, therefore, were not only

surprised and keen to learn more about tuberculosis, but were also made aware about the TB/HIV co-infection.

Key lessons learned so far and unforeseen challenges

- Key lessons:
  - Partnerships between public health sector and the private sector can be very effective.
  - Each workplace can easily be provided with educational tools to disseminate information to staff.
  - On a global company level, the communication campaign induced debates among staff, and showed that staff are interested to learn more about TB, particularly in countries where tuberculosis is a public health issue. As the majority of our staff are younger than 30 years old, many young European staff were not familiar with the term tuberculosis and discovered its significance (also in relation with HIV) for the first time.
- Unforeseen challenges: the detection of one TB case among our staff in the Middle East; as an African citizen and according to local immigration laws, our staff member had to leave the hotel's country within 7 days of being well enough to travel. Kempinski took care of the employee's cure and convalescence in his home country, although this employee could not return to his position at the original hotel due once again to local immigration laws. He now works for Kempinski in Bahrain.

Innovative contribution to global health and development

1. Using the workplace as a platform to disseminate information about TB is easy to replicate and ultimately reaches out to family and local community, multiplying the campaign's impact.
2. The campaign showed that working in partnership with different stakeholders (Kempinski in partnership with Stop TB and others), each partner could bring in their specific competency and strengths to make the project reach further. Although our work was build on an existing campaign (Luis Figo), it was complementary and brought tremendous leverage. It opened up a new advocacy channel (luxury hotel guests), who were in many cases unaware of the burden of TB.
3. One awareness campaign reaches different audiences at the same time: (a) employer made aware of the burden of TB and the necessity to provide support and care to employees directly or indirectly facing TB and does not shrink from promoting donations for TB in luxury hotels; (b) after training, staff are able to show equal understanding and respect to and support colleagues/local community members directly or indirectly facing TB; (c) hotel customers may have become aware of TB and better understand what still has to be done to rid the world of TB.

Direct effect of Kempinski's support for the Stop TB Campaign:

Creation of BE Health Association

Even if Kempinski's employees in developing countries are provided with basic health coverage through their job, their family members and children often are not, as their communities do not always have access to health care services. The communication campaign demonstrated that the workplace is an ideal spring-board for reaching not only our employees, but also their households and local communities, through preventing, detecting and treating infectious diseases.

This is why Kempinski has co-founded a juridical independent, self-funding, non-profit organization, based in Switzerland, called BE. (Why BE? Without good health, we cannot 'be'. Good health gives people strength. It allows them to grow and to achieve their goals in life. It allows them to be.)

BE's mission is to prevent and to protect employees, their households and local communities from infectious diseases (tuberculosis, malaria and HIV/AIDS) by implementing prevention activities in the workplace and in the local community while facilitating health care support and services.

BE furthermore aspires to mobilize the corporate sector by inviting medium-sized companies to become members. BE will assist them in implementing prevention activities in their workplace and in the local community and facilitate health care support and services for their employees and members of local community.

BE's main objectives are to do the following:

- Create a network of peer educators by training and mobilizing employees to spread health and well-being in their local community and at their workplace.
- Facilitate detection and treatment of infectious diseases among employees, their household and the local community.
- Coordinate, facilitate and manage projects which support the prevention, detection and treatment of infectious diseases.
- BE's volunteers will also learn important skills to help them in their new role such as self-management and interpersonal skills.

Kempinski shares BE's values and sustainable approach. It brings management expertise, communication skills, gives BE access to fundraising and its hotels are an excellent platform from which to educate and reach large numbers of people. Most importantly, it brings a firm commitment across the group to tackling devastating infectious diseases such as HIV/AIDS, tuberculosis and malaria.

All Kempinski guests will have the opportunity to support BE by donating one euro (or local equivalent) per night.

Sources: Stop TB Partnership, http://www.stoptb.org/ and Kempinski, http://www.kempinski.com.

EXERCISES

1   **GROUP DISCUSSION, GROUP PROJECT OR WRITTEN ASSIGNMENT**

Hospitality stakeholders

- Map out who the key internal and external stakeholders are for a hotel or restaurant and identify the potential impacts on the business and wider communities.

2   **GROUP DISCUSSION OR GROUP PROJECT**

Non-governmental organizations and hospitality

- Find out what is the NGO's verdict on what is missing from the hospitality sustainability strategy. How much should a hotel engage with NGOs? What does an engagement deliver for the hotel company and for the NGO?

3   **GROUP PROJECT**

Embracing CSR in the hospitality industry

- Identify, categorize and describe the key responsibilities a hotel or restaurant takes when embracing corporate social responsibility.

4   **GROUP DISCUSSION**

Engaging green travellers as key stakeholders in the future of our industry

- Discuss how hospitality businesses can better collaborate with other consumer service and product providers to promote sustainability and engage with the sustainable travellers.

5   **GROUP DISCUSSION**

Multi-stakeholder approaches to sustainable hospitality

- Identify examples of public and private sector collaboration and multi-stakeholder approaches to sustainability challenges and opportunities in hospitality. Discuss whether those initiatives were successful (or not) from the sustainability viewpoint.

References

Boulding, K. E. (1966) 'The economics of the coming Spaceship Earth', in H. Jarrett (ed.) *Environmental Quality in a Growing Economy*, Baltimore, MD: Johns Hopkins University Press, 3–14. Available at: http://www.eoearth.org/article/The_Economics_of_the_Coming_Spaceship_Earth_%28historical%29.

Porter, M. and Kramer, M.R. (2011) 'Creating shared value', *Harvard Business Review*, 89(1/2): 62–77.

Richter, U. and Sigbjorn, T. (2012) 'The case of Inkaterra: pioneering ecotourism in Peru', in P. Sloan, C. Simons-Kaufmann and W. Legrand (eds), *Sustainable Hospitality and Tourism as Motors for Development: Case Studies from Developing Regions of the World*, Abingdon: Routledge, pp. 24–36.

Riedmiller, S. (2012) 'Can ecotourism support coral reef conservation? Experiences of Chumbe Island Coral Park Ltd in Zanzibar/Tanzania', in P. Sloan, C. Simons-Kaufmann and W. Legrand (eds), *Sustainable Hospitality and Tourism as Motors for Development: Case Studies from Developing Regions of the World*, Abingdon: Routledge, pp. 176–97.

Sebastian, L.M. and Rajagopalan, P. (2012) 'Tourist destinations with planned interventions: the success of Kumily in Kerala, India', in P. Sloan, C. Simons-Kaufmann and W. Legrand (eds), *Sustainable Hospitality and Tourism as Motors for Development: Case Studies from Developing Regions of the World*, Abingdon: Routledge, pp. 402–21.

World Commission on Environment and Development (WCED) (1987) *Our Common Future*. Available at: http://www.un-documents.net/wced-ocf.htm.

Resources

Chomsky, N. (1999) *Profit Over People: Neoliberalism and Global Order*, Westminster, MD: Seven Stories Press.

Green Hotelier (2005) 'Tourism today: how the agenda has evolved', *Green Hotelier*, 36: 6–15.

Green Hotelier (2006a) 'Sustainable supply chains', *Green Hotelier*, 38: 1–4.

Green Hotelier (2006b) 'The power of partnerships', *Green Hotelier*, 41: 12–19.

Green Hotelier (2006c) 'Environmental awareness and training', *Green Hotelier*, 41: 1–4.

Green Hotelier (2007a) 'What does it mean to be a sustainable hotel?', *Green Hotelier*, 44: 24–6.

Green Hotelier (2007b) 'Greening the urban jungle', *Green Hotelier*, 43: 12–18.

Harris, R., Griffin, T. and Williams, P. (2002) *Sustainable Tourism: A Global Perspective*, Oxford: Butterworth-Heinemann.

Sloan, P., Simons-Kaufmann, C. and Legrand, W. (eds) (2012) *Sustainable Hospitality and Tourism as Motors for Development: Case Studies from Developing Regions of the World*, Abingdon: Routledge.

United Nations (2008) *The Millennium Development Goals Report*, New York: United Nations. Available at: http://www.un.org/millenniumgoals/pdf/The%20Millennium%20Development%20Goals%20Report%202008.pdf.

Additional material

Go to www.routledge.com/cw/sloan to find PowerPoint slides of all the figures and tables from the book, additional case studies, a test bank of questions and extra links to useful videos.

Hospitality industry environmental management systems

CHAPTER OBJECTIVES

The objectives for this chapter are:

- To define environmental management systems (EMS)
- To review ISO and EMAS
- To understand the EMS methodology
- To identify the key benefits in establishing an EMS
- To discuss the implementation of EMS in hospitality
- To draw up a set of recommendations for the successful implementation of an EMS

Environmental management systems (EMS)

A corporate **environmental management system (EMS)** embraces both technical and organizational activities aimed at reducing the environmental negative **impacts** caused by a company's operations. EMS is a management tool that allows a company to be organized in a way so as to control and reduce its **environmental impacts**. An EMS is also an engagement towards continuous environmental improvement. The five principal objectives of the EMS are:

1. To identify and control the environmental impact of activities, products or services.
2. To respect regulations and go beyond the initial objectives set out in the company's environmental policy.
3. To implement a systematic approach to setting environmental objectives and targets.
4. To continuously improve environmental performance.

5. To ensure transparent communication towards employees, communities and consumers.

Examples of EMS

The International Organization for Standardization (ISO) as well as the **European Union Eco-Management and Audit Scheme (EMAS)** are two established management tools for hotel companies to evaluate, report and improve their environmental performance.

ISO 14000

ISO functions are classified into family and number system. For example, ISO 9000 is a family of standards which is related to quality management systems in companies and the ISO 14000 family addresses various aspects of environmental management. The first two standards within that family, ISO 14001 and ISO 14004 are particularly concerned with environmental management systems (EMS). The International Organization for Standardization published the first edition of ISO 14001 in 1996. ISO 14001 provides a framework for a strategic approach to the organization's environmental policy, plans and actions rather than setting the level of environmental performance of an individual business. ISO 14004 focuses on the general EMS guidelines. ISO 14001 is considered the foundation document of the entire series within the 14000 family. A second edition of ISO 14001 was published in 2004, hence the current full name ISO 14001:2004. Within the 14000 family, other standards are available, each with a particular focus from labelling to communication, from performance evaluation to auditing as shown in Table 13.1.

With the increased public attention to matters surrounding climate change, ISO has developed another set of standards under the 14000 family for **greenhouse gas** (GHG) accounting, verification and emissions trading, and for measuring the **carbon footprint** of products as shown in Table 13.2.

The Plan-Do-Check-Act Cycle

The ISO 14000 family follows the **Plan-Do-Check-Act Cycle (PDCA)** as shown in Table 13.3. The PDCA reached a broad audience in many industry circles through the work of the twentieth-century American statistician, William Edwards Deming, who is regarded as having had a great impact on modern quality control in manufacturing and business in general. The PDCA cycle is also referred to as the Deming Cycle.

1. *PLAN*: the cycle starts with planning (**P**DCA) whereby objectives are established and processes designed in line with the expected output or goals.
2. *DO*: doing (P**D**CA) is about implementing the plan and executing the processes. This stage also includes collecting data which will be analysed in the following sequence.

TABLE 13.1 The ISO 14000 family of International Standards

ISO 14000 Family	General focus	Standard details
ISO 14001:2004	EMS implementation	EMS – Requirements with guidance for use
ISO 14004:2004	EMS implementation	EMS – General guidelines on principles, systems and support techniques
ISO/DIS 14005	EMS implementation	EMS – Guidelines for the phased implementation of an environmental management system, including the use of environmental performance evaluation
ISO 14050:2009	EMS implementation	Environmental management – Vocabulary
ISO 14040:2006	Conduct LCA/Manage environmental aspects	Environmental management – Life cycle assessment (LCA) – Principles and framework
ISO 14044:2006	Conduct LCA/Manage environmental aspects	Environmental management – Life cycle assessment – Requirements and guidelines
ISO/TR[1] 14047:2003	Conduct LCA/Manage environmental aspects	Environmental management – Life cycle impact assessment – Examples of application of ISO 14042
ISO/TS[2] 14048:2002	Conduct LCA/Manage environmental aspects	Environmental management – Life cycle assessment – Data documentation format
ISO 14015:2001	Conduct audits/ Evaluate performance	Environmental management – Environmental assessment of sites and organizations
ISO 14015:2001	Conduct audits/ Evaluate performance	Environmental management – Environmental performance evaluation – Guidelines
ISO 19011:2002	Conduct audits/ Evaluate performance	Guidelines for quality and/or environmental management systems auditing
ISO 14020:2000	Communication/ Declaration	Environmental labels and declarations – General principles
ISO 14021:1999	Communication/ Declaration	Environmental labels and declarations – Self-declared environmental claims – Type II environmental labelling
ISO 14024:1999	Communication/ Declaration	Environmental labels and declarations – Type I environmental labelling – Principles and procedures
ISO 14025:2006	Communication/ Declaration	Environmental labels and declarations – Type III environmental declarations – Principles and procedures
ISO/AWI[3] 14033	Communication/ Declaration	Environmental management – Quantitative environmental information – Guidelines and examples
ISO 14063:2006	Communication/ Declaration	Environmental management – Environmental communication – Guidelines and examples

Source: Adapted from Environmental Management: The ISO 14000 family of International Standards, http://www.iso.org/iso/theiso14000family_2009.pdf.

Notes: 1 Technical report. 2 Technical specification. 3 Approved work item.

TABLE 13.2 The ISO 14000 family of International Standards for GHG and carbon footprint

ISO 14000 Family	General focus	Standard details
ISO 14064-3:2006	Evaluate GHG performance	Greenhouse gases – Part 3: Specification with guidance for the validation and verification of greenhouse gas assertions
ISO 14065:2007	Evaluate GHG performance	Greenhouse gases – Requirements for greenhouse gas validation and verification bodies for use in accreditation or other forms of recognition
ISO/CD[1] 14066	Evaluate GHG performance	Greenhouse gases – Competency requirements for greenhouse gas validators and verifiers document
ISO 14064-1:2006	Manage GHG	Greenhouse gases – Part 1: Specification with guidance at the organization level for quantification and reporting of greenhouse gas emissions and removals
ISO 14064-2:2006	Manage GHG	Greenhouse gases – Part 2: Specification with guidance at the project level for quantification, monitoring and reporting of greenhouse gas emission reductions or removal enhancements
ISO/WD[2] 14067-1	Manage GHG	Greenhouse gases Part 2: Specification with guidance at the project level for quantification, monitoring and reporting of greenhouse gas emission reductions or removal enhancements
ISO/WD[2] 14067-2	Manage GHG	Greenhouse gases Part 2: Specification with guidance at the project level for quantification, monitoring and reporting of greenhouse gas emission reductions or removal enhancements

Source: Adapted from Environmental Management: The ISO 14000 family of International Standards, http://www.iso.org/iso/theiso14000family_2009.pdf.

Notes: 1 Committee draft. 2 Working draft.

3. *CHECK*: checking (PD**C**A) includes the conduction of analysis based on data collected or measured in the previous stage. Checking is also about comparing the actual results to the expected output as planned in the very first PDCA stage and check for variances.
4. *ACT*: the cycle concludes with acting (PDC**A**) on the significant differences between actual and planned results. Acting also means the identification of the root causes to differences and the establishment of corrective actions.

TABLE 13.3 Comparing the PDCA cycle to the ISO 14001 Standard

PDCA cycle	ISO 14001 Standard
	4.2. Environmental Policy
PLAN	4.3. Planning
	4.3.1. Environmental Aspects
	4.3.2. Legal and Other Requirements
	4.3.3. Objectives, Targets and Programme(s)
DO	4.4. Implementation and Operation
	4.4.1. Resources, Roles, Responsibility and Authority
	4.4.2. Competence, Training and Awareness
	4.4.3. Communication
	4.4.4. Documentation
	4.4.5. Control of Documents
	4.4.6. Operational Control
	4.4.7. Emergency Preparedness and Response
CHECK	4.5. Checking
	4.5.1. Monitoring and Measurement
	4.5.2. Evaluation of Compliance
	4.5.3. Nonconformity, Corrective Action and Preventive Action
	4.5.4. Control of Records
	4.5.5. Internal Audit
ACT	Management Review

Source: Adapted from Generic ISO 14001 EMS Templates User Manual.

Since the PDCA is based on a system of continuous improvement and on a cycle, once the four stages have been completed and improvement applied, the cycle repeats itself to improve other processes, products or services.

EMAS

EMAS comes under European Regulation but, similar to the ISO family of international standards, is globally applicable. Equally similar to ISO, EMAS is based on the voluntary participation of companies and organizations with a similar focus on continuous improvements.

The ISO 14001 EMS requirements are an integral part of EMAS. Consequently, a company deciding to register with EMAS may be additionally issued with an ISO 14001 certificate from the environmental verifier. While some differences do exist

13

Initial environmental review
EMAS requires an initial environmental review to identify an organization's significant impacts

↓

Environmental policy
The environmental policy has to include a provision for legal compliance and a commitment to continual improvement of the environmental performance

↓

Planning
Proof of legal compliance and all items identified in the environmental review have to be addressed at this step

↓

Implementation
EMAS requires active employee involvement to improve environmental performance. Suppliers and other contractors should comply with the organization's environmental policy. Open communication with external stakeholders is required

↓

Management review
Relevant information will need to made available to top management

↓

Registration
Registration must be with national competent body in publicly accessible register

↓

Environmental statement
EMAS requires an environmental statement, which must be externally validated on an annual basis and accessible to the public

FIGURE 13.1 Main stages in EMAS
Source: Adapted from EMAS-Factsheet, http://ec.europa.eu/environment/emas/pdf/factsheet/EMASiso14001_high.pdf.

between EMAS and ISO 14001, principally in the initial environmental review process and the issuing of the environmental statement as shown in Figure 13.1, both include a full audit of a company or an organization on a three-yearly basis.

EMS: a methodology

The methodology followed by both EMAS and ISO is very similar. An EMS generally consists of the three generic stages: the preparation, the implementation and the follow-up. In more detail, the three generic stages encompass the following eight phases. Splitting the EMS development into smaller phases allows an organization to take an incremental approach to the introduction of an EMS into its mainstream management processes.

Phase I: initial review

- The purpose of the initial review is to find out about existing EMS and about the organizational commitment. Questions should be asked such as: do we have an environmental policy? Do we have documented procedures and responsibilities with regards to environmental matters? Are activities mitigating environmental impacts in place?
- The initial review is also there to investigate the trends that affect the business **environment**. This may include matters related to: (1) legal aspects including developments in environmental legislation; (2) competitive aspects including keeping up or surpassing the latest industry **best practices**; (3) fiscal trends such as the increasing financial implications of energy prices and waste disposal costs; and (4) marketing implications, including managing the public concern with the environment.
- The initial review helps to explain the main options available for EMS **certification** and consider the benefits and costs attached to each EMS option.
- Finally, the initial review is about securing appropriate commitment at the senior management level for EMS development.

Phase II: information and commitment

- Phase II aims at the definition of the EMS project. In this phase employees and managers are informed and sensitized to the tasks ahead and the approaches and expectations are described. This is also the phase where goals are set and a project team is formed.

Phase III: planning and organization

- In Phase III, processes relevant to the appropriate environmental aspects are analysed with the help of available documents. An input-output framework is designed and detailed planning settled. This all serves the preparation of the status quo analysis. Identifying and ensuring compliance with legal and other requirements (as researched in Phase 1) is critical for this stage.

Phase IV: data assessment

- This phase is also referred to as the *mini-audit stage*, since the goal is to examine and analyse, with the help of data gathered in Phase III, the status quo within the company. Phase IV includes the inspection of documents and evaluation of checklists as well as qualitative interviews. This provides the company with a full diagnosis of its operations in relation to environmental matters.

Phase V: analysis and training

- Based on the findings in Phase IV, weaknesses are investigated and an input–output analysis developed. Along with a cost-benefit analysis, possible savings and potentials for optimization are revealed. This phase also includes the development of an environmental programme, training sessions for employees and auditors and the development of an audit report. The overall aim of this phase is the verification of data, the completion of a strength and weaknesses analysis and the development of an action plan.

Phase VI: management system and documentation

- Phase VI is concerned with the documentation surrounding the EMS to ensure a continuous improvement of the organizational mitigation of environmental impacts. This phase also sets the premise for the company's environmental declaration and establishment of a controlling system.

Phase VII: management review

- Phase VII focuses on measuring the extent to which the action plan developed in the previous stages has been implemented and possibly aims at the certification/registration of the organization.

Phase VIII: certification/registration

- A company may decide to have an external body confirm that their EMS meets the requirements of standards such as ISO 14001 or EMAS. This process is known as certification or registration. The certification is carried out by an environmental certification body (this is also known as independent or third-party certification) and involves a visit to the organization, examining documents/records and interviewing personnel. The goal is to ensure that the EMS installed by the organization: (1) conforms to specified requirements; (2) is capable of achieving its objectives; and (3) is effectively implemented with a system of continuous improvement in place.

EMS: the benefits

The benefits for businesses implementing EMS are many, including:

- Image profiling.
- In light of public scrutiny, showing engagement as a responsible business is good for a company's image which can be used to differentiate itself from the competition.
- Tool for dialogue.

- An EMS reinforces partner confidence and solidifies relationships with **stakeholders** (consumers, investors, communities, associations and organizations for environmental protections and public authorities) by ensuring transparency and willingness for two-way communication.
- Prevention.
- While preventing waste of non-renewable resources, a company can ensure a **return on investment** on the design and implementation of an EMS and on the long-term day-to-day operations.
- Internal motivation.
- Employees join in a project which has **direct impact** on their professional lives particularly from the health and safety angle but also in promoting a 'feel-good' factor among the employees.
- Anticipating environmental and **sustainable development** trends.
- In light of a global and intensive competitive hospitality market, the rise in awareness of the concept of sustainable development allows the companies that have anticipated the environmental protection development to profit from a first mover advantage.

EMS: must it be EMAS or ISO 14001?

Any management action or set of actions that benefit the environment can be called an EMS. However, as it is unlikely that hotel executives have either sufficient knowledge or the luxury of unlimited time and other resources to install a set of measures that comprehensively address all the environmental impacts of their establishment, so most companies turn to a recognised environmental standards organization. The standards most commonly used are the globally valid ISO 14000 series of environmental standards and the EU EMAS directive.

The use of either of those two recognised standards can help a hotel company to meet internal as well as external objectives such as:

- *Internal objectives*
  - ensuring that management it is in control of the organizational processes and activities that have an impact on the environment;
  - assuring employees that they are working for an environmentally responsible organization.

- *External objectives*
  - providing assurance to external stakeholders (such as customers, local communities or governmental bodies);
  - complying with environmental regulations;
  - supporting the company's claims and communication about its own environmental policies, plans and actions;
  - providing a framework for certification by a third party organization.

Implementing an EMS in the hospitality industry

The differences in the environmental management strategies between the largest companies in the hotel industry with respect to the environment, are striking. Individual hotel properties or hotel chains that are performing well in the domain of environmental management used to have a real *competitive advantage* both in terms of monetary savings, from reduction in energy, water and waste costs, and market attractiveness. The competitive advantage is slowly eroding since the majority of national and international hotel players have adopted some environmental mitigation activities. Hotels having yet to embark on any environmental management system have been moved into a *competitive disadvantage* category.

Implementing an EMS requires a systematic approach to achieve the environmental goals in a company. The principal idea of environmental management is that a company's environmental impacts are managed in the same way that production of food in the restaurant, quality of the overnight stays and check-ins and check-outs are managed: with clear goals, set processes and measurable outputs. The working procedure for implementation of an EMS in nine stages is shown in Figure 13.2.

It is important to realize that despite the size of the hotel property, the success of any EMS will depend on the involvement, commitment and motivation of hotel employees and the support of management. Therefore, as a summary towards a successful implementation of an EMS, the following four aspects need to be considered:

Involve staff in 'greening' activities

Starting at the top, having dedicated managers and Chief Executive Officers (CEOs) who understand that ecology and economy no longer require a trade-off will boost a company's green endeavours. CEOs will be confronted with an increasing demand for **sustainability** from many stakeholders and they will be expected to have the answers to those issues at hand. The staff at all levels need to be encouraged to take on leadership roles in the sustainability process. Strategic decisions must be supported by the entire organization. Convincing employees to apply 'greener' processes, which save resources and help the environment, should be at the top of the hotel executives' agenda. Raising the awareness of the staff is the first step. The term 'greening' does not always and automatically involve technology or capital investment. Small steps lead to greater efficiency, resource efficiency and financial savings. Being 'green' is a mind-set, and positive outcomes will happen when mind-sets evolve. So much attention is focused on the plight of our planet by the media that a momentum for change is developing in society; hotel executives are advised to follow this movement. Once inspiring leadership has captured enthusiasm, environmental training procedures need to be installed. Only regular ongoing training sessions ensure that 'greener' processes become a matter of course. A 'green team'

Stage 1: Involve staff and assemble team
Members representing the executive committee (Finance, Sales and Marketing, Accounting, General Manager) as well as members representing the operations (Housekeeping, Food and Beverage, Front Office, Purchasing, Engineering) should be represented on the EMS team. It is also essential to organise the responsibilities (analysis, implementation, control) amongst the team.

Stage 2: Analyse status quo
This is initial review gathering information on the current status. Information should encompass the following three areas: (1) status on legal compliance, (2) evaluation of environmental impacts, (3) review of current environmental management practices.

Stage 3: Design an environmental policy
This is an essential document which should be communicated to all team members at the property and be publicly available. The core of an environmental policy should contain a statement on the commitment to (1) complying with legislation, (2) preventing pollution and (3) improving environmental performance of all operations within the hotel.

Stage 4: Evaluate environmental impacts
Both the direct and indirect impacts must be evaluated and assessed. These include (1) carbon emissions, (2) solid and other waste, (3) water usage, (4) energy usage, (5) use of land surrounding the hotel, (6) noise, odour, dust and visual impact, (7) other indirect impacts (for example guest and staff commuting) and (8) positive impacts.

Stage 5: Set environmental objectives and targets
Once all data at the hotel has been recorded, targets should be set to mitigate the impacts. The targets should follow the SMARTER guideline which stands for Specific and Significant, Measurable and Motivational, Attainable and Agreed, Relevant and Realistic, Traceable and Tangible, Engaging and Enjoyable and finally Rewarded and Recordable.

Stage 6: Maintain documentation
Documenting the progress based on the targets is important, but it is equally important to have an up-to-date listing of the key roles and responsibilities. Documentation should also comprise the environmental policy and any other documents pertinent to the establishment of the EMS.

Stage 7: Implement training
Training on the purpose of the EMS as well as the changes in the operational duties is essential to ensure improvement and successful implementation of the EMS. Training is not limited to operational staff but to middle and senior management teams. Information should be provided to suppliers and customers.

Stage 8: Continue recording and establish auditing
It is important to continuously record the actual performance. Once data is gathered, comparison to the targets can be accomplished. The audit will then determine whether the environmental management activities are in line with the programme and whether the system is effective in relation to the policy.

Stage 9: Conduct review and apply for registration/certification
The management team and the EMS team should review the results from the audits and decide whether to continue with the current set of targets or whether any changes need to be instilled in certain areas. The management team may decide to apply for an assessment by a third-party certification agency recognizing the effort undertaken to manage the environmental impacts.

FIGURE 13.2 EMS implementation stages

or a manager responsible for sustainability issues should look at operational areas that can be improved. Departmental heads should be made responsible for the implementation of improved processes and staff feedback should be encouraged. An assessment of environmental attitudes could become part of the recruitment process in human resource departments. Employees who are sensitive towards environmental issues are more willing to apply new environmental standards. Industry analysts point out that employees are often more satisfied working for an employer that has concern for the environment. Staff environmental initiatives improve company morale, decrease staff turnover and consequently enhance guest satisfaction. Employees who are eager to act on environmental issues increase the likelihood of greater efficiency and greater financial returns.

Consider types of technologies and initiatives

Before actually thinking about the promotion of their efforts in sustainability, hotel companies must make sure that the green technologies and initiatives they wish to install keep their promise. The alternative is to be accused of **greenwashing**, thus damaging their valuable brand image. Many new technologies require high capital investments and their true cost/benefits are sometimes not sufficiently researched.

Know your customers

Hospitality operations are not always well equipped to attract environmentally sensitive consumers. Hotel companies would be well advised to gain feedback from guests on their behaviour concerning environmental initiatives. At the very least, such enquiries sensitize customers to responsible marketing activities and 'green' branding. Although hotel sustainability might never become a unique selling proposition, it adds extra value in some sectors. A similar approach influences the guests' choice of holiday decisions. **Tourists** are more sophisticated than ever before, **sustainable** holiday destinations are in vogue. However, society is not ready for a bulldozer approach to sustainability, as environmental concern is the right of the individual. While fulfilling the expectations of guests is paramount in the job of all hospitality professionals, comfort and satisfaction can never be sacrificed. Fortunately, environmental concern is no longer a marginal activity, and care must be taken to ensure that guests become partners in environmental policy-making. The role of hoteliers as educators should not be underestimated, and once hotels are clear about their customers' views, the management can then start to satisfy their curiosity as to what the establishment is doing in this domain.

Establish centralized actions

With the extensive organizational resources hotel chains have at their disposal, they have the power to bring about change on a large scale. Strong franchise systems

and tight control systems ensure success. If individual units in hotel chains act independently on environmental issues, without special focus, short-term financial returns might be achieved but chain branding opportunities will be lost. Actions must be centralized and consistent from unit to unit in order to create internal and external awareness.

Moreover, a centralized approach reduces bureaucracy and repetition. Finally, centralization of actions facilitates strategic adjustments once the programme is running.

CASE STUDY 13.1 Ibis and ISO 14001

Ibis is Accor's leading economy hotel brand. Since inaugurating its first hotel in 1974, Ibis has developed to be a market leader in Europe and a large player globally in the economy hotel segment with more than 900 hotels and 107,000 rooms in 51 countries as of the start of 2012.

Ibis made the conscious choice of implementing a recognised EMS and became the world's first hotel chain to have secured the ISO 14001 in 2004. One-third of all Ibis hotels have been certified ISO 14001 to date (2012).

Why implement an EMS?

According to Accor, the global **hospitality industry** is increasingly aware of its environmental impact and is taking more and more action to reduce it. This is for two reasons.

1. Changes in customers' attitudes require initiatives that show respect for the planet. The chains that really pay attention to global consumer trends have recognised the emergence of a new kind of consumer. Aided by the now ubiquitous Internet, this pro-active (and even activist) consumer still looks for the best value in terms of price, quality and service but does so as a 'responsible consumer'. The ethics of the brand he or she buys, especially the respect for the environment, is no longer just a matter of image but an actual selling point. This responsible consumer is very real.
2. The hotel industry's business model must take into consideration customers' new expectations without making them pay the price. The growing influence of environmentalism still comes with a limit to the premium customers are willing to pay. Environmental programmes in the hotel industry should also generate competitive advantages – by lowering operating costs, improving guest and employee satisfaction and helping to advance the brand's reputation as an environmentally responsible company.

The challenge for the hotel industry is therefore to implement, in the course of its expansion, genuine environmental programmes that can produce precisely measurable ecological improvements.

Moving forward and accelerating the deployment of its environmental strategy, Ibis decided to begin a long process to get its hotels certified. By 2004, the chain had earned the ISO 14001 certification from Bureau Veritas Certification for 19 hotels in France. The effectiveness of the standardized Ibis model enabled the brand to further accelerate this programme and by January 2010, 2864 hotels in 17 countries are ISO 14001 compliant, or 33 per cent of the Ibis network.

Getting and working with ISO 14001

ISO 14001 is something you earn through a long-term process, and requires considerable effort. It is awarded by Bureau Veritas Certification, the world's leading certification firm, after **auditing** each hotel's environmental commitment and following updates made to environmental regulations in each country.

The ISO 14001-certified Ibis hotels adopt action plans to reduce their environmental impact, and monitor and analyse their performance continually. They also prove to the relevant authorities that they are in compliance with the European, national and local environmental regulations related to hotel and restaurant operations.

The ISO 14001 certification is therefore not an end but a means for Ibis hotels to make progress each day on their environmental performance. Ibis's four pillars of commitment are:

- Reduce usage of water.
- Reduce energy consumption and promote **renewable energy**.
- Perform selective sorting of waste.
- Educate and inform employees and suppliers about the environment and the need for day-to-day concrete actions, and raise the environmental awareness level of guests during their stays.

It is the goal that every Ibis hotel, by observing ISO 14001, involves itself in a long-term process of eco-citizenship. For the guests, this is a welcome development that gives them an assurance that the money they are spending is supporting a responsible company.

Source: Ibis Hotel, http://www.ibishotel.com.

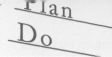

EXERCISES

1   **GROUP PROJECT**

Develop and implement EMS in a hospitality business

- Ask hotels and restaurants in the region if they would be interested in having a group of students develop an EMS for their business. This will provide a hands-on practical project for several groups of students (5–6 students per group), and help local businesses improve environmental performance.

The first group of students would visit the property, interview the owner and employees, and then do the following:

- prepare and conduct a preliminary environmental review (including level of compliance, fines);
- review charges, costs of resource use and waste disposal;
- analyse the findings of the review;
- develop an environment policy;
- establish environmental objectives and targets;
- develop a baseline environmental management programme.

A group of students from the next semester could:

- help the business further develop the environmental management programme;
- implement the programme;
- set up regular performance-monitoring practices;
- analyse environmental progress.

A group of students from the next semester could then:

- carry out an environmental audit;
- assess the findings of the audit;
- make recommendations on further improvements, revise targets and objectives for continual improvement, and investigate how to maintain environmental enthusiasm within the business.

2   **GROUP PROJECT**

Develop an EMS training programme

- Develop an EMS training programme for a small hotel or restaurant in the region. The exercise should involve site visits, a short preliminary environmental review and interviews with management and staff.
- Make a presentation describing the programme. Managers of the business could be present during the presentation.

3 GROUP DISCUSSION OR GROUP PROJECT

- Consider the environmental management concepts and tools, cleaner production, eco-efficiency, industrial ecology and life cycle analysis.
- Devise examples of the application of each of these concepts in the hospitality businesses.
- Make a presentation of your examples.

4 WRITTEN ASSIGNMENT

Critically discuss the following statements. Your answer should be about 1500 words long.

- Who is responsible for environmental quality? The tourism industry, the hospitality businesses, the tourists, the suppliers or everybody?
- Tourism and hospitality trade associations can be very effective in promoting EMS in the industry.
- EMS is equally important for small-to-medium-sized businesses and large companies.

5 GROUP PROJECT

Develop an environmental status review

Develop and carry out an environmental status review of your hotel school or the hotel and hospitality department (if it is part of a larger college or university). Based on the findings of the review:

- Create an environmental policy for the school or department.
- Establish environmental objectives and targets.
- Develop an environmental management checklist.

6 GROUP DISCUSSION OR WRITTEN ASSIGNMENT

- Select an article related to a hotel property or tourism business that discusses their environmental management system. Critically review the article and then consider this question: 'What EMS steps and wider sustainable tourism actions could be taken in the hotel property or tourism business as a whole to improve conservation and environmental protection?'

Acknowledgments

The exercises proposed in this chapter were originally created by the International Association of Hotel Schools (EUHOFA), the International Hotel & Restaurant Association (IH&RA) and the United Nations Environment Programme (UNEP) in a document entitled *Sowing the Seeds of Change: An Environmental Teaching Pack for the Hospitality Industry* published in 2001 and updated in 2008. Thank you to EUHOFA (http://www.euhofa.org/), IH&RA (http://www.ih-ra.com/), UNEP (http://www.unep.org) and François-Tourisme-Consultants (http://www.francoistourisme consultants.com).

Resources

On environmental management systems

Eco-Management and Audit Scheme (EMAS) *Guidance Documents*, Brussels: European Commission Environment. Available at: http://ec.europa.eu/environment/emas/documents/guidance_en.htm.

International Standard Organization (ISO) *ISO and the Environment*. Geneva: International Standard Organization. Available at: http://www.iso.org/iso/iso_catalogue/management_standards/iso_9000_iso_14000/iso_and_the_environment.htm.

On hospitality industry environmental and/or sustainability policies

Accor: *Sustainable Development*. Available at: http://www.accor.com/en/sustainable-development.html.

Fairmont Hotels & Resorts: *Environmental Policy*. Available at: http://www.fairmont.com/EN_FA/AboutFairmont/environment/EnvironmentalPolicy/.

Hilton Worldwide: *Travel with Purpose*. Available at: http://www.hiltonworldwide.com/corporate-responsibility/.

InterContinental Hotels Group: *Corporate Social Responsibility Approach*. Available at: http://www.ihgplc.com/index.asp?pageid=740.

Marriott Hotels: *Marriott Social Responsibility Report*. Available at: http://www.marriott.com/Images/Text%20Images/US/MarriottSocialResponsibilityandCommunityEngagement.pdf.

Scandic Hotels: *Sustainability and the Environment*. Available at: http://www.scandichotels.com/settings/Side-foot/About-us-Container/Responsible-living/.

Six Senses Resorts & Spas: *Sustainability Policy*. Available at: http://www.sixsenses.com/environment/six-senses-sustainability-policy.php.

Additional material

Go to www.routledge.com/cw/sloan to find PowerPoint slides of all the figures and tables from the book, additional case studies, a test bank of questions and extra links to useful videos.

CHAPTER

Certification processes and eco-labels

CHAPTER OBJECTIVES

The objectives for this chapter are:

- To define certification
- To define, discuss and review the development of eco-labels
- To distinguish the different types of eco-labels pertaining to the hospitality industry
- To introduce a categorization system for hospitality-related eco-labels
- To discuss trends in eco-labelling
- To understand the major benefits associated with eco-labelling
- To introduce the Green Key and Green Globe standards
- To discuss how hotels communicate performance
- To introduce the Global Reporting Initiative and AccountAbility Standards

Certification and eco-labels

Defining certification

Certification is a procedure by which a third party, the certifier, provides a written insurance that a system, a process, a person, a product or a service have conformed to the requirements specified in a standard or a reference frame. Certification is a voluntary act. It is a tool of competitiveness and differentiation, which establishes consumer confidence.

Certification and quality

Certification and quality are often perceived as being complementary. This is in part due to the fact that certification recognises that a company has made or is making efforts towards higher quality levels. It is important to note that the implementation of processes towards higher quality is not always related to the search for certification. Likewise, obtaining certification is not inevitably a pledge for the quality of the products or services offered by the company. Certification is a stamp of approval noting that a business is in conformity with the specified requirements dictated by the certifier.

Definition and concept of eco-label

Certification schemes with a clear focus on environmental management and **sustainability** issues are called **eco-labels**. According to the Global Eco-labelling Network:

> Eco-labelling is a voluntary method of environmental performance certification and labelling that is practised around the world. An eco-label is a label which identifies overall, proven environmental preference of a product or service within a specific product/service category.

Eco-labels are basically a brand placed on a product, service or organization. The characteristics of an eco-label include:

- the measurement of environmental performance of a product or service;
- the evaluation of the environmental performance of a product or service benchmarked against criteria and standards set by the certifying agency;
- the presentation and diffusion of environmental information and performance of a product or service through a label and/or logo.

Eco-labels are voluntary schemes open to all businesses. Some eco-label schemes allow a company to **self-audit** its activities and certify itself with an eco-label. This approach is called first-party certification. In some industry sectors, second-party certification allows wholesalers to have their own **auditing** schemes to certify suppliers' products and services such as accommodation facilities and transportation in the tourism industry. Third-party certification involves an independent certifier which is responsible for the measurement, assessment and evaluation of results as well as the decision on the attribution of the eco-label. Third party organizations are typically governmental or non-profit organizations, industry associations, private companies and other non-governmental organizations (**NGOs**). For the sake of credibility of an eco-label and transparency of measurement and evaluation, the certification procedure should be undertaken by an independent third party to ensure that the standards of a certain eco-label are met.

Aims of eco-labelling

Eco-labels have four aims:

1. The authentication of a product's or service's environmental performance.
2. The promotion of information about a product's or service's environmental performance, allowing consumers to make an informed purchasing decision.
3. The ability to gain a competitive advantage in the market over other companies which are not certified.
4. The assurance that **environmental impacts** have been mitigated.

History and development of eco-labels

Stricter governmental regulations, combined with increased public interest in environmental affairs, have acted as a push factor for the steady development of eco-labels in various types of industries. Eco-labelling programmes started in Europe and their use has spread across the globe. This rapid development is also due to the fact that businesses have recognised that environmental concerns can be translated into a market advantage. Businesses' claims and declarations are reinforced by the introduction of eco-labels.

The German Blue Angel (*Der Blaue Engel*) is the world's first eco-label, created at the end of the 1970s to promote environmentally friendly products and services. The label is awarded by a jury composed of **environment** and consumer protection groups, industry, unions, trade, media and churches. The basic criteria forming the eco-label are: (1) the efficient use of fossil fuels; (2) products with less of an impact on the climate; (3) reduction of **greenhouse gas** emissions; and (4) **conservation** of resources. The eco-label currently covers some 10,000 products in some 80 product categories.

In the hospitality and tourism sector, one of the very first eco-labels was the Blue Flag label, established in France in 1985. The Blue Flag eco-label was awarded to coastal municipalities in recognition of the efforts made to preserve the beach and coastal fragile environment. The Blue Flag eco-label is now an internationally recognised eco-label managed by the Foundation for Environmental Education (FEE), an independent and not-for-profit organization.

Launched in 1992, the European Union (EU) Eco-Label is a voluntary product label. The main goal, similar to most eco-labels, is to encourage businesses to market products and services that meet certain standards of environmental performance and quality. The labels are awarded according to environmental criteria set by the member states of the EU with the involvement of industry and consumer and environmental NGOs. One particular advantage of this label resides in its European dimension. In other words, once approved by a member state, the label can be used throughout the other EU states, eliminates costly and redundant applications.

Eco-labels have since mushroomed. In the United States, the US Environmental Protection Agency (EPA) developed the Energy Star label in the early 1990s to estimate and compare the amount of energy used for similar products. The Energy Star programme was significantly expanded by the mid-1990s, by introducing labels for residential heating and cooling systems for industrial and commercial buildings as well as new homes. Energy Star is now considered an international standard for energy-efficient consumer products and buildings.

The Leadership in Energy and Environmental Design (LEED) programme developed by the United States Green Building Council (USGBC) in 1998 is another well-established example of an eco-label, consisting of a rating system for the design, construction and operation of green buildings and homes.

The common goal of these labels is to inform consumers about environmentally friendly products, thereby giving global support to product-related environmental protection. While the many eco-labels available have managed to attract consumers, the propagation of logos and claims for all categories of products and services has also led to some confusion and scepticism. Without guiding standards and investigation by an independent third party, consumers may not be certain that a labelled product or service is a truly environmentally preferable alternative. This concern with credibility and impartiality has led to the formation of both private and public organizations providing third-party labelling.

The Global Eco-labelling Network (GEN) was established in 1994 with the goal of improving, promoting and developing the eco-labelling of products and services. GEN is a non-profit association of third-party, environmental performance recognition, certification and labelling organizations.

Eco-labels in hospitality and tourism

According to the United Nations Environment Programme (**UNEP**), eco-labels were designed to improve environmental performance in the tourism industry. There is a wide diversity of hospitality and tourism initiatives related to environmental concerns but also to societal issues.

Home-made seal of approval

A company may decide to draw up an environmental charter for its operation and devise codes of conduct showing commitment towards managing the environmental and/or **social** impact. In the same vein, a company may then decide to apply its own 'seal of approval' which advertises superior environmental performance. This strategy is quite common in the tourism and **hospitality industry**. The vertically-integrated global tourism player TUI has developed the TUI Environmental Champion Award. TUI's hotel partners compete for the award by being **benchmarked** on the environmental and social performance as well as guest satisfaction with the environmental measures undertaken at the individual properties. One of the prerequisites for taking part in the contest is to reach a minimum score in the Travelife check list. Established in 2007, Travelife is a wholly owned subsidiary of the Association of British Travel Agents (ABTA) and supported by tour operators such as Thomas Cook, TUI and Kuoni.

Similar to the TUI Environmental Champion Award, DoubleTree by Hilton Hotels awarded its first Environmental CARE Award in 2007. The DoubleTree Environmental CARE Award is presented to one individual hotel, selected from the brand's collection of hotels that demonstrates a commitment to implementing and demonstrating sustainability and environmental outreach efforts.

One of the main drawbacks of home-made awards, certification or eco-labels is the lack of independence in the process of awarding the recognition which directly affects the credibility of the certification or label.

Third-party awards

Businesses and consumers have shown an increased interest in environmental awards. As **sustainable tourism** and hospitality practices increasingly gain momentum around the world, organizations and destinations are raising the bar on **best practices**. The basic concept behind an award is to recognise the attempt by a company or organization to find innovative solutions in enhanced environmental management. The award schemes can be managed and awarded by industry peers, trade associations, consumers, NGOs, governmental authorities or publishers. The awarding bodies are looking for applicants that want to participate and be promoted as a best practice example. Depending on the award, professionals from the industry or independent organizations may be asked to verify the judging and award process. Today there is a plethora of award events and ceremonies in the hospitality and tourism industry, here are a few notable examples:

- *Tourism for Tomorrow Awards*: the World Travel and Tourism Council (WTTC) has developed the Tourism for Tomorrow Awards. The awards represent accolades from industry peers for sustainable tourism achievements among businesses and destinations.
- *Worldwide Hospitality Awards*: the Worldwide Hospitality Awards, created by MKG Group in association with the *Hotel, Tourism and Restaurant* (HTR) magazine, is an annual event where individual hotels and hotel groups compete in various categories. One category is the Best Initiative in Sustainable Development. This is awarded to an initiative that demonstrates active involvement in the **sustainable development** of a hotel or hotel group.
- *World Travel Awards*: established in 1993, the World Travel Awards acknowledge and recognise excellence in the global travel and tourism industry with categories such as the World's Leading CSR Programme, the World's Leading Eco-Lodge, the World's Leading Green Resort and the World's Responsible Tourism Award. The judges are made up of international industry peers, including professionals from travel agencies, hotel groups, tour and transport companies and tourism organizations.

- *EcoTrophea*: another example of a third-party award is the EcoTrophea, organized by the German Travel Association (Deutscher Reise Verband or DRV). Established in 1987, the EcoTrophea awards exemplary international projects in tourism showing commitment to environmental protection and social responsibility in destinations.
- *Good Earthkeeping Stars of the Industry Award*: the American Hotel & Lodging Association (AH&LA) awards the Good Earthkeeping Stars of the Industry Award.
- *Consumer and trade publication awards*: professional and trade publications are also behind some industry awards. The Green Leadership Award is sponsored by Kostuch Publications, active in Canada's food service and hospitality industry and publisher of the *Hotelier* magazine. The Mother Nature Network (MNN) publishes the annual Top 10 Green Hotels in the United States. There are also online review sites such as TripAdvisor with its regular Travelers' Choice Winner of the Top List of Eco-Friendly Hotels.

Third-party certification and eco-labels

Similar to home-made seals of approval or third-party awards, third-party certified eco-labels are a tool to help consumers make informed purchasing decision. And similarly, there is an abundance of eco-label programmes and certification schemes around the world for the tourism and hospitality industry, let alone for all other consumers' goods and services. These eco-labels are usually designed to promote products that reduce the environmental impacts of an activity, service, product or particular set of operations. However, many of those eco-labels were designed in closed settings, usually at a local, regional or possibly at a national level. The international nature of the tourism and hospitality industry means that information portrayed by an eco-label should mean the same thing to all travellers around the globe, thus ensuring that travellers make informed decisions regardless of where they are. This is, however, not the case in the hospitality industry. There are several voluntary regional, national and international eco-labelling programmes available to the hospitality industry (see Table 14.1).

The establishment of an eco-label requires clear design criteria to be met, in other words, the necessary performance of a product or service in order to gain the eco-label. The ideal eco-label has stricter standards than current application government legislation and is available to a range of tourism suppliers and facilities where performance can be measured, compared and benchmarked. As a general rule, the more stringent the criteria, the more selective the eco-label scheme will be. The criteria should guide applicants and their facilities to mitigate the environmental impacts.

Eco-labels can be divided into two types of categories: (1) process-based; or (2) performance-based. An eco-label may also consist of a combination of both categories.

1. *Process-based categories*: this category is based on environmental management systems (EMS, see Chapter 13) such as the ISO 14000 family of environmental

TABLE 14.1 Categorization of hospitality-related eco-labels[1]

Evaluation category / Eco-label	Environmental management	Socio-cultural concerns	Construction and buildings	Energy efficiency	Carbon dioxide emissions	Resource conservation	Pollution prevention	Sourcing and supply chain management	Food and beverage management	Community involvement	Life cycle assessment
Audubon Green Leaf	X			X		X	X	X			
B Corporation	X	X		X		X	X	X		X	X
Building Research Establishment Environmental Assessment Method (BREEAM)	X		X	X		X	X				
Carbon Neutral Certification	X				X	X	X	X			
Carbon Reduction Label	X				X	X	X	X			
Certified Green Restaurant	X			X		X	X	X	X		
German Sustainable Building Council (DGNB)	X	X	X	X	X	X	X	X			X
EarthCheck	X	X		X	X	X	X	X		X	
Eco Hotels Certified (EHC)	X			X	X	X	X	X			
EU Ecolabel Tourist Accommodation	X	X		X	X	X	X	X			
Green Globe Certification	X	X	X	X	X	X	X	X	X	X	
Green Key	X	X		X		X	X	X	X	X	
Green Key Eco-Rating Program	X	X		X		X	X	X	X	X	
Green Seal	X			X	X	X	X	X			
Green Tourism Business Scheme	X	X		X		X	X	X		X	
Haute Qualité Environnementale (HQE)	X		X	X	X	X	X				X
International Eco Certification Program	X	X				X	X	X	X	X	
Klima Haus	X		X	X	X	X	X				X
Leadership in Energy and Environmental Design (LEED)	X		X	X	X	X	X				X
Legambiente Turismo	X	X		X		X	X	X	X	X	
National Green Pages™ Seal of Approval	X	X		X		X	X	X		X	
Nordic Ecolabel/Swan	X			X	X	X	X	X	X		
Singapore Green Label Scheme (SGLS) Hotel Certification	X			X		X	X	X			
Steinbock	X	X		X		X	X	X	X	X	
Sustainable Tourism Education Program (STEP)	X	X		X	X	X				X	
Viabono	X	X		X	X	X	X	X	X	X	

Note: 1 Evaluation categories for listed label may change (valid as of Spring 2012).

standards and the **European Union Eco-Management and Audit System (EMAS)**. Process-based approaches tend to focus on the operating processes and are not a direct guarantee of improved environmental performance.

2. *Performance-based categories*: performance-based categories consist of set criteria, benchmarks and objectives that must be achieved to obtain certification. A company wanting such an eco-label must fulfil the very same criteria as all other companies applying for that particular eco-label. The ranking and comparison of performances thus motivate companies to continuously improve performances.

The trend is to have eco-labels built upon the two categories of performance-based and process-based approaches. The certification using such an eco-label starts with the implementation of EMS and continues by setting performance measures.

The hospitality industry does not produce, make or grow any products in the traditional sense. Nevertheless, hospitality firms consume natural resources and products on a large scale. Specifically, hotels consumption includes:

- land
- construction materials
- fixtures and furnishings
- cleaning supplies
- food and beverages
- technical equipment
- energy and water.

Eco-labels assess hotels regarding their environmentally sound performance in the above-mentioned areas. After having reached all required benchmarks, the hotel is awarded the particular logo of the eco-label organization and can use this to promote its environmental efforts.

Eco-labels can have a built-in rating or ranking structure and indicate different levels of performances. For example, a particular eco-label defines different levels for certification with the words or categories Bronze, Silver and Gold which is the case for Leadership in Energy and Environmental Design (LEED) certification scheme.

Trends in eco-labelling

The trend towards environmental certification or eco-labelling as it is commonly known has increased greatly in the past 20 years primarily because it is an important promotional tool for sustainable tourism and hospitality. Eco-labels have three key functions for organizations: (1) environmental standard setting; (2) third party certification of these standards; and (3) **value-added** marketing or **environmental communication**. However, with the sheer quantity of various eco-labels on the market, the hotel or restaurant guest may struggle to identify which labels are valuable and credible and which are not. Presently the global tourism sector can choose between hundred of different eco-labels, Europe alone has 60 labels available to hoteliers and restaurateurs. Ideally, local and regional certification programmes should be linked to an international **accreditation** system. Established in 2004, the Voluntary Initiatives for Sustainability in Tourism (**VISIT**) is an example of such a scheme whereby various eco-labels can be promoted via VISIT only if they meet a particular requirement level. VISIT was developed under the EU LIFE programme. The LIFE programme is the EU's funding instrument for the environment. VISIT's main objective is to foster a fruitful cooperation between distinct initiatives working towards achieving sustainability in tourism. It states its aim is:

> to promote and support sustainable tourism development through the representation, promotion and mutual co-operation of international, national and regional certification schemes and other voluntary initiatives for sustainable tourism at an international level.

Seven labels are currently represented under VISIT (from the Netherlands, Italy, Denmark, Latvia, the United Kingdom, Switzerland and Luxembourg) representing some 2000 participating tourism businesses. While VISIT is unique in its form, the success of VISIT is, however, limited.

As summarized in Figure 14.1, eco-labels are often seen as being too expensive for individual hotels especially when the ratio costs to benefits are not properly understood. They also tend to attract customers just interested in eco-tourism and have limited marketing power. Lastly, there is a risk that with the existence of such a large number of certificates, companies will choose those that are the least demanding.

In some unfortunate circumstances some establishments have used the lax control mechanisms associated with some eco-labels to make fraudulent claims. Consequently, consumer recognition has again suffered. However, some eco-labels have obtained increased international notoriety in the hospitality industry over the past decade following the constant update of standards and increased industry recognition such as the **Green Globe** and the Green Key standards.

Disadvantages:
- Many eco-labels overlap, making it difficult to choose the right one
- General proliferation of eco-labels leaves consumers confused
- Abuse of eco-label claims by unscrupulous hoteliers
- Cost of application, implementation and assessment

Advantages:
- Cost savings can be achieved through implementation of eco-label's guidelines and standards
- Eco-label provides enhanced visibility and marketing opportunities
- Eco-label allows for industry benchmarking and recognition
- Implementation of eco-label's guidelines and standards boosts employees' morale and motivation
- A hotel's economic, environmental and social performance following the implementation of an eco-label's guidelines and standards increases

---

FIGURE 14.1 Summary of advantages and disadvantages of eco-labels

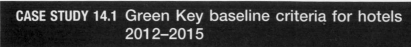

CASE STUDY 14.1 Green Key baseline criteria for hotels 2012–2015

The Green Key

Aim

The aim of the programme is to develop and manage an eco-label for leisure organizations.

Green Key is conducted as a certification programme intended to increase the awareness of the owners, staff, **stakeholders** and clients of their potential for action towards environmental and sustainability issues.

Goals

Green Key pursues four goals:

1. **Environmental education** for sustainable development of the owner, the staff, the stakeholders (suppliers, etc.) and the client.
2. Reduction of the **impacts** of the facility.
3. Economic management as a reduction of consumption induces the reduction of costs.
4. Marketing strategy with the promotion of the label and the facilities awarded.

Criteria

The criteria are divided into two categories:

- imperative to be fulfilled in every Green Key hotel
- guideline (G): designed to be part of the point system

Proposed point system

Establishments have to match some guideline criteria every year (except the first year for newcomers) (Table 14.2).

TABLE 14.2 Year and guideline criteria for Green Key award

Year	Number of guideline criteria	Percentage of total guideline criteria
1	0	0
2	3	5
3	6	10
4	9	15
5	12	20
10 and +	30	50

The international criteria will be revised every three years. This set of criteria is for the period 2012–2015 (Table 14.3).

TABLE 14.3 International criteria for Green Key award

I. ENVIRONMENTAL MANAGEMENT

I.1 The Management must be involved and they should appoint an environmental manager from among the staff of the facility

I.2 The establishment must have an environmental policy and present it in the application

I.3 The establishment must formulate objectives and an action plan for constant improvement and present it in the application

I.4 All documentation concerning the Green Key must be kept and maintained in a binder ready for inspection

I.5 The establishment must comply with the national environmental legislation

I.6 The environmental manager must ensure that the Green Key criteria are reviewed annually

I.7 The surroundings of the establishment must not be polluted and/or present a major risk for the health and the safety of the guests

I.8 Active collaboration with relevant stakeholders is established (G)

II. STAFF INVOLVEMENT

II.1 The management must hold a meeting/s with the staff in order to brief them on issues concerning existing and new environmental initiatives

II.2 The environmental manager must participate in meetings with management for the purpose of presenting the environmental developments of the establishment

II.3 The environmental manager and other staff members assigned with environmental duties must receive training on environmental issues

II.4 The environmental manager must ensure that the employees are aware of the establishment's environmental undertakings

II.5 The procedure regarding towels and sheets re-use must be known and accepted by the housekeeping service

II.6 The establishment has a CSR policy, covering the areas of Human Rights, Labour Equity Environmental Education and Anti-corruption (G)

III. GUEST INFORMATION

III.1 The Green Key award must be displayed in a conspicuous place

III.2 The establishment must keep the guests involved and informed about its environmental policy and goals and encourage guests to participate in environmental initiatives

III.3 Information material about Green Key must be visible and accessible to the guests, including on the establishment's website (the use of Green Key logo is optional)

III.4 Front desk staff must be in a position to inform guests about the current environmental activities and undertakings of the establishment

III.5 The establishment must be able to inform guests about local public transportation systems and alternatives

III.6 Signs about energy and water saving should be visible for guests and staff. (e.g., television in room, lights, heat, taps, showers, etc.)

III.7 The establishment provides its guests with the opportunity to evaluate its environmental undertakings (questionnaire, link to homepage, . . .) (G).

IV. WATER

IV.1 The total water consumption must be registered at least once a month

IV.2 Newly purchased toilets are not allowed to flush more than 6 litres per flush

IV.3 The staff and cleaning personnel must regularly check for dripping taps and leaky toilets

IV.4 Each bathroom must have a waste bin

IV.5 Water flow from at least 50% of the showers must not exceed 9 litres per minute

IV.6 Water flow from at least 50% of the taps must not exceed 8 litres per minute

IV.7 Urinals are not allowed to use more flushing water than necessary

IV.8 Newly purchased cover or tunnel dishwashers are not allowed to consume more water than 3.5 litres per basket

IV.9 Instructions for saving water and energy during operation of dishwashers must be displayed near the machine

IV.10 All wastewater must be treated. When treatment of wastewater is regulated by national or local regulations, then it must comply with these regulations

IV.11 Hazardous liquid chemicals must be stored, avoiding leaks that can damage the environment

IV.12 Newly purchased dishwashers are not allowed to be conventional domestic appliances (G)

IV.13 Separate water metres are installed in areas with a high degree of water consumption (G)

IV.14 Water flow from taps and toilets in public areas should not exceed 6 litres per minute (G)

IV.15 Wastewater is re-used (after treatment) (G)

IV.16 Toilets are flushed with rain water (G)

IV.17 Newly purchased toilets are dual flush type 3/6 litres (G)

IV.18 Purified tap water is offered to the guests (G)

IV.19 The swimming pools are covered to limit evaporation (G)

IV.20 Regular controls shows that there is no leak in the swimming pool (G)

V. WASHING AND CLEANING

V.1 There must be signs in bathrooms and restrooms informing guests that sheets and towels will only be changed upon request (e.g., place your towel in the shower if you need a new one)

V.2 Newly purchased chemical cleaning products and products for washing have a national or internationally recognised eco-label or are not allowed to contain agents that are listed in Green Key's 'Requirements related to cleaning and washing articles in Green Key establishment'

V.3 In European countries, paper towels and toilet paper must be made of non-chlorine bleached paper or must be awarded with an eco-label. This criterion must be effective next time the hotel buys paper towels and toilet paper

V.4 Fibre cloth is used for cleaning to save water and chemicals (G)

V.5 In non-EU countries, paper towels and toilet paper are made of non-chlorine bleached paper or are awarded with an eco-label (G)

VI WASTE

VI.1 The establishment must separate waste into the categories that can be handled separately by the local or national waste management facilities

VI.2 If the local waste management authorities do not collect waste at or near the establishment, then the establishment must ensure safe transportation of its waste to the nearest appropriate site for waste treatment

VI.3 Instructions on how to separate and handle waste must be easily available to the staff and guests in an understandable and simple format

VI.4 Disposable cups, plates and cutlery must only be used in the pool areas, at certain music arrangements and in connection with transportable diner

VI.5 Hazardous waste (such as batteries, fluo compact bulbs, paint, chemicals, etc. . . .) should be secured in separate containers and taken to an approved reception facility

VI.6 Toiletries such as shampoo, soap, shower caps, etc. in rooms are not packaged in single dose containers. If so, they must be packaged in material that can be recycled or biodegradable (G)

VI.7 Guests have the possibility to separate waste into the categories that can be handled by the waste management facilities as per VI.1 (G)

VI.8 Single dose packages for cream, butter, jam, etc. are either not used, reduced or packaged in material that can be recycled (G)

VI.9 The establishment makes arrangements for the collection and disposal of packaging with an appropriate supplier (G)

VI.10 The establishment uses biodegradable disposable cups, plates and cutlery (G)

VII. ENERGY

VII.1 Energy use must be registered at least once a month

VII.2 Heating and air-conditioning control systems must be applied when the accommodation facilities are not in use. A one-year grace period is granted for compliance with this criterion from the date the Green Key is awarded

VII.3 At least 50% of the light bulbs are energy-efficient. Reasons for not having energy-efficient light bulbs must be clearly explained

VII.4 The surfaces of the heating/cooling exchanger of the ventilation plant must be regularly cleaned

VII.5 Fat filters in the exhaust must be cleaned at least once a year

VII.6 The ventilation system must be controlled at least once a year and repaired if necessary in order to be energy-efficient at all times

VII.7 Refrigerators, cold stores, heating cupboards and ovens must be equipped with intact draught excluders

VII.8 Newly purchased pumps and refrigeration plants must not use CFC or HCFC refrigerants. All equipment must always comply with national legislation on phasing out refrigerants

VII.9 Newly purchased mini-bars must not have an energy consumption of more than 1 kWh/day

VII.10 There is a written procedure regarding electric devices in empty bedrooms based on time schedules: how refrigerators, televisions, are turned off when hotel bedrooms, holiday flats and holiday houses are not being let

VII.11 All windows have an appropriately high degree of thermal insulation in compliance with the local climate (G)

VII.12 The establishment is 90% equipped with energy-efficient light bulbs (G)

VII.13 An energy audit is carried out once every 5 years (G)

VII.14 The business shows efforts concerning savings of water or energy consumption, i.e. sauna, hammam, swimming pool, spa, solarium, etc. (G)

VII.15 Heating from electric panels or other forms of direct functioning electric heating is not allowed (G)

VII.16 The establishment uses renewable energy (G)

VII.17 Ventilation plants are equipped with an energy-optimum ventilator and an energy-saving engine (G)

VII.18 Automatic systems that turn the lights off when guests leave their room are installed (G)

VII.19 Unnecessary outside lights have an automatic turn-off sensor installed (G).

VII.20 Separate electricity meters are installed at strategically important places for energy monitoring (G)

VII.21 Air-conditioning automatically switches off when windows are open (G)

VII.22 The building is insulated above the minimal national requirements to ensure a significant reduction of energy consumption (G)

VII.23 A heat recovery system for refrigeration systems, ventilators, swimming pools or sanitary wastewater is installed (G)

VII.24 Hot water pipes are integrally insulated (G)

VII.25 Automatic systems are installed in public areas for energy-efficient lighting (G)

VII.26 The accommodation has a key card system to ensure that electrical appliances are switched off in rented rooms when the occupants are out (G)

VII.27 Computers and copying machines switch off after a maximum of one non-used hour

VIII. FOOD AND BEVERAGE

VIII.1 When it is possible, the establishment must purchase and register the amount of labelled (organic or other acknowledged eco-label) foods, and focus on buying locally produced product, when they have less impact on the environment than non-local products

VIII.2 The share of labelled foods must be maintained or increase each year. If not, the reasons must be communicated to Green Key national operator

VIII.3 A vegetarian alternative menu is proposed in the restaurant (G)

VIII.4 In conference rooms, where water quality is of an adequate standard, then tap water is used instead of mineral bottled water (G)

IX. INDOOR ENVIRONMENT

IX.1 The establishment must respect legislation regarding polluting elements within its premises

IX.2 A non-smoking section must be available in the restaurant

IX.3 The majority of the rooms must be non-smoking

IX.4 When the establishment makes extended interior changes it must ensure that the indoor climate is taken into account

IX.5 The establishment has a personnel policy concerning smoking during working hours

IX.6 In case of refurbishing or new building, the establishment uses environmental procedures

X. PARKS AND PARKING AREAS

X.1 Chemical pesticides and fertilizers cannot be used more than once a year, unless there is no organic or natural equivalent

X.2 Newly purchased lawnmowers must either be electrically driven, use unleaded petrol, be equipped with a catalyst, be awarded with an eco-label or be manually driven

X.3 Flowers and gardens must be watered in the early morning or after sunset

X.4 Garden waste is composted (G)

X.5 Rainwater is collected and used for watering flowers and gardens (G)

X.6 Gardens are watered by a drip system (G)

X.7 When planting new green areas, endemic or native species are preferred (G)

XI. GREEN ACTIVITIES

XI.1 Information material about nearby parks, landscape and nature conservation areas must be readily available to the guests

XI.2 The establishment must provide information about the nearest place to rent or borrow bicycles

XI.3 The guests have the opportunity to borrow or rent bicycles (G)

XI.4 The establishment financially sponsors green activities in the local area (G)

XI.5 The establishment provides activities for raising awareness, focused on sustainable development, environment and nature in or around the premises (G)

XI.6 The establishment provides information to their guests regarding close by Blue Flag-awarded marinas and beaches (G)

XII. ADMINISTRATION

XII.1 All staff areas must fulfil the same criteria as guest areas

XII.2 The stationery, brochures, etc. produced or ordered by the establishment must be awarded with an eco-label or produced by a company with an environmental management system

XII.3 Hairdresser salon, spa facilities or the like, which are on the premises of the establishment, must be informed about its environmental initiatives and Green Key and encouraged to manage their activities in the spirit of Green Key

XII.4 Newly purchased durables have an eco-label or must be produced by a company with an environmental management system (G)

XII.5 The use of environmentally friendly means of transport by guests and staff is encouraged (G)

XII.6 The management encourages the use of less paper in conference rooms (G)

Source: Green Key International/Foundation for Environmental Education (FEE), http://www.green-key.org/.

CASE STUDY 14.2 Green Globe Certification Standards

The Green Globe Standard is a structured assessment of the sustainability performance of travel and tourism businesses and their supply chain partners. Businesses can monitor improvements and document achievements leading to certification of their enterprise's **sustainable** operation and management.

The Green Globe Standards is a collection of 337 compliance **indicators** applied to 41 individual sustainability criteria. The applicable indicators vary by type of certification, geographical area as well as local factors. The Green Globe Standard is reviewed and updated twice per calendar year.

Green Globe Certification is active in harmonizing with other established sustainability certification programmes around the world. The process of harmonization contributes to maintaining core criteria and at the same time addresses regional issues through the adoption of locally developed standards.

The Green Globe Standard is based on the following international standards and agreements:

- Global Sustainable Tourism Criteria
- Global Partnership for Sustainable Tourism Criteria (STC Partnership)
- Baseline Criteria of the Sustainable Tourism Certification Network of the Americas
- Agenda 21 and principles for Sustainable Development endorsed by 182 governments at the United Nations Rio de Janeiro Earth Summit in 1992
- ISO 9001/14001/19011 (International Standard Organization)

To guarantee compliance to the highest international standards, a third-party independent auditor is appointed to work with clients on-site. The international standard ISO 19011 provides guidance on the management of audit programmes, the conduct of internal and external management systems as well as the competence and evaluation of auditors. Green Globe Certification has drawn on ISO 19011:2002 in the development of its audit programme (see Appendix).

Communicating performance

A factor of differentiation for hotels and restaurants is the way they communicate their environmental commitment. For many hospitality entrepreneurs, the reduction of environmental impacts and the increase in societal involvement are the credo for successful business management. However, the level of implication in this new approach to business management depends a lot on the hotel brands and the type of ownership. Indeed, the implementation of environmental charters is often the responsibility of individual hotel or restaurant directors, who may have other priorities in mind. One of the main objectives sought by implementing environmental and societal initiatives is, besides the observance of legislation, the potential reduction in operating costs. Additionally, good environmental communication can become an advantageous differentiation factor and create a positive brand image.

It is becoming clear from the demand of stakeholders that the hospitality industry needs to communicate effectively on their environmental and social commitment in addition to their economic prosperity. Mandatory reporting is only required for financial information. The communication of sustainability efforts or results, however, is far from being as regulated. Great diversity can be noted with regard to the way environmental and social justice information is disseminated and the reasons for publication. However, the reporting of environmentally sustainable efforts is essential to attract capital from block investors with specific investment guidelines.

Three ways of communication are described in this chapter:

1. certification
2. **benchmarking**
3. reporting.

Certification

Certification, as stated in the first section of this chapter, is often considered to be a communication effort by the company to potential customers voluntarily advertising the company's adherence to certain standards.

Benchmarking

Benchmarking is a process that is increasingly being incorporated into environmental certification. The main aim of benchmarking is to compare operational efficiency and environmental impacts within facilities having a similar portfolio and to indicate possible improvements in business activity, processes and management by establishing more efficient operational standards. Benchmarking is either internal between different departments or sections or external and compares performance data with other organizations at different levels. This comparison can be either between environmental items such as energy, waste and water consumption or social initiatives such as employee satisfaction or participation in local charity events.

Benchmarking typically involves the comparison of processes within one's own business and those in other businesses. The development of measures aimed at closing performance gaps are then identified and put into action.

CASE STUDY 14.3 The Sustainability Performance Operation Tool (SPOT)

The Sustainability Performance Operation Tool (SPOT), developed by the International Tourism Partnership, is an easy-to-use sustainability check for business operations. SPOT graphically demonstrates the sustainability of an operation, which can be used either as a management information tool or as part of a training process. SPOT structures key principles and indicators of sustainability into a robust framework, against which an appraisal of performance can be undertaken and reported. The tool also includes a comprehensive resource library to assist you in assessment and help with further learning.

SPOT allows the sustainability of an operation to be measured and illustrated graphically at all stages. The tool is divided into 15 sustainability indicators or sub-categories:

1. Environmental management
2. Energy use
3. Water use
4. Waste control
5. Pollution protection
6. Habitat protection
7. Purchasing and sales
8. Local community
9. Education/training
10. Culture and heritage
11. Health and safety
12. Business ethics
13. Monitoring and assessment
14. Supply chain
15. Work and employment.

The assessment allows optimization of the key elements of sustainability: environmental, social and economic (Figure 14.2). The simple, logical and transparent methodology is fully adaptable to all types of projects. SPOT also features a resource library of practical information, good practice and other educational materials to provide continuous education and improvement.

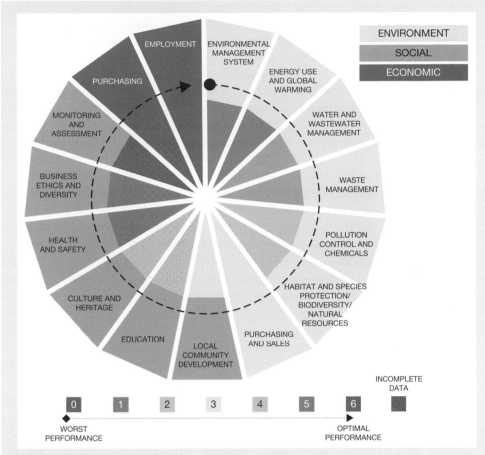

FIGURE 14.2 SPOT: key elements of sustainability
Source: International Tourism Partnership, http://www.tourismpartnership.org/.

SPOT can be used as an effective comparator of options to help lead strategic management decisions. The assessment can also be used to demonstrate to both internal (executive management, workforce, etc.) and external (planning authority, insurers, public, etc.) stakeholders the overall performance of the operation in terms of sustainability.

Reporting

Reporting is more concerned with publishing detailed information accounting for a company's individual efforts to a wider range of stakeholders. Traditionally, businesses and particularly the hospitality industry published very little 'non-financial' information. With growing pressure from environmental lobby groups and other stakeholders in recent years for more transparency, a lot of companies have started to provide some environmental and social information. **Agenda 21**, signed by 178 member countries of the United Nations, also requested businesses to report on their environmental performance records.

With growing recognition of concepts such as sustainable development, the **carbon footprint** and the **triple bottom line**, environmental reporting began to evolve into **corporate social responsibility (CSR)** reporting but also under names such as *sustainability reporting*, *responsible reporting* or *triple bottom line reporting*. The aim remains the same, however: 'to expand traditional reporting on the financial dimension to provide information also on environmental and social dimensions giving a more balanced view of overall corporate performance'.

Many companies from all sections of industry including hospitality, now publish stand-alone sustainability reports. Standards of sustainable reporting have started to emerge, although little legislation exists. A major contribution to sustainable reporting was made by the **Global Reporting Initiative (GRI)** in 2002, launching globally applicable sustainability reporting guidelines. GRI's reporting guidelines encompass 84 different indicators to assess a company's sustainability performance. These indicators are classified into three standards disclosures: economic, environmental and social. The social standard disclosure is further divided into labour practices and decent work, human rights, society and product responsibility. The most recent version of the guidelines – G3.1– was released in March 2011. GRI is currently working on the development of the fourth generation of the guidelines – G4, which is due for release in May 2013. The guidelines are freely available to the public.

According to the GRI, a sustainability report is: 'an organizational report that gives information about economic, environmental, social and governance performance [. . . whereby . . .] a sustainability report is the key platform for communicating positive and negative sustainability impacts' (https://www.globalreporting.org/information/sustainability-reporting/Pages/default.aspx, on 11 April 2012).

Companies need to keep a large diversity of stakeholders up to date about their performance. In communicating to those stakeholders, a sustainability report should provide a balanced and reasonable representation of the sustainability performance of a reporting organization – including both positive and negative performance.

Primary stakeholders including shareholders, customers, personnel and suppliers play an active role in the survival of the company. Secondary stakeholders affect and are affected by the company but are not considered to be essential for the survival of the company. However, those stakeholders such as the media and non-governmental organizations have a considerable influence on the content and presentation of sustainable reporting.

For example, shareholders have to be informed about company performance and earnings and governmental authorities about tax obligations. For legal reasons, as well as voluntarily, companies publish financial data in balance sheets, income statements and cash flow statements. Besides this external function, reporting also serves as an internal communication and management tool. The most important reasons for publishing sustainability reports with the exception of financial reports are still **public relations** and reputation management.

CASE STUDY 14.4 Global Reporting Initiative (GRI)

The Global Reporting Initiative (GRI) is a non-profit organization that promotes economic, environmental and social sustainability. GRI provides all companies and organizations with a comprehensive sustainability reporting framework that is widely used around the world.

GRI works towards a sustainable global economy by providing organizational reporting guidance. A sustainable global economy should combine long-term profitability with social justice and environmental care. This means that, for organizations, sustainability covers the key areas of economic, environmental, social and governance performance.

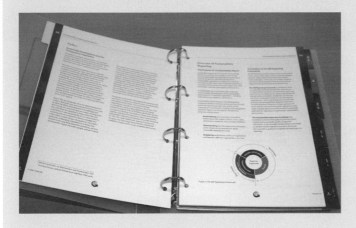

PICTURE 14.1 GRI Guidelines are freely available to the public

GRI's Sustainability Reporting Framework enables all companies and organizations to measure and report their sustainability performance. By reporting transparently and with accountability, organizations can increase the trust that stakeholders have in them, and in the global economy.

GRI is a network-based organization. A global network of some 30,000 people, many of them sustainability experts, contributes to its work. GRI's governance bodies and Secretariat act as a hub, coordinating the activity of its network partners.

- *Vision*: a sustainable global economy where organizations manage their economic, environmental, social and governance performance and impacts responsibly and report transparently.
- *Mission*: to make sustainability reporting standard practice by providing guidance and support to organizations.

Source: Global Reporting Initiative (GRI) (2012). Retrieved from: https://www.global reporting.org/information/about-gri/Pages/default.aspx, on 15 February 2012.

Within the GRI system, sector supplements are available for several different industry sectors; unfortunately no separate sector supplement has been created for hospitality operations. The Institute of Social and Ethical Accountability has created the AA1000 series. This set of corporate responsibility standards is an open source framework for organizational accountability developed through multi-stakeholder consultation and review process. These standards are designed to be compatible with other key standards in the area of sustainable development, including the GRI guidelines. As the verification of sustainability reports is not compulsory, unlike the verification of financial reports, management still has a large degree of control over the verification process, the selection of the auditor, the actual contents and the confidentiality of the auditor's report.

CASE STUDY 14.5 AccountAbility's AA1000 series of standards

AccountAbility's AA1000 series are principles-based standards to help organizations become more accountable, responsible and sustainable. They address issues affecting governance, business models and organizational strategy, as well as providing operational guidance on sustainability assurance and stakeholder engagement. The AA1000 standards are designed for the integrated thinking required by the low carbon and green economy, and support integrated reporting and assurance.

The standards are developed through a multi-stakeholder consultation process which ensures they are written for those they impact, not just those who may gain from them. They are used by a broad spectrum of organizations – multinational businesses, small and medium-sized enterprises (**SMEs**), governments and civil societies.

The AA1000 standards are:

- The AA1000 AccountAbility Principles Standard (AA1000APS) provides a framework for an organization to identify, prioritize and respond to its sustainability challenges.
- The AA1000 Assurance Standard (AA1000AS) provides a methodology for assurance practitioners to evaluate the nature and extent to which an organization adheres to the AccountAbility Principles.
- The AA1000 Stakeholder Engagement Standard (AA1000SES) provides a framework to help organizations ensure stakeholder engagement processes are purpose-driven, robust and deliver results.

The AA1000 Principles

- *Inclusivity*: for an organization that accepts its accountability to those on whom it has an impact and who have an impact on it, inclusivity is the participation of stakeholders in developing and achieving an accountable and strategic response to sustainability.

- *Materiality*: materiality is determining the relevance and significance of an issue to an organization and its stakeholders. A material issue is an issue that will influence the decisions, actions and performance of an organization or its stakeholders.
- *Responsiveness*: responsiveness is an organization's response to stakeholder issues that affect its sustainability performance and is realized through decisions, actions and performance, as well as communication with stakeholders.

The value of these principles lies in their comprehensive coverage and the flexibility of their application. They demand that an organization actively engages with its stakeholders, fully identifies and understands sustainability issues that will have an impact on its performance, including economic, environmental, social and longer-term financial performance, and then uses this understanding to develop responsible business strategies and performance objectives. Being principles rather than prescriptive rules, they allow the organization to focus on what is material to its own vision and provide a framework for identifying and acting on real opportunities as well as managing non-financial risk and compliance.

Source: AccountAbility, www.accountability.org.

The four Cs of sustainable reporting

All sustainable reports should incorporate the four Cs of credible reporting:

1. *Clear presentation*: the report should be user-friendly, illustrating programmes and results with tables, figures and graphs.
2. *Comprehensive coverage*: the report should address all issues that are relevant to the company. Addressing only a few issues will send a positive signal to those stakeholders involved in these issues, but a negative signal to those involved in other, unaddressed, issues.
3. *Consistent inclusion*: enable comparison of results, reports should address the same issues over time.
4. *Comparable measurement and reporting techniques*: increase the reliability of reported progress.

CASE STUDY 14.6 Fairmont Hotels & Resorts expands Green Key Eco-Rating Program worldwide

About Green Key

The Green Key Eco-Rating Program is the first of its kind to rank, certify and inspect hotels and resorts in North America based on their commitment to sustainable 'green' operations. The programme was originally developed for the Hotel Association of Canada by a leading environmental engineering firm with funding from the Canadian government. Designed specifically for hotel operations, the Green Key Eco-Rating Program is a comprehensive environmental self-assessment that will allow each participating property to benefit on several fronts – cost savings, increased bookings from environmentally conscious consumers and meeting planners and responsible corporate citizenry. In the United States Green Key is a joint partnership between the Hotel Association of Canada and LRA Worldwide, Inc.; for more information, visit www.GreenKeyGlobal.com.

Toronto, 21 September 2010 – Fairmont Hotels & Resorts is proud to announce that it has committed its global portfolio of landmark properties to becoming members of The Green Key Eco-Rating Program (Green Key). As part of the luxury hotel brand's 20-year commitment to **environmental stewardship**, sustainability and **responsible tourism**, the extension of this highly-respected programme to its properties outside of North America will provide guests with an unbiased guarantee that no matter where they are in the world, a stay with Fairmont will be as green as possible.

The partnership between Green Key and Fairmont dates back to the original development of the programme in the mid-1990s. In 2009, the brand committed its entire North American portfolio to the Green Key system, and the success of the initiative led to a brand-wide extension that will include hotels from Scotland to Shanghai.

'Guests around the world continue to demand environmental sensitivity when they travel, so when the Green Key Program expanded internationally from its Canadian roots it made perfect sense to enroll our entire portfolio of hotels,' said Chris Cahill, President, Fairmont Hotels & Resorts. 'Our hotels have implemented an incredible number of green initiatives over the past 20 years, and this rating system is a great way for them to audit, benchmark and even further reduce their environmental footprint.'

The Green Key evaluation is a comprehensive 150-question self-assessment that is administered by the staff at the participating property, covering a broad range of operational areas and sustainable practices. Upon completion, the answers are tabulated and the property is awarded a ranking of 1–5 Green Keys and a corresponding display plaque. The property also receives a comprehensive report that includes recommendations, best practices and potential areas for improvement and savings and a listing on the www.greenkeyglobal.com website, a valuable resource for environmentally conscious travelers. Unlike other programmes of this nature, Green Key includes random, on-site verification of self-assessment results, mitigating the risk of score inflation.

The cornerstone of the programme is its focus on sound sustainable practices specifically for the lodging industry. Green Key was developed by a leading environmental engineering firm with support from the Canadian government to withstand the scrutiny of a wide range of environmental experts. The programme has also received praise from the U.S. Office of the Federal Environmental Executive (OFEE), the Partnership for Global Sustainable Tourism Criteria and the Rainforest Alliance and is the American Hotel & Lodging Association's (AH&LA) programme of choice.

For close to two decades, Fairmont has strived to minimize its impact on the planet through its award-winning Green Partnership programme, a comprehensive platform focused on key areas such as waste reduction, **energy management**, water conservation, and innovative community outreach programmes. In a sign of corporate leadership, the company also encourages others to follow in its footsteps and has developed the Green Partnership Guide, a how-to text that any company can obtain to create or grow their environmental programming. For more information on Fairmont's Green Partnership programme, please visit www.fairmont.com/environment.

CASE STUDY 14.7 Green Key Eco-Rating Program: helping hotels' performance

The Green Key Eco-Rating Program is a graduated rating system designed to recognise hotels, motels and resorts that are committed to improving their environmental and fiscal performance.

Based on the results of a comprehensive environmental self-assessment, hotels are awarded a 1–5 Green Key rating and provided with guidance on how to 'unlock' opportunities to reduce environmental impacts and operating costs through reduced utility consumption, employee training and supply chain management.

The programme assesses the five main operational areas of a property and covers nine areas of sustainable practices:

Operational areas

- Corporate environmental management
- Housekeeping

- Food and beverage operations
- Conference and meeting facilities
- Engineering

Sustainable practices

- **Energy conservation**
- Water conservation
- Solid **waste management**
- Hazardous waste management
- Indoor air quality
- Community outreach
- Building infrastructure
- Land use
- Environmental management

Upon completion of the programme and being awarded their Green Key Rating, an on-site inspection may be conducted to confirm the rating.

As of March 2012, there were 2849 hotels participating in the Green Key Program. Of those members that have completed and submitted the assessment, the Key Rating breakdown is as follows:

Green Key rating	Hotels
1 Green Key	23
2 Green Keys	413
3 Green Keys	1444
4 Green Keys	745
5 Green Keys	52

Note: The number of active hotels in the Green Key Program changes almost daily as new properties join and complete the self-assessment.

How are the ratings determined?

The Green Key Self-Assessment consists of approximately 160 questions related to various areas of sustainable hotel operations. Each question has been assigned a specific point value based on the environmental and social impacts a particular action has and its associated impact on guests, employees, management and the local community.

When a hotel completes the self-assessment, their answers are evaluated and their final score is converted to a percentage. Green Key Ratings are then awarded as follows:

Final score	(%)	Green Key rating
1	19.9	1 Green Key
20	39.9	2 Green Keys
40	59.9	3 Green Keys
60	79.9	4 Green Keys
80	100	5 Green Keys

Based on the fact that ratings are awarded based on a percentage range, not every hotel in a specific rating level will be doing exactly the same things. For example, one 3 Key property may have recycling bins in each guest room; another 3 Key property may not have **recycling** bins in each room but staff separate recyclables from the garbage in the back-of-house area.

The Green Key Eco-Rating Program is currently active in Canada, the United States and 15 other countries throughout the world.

Source: Green Key Eco-Rating Program, http://www.greenkeyglobal.com/.

EXERCISES

1   SMALL GROUP PROJECT AND DISCUSSION

Eco-labels in hospitality industry: the best option?

Sustainable development calls for a wide range of incentives and sound legislation. Voluntary self-regulation initiatives are now becoming a popular force for sustainability-related improvements in the hospitality industry. Eco-labels are voluntary initiatives whereby sustainability is based on voluntary agreements and voluntary standards.

- In small groups, research and define the following eco-labels and provide for each eco-label an industry example (at best from the hospitality industry).

- Each group should then discuss whether the hospitality industry should seek to obtain this particular eco-label or not. Findings will be presented to the class:

    – Carbon Neutral Certification

    – Certified Green Restaurant

    – Climate Neutral label

    – The Green Key

    – Green Globe

    – Leadership in Energy and Environmental Design (LEED)

2 SMALL GROUP PROJECT AND DISCUSSION

Working with certified suppliers

Sustainability in hospitality requires a holistic approach to management, looking upwards into the supply chain and downwards into the distribution channels.

- In small groups, research and define the following eco-labels and provide for each eco-label an industry example.
- Each group should then discuss whether the hospitality industry should seek to work with suppliers being certified with one of those labels or not. Findings will be presented to the class.
  - Energy Star
  - Organic Certified
  - Forest Stewardship Council
  - Marine Stewardship Council
  - Blue Angel
  - Demeter Certified[SBLX]

3 WRITTEN ASSIGNMENT

- Critically discuss the following statements. Your answer should be about 1,500 words long.
  - Hotels and restaurants should carry environmental labels with data on carbon emissions and other impacts.
  - A certified hotel should provide information about the carbon footprint for an overnight stay to its guests.
  - A certified hotel should have water and energy meters installed in the rooms metering consumption from a hotel guest and the room rate should reflect consumption level.

4 GROUP DISCUSSION OR WRITTEN ASSIGNMENT

- Select an article related to a hotel property that discusses their commitment to sustainability and their recent acquisition of an eco-label.
- Critically review the article and then consider this question (from the customer point of view): Would you rely on this eco-label to make your purchase decisions?

Appendix: Green Globe sustainable management audit

A. Sustainable management

A.1 Implement a sustainability management system

Criteria: The business has implemented a long-term sustainability management system that is suitable to its reality and scale, and that considers environmental, socio-cultural, quality, health, and safety issues.

The first step toward embracing sustainable business practices entails creating a sustainability management system (SMS) that includes transparent, documented policies and procedures, implementation and communication plans. A well-written sustainability policy will define and clearly communicate organizational goals and objectives as they relate to the business, environmental, socio-cultural, and economic performance. The primary purpose of the sustainability management plan is to guide decision-making, management, and the daily operations of the business in a sustainable manner.

A.2 Legal compliance

Criteria: The business is in compliance with all relevant international or local legislation and regulations (including, among others, health, safety, labor, and environmental aspects).

International and local legislation and regulation address many of the social and environmental negative practices associated with tourism operations. These include major labor conventions of the International Labor Organization (ILO) covering freedom of association, no child labor, no forced or bonded labor, no discrimination, health and safety, work hours and minimum pay. This criteria is not an alternative to government regulation and national labor legislation, rather it is a complementary instrument that fills voids in the application, adherence and enforcement of critical social and environmental protections.

A.3 Employee training

Criteria: All personnel receive periodic training regarding their role in the management of environmental, socio-cultural, health, and safety practices.

The success of the business's sustainability management system depends on the effective integration and internalization of the system by employees at all levels. A defined training program for all employees on the SMS aspects will enable employees to understand the business' goals and objectives, why they are important, and how they can positively contribute to the business's efforts in each of their individual roles.

A.4 Customer satisfaction

Criteria: Customer satisfaction is measured and corrective action taken where appropriate.

The customer is the central focus of the tourism experience. Their satisfaction should be eagerly sought in order to foment continued travel to a destination through return visits and word of mouth communication. Additionally, the customer provides a unique vantage point on the business's operations that the management and business employees may not be able to provide. The business tools used to monitor customers' satisfaction with internal operations, relations with the community and other stakeholders, and the effectiveness of sustainable programs enable the business to make improvements on a regular basis.

A.5 Accuracy of promotional materials

Criteria: Promotional materials are accurate and complete and do not promise more than can be delivered by the business.

Ethics in marketing dictate that all promotional tools should provide an honest representation of what services the business provides. In addition, they reflect the responsible and sustainable strategies that the business undertakes. Accurate information improves customer satisfaction by ensuring that expectations can be met.

A.6 Local zoning, design and construction

A.6.1 Design and construction – compliance with legal requirements

Criteria: Comply with local land acquisition and land rights legislation and local zoning and protected or heritage area requirements.

Land used for buildings and operations should be acquired respecting traditional rights and local legislation. Local zoning defines how activities can be carried out in a community reflecting the community's social, economic, and environmental needs, balanced with long-term sustainability. Alteration of protected and designated heritage sites is regulated through local zoning and legal requirements (local, national, and international conventions). Tourism operations must consider these zoning and area requirements to optimize community development plans, while minimizing impact.

A.6.2 & 3 Sustainable design and construction of buildings and infrastructure – new and existing buildings

Criteria: Use locally appropriate principles of sustainable construction and design while respecting the natural and cultural surroundings.

Local environmentally and economically sound design and development techniques should be integrated into the design and construction phase of the tourism operation to minimize natural resource impacts as well as consideration of the potential socio-cultural and economic benefits. This includes:

- locally appropriate tools and materials that minimize environmental impact;
- locally appropriate technologies that are used in buildings and for construction, including indigenous materials and technologies;
- development of local capacity – education, knowledge and experience – to use the materials, technologies, tools for sustainable construction;
- local involvement of all concerned stakeholders in the process of adoption and implementation of sustainable construction principles.

Enhancing the aesthetic, cultural, historic, and natural assets of a destination as well as ensuring that built structures and operations do not negatively impact adjoining areas and people is also an important factor in sustainable design. Businesses must also ensure universal access to their facilities and services to people with special needs.

A.7 Interpretation

Criteria: Information about and interpretation of the natural surroundings, local culture, and cultural heritage is provided to customers, as well as explaining appropriate behavior while visiting natural areas, living cultures, and cultural heritage sites.

Interpretation of the natural and cultural environment is not only important for educating visitors and protecting heritage, but a key factor for a high quality tourist experience marked by a high level of satisfaction (criterion A.4 addresses the need to measure it). Providing information to the customer to inform them about the surroundings is a key factor for tourism businesses.

A.8 Communications strategy

Criteria: The business has to implement a comprehensive communications strategy to inform visitors and guests on its sustainable policies, programs and initiatives.

A well-written Communications Strategy will clearly communicate organizational goals and objectives as they relate to the business' environmental, socio-cultural, and economic performance. It is important that all stakeholders including management, employees, customers and the local community understand the business's goals and objectives, why they are important, and how they can positively contribute to the business's efforts in each of their individual roles.

A.9 Health and safety

Criteria: The business complies with all relevant health and safety measures to ensure the well-being of its customers, staff, and local community.

International and local legislation and regulation address many of the health and safety obligations associated with tourism operations. This criteria is not an alternative to government regulation and national health and safety legislation, rather it is a complementary instrument that fills voids in the application, adherence and enforcement of critical health and safety protections. The health and well-being of all stakeholders is a prime responsibility of all tourism businesses.

B. Social/economic

B.1 Community development

Criteria: The business actively supports initiatives for social and infrastructure community development including, among others, education, health, and sanitation.

Linkages to the local community should exceed employment and economic growth through the development of the business. Opportunities should be undertaken on a regular basis to provide resources, education, training, financial assistance, or in-kind support for initiatives in accordance with community priorities to improve the local livelihoods, thereby engendering community support for operations and creating a better customer experience.

B.2 Local employment

Criteria: Local residents are employed, including in management positions. Necessary training is offered.

Local hiring and training are the key to maximizing community economic benefit and fostering community involvement and integration for the business. In addition, the tourism operation establishes a long-term stable labor relationship while enhancing the local authentic character of the tourism service and product. Providing jobs at all levels of management ensures that the local population does not feel disenfranchised and can provide a sufficient dialogue between the business' ownership and the community. The business should support programs – internal or external – that will allow employees to develop beneficial skills for upward mobility.

B.3 Fair trade

Criteria: Local and fair-trade services and goods are purchased by the business, where available.

Using goods and services produced locally or with 'fair-trade' principles has numerous social, economic and environmental benefits:

* Supports local businesses and provides jobs.
* Higher percentage of the price paid is transferred directly to the provider of the goods and services which is then re-circulated several times in the community.

- Reduced ecological **footprint** due to fewer greenhouse gases being burned in the transportation of the goods.
- Fair prices and wages are received by the producers.
- The visitor experience is enhanced.
- Local goods and services can substantially lower costs with fewer middlemen and transportation costs.

B.4 Support local entrepreneurs

Criteria: The business offers the means for local small entrepreneurs to develop and sell sustainable products that are based on the area's nature, history, and culture (including food and drink, crafts, performance arts, agricultural products, etc.).

Programs that expose customers to the local culture and encourage the purchase of local crafts, goods and services help increase positive economic benefits to the community while engendering a sense of pride in cultural heritage. Working with local small entrepreneurs can help diversify the product, thus increasing spending and length of stay. In some cases this can include designating a specific area on the premises for use by local entrepreneurs or promoting local cultural activities that are open to the public.

B.5 Respect local communities

Criteria: A code of conduct for activities in local communities has to be developed, with the consent of and in collaboration with the community.

Respecting and preserving the traditions and property of local populations is an important aspect in terms of today's globalization. Codes of conduct for tourism activities that are developed in concert with local communities, respecting the principle of prior informed consent and the right of communities to say 'no' to tourism activities is key to the long-term viability and sustainability of the community and its environment. Tourism businesses should develop a plan to maintain regular and open communication with community officials to create a cooperative agreement that allows for tourist interaction with local people in those communities.

B.6 Exploitation

Criteria: The business has to implement a policy against commercial exploitation, particularly of children and adolescents, including sexual exploitation.

Children, adolescents, women, and minorities are particularly vulnerable to abusive labor practices, including sexual exploitation. Weak law enforcement, corruption, the Internet, ease of travel, and poverty have created an underground industry which creates devastating immediate and long-term community impacts in terms of disease, pregnancies, trauma, ostracism and even death. Many codes and international initiatives within the tourism industry have appeared in recent years as a result of this growing threat. Tourism businesses can play a key role in ensuring the protection of local populations at the destination by not buying products produced with child labor; not allowing use of tourism premises for sexual exploitation of minors and denouncing these practices to local authorities.

B.7 Equitable hiring

Criteria: The business is equitable in hiring women and local minorities, including in management positions, while restraining child labor.

While major international labor conventions and norms address discrimination and child labor, women and local minorities often have unequal access to job opportunities, particularly in management, and child labor is still pervasive in many areas. Equality in hiring policies encourages an equitable distribution of wealth and closes income gaps along gender and ethnic lines. Adherence to international guidelines concerning the employment of children ensures their education, enabling them to be future productive members of their community and enhances their quality of life.

B.8 Employee protection

Criteria: The international or national legal protection of employees is respected and employees are paid a living wage.

Treating workers humanely and fairly makes good business sense by establishing stable labor relationships. International and national regulations and conventions (including ILO) establish the minimum baseline for respecting worker's rights. Wages that allow employees to afford – at minimum – provision of basic needs such as food, health care, shelter and education are critical for alleviating poverty and improving the quality of life in the local population as well as increasing productivity and employee retention.

B.9 Basic services

Criteria: The activities of the business must not jeopardize the provision of basic services, such as water, energy, or sanitation, to neighboring communities.

Tourism businesses can alter, disrupt or strain community infrastructure and basic services, adversely impacting local users and communities. In some cases, service providers, such as utility suppliers may favor businesses over local populations. Regular communication with local communities is required to ensure that normal business operations enhance the socio-economic and environmental character of the destination and do not reduce services available to the community or increase their cost.

C. Cultural heritage

C.1 Code of behavior

Criteria: The business follows established guidelines or a code of behavior for visits to culturally or historically sensitive sites, in order to minimize visitor impact and maximize enjoyment.

Respect for local cultures and historic locations must be observed. Businesses must also understand and actively seek to minimize the impact on built and natural environments caused by increased visitor activity. Education about local people's cultural customs, mores, and beliefs as well as appropriate verbal and non-verbal behavior will contribute to overall appreciation of the site and local community pride.

C.2 Historical artifacts

Criteria: Historical and archeological artifacts are not sold, traded, or displayed, except as permitted by law.

Sustainable tourism aims to protect and embrace the uniqueness of a destination. Norms, regulations and conventions exist to protect historical and archeological artifacts from international trade exploitation. With lax enforcement and interested markets, tourism businesses are critical in protecting artifacts while promoting the area's heritage.

C.3 Protection of sites

Criteria: The business contributes to the protection of local historical, archeological, cultural, and spiritually important properties and sites, and does not impede access to them by local residents.

Cultural and historical heritage are important components of a destination's attractiveness and should be conserved to ensure their enjoyment for future generations. Collaboration with local residents and preservation bodies ensures that tourism-related activities do not damage sites or prevent local people from visiting or using them. Preservation and enhancement of local cultural and historical assets increase the tourism experience and make the product offering stronger.

C.4 Incorporation of culture

Criteria: The business uses elements of local art, architecture, or cultural heritage in its operations, design, decoration, food, or shops; while respecting the intellectual property rights of local communities.

Utilizing aspects of local culture wherever possible increases ties to the neighboring community and promoting the destination's unique character provides an incentive to preserve unique skills that may otherwise vanish. The communication between community leaders and companies is the key point to ensuring a respectful use of local culture (e.g. sacred elements) and avoiding possible wrong interpretations, conflicts, and undesirable commoditization.

D. Environmental

D.1 Conserving resources

D.1.1 Purchasing policy

Criteria: Purchasing policy favors environmentally friendly products for building materials, capital goods, food, and consumables.

The economic leverage of purchasing by a tourism business can produce positive impacts by encouraging sustainably produced goods and services. Responsible purchasing is a powerful means to reduce negative environmental impact. This can be done by favoring certified environmentally friendly products and/or regularly evaluating providers that seek to conserve energy, utilize recycled materials, responsibly manage waste, and minimize greenhouse gas emissions.

D.1.2 Consumable goods

Criteria: The purchase of disposable and consumable goods is measured, and the business actively seeks ways to reduce their use.

Responsible consumption and frequent monitoring of waste can help businesses achieve cost savings as well as minimize environmental impact of the waste streams production.

D.1.3 Energy consumption

Criteria: Energy consumption should be measured, sources indicated, and measures to decrease overall consumption should be adopted, while encouraging the use of renewable energy.

Energy use is one of the most damaging activities on the planet with adverse impacts degrading air, water, soil quality, human and ecological health. Energy efficiency through sustainable technology and effective waste management is a key to reducing negative impacts. The greatest environmental and financial benefits related to business operations are achieved by frequently monitoring utility bills, effectively training and providing incentives for staff to implement energy-efficiency programs, and routine preventive maintenance of mechanical equipment. By applying energy-efficient practices to the operations and investing in renewable energy technologies (e.g., solar, wind, micro-hydro, and bio-mass), the business can help conserve natural resources, promote energy independence, and reduce greenhouse gas emissions.

D.1.4 Water consumption

Criteria: Water consumption should be measured, sources indicated, and measures to decrease overall consumption should be adopted.

Water is precious and, in many regions, an increasingly scarce resource with many countries facing moderate or severe water shortages. Year-round or seasonal water shortages are expected to increase with climate change. Overall water consumption should be reduced to the minimum possible level necessary for adequate operation. Reducing water consumption also has financial and environmental benefits for tourism businesses.

D.2 Reducing pollution

D.2.1 Greenhouse gas

Criteria: Greenhouse gas emissions from all sources emitted by the business are measured, and procedures are implemented to reduce and offset them as a way to minimize climate change.

The principal emissions from tourism businesses are from transportation (especially by air), heating, cooling, electricity use, and methane emissions from sewage and organic wastes. Except for air transport, most of these emissions can be directly reduced by actions from the business. Those emissions that are not reduced can be offset using properly regulated projects. Proper emission management practices will help reduce global warming, promote energy independence from foreign non-renewable sources, and may substantially reduce operational costs.

D.2.2 Wastewater

Criteria: Wastewater, including grey water, is treated effectively and reused where possible.

Wastewater management reduces aquatic pollution, protects aquatic ecosystems, and reduces risks to human health. Re-using wastewater increases the availability of drinking water for human consumption (see criterion D.1.4) as well as reducing a business's sewage and treatment costs.

D.2.3 Waste management plan

Waste has become a major pollutant affecting both environmental aspects (land degradation, water quality) and socio-economic factors such as health and public dumps. Reducing potential waste streams, re-using what cannot be avoided and recycling what is not re-usable is critical factor in sustainable tourism operations. Minimizing the amount of solid waste that goes to landfills and incinerators helps reduce negative environmental impacts. Additionally, minimizing waste reduces the need for virgin materials and limits the amount of greenhouse gases that are released throughout a product's lifecycle (i.e., extraction, manufacturing, distribution, use, and disposal). A lifecycle approach to waste management begins with the purchasing practices (D.1.1 and D.1.2) through coordination with local authorities for appropriate disposal.

D.2.3.1 Plan and reduce

Criteria: A solid waste management plan is implemented, with quantitative goals to minimize waste that is not reused or recycled.

D.2.3.2 Reuse

Criteria: A comprehensive strategy of reuse exists to reduce waste to landfill.

D.2.3.3 Recycle

Criteria: A comprehensive recycling strategy exists to reduce waste to landfill.

D.2.4 Harmful substances

Criteria: The use of harmful substances, including pesticides, paints, swimming pool disinfectants, and cleaning materials, is minimized; substituted, when available, by innocuous products; and all chemical use is properly managed.

Chemicals and other non-organic materials slip into the environment during application and storage via evaporation, run-off, spills, leaks and over-application. Such practices lead to air, soil and water pollution, adversely affecting the local environment, harming flora and fauna, contaminating water supplies for local communities and causing serious health problems. The misuse and improper handling of potentially toxic substances create additional threats to the environment and human health. Many 'natural' substitutes exist which not only have less impact on the environment and human health, but are often cheaper. Technology has also developed various alternatives. Where no alternatives are possible, the proper storage, handling and use of chemicals will reduce potential impacts.

D.2.5 Other pollutants

Criteria: The business implements practices to reduce pollution from noise, light, runoff, erosion, ozone-depleting compounds, and air and soil contaminants.

Environmental pollution can occur from several sources and have long-term, damaging effects on local ecosystems and human populations. The business should regularly perform site audits to identify sources for potential pollution while educating and empowering staff to identify potential pollution during daily activities. Particular attention should be paid to special local conditions, such as damage to coral reefs from sediments, eutrophication of rivers and lakes from runoff, melting of permafrost, and light pollution of marine nesting sites, among others.

D.3 Conserving biodiversity, ecosystems, and landscapes

D.3.1 Wildlife species

Criteria: Wildlife species are only harvested from the wild, consumed, displayed, sold, or internationally traded, as part of a regulated activity that ensures that their utilization is sustainable.

Tourism businesses sometimes use precious woods, palm thatch, or coral for buildings, furniture, or exhibitions. Shops often sell items harvested from the wild, such as black coral or carey (from endangered sea turtles). Restaurants may serve food harvested from the wild. These and other uses may be sustainable or not. Non-sustainable consumption should be avoided and other uses should be in accordance with local regulations and conservation practices.

D.3.2 Wildlife in captivity

Criteria: No captive wildlife is held, except for properly regulated activities, and living specimens of protected wildlife species are only kept by those authorized and suitably equipped to house and care for them.

In general, tourism businesses should not maintain wildlife in captivity – for example as pets or in cages – unless these activities enhance conservation. In that case, the activity should be in accordance with local regulations and international conservation.

D.3.3 Landscaping

Criteria: The business uses native species for landscaping and restoration, and takes measures to avoid the introduction of invasive alien species.

Native flora is adapted to local conditions (drought, temperatures, etc.) and local pests, reducing the need for irrigation (reducing water use D.1.4) and chemicals (criterion D.2.4). The character of the natural environment can be preserved by utilizing sustainable landscaping techniques that incorporate local flora. Non-local species that are used should be screened to avoid introducing potentially invasive plants and animals, which have negative impacts on the biodiversity and local ecosystems.

D.3.4 Biodiversity conservation

Criteria: The business contributes to the support of biodiversity conservation, including supporting natural protected areas and areas of high biodiversity value.

Tourism activities outside of urban areas generally depend, directly or indirectly, on natural resources. Even those in urban areas can benefit their society by indirect support of their country's natural areas or urban parks. Contribution can range from active participation in projects to financial contributions.

D.3.5 Interactions with wildlife

Criteria: Interactions with wildlife must not produce adverse effects on the viability of populations in the wild; and any disturbance of natural ecosystems is minimized, rehabilitated, and there is a compensatory contribution to conservation management.

Tourism activities outside of urban areas frequently affect plants and animals in the wild. These activities can be passive, such as building construction or trail use, or active, such as hunting and fishing. In all cases, the disturbance created should be minimized. In addition, compensatory conservation activities should be supported.

Resources

Building Research Establishment Environmental Assessment Method (BREEAM): *What is BREEAM?* Available at: http://www.breeam.org/page.jsp?id=66.

Ecolabel Index: http://www.ecolabelindex.com/.

ECOTRANS: *The VISIT Initiative: Tourism eco-labelling in Europe – moving the market towards sustainability*. Available at: http://www.ecotrans.org/visit/docs/pdf/visit_en.pdf.

Green Globe: *Green Globe Certification Standard*. Available at: http://greenglobe.com/register/green-globe-certification-standard/.

Green Key Eco-Rating Program: *About The Green Key Eco-Rating Program.* Available at: http://www.greenkeyglobal.com/about_the_program.asp.

The Green Key: *Criteria Hotels*. Available at: http://www.green-key.org/Menu/Criteria/Hotels.

United States Green Building Council: *What LEED Is.* Available at: http://www.usgbc.org/DisplayPage.aspx?CMSPageID=1988.

Additional material

Go to www.routledge.com/cw/sloan to find PowerPoint slides of all the figures and tables from the book, additional case studies, a test bank of questions and extra links to useful videos.

CHAPTER **15**

Financing, investing, measuring and accounting in sustainable hospitality

CHAPTER OBJECTIVES

The objectives for this chapter are:

- To understand the barriers and motivators pertaining to implementation of sustainability strategies
- To review the concepts of green financing and green investment schemes available to hoteliers
- To review the concept of green accounting
- To understand the meaning of externalities
- To identify ways of measuring and accounting for externalities
- To identify and discuss environmental performance indicators (EPI)
- To define and analyse the concept of sustainability performance indicators (SPI)
- To review the basic calculation of return on investment (ROI) of environmental measures
- To establish and discuss a sustainability performance framework
- To discuss auditing and environmental auditing
- To appreciate the value of self-auditing
- To introduce cutting-edge online environmental self-auditing tools
- To discuss the importance of eco-innovation

Investing in sustainable hospitality

Barriers and motivators

The top five barriers are:

1. perceived high capital costs
2. doubts of return on investment
3. lack of time
4. requires too much management
5. limited interest/knowledge.

Traditional barriers for hoteliers to invest in **sustainability** matters are perceived to be high capital costs, reservations concerning improved profitability resulting from the implementation of **environmental management systems** and a general lack of knowledge of environmental issues. Indeed, business executives believe that they must decide between **social** and environmental benefits to sustainability and the costs of implementing such schemes. Few hotel owners and managers recognise the financial benefits associated with the implementation of environmental initiatives. The notion that sustainability is expensive is deeply anchored in society and has become a widespread fallacy. Despite the common belief that high investment is required for the creation of **sustainable** buildings and facilities, it has been proven that by employing an integrated, holistic building design strategy early in the planning process, sustainability of the structure is maximized without a considerable increase in costs. Furthermore, a net reduction in the initial cost of a sustainable building can be achieved, while in cases where the capital cost is higher, the investment typically pays off during the first few years of operation. In addition, lower operating costs lead to savings throughout the building's **life cycle**. Moreover, certain sustainable features can be incorporated into the design at minimal or even zero up-front costs, and consequently lead to significant savings.

Apart from the financial aspect, the time invested as well as the management required to implement a sustainability strategy also greatly contributes to the resistance felt by hoteliers. Finally, the lack of interest and knowledge in the topic of sustainability coupled with the missing business relevance are further barriers.

On the other hand, the top five motivators are:

1. potential cost savings
2. increased market share and image improvement
3. acquiring competitive advantage
4. intrinsic motivation ('doing something good')
5. enhanced employee morale.

While the general perception that financial constraints resulting from investing in sustainability is one of the greatest barriers, the possible long-term cost savings as well as the incentives offered to companies investing in green technologies are perceived as strong motivators. Hoteliers seem to be in a typical causality dilemma, whereby money must be invested in order to save money. The increased energy costs for hoteliers over the past decade may explain the increased importance of the 'energy-efficiency' factor as a motivator for investment.

Companies also embrace sustainability trying to make use of a potential image improvement. With increased public scrutiny, it does not come as a surprise that positive activities are rewarded with peer and consumer recognition. A hotel implementing sustainability can also benefit from an improved competitive position when entering a market niche of environmentally friendly products and services. The corporate decision to move towards sustainable or responsible management may equally be fostered by ethical motives or institutional pressures or simply by a 'feel-good factor'. Since overall positive work satisfaction and enhanced employee moral were short-term benefits encountered in companies implementing a sustainability strategy, those components are also considered to be motivators.

Financing and investment schemes

Financing schemes have been created specifically for the promotion of more environment-friendly, sustainable building practices. The sustainable financing instruments available include green financing and green investment schemes initiated by governments to attract funding at reduced interest rates.

Green financing

Green financing initiatives encompass all investing or lending programmes focusing on mitigating **environmental impacts** or ensuring the inclusion of environmental impacts into the risk assessment. Green financing takes place in both consumer markets and producer markets.

In the consumer market, the efforts of a lending company providing other businesses with quick and easy financing solutions and various incentives to reduce emissions via **retrofitting** in the existing hotel property to achieve optimum energy efficiency and cost savings would be an example of green financing.

In the producer market, green financing is used by banking or governmental institutions either to discriminate in investing or lending practices in favour of sustainable ventures or against environmentally damaging projects.

Banks operating green financing schemes can offer loans designated for projects that respect the principles of **sustainable development**, or those facilities that wish to install environment-friendly systems (improving energy-efficiency or incorporation of **renewable energy**, for example).

Most industrialized countries have developed special financing schemes to encourage the development of structures compatible with the local natural **environment**, as well as the socio-cultural context, not only in their own countries, but also in developing countries and countries with economies in transition.

Funding for specific end-of-pipe measures to reduce water **pollution** and airborne pollution and cut the use of non-renewable energy resources is widely available. Legislation to curb pollution has increased in recent years and companies are obliged to modify their activities. However, legislation compelling individuals and companies to use alternative energy resources are few and far between. Some countries in Europe have introduced eco-taxes to penalize heavy users of fossil fuels.

Many **subsidies** exist in Germany and France to encourage companies to use alternative forms of energy. In Germany, these grants and tax reductions come mainly from regional governments and in France from the *Agence de l'Environnement et de la Maîtrise de l'Energie* (Environment Agency for Energy Management or ADEME). Countries throughout the European Union can also benefit from the LIFE programme for financing. LIFE is an EU financial instrument supporting environmental and nature **conservation** projects. Since 1992, LIFE has co-financed thousands of projects geared towards the protection of the environment. The Competitiveness and Innovation Framework Programme (CIP) of the EU is particularly of interest to the **hospitality industry**. The CIP aims to encourage the competitiveness of European enterprises. With small and medium-sized enterprises (**SMEs**) as its main target, the programme supports innovation activities (including eco-innovation), provides better access to finance and delivers business support services. The programme's particular objective is to promote the increased use of renewable energies and energy efficiency. Pilot eco-innovation projects may be eligible for funding under the Entrepreneurship and Innovation Programme (EIP), a sub-programme of the CIP. The EIP sub-programme ensures better access to finance for SMEs through venture capital investment and loan guarantee instruments. It also supports the promotion of entrepreneurship and innovation in the world of eco-innovation. The funding priorities are buildings, food and drinks, greening businesses and smart purchasing.

It is recommended that hoteliers inform themselves about the current financing opportunities available to them within the local, regional or national boundaries. A good place to start searching for information is usually the hoteliers' national trade association.

CASE STUDY 15.1 KFW offer new sustainability financing in Germany

The German KfW (Kreditanstalt für Wiederaufbau) banking group is providing a new financing vehicle for renewable energies, energy efficiency and innovations for Germany's energy turnaround across the private and public sectors.

The expanded range of energy and environmental financing, 'KfW Energy Turnaround Action Plan' for enterprises starts on 1 January 2012 and will be broad-based financing for enterprises, municipalities and even individuals.

The 'Plan' has numerous financing offers in order to accelerate the transformation of the German energy supply system. Already, investments have been provided for energy-efficient construction and in support of renewable energies such as offshore wind farms, as well as large investments by municipalities in the area of energy efficiency.

KfW will be offering another important component. It will considerably expand the range of products for enterprises to improve operational energy efficiency, utilize renewable energies and finance innovation projects for (further) development of technologies to save energy, for efficient energy generation, energy storage and transmission.

According to the website:

> The energy turnaround is an immense challenge for the entire society which we are tackling, also to take responsibility for coming generations. With the 'Energy Turnaround Action Plan', KfW is providing important building blocks to meet the enormous financing needs to transform the energy supply system in Germany.

The promotion of energy-efficiency measures in enterprises will be combined in the new KfW Energy Efficiency Programme. In individual cases, large enterprises with a turnover of up to €3 billion can also receive support.

In the framework of the Renewable Energies programme (standard), the maximum loan amount will increase to €25 million. In this way, renewable energy, such as onshore wind farms, can be even better supported.

Larger innovation projects for energy savings, production, storage and transmission can be promoted by the ERP Innovation Programme in the future with loans and subordinated capital of up to €25 million.

In the framework of a pilot model, KfW is starting the 'KfW Energy Turnaround Financing Initiative' which particularly targets large enterprises. Upon the request of banks, KfW provides direct loans in the framework of syndicated financings. Financings are provided for larger projects of enterprises to increase operational energy efficiency, innovation projects (research and development expenditures) in the areas of energy savings, production, storage and transmission, as well as investments for utilizing renewable energies.

General corporate environmental protection measures can also be financed from the new KfW Environmental Protection Programme. This applies to enterprises of any size. In the future, this programme will also promote measures of resource efficiency or material saving, for example, the reduction of waste material or the optimization of production processes.

Source: © 2011 The Energy Saving Association.

Green investment

In its traditional meaning, green investments are investment instruments such as stocks or funds involving the underlying company or businesses in environmental improvement operations. Those businesses could be companies that are developing renewable energy technology or that have an excellent environmental track record.

Of course, the range of companies involved in environmental initiatives represented on the stock market is wide. Investors will be looking both at cutting-edge start-up companies in the field of solar technologies but also at more traditional companies which are expanding their portfolio to attract the environmentally concerned citizen and thus obtain new market shares.

Sustainable funds guidelines

Funds with a focus on responsible or green companies have also been established. There is no strict or universally accepted definition of what typifies a green or sustainable fund. However, green funds can be characterized as mutual funds that invest in socially and environmentally responsible companies.

We can discern five categories of sustainable or green funds (each category is also applicable to tourism companies):

- *Environmental leaders*: companies whose core products are environmentally friendly.
- *Environmental pioneers*: small innovative companies that are developing environmentally and socially friendly products.
- *Ethically minded companies*: companies that have a strong ethical policy.
- *Environmental technology companies*: companies that are involved in sewage and rubbish disposal or wind energy.
- *Sustainable companies*: companies that incorporate the principles of sustainability at all stages of the business cycle.

Many banks offer sustainable investment funds to investors, and 'green' bonds to private individuals who want to save money in an environmentally friendly manner. Unfortunately, some of the banks offering green funds can give hardly any information why these funds are called 'green' and on which sustainability principle they rely. The consumers may often have to study information further before understanding the underlying purpose of funding and the relevant qualifications attached to the application.

CASE STUDY 15.2 Sustainable investment scheme

Jupiter Investment Management Group Limited is among the institutions offering green financing to companies all over the world. Jupiter has been managing environmental solutions funds for over 20 years and launched one of the first authorized socially responsible unit trusts in the UK in 1988, the Jupiter Ecology Fund. Since then, the company has developed a leading knowledge of environmental investing across a range of products with three distinct funding schemes:

Jupiter Ecology Fund

The objective of the Jupiter Ecology Fund is to achieve long-term capital appreciation together with a growing income consistent with a policy of protecting the environment. The Fund's investment policy is to invest worldwide in companies which demonstrate a positive commitment to the long-term protection of the environment.

Jupiter Green Investment Trust

The investment objective of the Jupiter Green Investment Trust PLC is to generate long-term capital growth through investing in a diverse portfolio of companies providing environmental solutions.

The Jupiter Green Investment Trust PLC's portfolio is biased towards small and medium-sized companies. Investments are made predominantly in stocks which are quoted, listed or traded on a recognised investment exchange.

Jupiter Responsible Income Fund

The Jupiter Responsible Income Fund has a predominantly UK bias with fewer ethical restrictions than The Jupiter Ecology Fund. The Fund focuses on investing in UK companies that are actively managing their environmental and social impact: good governance companies. The Fund will specifically avoid investing in companies associated with armaments, tobacco and nuclear power.

The Fund's objective is to provide income and long-term capital growth through investing primarily in UK equities.

Source: Jupiter, http://www.jupiteronline.co.uk/.

Green accounting

Better known as *environmental accounting*, this is a technique to measure the cost of the environment stemming from a company's operations. Those costs, once identified, are to be included in the annual company accounts, and communicated to **stakeholders**. The main concept is the internalization of external environmental and social costs.

Externality

An external cost, also known as an externality, arises when the social or economic activities of one company has an impact on another company or group of people whereby that impact is not fully accounted, or eventually compensated for. The hospitality industry produces negative socio-environmental **externalities** in the areas of (1) water; (2) energy; (3) **waste management**; (4) air pollution; as well as (5) socio-cultural environment.

- Water externalities:
  - water wastage from improper usage
  - production of grey and black water necessitating treatment
  - decrease in water quality
  - quantity of water used
  - effects on **flora** and **fauna**.

- Energy externalities:
  - production of **greenhouse gases** from non-renewable energy sources
  - increased need for energy for operations leading to more demand and increased pressure on energy sources
  - use of fossil fuel-based energy sources causes respiratory and other health problems
  - effects on flora and fauna.

- Waste externalities:
  - solid waste accumulates in landfill, increasing soil and water pollution
  - liquid waste increases waterborne illness
  - liquid waste negatively influences aquatic habitat
  - overall effects on **ecosystem**, flora and fauna.

- Air pollution externalities:
  - transport to and from a hotel produces emissions increasing the **greenhouse effect**
  - burning of fossil fuel negatively **impacts** air quality
  - effects on health issues and fauna and flora.

- Socio-cultural externalities:
  - increased construction of hotels at a destination changes the land tenure and ownership with less opportunities for local residents
  - concentration of tourism infrastructures, including hotels, creates overcrowding of public spaces and road congestion
  - tourism is reported to have introduced increased alcoholism, prostitution and drug abuse among local residents with direct link to crime rate and health concerns
  - hospitality and tourism encourage the development of pseudo-art forms and commercialize traditional ceremonies catering to **tourists** and guests, devaluing the traditional practices and cultures of the destinations.

In many cases, hotels are based in pristine destinations and the quality of a natural resource is taken free of charge by the owners, investors and managers of hospitality operations. As long as the externalities are kept to a minimum, businesses and the destination in general benefit from this free-of-charge resource. However, a drastic increased visitation rate at a destination usually equates to a diminution of the destination quality. As the quality of the destination – in other words, the natural resources – decreases, the value of each additional visit can be affected negatively by increased pressure on those natural resources, such as water and energy, along with an increase in air pollution and waste generation. In this example, the environmental and social costs are *external* because, although they are real costs to all members of a society (or in this case all residents at the destination), the owners of tourism and hospitality businesses are not taking these externalities into account either in terms of financial constraints or when making decisions about future development of their businesses. In other words, the environmental and socio-cultural impact is an externality of the hospitality products and services if not accounted for in the price of those products or services.

Measuring and accounting for externalities

There are several ways to measure environmental costs and try to reduce them. Depending on whether one seeks to incorporate environmental costs according to activities or processes or to simply record all costs, whether internal or external to the hotel, and to consider the life cycle of the products and services produced, the practices vary, usually at the discretion of the business owners and accountants and are far from being standardized.

In practice, accounting for externalities requires a set of market interventions by governmental authorities via some combination of regulations and **environmental taxes**. In hospitality and tourism, the situation is even more complicated since many stakeholders do benefit from the tourism activities. Thus, the question often asked is: if many players do benefit from the activities of tourism and hospitality, who should then pay for the environmental and socio-cultural impacts?

Tourists and guests are the users of products and services and thus producers of waste and users of resources. It is argued that the price paid for their stay should reflect the environmental impacts incurred by the consumption of those products and services they consume. This is clearly not the case in the hospitality industry since very few, if any, of the products and services offered on the market have undertaken a detailed **life cycle assessment**. The hoteliers, being the product and service producers, have a responsibility, since the very base of their business model rests upon responsible environmental management and should therefore contribute to the externalities created by their businesses. Many other businesses (suppliers and distributors) clearly benefit from the hospitality and tourism industry and should carry an equal accountability for the externalities. Finally, government authorities have an equal responsibility towards communities regarding public health issues and other environmental compliances within national and international agreements and are equally responsible for the externalities. The tourism industry as a whole clearly creates a set of indirect benefits in terms of business creation.

Three concepts linked to internalizing externalities are presented here:

- **Polluter pays principle (PPP)** – *user pays*: PPP implies that the party responsible for producing pollution or causing environmental damage should bear the costs of avoiding the damage or of compensating for it. Governments have used the PPP to establish various forms of eco-tax. For example, in order to mitigate the environmental impacts created by the tourism industry and with limited public finances available, some regional authorities have established eco-taxes on overnight stays. The users of overnight stays, guests, act as the taxpayer and the hoteliers assume the tax collection role.
- **Extended producer responsibility (EPR)**: similar to PPP where users pay, EPR seeks to shift the responsibility of externalities from governments to the businesses (suppliers, manufacturers and distributors) producing externalities. This requires businesses to complete a life cycle assessment, from the selection of raw materials to the final disposal of the product, of all environmental impacts. In theory, under the PPP, the externalities should then be included in the cost of the products and services. In theory again, since businesses operate in competitive environments where price often plays a determining role in market share, and in order to stay competitive, the internalization of externalities should act as a push factor for businesses to improve all aspects related to the sustainability profile of products and services. For example, waste should be decreased, reuse and **recycling** possibilities increased, thus enhancing costs savings in the life cycle analysis and helping the business to remain competitive from a price point of view.
- **Carbon credits** – *internalizing the cost of air pollution*: the basic concept behind carbon credits is valuing the cost of greenhouse gas emissions and creating a market in the form of carbon credits to reduce those emissions. In practice, the greenhouse gas emissions become an internal cost of doing business. The cost is presented on the company's balance sheet alongside materials and other

liabilities or **assets**. Purchasing carbon credits allows a business to offset the excess emissions or to buy its way towards zero-emission, without necessarily undertaking emission efficiency measures.

While the methods in measuring and accounting externalities differ from one company to another, and rendering any form of comparisons between companies or across the industry is unreliable and not recommended, the need to internalize external costs is well recognised.

One of the most recent green accounting initiatives has been created by the World Bank under the acronym Waves, or Wealth Accounting and Valuation of Ecosystem Services. Waves' basic concept is for companies to apply green accounting principles to their own business strategies. While the project is in its first phase of creating a common methodology for national ecosystem accounting, many countries across the globe have provided support in the development phase of the system. The system is also based on the belief that it is by putting an economic value (hence a price tag) on nature (land, forest, ocean and air), that changes and responsible handling of scarce resources can be achieved. A proper accounting system not only takes externalities into consideration when doing business, thus facilitating the decision-making process in designing new products, services or building new hotels, but also helps companies to assess potential liabilities and reduce operational costs.

The introduction of **environmental performance indicators (EPI)** is yet another proof of the general acceptance of environmental accounting. The scope of environmental accounting is no longer confined to large companies but includes at a growing rate small and medium-sized enterprises (SMEs).

Environmental performance indicators (EPI)

Once all the operational activities that could cause environmental damage are recorded for an individual hotel or a group of hotels, it is necessary to identify which activity poses a significant impact on the natural environment. It is then necessary to regularly monitor the key parameters (e.g. waste output, water usage energy consumption, etc.) in order to monitor the performance of the company. This requires that operational **indicators** and environmental conditions must be established. Within the ISO14000 series of standard, the ISO14031 provides guidance on the design and use of environmental performance evaluation, and on identification and selection of environmental performance indicators. Those environmental metrics provide a clear indication of the performance of an environmental management system, of the activities of production and of the state of the environment with which the company interacts. However, the standard does not establish any level of performance. Different types of indicators are used to measure the performance of the company as shown in Table 15.1.

TABLE 15.1 Examples of environmental performance indicators

Environmental impact	Indicator examples
Waste output	Total annual waste output in tonnes Waste output per employee Waste output per overnight stay Amount of waste produced per quantity of meal produced Percentage of waste recycled
Greenhouse gas emissions	Total annual quantity of specific pollutants (e.g. carbon dioxide, nitrogen dioxide or sulphur dioxide) Carbon dioxide emitted per guest Carbon dioxide emitted per overnight stay
Water usage	Total annual water consumption Water consumption per employee Water consumption per guest Water consumption per overnight stay
Wastewater discharge	Total discharge of wastewater in m^3 Wastewater discharge per overnight stay in m^3
Energy	Hotel total energy performance in kWh per m^2 per year Carbon dioxide emission by energy type
Transport	Total annual fossil fuels consumed for employee commuting and shuttling Proportion of employee travelling alone by car when commuting Employee kilometres on business travels Carbon dioxide emissions per kilometre travelled Guest kilometres on travel to and from a destination
Hazardous waste	Total quantity of hazardous waste generated Hazardous waste produced per overnight stay
Incidents	Total annual number of incidents related to the environment Total annual number of prosecutions

Sustainability performance indicators (SPI)

Since sustainability is built upon three pillars, namely: (1) the environmental; (2) the social; and (3) the economic pillars, measuring the EPIs or the traditional **return on investment (ROI)** can only provide part of the sustainable picture. Each pillar will necessitate its own set of metrics to ensure a clear and measured perspective on sustainability endeavours within a hotel or hotel chain. One of the greatest challenges faced by hoteliers is to reduce the amount of information and data collected into a manageable number of key indicators. Similar to EPI, **SPI** is a tool gathering data and classifying those in three distinct areas covering the economic, environmental (in form of EPIs) and social dimension of sustainability. The **Global Reporting Initiative (GRI)**, presented in Chapter 14, provides a SPI framework and guidance for the reporting on those SPI. A short description of the three groups of SPIs under the GRI is provided here.

The environment pillar

As stated in Chapter 14, an organization's impacts on ecosystems, land, air and water are measured using EPIs. Examples of indicators under the GRI include:

- total direct and indirect greenhouse gas emissions;
- energy consumption by primary source;
- energy saved through conservation and efficiency improvements;
- initiatives to reduce energy consumption;
- total water consumption;
- total water recycled and reused;
- waste output.

The social pillar

An organization's impacts on the social systems within which it operates are measured using social performance indicators. Within the GRI framework, examples of social performance indicators are categorized under labour practices and human rights issues. Examples of specific indicators include:

- incidents of **discrimination** and actions taken;
- total workforce by employment type, employment contract and region;
- employee turnover rates by region and according to indicators of diversity;
- workforce representation in health and safety committees and injury rates;
- employee training, programmes for skills management and lifelong learning;
- percentage of employees receiving regular performance and career development reviews;
- participation in international organizations to improve conditions for people, as well as local community partnerships.

The economic pillar

All areas of a business pertaining to the economic performance as a consequence of the business's activities are measured using economic performance indicators. Examples of indicators include:

- company revenues;
- operating costs;

- company profits;
- employee compensation;
- donations and other community investments;
- retained earnings;
- payments to capital providers and governments;
- proportion of spending on locally-based suppliers.

Evaluating sustainability performance

The **Dow Jones Sustainability Index (DJSI)** evaluates the sustainability performance of the largest companies listed on the Dow Jones Index. A defined set of criteria and weightings is used to assess the opportunities and risks deriving from the economic, environmental and social activities of the eligible companies. Further screening is made of the company and third-party documents as well as personal contacts between the analysts and companies. An external review ensures that the corporate sustainability assessments are completed in accordance with the defined rules. Companies are assessed in equal proportion on the three pillars of sustainability. Within the economic pillar, issues surrounding corporate governance, risk and crisis management and anti-corruption as well as industry-specific criteria are used to monitor companies. Within the environmental pillar, environmental reporting as well as industry-specific environmental criteria are used to assess the performance. Finally, within the social pillar, issues such as human capital development, talent attraction and retention, labour practices, corporate philanthropy, social reporting and industry-specific criteria are used to evaluate the performance.

However, small and medium-sized businesses, a core of the hospitality industry on most continents (particularly in Europe and Asia), are not represented within the DJSI and require other methods of evaluation. Most hoteliers will be interested in calculating a return on investment for the planned sustainability projects to make better and informed decisions.

Return on investment (ROI)

Return on investment (ROI) is a performance measure used to evaluate the efficiency of an investment. To calculate ROI, the benefit – in other words, the return – of an investment is divided by the cost of the investment. The following result is expressed as a percentage or a ratio.

ROI calculation helps to evaluate each alternative investment possibility for each sustainability solution. ROI is a quick and very popular metric because of its versatility and simplicity. In other words, if an investment does not have a positive ROI, or if there are other opportunities with a higher ROI, then the hotelier will simply not undertake the investment.

What is the optimal ROI for a particular project, in one, two, five, ten or more years? The answer to this question greatly depends on the type of investment required, type of hotel, ownership situation (is the building leased or owned?) as well as a series of other local, regional or global factors anchored in the macro-economic situation. However, there are some very broad, very general categories of acceptable ROI periods depending on the type of investment:

- *ROI within a two-year period*: the focus of investments with a ROI period of two years will be on creating a clear diagnostic of the operations and investing in general maintenance while setting parameters regarding sustainability measures. These will usually be in the realm of training, preventive maintenance and retrofitting (e.g. **water management**: training staff on water conservation, inspecting and repairing water pipes' leakages, investing in low-flow water taps.
- *ROI within a five-year period*: these investments include changes such as the renewing of some equipment (compressors, chillers, pumps and motors), changes in lighting technologies and installing motion sensors or ensuring heat recovery using heat exchangers.
- *ROI within a 10- to 15-year period*: in a longer timeframe, the focus of investments will lie on changing equipment to increase energy efficiencies (e.g. HVAC), on installing equipment to include renewable technologies (e.g. photovoltaic panels) and renovating the building interior and envelope (e.g. thermal renovations).

ROI on photovoltaic panels

Photovoltaic panels convert sunlight into electricity using cells made from two layers of silicon. One photovoltaic panel consists of 20 cells generating an average voltage of 12 volts. Therefore, the intensity of electrical energy produced largely depends on the amount of sunshine. Long hours of sunlight equate to more power produced by the panels, this is an optimal situation. However, photovoltaic electricity is highly dependent on weather conditions and the succession of seasons. The size of the initial investment varies depending on the facilities used and energy needs.

There are five steps to consider when calculating the ROI on photovoltaic panels:

1. *Establish the purchasing costs.* These costs include the panels, installation and maintenance.
2. *Calculate the tax credit amount.* National governments across the globe allow businesses to file tax credits on the purchase of renewable energy equipment, but also in energy efficiency measures such as window, wall and roof insulation. Consequently, the total purchasing costs should be reduced by the tax incentives offered in the region.
3. *Estimate the energy produced.* Based on the geographical location and the placement of the panels, an estimation of the energy produced in kilowatt-hour (kWh) per day must be completed. The manufacturer or distributor of the photovoltaic panels can help with the estimation.

4. *Find out current kWh rate*. The most recent bill or receipt from the local electrical power provider is the best source to find out the rate paid per kWh.
5. *Compute the ROI*. With the information above, the ROI can be calculated. Knowing how much is to be paid per kWh and the amount of kWh collected every day helps to estimate the daily savings. Those savings can be extrapolated to a monthly basis. In order to calculate the ROI, the total purchasing costs after tax incentives must be divided by the total savings per month. The amount obtained is then the number of months to amortise the investment.

In some countries, national schemes have been put in place whereby the electricity produced by photovoltaic panels by homeowners and/or businesses can be sold back to the power companies for a higher rate per kWh than purchased from the national electrical grid. If this is the case, the payback or ROI will be greatly shortened. The revenues from electricity sold to the power company are exempt from income tax under some national schemes. Some governments also offer tax incentives and subsidies with the goal of encouraging the use of renewable energy.

CASE STUDY 15.3 Calculating ROI on photovoltaic panels

Following the five steps above, here is a simple calculation. The following figures are based on a northern European scenario but are neither representative of any country in particular, nor transferable.

1. *Establish the purchasing costs*. The cost of panels, installation, maintenance, as well as connection and meter rentals adds up to approximately €1000 per square metre of panel. Six square metres have been installed for a total investment of €6000.
2. *Calculate the tax credit amount*. The government in this case allows business owners a 30 per cent tax incentive on the purchase price; 30 per cent of €6000 comes to a tax credit of €1800, bringing down the investment costs to €4200.
3. *Estimate the energy produced*. The 150-watt photovoltaic panels are expected to produce 1 kWh/m²/day. In this case, the panels will collect 6 kWh of electricity per day.
4. *Find out current kWh rate*. The current rate is €0.20 per kWh.
5. *Compute the ROI*. Since 6 kWh of electricity is collected per day, the daily savings add up to €1.20 or approximately €36 per month. The total cost for the panels (minus tax credits), €4200 is then divided by the total savings per month of €36. The result, approximately 117 months, (or 9 years and 11 months) represent the time to break even on the original investment.
6. *Extra step: selling electricity to power company*. If the electricity produced is then sold back to the power company and regular electricity is purchased at

a lower rate from the national grid, the added savings must be computed. In this case, pretend the power company buys solar-produced electricity for a price three times more expensive than the current electricity price for the next 20 years. As such, the power company purchases solar-produced electricity at €0.60 per kWh and the business buys back electricity from the grid at a rate of €0.20 per kWh. The difference, €0.40 kWh, represents savings. The revenues from electricity sold to the power company are exempt from income tax. The photovoltaic panels produce 6 kWh per day, thus the daily saving from electricity sold to the power company per day adds up to €2.40 per day or €72 per month. The total cost for the panels (minus tax credits), €4200 is then divided by the total savings per month of €72. The result, approximately 58 months, (or 4 years and 10 months) represents the time to break even on the original investment.

Photovoltaic life expectancy

Knowing that the life expectancy of solar panels is anywhere between 25 and 35 years, any electricity produced after the 9 years and 11 months is free of charge. Some photovoltaic panels are still producing electricity some 40 years after installation. However, the common view is that solar panels' production drops to 80 per cent of their rated capacity within about 20 years.

General considerations on ROI

Currently, ROI on photovoltaics is in the 15-year range. However, the term ROI also depends on the amount of incentives, grants and aid as well as tax credit offered. The calculation should consider each situation as being unique.

General consideration on sustainability of solar panels

It is important to note that a solar panel requires a period of 10 to 15 years to produce as much energy as it has required in its manufacturing. It is thus a long-term approach both in economic profitability and in terms of mitigation of environmental impact.

The sustainability performance framework

Beyond the traditional ROI calculation, a framework is needed to evaluate the costs, benefits and return on all activities under the three pillars of sustainability (see Figure 15.1). In other words, while some activities are still difficult to quantify in terms of financial or monetary gains (e.g. reduction of **carbon dioxide** emission or greater **biodiversity** conservation) although progress in that field has been made over the past decade, by measuring the effect of their action, owners and managers of hospitality businesses require a more holistic approach to their operations. Greater awareness of the effects of business decisions on the larger ecosystem, environmental or social, can ensure a shift from the tradition *make-the-most-money-in-the-shortest-time* paradigm towards a long-term approach, which is the very basis of sustainability thinking.

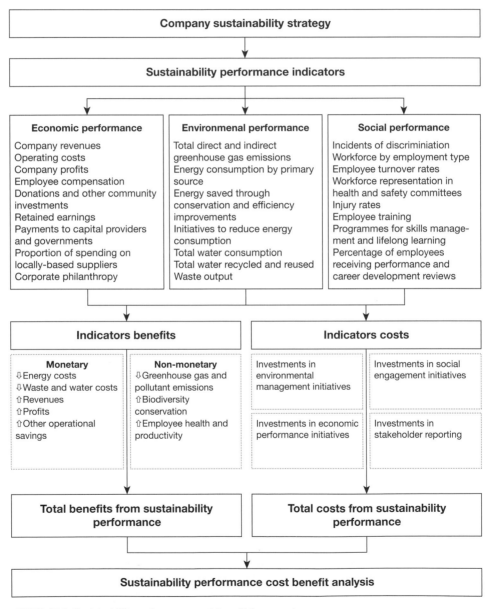

FIGURE 15.1 Sustainability performance cost benefit framework

Auditing

Different types of audits exist. Financial **auditing** is probably the most common form of auditing in business whereby an audit is performed to ascertain the validity and reliability of the information presented. Audits also exist covering non-financial information such as **environmental auditing**, quality auditing and safety or health auditing.

Environmental auditing

Also known as *green audit* or *eco-audit*, the **International Chamber of Commerce (ICC)** defines environmental auditing as:

> A management tool comprising systematic, documented, periodic and objective evaluation of how well environmental organization, management and equipment are performing with the aim of helping to safeguard the environment by: (i) facilitating management control of environmental practices; (ii) assessing compliance with company policies, which would include regulatory requirements.

In other words, an environmental audit is a tool to support the management of environmental practices, goals and the fulfilment of those goals by a company with the overall aim of protecting the environment. Essential to auditing is the unbiased and systematic approach to procedures and documentation. Audits are undertaken by independent and autonomous auditors. The audit process leads the auditors to state whether the environmental performance complies with the environmental policy and goals set by the company.

Benefits of environmental auditing

Environmental audits provide the organization with a clear and independent analysis and understanding of their current environmental efficiency and allow them to evaluate to what extent their set goals have been met. Room for improvement is brought to light and any deviations from the environmental legislation are reported. This information is information upon which a company can act. Furthermore, an audit is an official stamp of approval, recognised by industry peers and consumers, which also acts as a motivating tool for further initiatives towards better environmental performance.

Self-auditing

A self-conducted or self-administered audit is an alternative to the traditional third-party audit whereby information is verified against some audit criteria by the same party producing the information. In other words, the company gathering the data, analysing the data using various indicators and producing the results on which it is to be evaluated, is the same company undertaking the audit. To ensure the minimum level of credibility, the audit of a particular item is undertaken by someone independent to that particular item. Once the **self**-**audit** has been completed, the findings are disclosed and corrective action is undertaken that will lead to a continuous improvement scenario.

Benefits of self-auditing

Self-audits are less costly than the traditional audits performed by regulators and provide a business with the same benefits as the traditional audits, including an increased awareness of the environmental impact of the operation and the chance to improve the environmental performance of the company.

Online environmental self-auditing

The use of information technology can greatly contribute to the overall reduction in the environmental impacts of hoteliers. Beside the general advantages such as increased efficiencies in all processes in hotels (e.g. reservation, check-in/out, housekeeping and maintenance management schedule), the hospitality industry benefits from the use of online content on the long road to sustainability. On that bumpy path, self-help online tools support hoteliers in auditing their operations and lead to informed decision-making. One of the most recent online tools is the free Hotel Energy Solution (HES) online toolkit. The HES toolkit is the result of a partnership between the United Nations World Tourism Organization (**UNWTO**), the United Nations Environment Programme (**UNEP**), the International Hotel and Restaurant Association (**IH&RA**), the French *Agence de l'Environnement et de la Maîtrise de l'Energie* (Environment and Energy Management Agency or ADEME) and the European Renewable Energy Council (EREC). HES helps small and medium-sized hoteliers to measure, analyse and reduce energy consumption and CO_2 emissions in their operations. The basic concepts behind HES and other online tools are for hotels to enter specific details into the online tool, including, for example, the occupancy rate, energy usage, energy costs, resources used maintaining the buildings and efforts already undertaken to improve sustainability. The tools consequently evaluate energy efficiency and the respective **carbon footprint** created by the hotel(s). In addition, tips and recommendations for investment with estimated returns on investment are presented, helping the managers and owners of hotel properties to achieve a higher level of energy efficiency. Online self-reporting software also serves as an industry **benchmarking** tool.

There are quite a few online tools available to hoteliers to measure, benchmark and conduct self-audits of their property and operations. Among the most prominent online tools available to hoteliers and with a particular focus on **energy management** are:

- Hotel Energy Solutions (http://hes.e-benchmarking.org/);
- Hotel Energy Check (http://www.hotelenergycheck.ch);

- Energy Star (http://www.energystar.gov);
- GreenQuest (http://www.mygreenquest.com/app.php);
- Smart Energy Analyzer (http://www.pge.com/energysurvey/);
- Energie-Sparprogramm (http://energiekampagne-gastgewerbe.de).

Those online tools are one of the latest set of innovations offering guidance for hoteliers, many free of charge, in mitigating environmental impacts at their properties.

Financing, investing, measuring, accounting and eco-innovating

It is no surprise to today's managers that innovation in products, services and processes is one of the key ingredients to long-term business success. In the hospitality industry, one of the core innovation sectors is the development of new services and the main drivers are employees. However, in the span of one decade, hotels have been the stage of numerous innovations and test tubes for design, architecture and technology implementation, mostly related to eco-innovation. While the hotel operator ensures a viable business with efficient processes, its facilities are being used to experiment. A hotel is a synthesis of societal ecosystems, where a multitude of products and services are on offer, where consumption happens round-the-clock, round-the-year, where processes are far from static and where success stories are soon to be found that spread to other businesses or individual homes.

Innovation is the key to hospitality growth. With the rising cost of primary resources due to increased **scarcity** of those resources, some hoteliers have decided to meet this challenge face on by developing and incorporating eco-innovation. However, since the hospitality industry relies on a multitude of other sectors to operate, such as agriculture, transport and technology, eco-innovation must be embraced across industries.

A great number of businesses in developed countries consider the access to restricted materials or raw resources coupled with the increases in the current and expected energy prices as key drivers of eco-innovation. And the very same factors are the main incentives for the use of eco-innovation, as often demonstrated in the hospitality industry.

Hospitality developments fall into the category of capital-intensive undertakings that require the active cooperation of all actors on financial markets. Governmental authorities have a role to play in the adoption of eco-innovation. Obstacles such as economic constraints and lack of external financing are perceived dampers in embracing eco-innovation. Therefore, the issue of project financing is among the most important aspects of hospitality development as well as development and adoption of eco-innovation.

Furthermore, the understating of sustainability by major decision-makers in the financial markets, such as company executives, investors and analysts, bankers, insurers and accountants differ often significantly. The abuse of the term sustainability by all stakeholders and in the media is partly to blame for the confusion.

There is a difference in the term 'sustainability' if used in the following context:

This company is showing sustainable earnings

compared to this context:

This company is engaging in sustainability.

In many instances, the division of facility ownership, operation and management among different stakeholders is an additional barrier to the implementation of eco-innovation and sustainable business practices. When a hospitality operator contracts a building on a fixed monthly rent, regardless of the water and energy quantities consumed, the building owner may not be willing to invest in additional energy-saving and/or water-saving measures. While retaining a time-limited contract, the operator may not be willing to initiate a possibly risky investment. The mutual and close cooperation of all stakeholders involved in finding a solution beneficial to all partners is ultimately required.

EXERCISES

1 SMALL GROUP REVIEW QUESTIONS AND DISCUSSION

Paying for environmental and sustainability accounting

In small groups, students should find answers to the following questions and be ready to discuss their findings.

- How can environmental matters be evaluated in money?
- How can societal matters be evaluated in money?
- Should society or companies pay for externalities?

2 SMALL GROUP PROJECT AND DISCUSSION

Financing green opportunities for a small business

Students build small groups of 3–5 individuals. Each group will develop a restaurant or hotel concept. The concept should include green technologies. Each group will need to find out:

- Are there any special grants for start-up companies wanting to implement green technologies within its operation?
- Are there specific loan programmes available for small businesses wanting to invest in green technologies or efficiency upgrades?

- Are there any cost benefits to be expected in terms of tax incentives from the green investments in the operation?
- Are there financial incentives offered to companies offering public transport advantages to its employees?

3   WRITTEN ASSIGNMENT

- Critically discuss the following statements. Your answer should be about 1500 words long.
  - The hotel industry needs a global scoring system in order to report to stakeholders on the sustainability performance of the industry as a whole, allowing also a comparative analysis of individual properties.
  - It is relatively easier to invest and implement green technologies when building a new hotel compared to undertaking efficiency upgrades in an established hotel.
  - Online self-audit tools are useful to measure and audit the environmental performance of an hotel, but an expert consultant should definitely double-check the results from the online tool.

4   GROUP DISCUSSION OR WRITTEN ASSIGNMENT

- Select an article related to a hotel property that discusses investment in green technology or efficiency upgrades.
- Critically review the article and then consider this question:
- How would you estimate the return on investment on the investment undertaken by the hotel?

Resources

Green investment, financing, funding and accounting

Jupiter: *Environmental and Responsible Investing*. Available at: http://www.jupiteronline. co.uk/PI/Our_Products/Environmental/Environmental.htm.

KfW Banking Group: *Domestic Loan Programmes*. Available at: http://nachhaltigkeit.kfw.de/ EN_Home/Programmes_and_products/Domestic_loan_programmes/index.jsp.

KfW Banking Group: *Sustainability Programmes and Products*. Available at: http:// nachhaltigkeit.kfw.de/EN_Home/Programmes_and_products/index.jsp.

Organization for Economic Co-operation and Development (OECD): *Environmental Indicators, Modelling and Outlooks*. Available at: http://www.oecd.org/topic/0,3699, en_2649_34283_1_1_1_1_37425,00.html.

The Sigma Project: *The Sigma Guidelines Toolkit: Sustainability Accounting Guide*. Available at: http://www.projectsigma.co.uk/Toolkit/SIGMASustainabilityAccounting.pdf.

United Nations Department of Economic and Social Affairs: *Integrated Environmental and Economic Accounting: An Operational Manual*. Available at: http://unstats.un.org/unsd/publication/SeriesF/SeriesF_78E.pdf.

U.S. Small Business Administration (SBA): *The Green Financing Guide for Small Businesses*. Available at: http://www.sba.gov/community/blogs/community-blogs/small-business-cents/green-financing-guide-small-businesses.

Online self-auditing tools

Energie-Sparprogramm: http://energiekampagne-gastgewerbe.de.

Energy Star: http://www.energystar.gov.

GreenQuest: http://www.mygreenquest.com/app.php.

Hotel Energy Check: http://www.hotelenergycheck.ch.

Hotel Energy Solutions: http://hes.e-benchmarking.org/.

Smart Energy Analyzer: http://www.pge.com/energysurvey/.

Additional material

Go to www.routledge.com/cw/sloan to find PowerPoint slides of all the figures and tables from the book, additional case studies, a test bank of questions and extra links to useful videos.

Epilogue
Sustainability education in hospitality

A description of issues and challenges in providing sustainability in hospitality curricula

As the need for **sustainable development** has risen to the forefront of the global hospitality industry, it is evidently necessary for students to be correctly prepared to tackle the challenges they will face in the business world. Unfortunately, the concept of **sustainability** is still frowned upon by sections of society because of its non-traditional approach to business. Sustainability involves issues that are about competing interests and values and requires all **stakeholders** to work together towards a common goal. Sustainability is holistic by nature and does not focus on short-term gains. It requires a long-term approach to profit that recognises that over-exploitation of resources will limit future economic viability and create irreparable damage to mankind in the process. Quite bluntly, sustainability has no place in any establishment, educational, business or otherwise, that seeks only short-term profitability with minimum expenditure. Sustainability requires a fundamental shift in thinking, values, ambitions and action by not only the general population but also by business leaders and educational establishments. Since it runs counter to the embedded values of the traditional business systems, it can be challenging for educators and students alike to embrace a different value system with the willingness to change.

We live in a time of cultural dissolution where shared academic culture rooted in recognised values is fading away. Role models are provided by mass media, where the **lifestyles** of a privileged few are glimpsed. The conveniences of communication systems and fast, easy travel make grasping the meaning of real culture tenuous. In societies which are increasingly secular and where communities are increasingly more fragile, the difference between right and wrong has become blurred for many. Young people need to learn the meaning and consequences of their behaviour and business ethics plays a fundamental part in any sustainability curriculum.

Education is critical for promoting sustainability and improving the ability of people to address business issues in the context of the **environment** and society. Both types of education, formal and non-formal, are indispensable to changing people's attitudes so that they have the power to assess and address sustainability concerns. Education is also critical to achieving environmental and ethical awareness and behaviour consistent with **sustainable** business development and for responsible decision-making. The importance of the role of education to stimulate change is widely recognised. For instance, the UN launched the Decade of Education for Sustainable Development (DESD) (2005–2014) as an attempt to further foster sustainable development by aiming to increase public awareness and reorienting education towards sustainability. Similar to the concept of sustainability, the concept of education is very wide and opinions differ. The increased pedagogical debate over sustainability's inclusion in undergraduate and graduate curricula has led to the creation of speciality journals such as the *International Journal of Sustainability in Higher Education* and the *International Journal of Sustainable Hospitality*.

Although there is huge interest in sustainability in hospitality businesses and universities alike, there is a gap between the demand for knowledge and what is on offer. A 2011 study by Barber revealed that three stakeholder groups (students, educators and industry practitioners) showed a real interest in environmental sustainability but that there are significant differences among them as to its level of importance. While hospitality educators had stronger environmental attitudes than industry professionals and students, the study found that industry practitioners were more likely to participate in environmentally friendly behaviour to save money. Despite the differences among the stakeholders, they agreed that teaching sustainability in hospitality curricula is necessary.

In a 2011 study carried out by Birk on the opinions of 250 tourism and hospitality students from Germany, sustainability is a topic that was shown to play an increasingly important role in their university education. The notion among hospitality and tourism students is widespread that universities should act as role models for sustainability: more than half of the respondents (52.9 per cent) 'totally agreed' with this notion and another third (36.9 per cent) 'agreed', showing that universities should aspire to this objective. Likewise the majority of the students in the survey considered this topic to be either important or highly important in their studies, both for their personal development (70.9 per cent) and for their future career (78.4 per cent). Findings in this study are in line with other previous studies carried out in other university disciplines on the importance of hospitality education. When asked if they believed that sustainability has sufficient focus in their university education, 46 per cent believe that it presently has only a minor focus. The remainder claimed that the teaching of sustainability was lacking. In a 2009 study by Deale it was found that 72 per cent of the hospitality educators sampled indicated that they felt it was important for students to be taught about sustainable issues, but that at best, only 12 per cent of them were actually teaching sustainability in the classroom. These discrepancies can be attributed to the lack of a coherent approach in incorporating sustainability into hospitality curricula.

In some quarters the debate on how best to teach sustainability is similar to teaching business ethics, which has been around in curricula for a lot longer. The discussion on ethics and sustainability centres on whether to limit its inclusion to one speciality class or to teach it across the whole curriculum. Since sustainability is holistic by nature, it is difficult to argue that it is of optimal benefit to students when taught as a stand-alone subject. Placing an emphasis on sustainability in all subject matters gives graduates a better, all-rounded understanding of the subject. It enables them to start work in hospitality businesses that embrace the **triple bottom line** with greater confidence. In fact, it may be argued that since the **hospitality industry** is gradually moving toward sustainability, curricula should move in the same direction. Nevertheless, as remarked in the (2009) Deale study, until now curricula have generally failed to do so.

The 'greening' of universities is seen by many as a means to 'practise what you preach'. It is now common for universities to create such initiatives as **greenhouse gas** inventories and comprehensive energy, waste and water usage efficiency programmes. Not only do these campus initiatives educate students about sustainability and improve relations in the university community, they can also provide large savings for the universities' operating budgets. However, in order to go 'green', universities have to embrace new ways of thinking. Reducing energy and waste requires commitment from all members of the institution, strong leadership and clear vision are always required. Financial considerations have to be made and effort must be made when implementing new environmentally friendly initiatives. Cash-strapped higher education institutions may struggle with management to prove that investments are worthwhile.

The many positive and negative **impacts** of the hospitality industry on the environment and society place an important responsibility on owners and managers to administer their properties to the best of their ability. Students are future agents of change and have the potential to herald a new era of sustainable hospitality management. It can be argued that sustainability should be at the centre of the debate that engages all of us in a fundamental rethink about the nature of higher education and its wider responsibilities. In an age of **greenwashing**, there is a danger that sustainability could still become just a buzzword devoid of any significant intellectual purchase if universities fail in their moral duty to penetrate the misty curtains of media spin, political rhetoric and corporate unethical practice.

Incorporating sustainability in hospitality education provides students with the opportunity to learn about complex world issues. In conventional hospitality curricula, students are not encouraged to see the link between hospitality and issues such as climate change, **food security** and the world economic crisis. The study of environmental politics has emerged as a result and has resulted in environmental issues being pushed to the top of the political agenda. This is called **environmental education**.

Another benefit of teaching sustainability is that it facilitates debate and allows students to critically form their own opinions. Universities, after all, are places of learning which involve the evaluation of information. Teaching sustainability requires students to move beyond just knowing and understanding, it requires them to apply concepts and ideas to complex problems and find sustainable solutions. As wealth increases for some, global poverty, insecurity and inequality are continuing reminders that economic development is far from even and fair. Higher education is implicated in all of these developments, for it no longer has the privileged position of simply observing, criticizing and evaluating what goes on beyond the seminar room or campus. It, too, is a global player involved in both the production of knowledge and wealth and the maintenance of poverty and insecurity through its growing role as servant to the global economy. Higher education therefore helps to shape the material reality in which we live and can guide present and future generations to attempt to understand, reflect on and, perhaps, even change it.

The results from the 2009 Deale survey on sustainability in hospitality education reveal that when sustainability is taught in 42 per cent of cases, it is left up to the instructor to decide whether or not it will be included. In 32 per cent of cases, specific sustainability classes were included in the curriculum and in only 13 per cent of hospitality curricula was sustainability integrated completely. While it might be the least common approach, the academic literature concerning the teaching of sustainability in higher education calls for full integration.

When a hospitality department decides that teaching sustainability is important, the decision on how to incorporate it into the curriculum may be based on several factors. Diverging opinions exist on how to teach sustainability, fortunately most instructors now follow the credo of the triple bottom line. The major challenge of universities is not the ability of universities to transform themselves into a sustainable institution but rather the will and the time frame for doing so. Of course, some universities face greater challenges than others depending on many factors (e.g. private or state funding, leadership, business culture). One of the key challenges is the unfamiliarity and the perception of intangibility of the sustainability concept even though a vast amount of subject matter covers it. Academics unfamiliar with sustainability have serious difficulties with integrating sustainability. Collaboration between disciplines is essential for course development. Not only is technical input required from eco-design architects and engineers but also from accountants versed in the principles of internalizing **externalities** and kitchen chefs with enthusiasm for recent trends in food foraging. Sustainable hospitality requires collaboration as well from economists, food scientists, urban planners and sociologists.

It is likely in the next few years that the demand for sustainable hospitality education will increase in response not only to the growing number of acute environmental and societal problems but also to a shift in consumer demand to more sustainable forms of hospitality operation. Universities that achieve this paradigm shift will undoubtedly be rewarded with greater student numbers and industry will benefit from well-rounded students able to apply their knowledge of sustainability to a variety of contexts.

EXERCISE

1 **GROUP RESEARCH, PRESENTATION AND DISCUSSION**

Bridging the gap between research and industry

Results of hospitality-based research often do not make it to the hospitality firms' boardrooms. However, a greater collaboration between researchers and practitioners could hasten the speed of change towards greater sustainability in the hospitality industry.

- Discuss how knowledge from research could better inform industry practices supporting sustainable management and operations strategies and practices and help to promote innovative solutions in hospitality.

References

Barber, N., Deale, C. and Goodman, R. (2011) 'Sustainability in the hospitality business curriculum: a pilot study of perspectives from three groups of stakeholders', *Journal of Hospitality and Tourism Education*. Forthcoming 2011.

Birk, A. (2011) 'The role of higher education in the transition to sustainable development', unpublished Diploma dissertation. Bad Honnef, Germany: International University of Applied Sciences, Bad Honnef, Bonn.

Deale, C.S., Nicholas, J. and Jacques, P.A. (2009) 'Descriptive study of sustainability education in the hospitality curriculum', *Journal of Hospitality and Tourism Education*. 22(4): 34–42.

Additional material

Go to www.routledge.com/cw/sloan to find PowerPoint slides of all the figures and tables from the book, additional case studies, a test bank of questions and extra links to useful videos.

Glossary

Accreditation: A procedure to establish if a tourism business meets certain standards of management and operation.

Active solar design: Active solar design uses technologies which consist of solar collecting devices that are designed to capture the sun's energy and convert it into heat or electrical energy.

Adventure tourism: A form of tourism in natural areas that incorporates an element of risk, higher levels of physical exertion and the need for specialized skills.

Agenda 21: Programme of action adopted by the 1992 United Nations Conference on Environment and Development.

Air pollutants: Particulates, sulphur dioxide, nitrogen dioxide, tropospheric ozone, carbon monoxide.

Alternative tourism: In essence, tourism activities or development that are viewed as non-traditional. It is often defined in opposition to large-scale mass tourism to represent small-scale sustainable tourism developments. AT is also presented as an 'ideal type', that is, an improved model of tourism development that redresses the ills of traditional, mass tourism.

Assets: Something of value that will provide future benefit or utility, that can be used to generate revenue. Usually owned, so simply described as 'things we own'.

Auditing: A process to measure and verify the practices of a business.

Benchmarking: Process of comparing performance and activities among similar organizations either against an agreed standard or against those that are recognised as being among the best.

Benchmarks: Points of reference or comparison, which may include standards, critical success factors, indicators, metrics.

Best practice: Operational standards considered the most effective and efficient means of achieving desired outcomes.

Biodiversity: Shorthand for biological diversity: the variability among living organisms. It includes diversity within species, between species and in ecosystems.

Biodynamic agriculture: A farming method that emphasizes the holistic development and interrelationships of the soil, plants and animals as a self-sustaining system.

Biomass: A renewable energy source from biological material such as wood or waste.

BRIC: Brazil, Russia, India and China.

Capacity management: A process that seeks to ensure that the organization operates at optimum capacity while maintaining customer satisfaction levels.

Capital expenditure: The cost of long-term assets, such as computer equipment, vehicles and premises. Importantly these are bought for use over several years and not to resell.

Carbon credits: The basic concept behind carbon credits is valuing the cost of greenhouse emissions and creating a market in the form of carbon credits for reducing those emissions (see carbon offset).

Carbon dioxide (CO_2): A greenhouse gas produced through the respiration and the decomposition of organic substances. The combustion of fossil fuels is primarily responsible for increased atmospheric concentrations of this gas.

Carbon footprint: A representation of the effect human activities have on the climate in terms of the total amount of greenhouse gases produced (measured in units of carbon dioxide).

Carbon neutrality: Carbon neutrality refers to achieving net zero carbon emissions by balancing the measured amount of carbon emitted with an equivalent amount sequestered or offset (see carbon offset), or buying enough carbon credits (see carbon credits) to make up the difference.

Carbon offset: A carbon offset is a reduction in emissions of carbon dioxide made in order to compensate for or to offset an emission made elsewhere. Carbon offsets are measured in metric tonnes of carbon dioxide-equivalent (CO_2e). Offsets are typically achieved through financial support of projects that reduce the emission of greenhouse gases in the short or long term. The most common project type is renewable energy.

Carrying capacity: In tourism, the number of travellers who can be supported in a given area within natural resource limits, and without degrading the natural, social, cultural or economic environment.

Cause-related marketing: Used where a company allies itself with a specific cause, and contributes money, time or expertise to an organization or event for that cause in return for the right to make publicity or commercial value from that involvement.

Certification: Certification is a procedure by which a third party, the certifier, provides a written insurance that a system, a process, a person, a product or a service has conformed to the requirements specified in a standard or a reference frame. Certification is a voluntary act.

Code of conduct: Guidelines advising a tourism stakeholder, including tourists, on how to behave in an environmentally responsible manner.

Code of ethics/practice: Recommended practices based on a system of self-regulation intended to promote environmentally and/or socio-culturally sustainable behaviour.

Composting: Biological process used to treat organic waste (green waste, fermentable fraction of municipal waste, sludge from urban treatment plants, etc.), by degrading them in an accelerated manner.

Concentrated animal feeding operation (CAFO): An industrial farming model based on concentrating farm animals in the smallest space possible, ensuring fast weight gain at the least cost.

Conservation: Can be broadly interpreted as action taken to protect and preserve the natural world from harmful features of tourism, including pollution and over-exploitation of resources.

Conventional agriculture: Also known as 'industrial farming', conventional agriculture is a form of modern farming heavily based on agrochemicals and refers to the industrialized production of livestock, poultry, fish and crops.

Corporate social responsibility (CSR): Corporate social responsibility is a concept by which companies integrate the interests and needs of customers, employees, suppliers, shareholders, communities and the planet into corporate strategies.

Creating shared value (CSV): Based on Michael Porter's research, CSV is a set of policies and practices that enhance the competiveness of a company while simultaneously advancing the economic and social conditions in the communities in which it operates.

Cultural tourism: Travel for the purpose of learning about cultures or aspects of cultures.

Deforestation: The removal or permanent destruction of indigenous forest for other purposes.

Degradation: Any decline in the quality of natural or cultural resources, or the viability of ecosystems, that is caused directly or indirectly by humans.

Demographic profile: Characteristics used in research such as age, gender, occupation, income, marital status, place of residence, etc.

Direct employment: In tourism, direct employment comprises all jobs where workers are engaged in the production of direct tourism output (hotel employee, restaurant servers, airline pilots).

Direct impact: The immediate consequence of an activity (e.g. tourism) on the environment, the community or the economy where the cause and effect relationship is generally clear.

Direct spending: Money that goes directly from a tourist into the economy of the destination.

Discrimination: Unequal treatment of persons on grounds which are not justifiable in law, e.g. in the UK, discrimination on the grounds of sex or race.

Dow Jones Sustainability Index (DJSI): The Dow Jones Sustainability Index is one of the first global indexes tracking the financial performance of leading companies with an emphasis on sustainability in economic, social and environmental capacities.

Eco-architecture: A term, also referred to as 'Sustainable Architecture', describing environmentally conscious design and architectural techniques.

Eco-label: Information (typically provided on a label attached to a product) informing a potential consumer of a product's characteristics, or of the production or processing method(s) used in its production.

Eco-procurement: Eco-procurement means choosing products and services that have the lowest negative impact on the environment while minimizing waste.

Eco-technology: A term depicting engineering practices that seek to help conserve and restore the environment through the integration of ecological principles.

Ecological monitoring: The action of developing indicators and using those to monitor the condition of ecological resources.

Ecologically sustainable: Using, conserving and enhancing the community's resources so that ecological development is maintained, and the total quality of life can be sustained now and in the future.

Ecosystem: A dynamic system of plant, animal, fungal and micro-organism communities, and the associated non-living physical and chemical factors.

Ecotourism: Ecologically sustainable tourism with a primary focus on experiencing natural areas that foster environmental and cultural understanding, appreciation and conservation.

Embodied energy: The quantity of energy required to manufacture and supply to the point of use, a product, material or service.

Energy conservation: Positive initiatives to reduce the consumption of energy to the minimum level required.

Energy management: In hospitality, energy management is the practice of controlling procedures, operations and equipment that contribute to the energy use in hotels.

Energy-plus building: A building that produces a surplus of energy during a portion of the year.

Energy security: Access by countries or regions to sufficient and affordable energy sources.

Environment: The ecosystem in which an organism or a species lives, including both the physical environment and the other organisms with which it comes in contact.

Environmental auditing: Inspection of a tourism organization to assess the environmental impact of its activities.

Environmental communication: Communication by enterprises or organizations about environmental affairs.

Environmental deterioration: The degradation of the environment through depletion of resources.

Environmental education: Formal and informal learning processes that are designed to raise awareness and teach new values, knowledge and skills, in order to encourage more sustainable behaviour.

Environmental impact: The effects that a community has on the environment as a consequence of its activities.

Environmental impact assessment (EIA): A study undertaken to assess the effect of an action upon a specific environment or the social or cultural integrity of a community.

Environmental impact statement: The report resulting from an environmental impact assessment.

Environmental management programme: Also labelled as environmental management plan, this is the procedure by which the environmental management system and policies are turned into activities.

Environmental management system (EMS): System that a tourism organization can use to implement its environmental policy and achieve associated objectives to control environmental impacts that are important to its activities and to respect regulatory requirements.

Environmental performance indicators (EPI): Environmental performance indicators simplify, quantify and communicate complex environmental data about the state or quality of the environment. EPIs facilitate the monitoring of environmental trends and the tracking of progress towards stated objectives and policy goals.

Environmental stewardship: Long-term management aimed at preserving and enhancing the quality of an environment.

Environmental tax: A tax that is of major relevance for the environment, regardless of its specific purpose or name.

European Union Eco-Management and Audit Scheme (EMAS): The EU Eco-Management and Audit Scheme is a management tool for companies and other organizations to evaluate, report and improve their environmental performance.

Extended producer responsibility (EPR): Similar to PPP where users pay, EPR seeks to shift the responsibility of externalities from governments to the businesses (suppliers, manufacturers and distributors) producing externalities.

Externalities: An external cost that arises when the social or economic activities of one company has an impact on another company or group of people whereby that impact is not fully accounted, or eventually compensated for.

Fauna: The animal characteristics and life of a region or particular environment.

Flora: The plant characteristics and life of a region or particular environment.

Food miles: A calculation of the distance and mode of transport foodstuffs have travelled throughout the complete production process until they reach the consumer.

Food security: When all people at all times have access to sufficient, safe, nutritious food to maintain a healthy and active life.

Footprint (ecological): A measure of the hectares of biologically productive area required to support a human population of given size.

Global Reporting Initiative (GRI): A private initiative offering sustainability reporting guidelines that take into account environmental, social and economic performance.

Global warming: Global warming refers to the rising average temperature of the Earth's atmosphere deemed to be caused by increasing concentrations of greenhouse gases produced by human activities.

Globalization: Generally defined as the network of connections of organizations and peoples across national, geographic and cultural borders and boundaries. These global networks are creating a shrinking world where local differences and national boundaries are being subsumed into global identities. Within the field of tourism, globalization is also viewed in terms of the revolutions in telecommunications, finance and transport that are key factors currently influencing the nature and pace of growth of tourism in developing nations.

Green Globe/Green Globe 21: Green Globe 21 is the worldwide benchmarking and certification programme which facilitates sustainable travel and tourism for consumers, companies and communities. It is based on Agenda 21 and the principles for Sustainable Development endorsed by 182 governments at the United Nations Rio de Janeiro Earth Summit in 1992.

Green marketing: Integrating business practices and products that are friendly to the environment while also meeting the needs of the consumers.

Greenhouse effect: The trapping of the sun's thermal radiation by gases and water vapour, keeping the surface of the earth warmer than it would be otherwise.

Greenhouse gas: A gas such as carbon dioxide or methane that reflects infrared radiation emitted by the Earth, thereby helping to retain heat in the atmosphere.

Greenwashing: The unjustified appropriation of an environmental virtue by a company, an industry, a government, a politician or even a non-government organization to create a pro-environmental image, sell a product or a policy.

Gross Domestic Product (GDP): A measure of the total value of goods and services produced by the domestic economy during a given period, usually one year.

Heritage: Things of value that are inherited which people want to keep. Heritage can be natural, cultural, tangible, intangible, personal or collective. Natural heritage is often conserved in places such as reserves and national parks. Cultural heritage practices are often conserved through ongoing traditions and practices.

Hospitality industry: An industry made up of businesses that provide accommodation, food and beverages, and entertainment.

HOTREC: The European Hotel and Restaurant Association is the representative body for hotels, restaurants and cafés at European institutional level.

IH&RA: The International Hotel and Restaurant Association.

Impacts: Effects, which may be either positive or negative, felt as a result of tourism-associated activity. Tourists have at least three kinds of impacts on a destination: economic, socio-cultural and environmental. Tourism also has effects on tourists, in terms of possible attitude and behaviour changes.

Indicator: A summary measure that provides information on the state of, or change in, a system.

Indirect impact: The secondary effects of an activity (e.g. tourism) on the environment, the community, the economy but the relationships are often misunderstood and/or difficult to establish.

Industrial agriculture: A form of agriculture where farming is industrialized to achieve economies of scale in production.

Integrated agriculture: Farms that work in an integrated manner try to minimize external farm inputs, such as fertilizers or pesticides, and take advantage of the synergies between a variety of livestock and plant production systems.

International Chamber of Commerce (ICC): The International Chamber of Commerce created a Business Charter for Sustainable Development comprising 16 principles for environmental management.

Kyoto Protocol: Protocol that came into force in 2005 as an extension of the United Nations outline agreement on climate change. In particular, it fixes limiting values for greenhouse gas emissions in industrial countries.

Life cycle: The particular pattern through which a destination evolves.

Life cycle assessment (LCA): LCA is the investigation and valuation of the environmental, economic and social impacts of a product or service. A product's life cycle starts when the raw materials are extracted from the earth through to processing, transport, use, reuse, recycling or disposal. For each of these stages, the impact is measured in terms of the resources used and environmental impacts caused.

Lifestyle: A person's pattern of living as expressed in his or her activities, interests and opinions.

LOHAS: Lifestyles of Health and Sustainability is a demographic defining a particular market segment related to sustainable living.

Mass tourism: Traditional, large-scale tourism commonly, but loosely used to refer to popular forms of leisure tourism pioneered in southern Europe, the Caribbean and North America in the 1960s and 1970s.

Millennium Development Goals (MDGs): Initiatives adopted by the United Nations in the year 2000 to tackle poverty and other related dimensions.

Minimal impact practices: Deliberate human behaviour that reduces the negative impact of people or objects on the environment to a minimum.

Monitoring: The ongoing review and assessment of the natural or cultural integrity of a place in order to detect changes in its condition with reference to a baseline condition.

Nature tourism (nature-based tourism): Ecologically sustainable tourism with a primary focus on experiencing natural areas.

NGO: Non-governmental organization refers to a non-profit-making, voluntary, service-oriented or development-oriented organization, either for the benefit of members or of other members of the population.

Organic agriculture: A production system that sustains the health of soils, ecosystems and people. It relies on ecological processes, biodiversity and cycles adapted to local conditions, rather than the use of inputs with adverse effects.

Organic farming: A form of agriculture based on farming techniques aimed at maintaining soil productivity without the use (or with limited use) of fertilizers, pesticides, herbicides and other non-natural additives.

Passive solar design: Passive solar design refers to the use of the sun's energy for the heating and cooling of living spaces.

PDCA (Plan, Do, Check, Act): The PDCA reached a broad audience in many industry circles through the work of the twentieth-century American statistician, William Edwards Deming, who is regarded as having had a great impact on modern quality control in manufacturing and business in general. The PDCA cycle is also referred to as the Deming Cycle.

Photovoltaic (solar) cell: Generally speaking, a device incorporating a semiconductor that generates electricity when exposed to (sun) light. The technology may be further sub-divided into crystalline, multi-crystalline, thin-film and concentrator variants.

Polluter pays principle (PPP): PPP implies that the party responsible for producing pollution or causing environmental damage should bear the costs of avoiding the damage or of compensating for it.

Pollution: Harmful effects on the environment as a by-product of tourism activity. Types include: air, noise, water and aesthetic.

Precautionary principle: An approach to risks that involves acting to avoid potential harm despite the lack of scientific certainty as to the likelihood or relative importance of that harm.

Public policy: This is whatever governments choose to do or not to do. Such a definition covers government action, inaction, decisions and non-decisions as it implies a very deliberate choice between alternatives.

Public relations: A set of activities with the goal of maintaining a chosen public image for a business or organization and enhancing its reputation.

Rainwater harvesting (RWH): Capturing and storing rain water for commercial, operational or personal use.

Recycling: The process by which discarded materials are collected, sorted, processed and converted into raw materials which are then used in the production of new products.

Renewable energy: Energy sources that are practically inexhaustible. For example, solar, hydro and wind energy.

Renewable resource: A resource that is capable of being replenished through natural processes or its own reproduction, generally within a time-span that does not exceed a few decades.

Responsible purchasing: Procurement deemed socially responsible and environmentally sustainable.

Responsible tourism: Type of tourism which is practised by tourists who make responsible choices when choosing their holidays. These choices reflect responsible attitudes to the limiting of the extent of the sociological and environmental impacts their holiday may cause.

Restoration: Returning existing habitats to a known past state.

Retrofit: The subsequent addition or implementation of new features to existing fixtures and facilities.

Return on investment (ROI): ROI is a performance measure used to evaluate the efficiency of an investment. To calculate ROI, the benefit – in other words, the return – of an investment is divided by the cost of the investment.

Scarcity: The concept which stems from unlimited wants but limited resources.

Self-auditing: A self-conducted or self-administered audit is an alternative to the traditional third-party audit whereby information is verified against some audit criteria by the same party producing the information. In other words, the company gathering the data, analysing the data using various indicators and producing the results on which it is to be evaluated, is the same company undertaking the audit.

SME(s): Small and medium-sized enterprises.

Social: Relating to human society and interaction between its members.

Stack effect: The movement of air into and out of buildings.

Stakeholder: Any person, group or organization with an interest in, or who may be affected by, the activities of another organization.

Subsidies: A subsidy is a financial incentive paid to a business or economic sector. Subsidies are often made by governments either to sustain industries in decline or to encourage the expansion of new or existing industries.

Sustainability: Sustainability is effectively the goal of sustainable development. It is the ideal end state to which we must aspire.

Sustainability performance indicators (SPI): Similar to EPI, SPI is a tool gathering data and classifying it into three distinct areas covering the economic, environmental (in form of EPIs) and social dimension of sustainability.

Sustainable: Something which can be kept in the same or a better condition for the future.

Sustainable architectural design: Architectural solutions that guarantee the well-being and coexistence of society, the environment and profitability.

Sustainable development: Development carried out in such a way as to meet the needs of the present without compromising the ability of future generations to meet their needs.

Sustainable food: Food which is safe, healthy and nutritious, which respects biophysical and environmental limits in its production and processing, providing a viable livelihood for farmers and other stakeholders in the supply and distribution chain as well as rural economies.

Sustainable tourism: Tourism that can be sustained over the long term because it results in a net benefit for the social, economic, natural and cultural environments of the area in which it takes place.

Thermal mass: The way in which a building can store and regulate internal heat.

Tourist: Anyone who spends at least one night away from home, no matter what the purpose.

Triple bottom line: An expanded baseline for measuring performance, adding social and environmental dimensions to the traditional monetary benchmark.

UNCED: The United Nations Conference on Environment and Development promotes global cooperation between developing and industrialized countries in planning and managing environmentally responsible development.

UNEP: The United Nations Environment Programme coordinates United Nations environmental activities.

UNWTO: The United Nations World Tourism Organization is a United Nations agency dealing with questions relating to tourism.

Value added: The additional value a product obtained through the different stages of production.

VISIT: The Voluntary Initiatives for Sustainability in Tourism promotes and supports sustainable tourism development through the representation, promotion and mutual co-operation of international, national and regional certification schemes.

Waste management: The collection, transport, processing, recycling or disposal, and monitoring of waste.

Water management: The planning, developing, distributing and managing of water resources.

WBCSD: The World Business Council on Sustainable Development is a global association of some 200 international companies dealing exclusively with business and sustainable development.

Western diet: A dietary habit characterized by high intakes of red meat, sugary desserts, high-fat foods and refined grains.

Willingness to pay: The amount an individual is willing to pay to acquire some good or service. This amount can be elicited from the individual's stated or revealed preferences.

WWF: The World Wide Fund for Nature aims to conserve nature and ecological processes by preserving biodiversity, ensuring sustainable use of natural resources and promoting the reduction of pollution and wasteful use of resources and energy.

Zero-energy building: A building with zero net energy consumption and zero carbon emissions annually.

Index